WALKING
IN THE WAY
OF LOVE

WALKING
IN THE WAY
OF LOVE

VOLUME ONE

A Practical Commentary on

1 Corinthians for the Believer

NATHAN J. LANGERAK

REFORMED
FREE PUBLISHING
ASSOCIATION
Jenison, Michigan

Reformed Free Publishing Association
1894 Georgetown Center Drive
Jenison, Michigan 49428
rfpa.org
mail@rfpa.org
616-457-5970

Cover design by Christopher Tobias/tobiasdesign.com
Interior design and typesetting by Katherine Lloyd/the DESK online.com

ISBN 978-1-944555-25-2 (hardcover)
ISBN 978-1-944555-26-9 (ebook)
LCCN 2017959011

This book is dedicated to my father and mother, Harry and Evelyn Langerak, who taught me to walk in the way of love, and to my wife, Carrie, who is my faithful companion on that way until death us do part.

CONTENTS

PREFACE

First Corinthians is scripture's detailed treatment of Christian love. According to the theme text of the epistle (12:21), love is "a more excellent way." It is more excellent in itself, and it is more excellent for all who walk on that way. In that more excellent way the believer, saved by grace alone, is called to walk. The way of love is described in painstaking detail by the Holy Spirit and applied to specific situations that arise in the lives of believers and in the church. These situations are set in the language of the time but have definite application to the church's situation today.

First Corinthians is not an abstract treatment of love, but a pointed application of the calling of the Christian to walk in the way of love as that must characterize the believer's whole walk in the world. Being the calling of believers, it is also the calling of the true church of Jesus Christ to walk in this way, to teach this way, and to demand of its members to walk in this way in the world. All who claim faith in Jesus Christ and confess to be Christians must acknowledge the way of love as the "excellent way" and out of that acknowledgement pursue the way of love in their lives.

The way of love the believer is called to confess as excellent and to pursue is totally antithetical to the man's idea of love, that is attractive to man's flesh and promoted by the world. In every situation man also has his word about what constitutes love. This word of man about love always contradicts the word of God and frequently involves ungodly toleration, lust, human affection, or selfishness that masquerades as love and that pushes itself on the church and believer as true love. It is false love, indeed, hatred. As ardently as the believer is called to pursue the way of love, he is also called to reject the way of love that man proposes and in which he is naturally inclined to walk.

Walking in the way of love is impossible for the natural man. The natural man slanders God's way of love as wrong, unloving, harsh, and even barbaric. It is exactly by their refusal to walk in this way of love that people reveal themselves to be carnal and unspiritual. Christians who claim faith in Christ but refuse to acknowledge the Spirit's way of love in 1 Corinthians and consequently refuse to walk in love also reveal themselves to be carnal and unspiritual and give the lie to their claim of faith in Jesus Christ. The justified believer alone, by the faith that justifies wholly apart from walking in this way of love, will acknowledge this way as the true way of love and by that faith will also walk in it.

Walking in the Way of Love is a commentary on and application of the words of 1 Corinthians for the believer and the true church of Jesus Christ to teach them about the vitally important way of love, as that contradicts the chatter of the world and apostate church about love. The commentary is laid out with believers in mind. Each chapter of the book focuses on a single aspect of the main theme of love. The chapters are designed to stand alone. Each chapter begins with an introduction to help the reader see the particular subject of the chapter in its immediate and larger context in the epistle of 1 Corinthians. This layout is not to discourage anyone from reading through more than one chapter at a sitting, but rather to aid those who prefer to read one chapter at a time, and especially for the purpose of Bible societies that may use the book as a guide in studying the epistle.

The publication of this commentary would not have been possible without the encouragement and support of the Reformed Free Publishing Association. I thank the men and women of the book and publication committee and the editing staff of the publisher for their encouragement and diligent work in this endeavor and pray that the fruit of their encouragement might be worthy of their trust. May the commentary serve the promotion of the way of love with the fruit that believers pursue it ardently in all their lives.

INTRODUCTION

The apostle Paul wrote the book of 1 Corinthians to the church of God in the city of Corinth, which was beautifully situated in the ancient landscape of Greece. Corinth sat atop two high plateaus on the Isthmus of Corinth, which separated mainland Greece and the Peloponnesus, a peninsula that formed the southern tip of Greece. The city proper was dominated by the steep-sided citadel of Acrocorinth, which towered 1,800 feet above the city and from whose heights the whole surrounding countryside was visible. Just to the north of the city, the isthmus narrowed to three miles and was somewhat of a strategic chokepoint. In the early sixth century BC a paved shipway was built across the isthmus to facilitate the transport of goods and ships across the narrow strip. Five miles to the east Corinth's port city, Cenchreae, lay on the Saronic Gulf. A mile northwest her other port, Lechaion, sat on the Corinthian Gulf. With the control of two major ports, numerous smaller local harbors, the paved shipway, and all land traffic to and from the Peloponnesus, the position of Corinth was economically and militarily advantageous.

The history of Corinth relevant to this commentary starts with the Roman Empire. In 146 BC the Roman consul Lucius Mummius destroyed the city, killed all the men, and sold all the women and children into slavery. For a century the city lay virtually uninhabited. Corinth's rebirth came in 44 BC when Julius Caesar rebuilt it as a special economic colony—a kind of transplanted Rome in miniature—to exploit Corinth's natural geographical advantages as the crossroads of east and west. By that time the Mediterranean Sea was a Roman lake, and Greece was a Roman province. The situation of Corinth no longer held any military value, but all the geographic characteristics that made the city strategically important in war made it economically important in peace.[1]

Initially three thousand Roman colonists formed the core of the city's population. The colonists included veterans, many freed slaves, and others from the lower social classes in Rome, mainly of Greek descent. The population was later supplemented by a large contingent of Roman merchants. The core of Roman colonists was surrounded by a large population of resident aliens, mainly Jews, Syrians, and native Greeks. Soon others were attracted by the economic opportunities of the city, and its population grew steadily. About 100,000 people lived in Corinth at the end of the first century AD. In 27 BC, when Achaea became a separate province, Corinth became the capital of the province, the seat of the governor, and the foremost city of Greece.

Because of its status as a colony, the political identity of the city was thoroughly Latin and Roman. After 27 BC and through the time of the apostle's labors in the city, its status as the seat of the provincial administration of Achaea reinforced that identity. Although Roman citizens dominated the city's political structure, they were far from the most numerous group. Corinth was a menagerie of ethnic groups: Romans, Greeks, Phoenicians, Anatolians, Jews, and Syrians, among many others. Those resident aliens formed the bulk of Corinth's population and made Corinth an ethnic melting pot.

The church in Corinth would have been surrounded by trade and industry. Usually each Roman colony directly controlled

---

1 Donald Engels, *Roman Corinth: An Alternative Model for the Classical City* (Chicago and London: University of Chicago Press, 1990), 22; Timothy E. Gregory, ed., *The Corinthia in the Roman Period* (Ann Arbor, MI: Cushing-Malloy, 1993), 34; James Wiseman, *The Rise and Decline of Roman Corinth* (Berlin: Walter de Gruyter, 1979), 462.

and administered a large surrounding territory. The territory of Corinth was about 500 square miles, but only about 120 square miles could be farmed. The business of Corinth was manufacture and trade. She was called "the common emporium of Asia and Europe."[2] Corinth filled the ancient world with pottery from her bustling terra cotta lamp industry, made possible by her skilled artists and a nearly limitless supply of clay within her territory. Corinthian bronze was highly prized, and objects made from it fetched fabulous prices in the early empire. The city was also known for its marble portrait sculpture, cloth manufacturing, and tent and sail industries.[3]

In addition to manufacturing businesses, Corinth had thriving service and trade industries. This had to do with its position as a religious, educational, cultural, and governmental center, as well as its control of a major shipping route. The provision of services to merchants, travelers, and tourists was Corinth's most important business. The voyage around the Peloponnesus involved six days of travel and treacherous winds off the Cape of Malea. It was much safer to unload at Lechaion and transport overland to Cenchreae, or vice versa. There were fees for the transport and money to be made warehousing goods, in financing and insurance services, cargo handling, and ship repair and refitting. Lodging had to be provided, and food and entertainment made available for the rowdy and restless crowd of sailors and merchants. Services provided to those merchants and travelers provided enormous wealth for Corinth.[4]

Corinth's values were basically a driven mercantilism, religious tolerance, and easy hedonism. She worked hard and played

---

2 Wiseman, *The Rise and Decline of Roman Corinth*, 502; Engels, *Roman Corinth*, 22; Simon Hornblower and Anthony Spawforth, eds., *The Oxford Classical Dictionary*, 3rd ed. (Oxford: Oxford University Press, 1999), 390–91.

3 Engels, *Roman Corinth*, 33–37.

4 Ibid., 39–50, 57–58.

hard. Corinth also loved—worshiped—sports. Corinth hosted the biennial Isthmian Games,[5] athletic contests second only to the Olympian Games in importance. The highest office with the highest honor in the city was the one responsible for the Isthmian Games. To those games the Corinthians added others, such as the quadrennial Caesarean Games and the Imperial Contest.[6]

Perhaps most importantly, Corinth was also a religious center for the worship of pagan gods, particularly Poseidon and Aphrodite. The isthmus had long been recognized by the Greeks as the special abode of the Greek sea and earthquake god, Poseidon. It was an area where so many made their livelihood from the sea and where the land was periodically torn by devastating earthquakes. There was a large sanctuary to Poseidon at Isthmia near Corinth. Corinth was also known—infamously—for its devotion to Aphrodite, the goddess of erotic love. There were three sanctuaries of Aphrodite within Corinth, two more each at Lechaion and Cenchreae, and one atop Acrocorinth—where the ancient rumors said there were one thousand sacred prostitutes. Corinth was infamous for her licentious lifestyle. The Greek poet Aristophanes coined the Greek word that means to act the Corinthian as a synonym for insatiable fornication and reckless hedonism.

In addition to the traditional Greco-Roman deities, the Roman elite favored Roman cults, such as the imperial cult that worshiped the Roman state and the emperor, the embodiment of the state. The many foreigners and religious seekers imported the exotic Eastern cults of Isis and Serapis. There was a large Jewish community at Corinth that traced its beginnings to early in the colony's history and was well established by the time of Paul's first visit. Corinth was a religious melting pot.[7]

---

5   Isthmian Games were a festival of athletic and musical competitions in honor of the sea god Poseidon held at his sanctuary on the Isthmus of Corinth.
6   Engels, *Roman Corinth*, 17–18.
7   Ibid., 95–107; Hornblower and Spawforth, *The Oxford Classical Dictionary*, 390–91; Wiseman, *Rise and Declines of Roman Corinth*, 465–91, 509–33.

The apostle Paul established the Corinthian congregation on his second missionary journey after nearly a year and a half of hard labor in that cosmopolitan metropolis of the Greek and Roman world. Paul was first in Corinth in the years AD 51–52. At first the work was so difficult and the fruit apparently so small that it was necessary for the Lord to encourage him by a special vision:

9. Then spake the Lord to Paul in the night by a vision, Be not afraid, but speak, and hold not thy peace:
10. For I am with thee, and no man shall set on thee to hurt thee: for I have much people in this city.
11. And he continued there a year and six months, teaching the word of God among them. (Acts 18:9–11)

In obedience to that vision and on the strength of that encouragement the apostle labored in Corinth, and as the fruit of that labor he established the Corinthian church.

While he was on his third missionary journey several years later, the apostle wrote 1 Corinthians to address certain problems that had arisen in the congregation. At the time Paul was laboring in Ephesus, across the sea. While he was there certain prominent members of the church at Corinth came to him, reporting a number of serious problems and bringing a list of questions from the Corinthian church. From Ephesus, or somewhere on his journey between Ephesus and Corinth as he hurried back to Corinth, the apostle penned the letter under the inspiration of the Holy Ghost and sent it to the church by Timothy. Paul would eventually come back to Corinth and labor there in the years AD 56–57.

The book of 1 Corinthians is the apostle Paul's second letter to the church of Corinth. The first letter to Corinth was a little missive that he refers to in 1 Corinthians 5:9 and that has been lost to the church: "I wrote unto you in an epistle not to company with fornicators." The book called 1 Corinthians is in fact his second letter, and 2 Corinthians is his third letter to that congregation.

The church of Corinth was gifted. She was a large congregation and had more than one pastor. She shared in the wealth enjoyed by the city. Besides, she overflowed with spiritual gifts. She had apostles, prophets, evangelists, and teachers. She had gifts of government and mercy. She had wisdom, understanding, eloquence, knowledge of all mysteries, and even the gifts of healing and of tongues. She came behind in no gift (1 Cor. 1:7).

Officially the church in Corinth was doctrinally sound. There were false apostles whom the apostle exposes in 1 Corinthians 15 for their denial of the resurrection, but they were only some in the church. They were being tolerated but had not yet gained the upper hand in the church.

Despite her gifts and apparent orthodoxy, Corinth was desperately sick. That sickness called forth from the apostle Paul one of the sharpest rebukes that a church could ever hear: "Ye are yet carnal" (3:3). As evidence of her carnality the Corinthian church was torn by cliques and division. Because of her carnality she was plagued by a host of practical problems. As a body sick from cancer has a host of other issues caused by the disease, so Corinth manifested her carnality by the many serious problems in the congregation.

Throughout the book the apostle addresses all those issues in an orderly and systematic way. Addressing Corinth's problems, the Holy Ghost gives much instruction to the church of Jesus Christ today.

This instruction is not merely a patchwork of different and disconnected themes. As all biblical books, 1 Corinthians has a theme, which as a golden thread runs through the entire book. In his glorious ode to love in 1 Corinthians 13 the apostle finally lays his finger on the heart of Corinth's problems and explains the theme that ran through all of his previous instruction in the epistle and that ties all of his instruction together into a coherent whole. The apostle Paul was a good physician who not only treated the various symptoms, but also rooted out the cancer that

6

was causing those things in the church. The theme of 1 Corinthians is love, specifically the calling of the church to walk in the way of love.

The apostle begins the explanation of his theme in 1 Corinthians 12:31: "And yet shew I unto you a more excellent way." That more excellent way is the way of love explained in chapter 13. Corinth's carnality and all her other problems were rooted in Corinth's lack of love and her refusal to walk in the way of love. That lack of love arose out of Corinth's lack of esteem for love. Her lack of esteem for love arose out of her lack of knowledge about love and its way. Because she did not know true love, she did not esteem love very highly; not esteeming love highly, she did not pursue love very ardently. Not pursuing it, she did not walk in the way of love, and things fell to pieces in the church, which is held together by the bonds of love.

This same ignorance of love and its way and the resultant chaos are characteristic of the churches today. How much sin is excused, tolerated, and even praised in the name of love? How often are not the words of one minister pitted against the words of another minister, or the words of one minister against the word of God, in the name of excusing ungodly toleration and fellowship? How many truly loving deeds are harshly criticized as foreign to love by those who have hardly an inkling of what true love is and reveal that by their failure to walk in the way of love as described by the apostle? What chaos has come to churches because of failure to walk in the way of love?

To mention only one example, one that is not an isolated occurrence but widespread, what of the wicked chaos that ensues when a husband abandons his wife of many years, lives with another woman, and then pleads for tolerance in the church in the name of love, and in the name of love the church capitulates to the pressure and sweeps the whole God-dishonoring, church-disrupting, family-destroying, and spirit-oppressing mess under the proverbial rug. The divorced husband sits with his new wife in the front pew of the church. The abandoned spouse and the children sit weeping in the back. From the pulpit the minister preaches a sermon on love. Is it love to tolerate and to condone such evil? Many professing Christians answer yes. That many professing Christians walk in this purported way of love illustrates the sad state of the church's knowledge of love, esteem for love, and pursuit of love. Because that is the "love" of many professing Christians, they do not walk in the way of love of the apostle Paul and the Holy Ghost.

In this epistle the apostle explains the way of love. The whole book is an exposition of the way of love. In the entire book the Holy Ghost calls the church to walk in the way of love as that way is carefully laid out and applied in many different situations. The way of love is "a more excellent way" (v. 31). Apart from walking in that way of love, the church is carnal and begins to disintegrate.

CHAPTER I

THE CHURCH OF GOD IN CORINTH

1 Corinthians 1:1–3

---

1. Paul, called to be an apostle of Jesus Christ through the will of God, and Sosthenes our brother,

2. Unto the church of God which is at Corinth, to them that are sanctified in Christ Jesus, called to be saints, with all that in every place call upon the name of Jesus Christ our Lord, both theirs and ours:

3. Grace be unto you, and peace, from God our Father, and from the Lord Jesus Christ.

The apostle Paul addresses the church. The word of God is always addressed to the church. The Bible is for the church. The epistle to the Corinthians was for the church in Paul's day and is also for the church today.

That there was a church in Corinth at all was an astounding work of God's grace. Corinth was a center of commerce, culture, religion, government, and learning in the Roman Empire. Wealthy from trade and famous for craftsmen, merchants, businessmen, and learning, Corinth was infamous for her addiction to pleasure, her toleration of every wicked perversion, and the access she offered to every pleasure to gratify man's insatiable lusts. Corinth was particularly devoted to Aphrodite, goddess of erotic love—lust, pleasure, and the gratification of man. In this city the antithesis between true Christian love and man's corruption of love stood out in the sharpest contrast.

God had an elect church in that worldly city. By means of Paul's preaching God gathered her out of the world and formed her into a church. Acts 18 relates the origins and establishment of the Corinthian church by Paul on his second missionary journey. Initially Paul met Aquila and Priscilla, Jewish refugees in the city due to the edict of Emperor Claudius expelling all the Jews from Rome. "Paul departed from Athens, and came to Corinth; and found a certain Jew named Aquila, born in Pontus, lately come from Italy, with his wife Priscilla; (because that Claudius had commanded all Jews to depart from Rome:) and came unto them." Paul stayed with them because they were tentmakers as he was: "And because he was of the same craft he abode with them, and wrought: for by their occupation they were tentmakers" (vv. 1–3).

Because of his preaching and teaching Paul encountered the fierce opposition of the unbelieving Jews of the city, who eventually managed to arraign Paul before Gallio the governor:

12. And when Gallio was the deputy of Achaia, the Jews made insurrection with one accord against Paul, and brought him to the judgment seat,
13. Saying, This fellow persuadeth men to worship God contrary to the law.
14. And when Paul was now about to open his mouth, Gallio said unto the Jews, If it were a matter of wrong or wicked lewdness, O ye Jews, reason would that I should bear with you:
15. But if it be a question of words and names, and of your law, look ye to it; for I will be no judge of such matters.
16. And he drave them from the judgment seat.
17. Then all the Greeks took Sosthenes, the chief ruler of the synagogue, and beat him before the judgment

seat. And Gallio cared for none of those things. (Acts 18:12–17)

Gallio saw through the trumped-up charges and dismissed them. Besides losing their case, the Jews saw Sosthenes—the chief ruler of the synagogue and probably the chief accuser of Paul at the time—badly beaten by the Greeks at Gallio's court. The reason no doubt was that the fashionable anti-Semitism of the capital, Rome, the same anti-Semitism that had resulted in the presence of Aquila and Priscilla, had spilled over into the provinces. Sosthenes is likely the same Sosthenes whom Paul mentions in 1 Corinthians 1:1. At the time of Paul's trial Sosthenes by religion was still a Jew and a chief leader of the synagogue. Sometime later he was converted and became a well-respected member of the church. He was probably connected with both reporting the situation of Corinth and delivering the letter with Timothy. By mentioning Sosthenes the apostle invests him with authority.

Against the stiff resistance from the Jews of the city and by the strength of an encouraging vision from God, the apostle labored diligently in Corinth for a year and a half. The fruit of his labors was a large and prosperous church.

The occasion of the letter was reports of schism and other problems in the church (v. 11) and a series of questions sent to Paul by the troubled church (7:1). What seems at first glance to be a series of disconnected and wide-ranging issues is tied together by the theme of love. From beginning to end he explains love and the calling of the church to walk in love as the answer to all her problems and questions. Love is the excellent way (12:31).

In the first three verses of chapter 1, the apostle begins his treatment on walking in the way of love by teaching the church who she is and whom she is especially called to love. It is necessary to teach the church who she is because love proceeds from faith. The Corinthian church's lack of love was due in part to her lack of knowledge—faith—about who she was. The apostle builds up the church's faith and thus her love by teaching the church the knowledge of herself. She was a divine creation, precious, and dear to God, and she must be so to the believer as well.

The Church in Corinth

The apostle calls the Corinthian congregation "church" and thereby graces the body of believers and their seed in Corinth with a glorious name. Paul uses "church" in 1:2 in three senses.

First, the church in Corinth was an institute. This is clear because she "call[ed] upon the name of Jesus Christ our Lord." Calling on the name of the Lord does not refer merely to any individual member's calling on the Lord. It is not a general reference to prayer. Rather, it refers to the church's calling on the name of the Lord as institute. By "call upon the name of Jesus Christ our Lord," the apostle refers to the public worship and activity of the church as institute.

The outstanding activity of the church institute by which she clearly manifests herself to be *church* in distinction from a sect or an organization that merely calls itself church, and by which she distinguishes herself from the false church that is no church at all, is that the true church of God calls on the name of Jesus Christ the Lord. She calls on him and acknowledges him as her Lord.

She calls on the name of the Lord when the Lord Jesus Christ is preached, when the testimony from the pulpit is the gospel of Jesus Christ revealed in the sacred scriptures, especially the truth of the cross of Christ as the only ground and foundation of the church's salvation, and the origin of that salvation in the eternal decree of predestination (vv. 17–18, 27). She calls on the Lord in that way because by that doctrine she calls on him to save her from her sins and ascribes all her salvation to God in Christ. She calls on the name of the Lord when the sacraments are administered according to the word and commandments of Jesus Christ and when the discipline in the church is carried out according to the will of Jesus Christ. She calls on the name of the Lord when his glorious name reigns supreme, when Jesus Christ is acknowledged as the only lord and king of the church, and when everything in the church is ordered and regulated by the word of Jesus Christ and done in Spirit and truth according to God's commands in scripture.

To call on the name of the Lord is the outstanding characteristic of the true church, just as the substitution of man's word and will for Christ's is the outstanding characteristic of the false and apostatizing church. When she departs from the true doctrine of the gospel, mal-administers the sacraments, and either sheathes the sword of discipline entirely or turns it on the people of God who rebuke her wickedness, she does not reveal herself as the church of God but shows she has taken the mark of the synagogue of Satan.

The name church, then, cannot be applied to just any gathering that calls itself church in the world. There cannot be a "house church," as it is meant today, in which there are no elders and deacons, no preaching of the word by God's ordained servant, no sacraments administered, and no discipline. This is not a church, and it is presumptuous to take the name. The institute that calls on the name of the Lord is the church.

How she calls on the name of the Lord—the kind of preaching, the way the sacraments are administered, the way discipline is carried out—is clearly seen and recognized in the world. This is how she becomes visible in the world.

Where these are done in agreement with the word of God, there is the church. To the degree that her life is according to the word and regulated by the word, publicly calling on the name of the Lord, she is church. To the degree that she departs, she departs from Christ her Lord and is no longer church.

That was the issue in Corinth. Corinth was threatening her very identity as church because she was toying with the gospel, the sacraments, and discipline. When the apostle calls her "church," he calls her to manifest the lordship of Christ by obedience to his word in preaching, sacraments, and discipline.

Second, "church" refers to the spiritual essence of the church. What is visible is not the full reality of the church. The church as institute has an invisible, spiritual essence. The apostle teaches this when he calls the church those who "are sanctified in Christ Jesus" (v. 2). To be sanctified in Christ is to be called out of the world and joined to Christ by true faith. "Church" refers to those who are called out from the world and who are joined to Christ really and actually by faith.

By nature according to her physical birth the church is joined to Adam, her head and representative. She is conceived and born in sin. She belongs spiritually with the world, she is one with the world, and in Adam she lies under the curse of God spoken in Eden. God calls her out of that world by the efficacious call of the gospel and joins her to Jesus Christ by a true and living faith. "Sanctified in Christ" refers to the church's real, invisible, spiritual communion with Christ Jesus, her new head. She is joined with him; she is bone of his bone and flesh of his flesh. In that union she is partaker of him and of all his riches and gifts. This is her salvation.

The local congregation as an institute has members and officebearers, who wield the power of preaching, government, and mercy; yet the spiritual reality of the church is her communion with Christ, and her spiritual essence is that she is sanctified in Christ. The devil always sows tares among God's wheat. Always mixed in the church are hypocrites and ungodly. Not all who are born into the church or join the church are church. The real essence of that local church is her union with Christ her head.

"Sanctified in Christ" means also that the visible life of the church flows from Christ as its spiritual source. Everything the church possesses flows from her head. This is the spiritual essence of the communion of the saints. Communion of the saints in the church does not refer first to individual gifts and the fellowship of the saints with one another, but to the fellowship all the saints have in common because they are joined to Christ. In common and in distinction from the world they are partakers of Christ.

Third, the full reality of the church includes the idea that the institute is a manifestation of the universal body composed of all the elect. The church is not exhausted by any one local congregation, but the church is the universal body of Jesus Christ consisting of all the elect gathered from the world throughout history and manifesting themselves in various local congregations. Paul makes clear that he speaks of other churches when he says that Corinth is church "with all that in every place call on the name of Jesus Christ our Lord, both theirs and ours" (v. 2). Corinth is church with all other churches that reveal themselves as such by calling on the name of the Lord Jesus Christ.

That Paul speaks of election in connection with the church is made plain by her name church. Her name church traces her origin back to election and the will of God because the calling of God proceeds from election. Those whom he calls church he predestinated to be the church from eternity. The universal elect body of Christ is the full reality of the church. The church in that sense has been gathered from the time of Abel and will be gathered to the end of the world.

The apostle joins all these ideas together and applies them all to the church in Corinth and thus to every true church of Christ. No one who is not a member of Christ's universal church is really a member in the institute at all. No one can claim to be a member of the universal church who despises the institute. The apostle does not allow anyone who lacks membership in a true church of Jesus Christ to claim membership in the universal body of Christ. The church is the universal body that manifests itself in a local congregation. If one has membership in a local congregation, and in his membership is sanctified in Christ, he may say, "I am a member of the universal body of the church of Jesus Christ." Apart from membership in the local church, one has no ground to claim membership in the universal body.

That church was in Corinth. It may seem that Corinth, torn by schisms, does not deserve the name church. It may seem that if there was one city where there could not be a church, it was Corinth. But God graced the body of believers and their children in Corinth with that glorious name church and thereby described in a single word a great wonder of grace. She was the gathering in the institute of those called out of the world by the efficacious call of the gospel according to the decree of predestination, joined in saving union to Christ, possessing the forgiveness of sins and the righteousness of Christ by faith only, sanctified by his Spirit, and calling on the name of the Lord.

If that is what the church is, the church is a glorious creation like no other institution in the world; a divine creation of God by his grace. She is not merely a society of likeminded individuals. The church does not exist because likeminded individuals got together and agreed to establish a church. The church is not a club. She is not a loose collection of friendly individuals. She is not a business. She is a church, the body of Jesus Christ gathered out of the world and manifesting itself in the institute, for the glory of God her creator. She is glorious.

God's Church

That church is God's church: "the church of God which is at Corinth" (v. 2).

The church is God's not merely in the sense that God creates and owns all things, but in the unique sense that she alone is the object of his grace and peace. Only within the church is God's grace and peace given. This is what the apostle means by "grace be unto you, and peace" (v. 3). God graciously conceived the church in eternity, graciously purchased her at the cross, graciously forgives her sins, graciously sanctifies her by Christ's

Spirit, graciously preserves her against all her enemies and all who seek to destroy her, and finally graciously perfects her in the assembly of the elect in life eternal. As the object of his grace she is at peace with God.

By mentioning grace and peace together, the apostle draws attention to the chief saving benefit of God's grace and to the way God's grace brings peace to the church, namely, justification by faith alone. In justification God forgives the sins of the elect but guilty sinner—his original and actual sins—imputes to him the perfect righteousness of Christ, and declares him righteous and worthy of eternal life. Being righteous, the church is the object of the unfailing grace of God and is blessed by him with every benefit of salvation. God blesses the righteous and only the righteous. So God blesses his church. He always blesses his church. He only blesses his church.

The first benefit of justification is peace with God in the sinner's own consciousness. This being the collective experience of every true member of Christ, the church's experience is that she is at peace with God. Being at peace with God, she is perfectly secure in the world and unto eternity since God is for her and nothing can be against her.

The truth of the preservation of the church and of each individual elect member is demanded by the statement that the church is God's. If God can be overcome and the church, or even a single member of Christ, can be wrested out of God's hands, then the church can fail and some member of the church who has received grace can fall from grace. If the church is God's, a fall from grace and the destruction of the church are as utterly impossible as a defeat of God. If the church is God's, she is perfectly secure in the face of every strife, division, and false doctrine. If the church is God's, the gates of hell cannot prevail against her. The church is wholly God's in every respect: individual elect member, as institute, as universal body, and regarding her spiritual essence of communion with Christ.

Since the church is God's, the church is not man's in any respect. The church is not the product of the will and work of man. She does not exist for man. The church does not belong to man or to any group of men.

Arminianism denies that. Arminianism teaches that the sinner by his free will must choose Christ offered in the gospel and that by virtue of his free will the power to believe is in every man. Any theology that teaches that salvation—being sanctified in Christ and thus being the church—is dependent on the work or the will of man not only corrupts the doctrine of salvation, but also overthrows the doctrine that the church is God's. If salvation is dependent on man's will or works, the existence of the church depends on man's will. If the existence of the church depends on man's will, the church is man's and not God's. Arminianism says not only that salvation is of man, but also that the church is of man.

Rome also teaches that the church is of man, because the church for Rome is synonymous with the pope and his curia of bishops, cardinals, and nuncios. Rome denies that the church's spiritual essence is communion with Jesus Christ and that the church is the elect body of Jesus Christ, gathered and defended throughout history. This corrupt doctrine that the church is man's and not God's leads Rome to introduce for truth the doctrines and commandments of men, bind men's consciences by her laws, make tradition equal to the word of God, make the believer's and thus the whole church's peace depend on man's works, and teach that the power to forgive sins resides in the church herself. Rome's church is man's church.

If a man teaches that God's grace is given wider than the church, which means wider than the elect of God, he denies that the church is God's unique creation and that she is God's. If all men have grace, are favored by God, or are offered grace, what is so special about the church?

The apostle's assertion that the church is God's contrasts not only with the *doctrine* that the church is man's, but also with the *practice* that the church is man's. This happens when a man's view of the church is that the church ought to serve him. When a man's desire and will, whether his own or another's, become most important in the church, that man has denied as thoroughly as a Roman Catholic that the church is God's.

That the church is God's means practically that she is precious and dear to God. One denies that the church is God's, then, when he does not regard the church as precious and dear. This lack of regard for the church is manifested especially when he refuses membership in her or easily forsakes her.

When the church herself or a member of the church behaves contrary to the will of God as revealed in the sacred scriptures or teaches contrary to his will in the scripture, there is also the practical denial that the church is God's. Especially a man who causes schism in the body of Christ denies that the church is God's.

God calls the church his to express his love for her. Here too we see that the source of all the church's love for herself is God's love for the church. In that love he is faithful to his church. That faithfulness of God in his love to his church is evident at the beginning of Corinthians when God addresses Corinth as his church. By her schism, disorder, doctrinal errors, laxity in discipline, and other sins, she had forfeited her right to be called church. In his faithfulness and love God calls her back to the consideration of who she is as church.

Grace by the Gospel

The church receives grace and peace from God the Father and Jesus Christ through the preaching of the gospel. Grace and peace mentioned together teach that the chief feature of the gospel that formed Corinth is the gospel of sovereign grace. This gospel is proclaimed in the preaching of the grace of God that forgives the sinner's sins without any works and constitutes that sinner righteous before him, so that it is as though the sinner never had any sin and has fulfilled all righteousness. This justified believer has peace with God.

The truth that the church receives grace and peace from God through the preaching of the gospel of grace makes plain both the reason for and the importance of the apostle's assertion of his apostleship in the first three verses: "Paul, called to be an apostle of Jesus Christ through the will of God" (v. 1). This means that he is an apostle who faithfully makes known Jesus Christ in the preaching of the gospel of saving grace. He is an apostle of Christ, and as such he makes Christ known as the only way of salvation, calls all men everywhere to believe in him, and declares the promise that all who do believe shall be saved by him from sin and wrath unto eternal life. By that preaching the Corinthians were formed as a church. By that preaching they continued to receive grace and peace from God.

"Through the will of God" means that Paul's call and commission to preach that gospel came from God, and thus the will of God in election is the ultimate source and explanation of the gospel itself and the existence of the church through his gospel. God sent Paul to preach the gospel. He sent Paul to preach Christ because God had an elect church that must be gathered and formed into an institute by that gospel.

The apostle shows himself to be very different in his thinking about missions than the proud men who would plant churches in this or that place of their choosing, not thinking for a moment to ask whether God has a church there. The apostle shows himself to be very different from those who in their self-will form congregations where God has clearly indicated that he does not have a church. God indicated this when the preaching of the gospel in that location did not call out God's elect church to be formed as an institute in that place because none or very few elect were there. The apostle had an election theology of missions, preaching, and the church.

God's eternal will in choosing the church is the truth that

God made fundamental to all of Paul's labors in Corinth and thus all his preaching. Before Paul had gathered hardly a convert in Corinth, God told him that he had much people in that pagan city.

When Paul teaches about the church and the preciousness of the church as the unique object of God's grace, Paul asserts his apostolic authority with a fervency second only to the opening of his letter to the Galatians. Some in Corinth were attempting to undermine Paul's apostleship and authority. By that attempt they were aiming at the apostolic gospel—the apostolic gospel that is preached now by the true church of Jesus Christ in the world—in order to make that gospel a mere word of man. By that tactic they were also attempting to take away from the church her divine origin and ownership and make the church an institution of man, an institution that they had designs on ruling.

The argument is this: if Paul's gospel is man's and not a gospel preached on the authority of God and consisting in the truth of Christ, all of his labors are also the labors of a mere man. Then the church he called out of the darkness of Corinth is also man's. If the word that called the Corinthian church into being is man's, the church is also man's, and she can depend for her existence on any man who shows himself to be more gifted, more eloquent, more understanding, or more favored than the apostle. If it is a man's church, it can be ruled by one man as well as another. However, if Paul's authority comes from God, the word that formed that church is God's word, and the church formed by that gospel is also God's.

Thus also by that gospel the church is the recipient of the grace and peace of God. Then the only lord in the church is Jesus Christ, and his word is the only rule. By that gospel God brings grace and peace to his elect people, calling them out of darkness and into the church. By God's will the church is gathered. By God's will the church is formed and fashioned. By God's will the church continues to exist in Corinth and to be the object of grace and peace.

This is the explanation of any church that is God's church, a true church. God wills it; therefore, it is church. Therefore, it is *his* church.

It is also necessary for a church that calls herself church to assert that her gospel is of Jesus Christ by the will of God and to vigorously insist that she preaches the truth. She may not give ear to those who call that pride and who would attempt to blunt that aspect of the church's proclamation. Paul does not, and he calls the church at Corinth to acknowledge that she is called of God because the gospel by which she was called is from God, so that she can see her origin in God. If she does not, cannot, or will not say that she preaches the truth, she is merely a man's church and not God's at all.

The Calling of the Church

This church is "called to be saints" (v. 2). The words *to be* do not appear in the original. The apostle is simply saying that as the objects of God's grace and peace the Corinthians are saints. By grace God graciously forgives their sins on the basis of Christ's perfect sacrifice and by faith alone. On that basis he also sanctifies them and makes them saints. Saints is their name because it describes their spiritual essence by God's grace. He made them saints by making them church; they are what they are by the grace of God.

The name saints also personalizes everything the apostle has said about the church. The individual believer's existence in the church is not a product of his will, works, or insights. It is the work of God, who calls the believer out of the world according to his will, joins him to the body of Jesus Christ that manifests itself as a church, and makes him a saint.

This name also expresses the saints' purpose in the world. A saint is wholly consecrated to God, his truth, and his glory. He separates from the world and impenitent sinners and loves God and hates sin. Here is also expressed the purpose of the church.

Since the church does not belong to man, she does not at all serve men or the will and desires of men. The church certainly does not serve the world, which thinking is the antithesis of what the apostle teaches here. The church serves God.

The knowledge of who the church is and who she is called to serve must regulate all of a believer's behavior in the church. A saint loves the church because he loves the God whose church she is and whose grace placed him in the church. Some who are vile in their speech against the church and refuse to associate with the church by having their membership there still claim to be saints. Saints love the church—especially in their church membership— because God loves the church and gave himself for the church and created her by a wonder of grace in the world. Loving the church, they are members in her.

Saints are devoted to the church. One who for personal gain, aggrandizement, or self-will divides, carves, tears, and rends the church has forgotten that the church is not his and that his existence in the church is not his doing. The church is God's. She exists because of God's good pleasure. She exists solely for God. Let all who are saints and who claim to love God so love the church, and their membership in her.

CHAPTER 2

ENRICHED
BY GOD'S GRACE

1 Corinthians 1:4–9

---

4. *I thank my God always on your behalf, for the grace of*
    God which is given you by Jesus Christ;
5. *That in every thing ye are enriched by him, in all utter-*
    ance, and in all knowledge;
6. *Even as the testimony of Christ was confirmed in you:*
7. *So that ye come behind in no gift; waiting for the coming*
    of our Lord Jesus Christ:
8. *Who shall also confirm you unto the end, that ye may be*
    blameless in the day of our Lord Jesus Christ.
9. *God is faithful, by whom ye were called unto the fellow-*
    ship of his Son Jesus Christ our Lord.

The teaching of these verses is important to understand the message of 1 Corinthians: walking in the way of love. In the context the apostle reminded the church of Corinth of her divine origin and ownership. As a church she is distinct from a society of men, a club, a clique, or a business. She is church. She is God's church. She is that because she is the object of God's grace. In verses 4–9 the apostle gives thanks that as the object of God's grace the Corinthians are enriched by that grace. Enriched by that grace, she is a gifted church.

It may seem strange in the face of the Corinthians' particular error that the apostle commends the church for her giftedness. Part of Corinth's problem was that the members horribly abused their gifts. They exalted one gift above another, praised the gifts that were the least praiseworthy, and esteemed as virtually of no account the gifts that were the best: faith, hope, and love. Besides, they used their gifts for their personal advancement and not for the church or the glory of God.

There is always the temptation present in the church to abuse gifts. Use of one's supposed giftedness is often the excuse to justify abandonment of the church. Giftedness is one of the arguments used to support the error that women may serve in church offices. "The sisters," they say, "are gifted. Therefore, they should be able to use their gifts in the offices." Because of his giftedness one lords it over another. Giftedness is still the occasion of evil in the church as it was in Corinth.

Someone might object then that it is harmful to speak of the giftedness of the church. Yet it is exactly instruction about her gifts that the Corinthian church needed. Exactly this same instruction corrects wrong thinking about gifts today. The abuse of gifts and giftedness does not overthrow the truth of the church's giftedness. The apostle uses the truth about the giftedness of the Corinthian church to begin to correct her abuse of gifts. She needed to know about her gifts. She especially needed to know where those gifts came from to set her again on a proper foundation from which to use those gifts lawfully in the church, for the church, and to the glory of God.

Enriched by Every Gift

When the apostle says to the Corinthians, "I thank my God always on your behalf, for the grace of God which is given you" (v. 4), he does not speak to every individual or even to every individual in the church in Corinth. Not all individuals and not all who are members of the church are recipients of the grace of God. Paul speaks to the church as elect, called, and gathered. This church manifested herself in Corinth as she does wherever there is a true church of Christ.

The apostle gives thanks to God "for the grace of God which is given you by Jesus Christ" (v. 4). The church alone is the object of the grace of God. That grace is God's favor shown to his elect people. It is an unmerited favor of God according to which he chose his church, called her out of the world, and bestowed on her every blessing of salvation in Jesus Christ, later summarized as "wisdom, righteousness...sanctification, and redemption" (v. 30). That grace of God is the power of God to save his church from sin, form her as church in the world, bestow on her every saving good, and bring her to heavenly perfection and glory in the day of Christ.

When the apostle speaks of the church as an object of grace, he is not vainly flattering the church, as some men flatter their victim before delivering a devastating criticism. The apostle looks at the church in Corinth from the viewpoint of her spiritual essence, as she exists in the world as church, and as she alone is the object of the grace of God.

By that grace the church is enriched. Enrichment of the church means that the grace of God bestows on the church every kind of gift. Paul makes that clear when he says, "The grace of God...enriched [you], in all utterance, and in all knowledge...so that ye come behind in no gift" (vv. 4–7). The grace of God not only bestows on the church every blessing of salvation in Jesus Christ, but also is the power by which the church is enriched and overflows with many other spiritual gifts for her use and the glory of God.

The apostle explains what he means when he says that the enrichment is "in every thing...in all utterance, and in all knowledge." Those phrases must be taken together. The grace enriched them in all things in their utterance and in their knowledge. "In utterance" literally means in word, that is, the word the church speaks in her united confession of the truth. The church as church speaks one word. She professes one doctrine. She preaches one truth. She agrees in true faith.

The word of God denies here the view of the church's giftedness that each church or denomination, no matter how corrupt and apostate, has a little giftedness to commend her to others. Someone might say, "Anglicans show liturgical beauty; Rome is committed to the past; Methodists are mission minded; and the Reformed have confessional beauty." Or if the idea is applied only to the Reformed community of churches, one might speak of denominational distinctives that commend each denomination to the others. But the giftedness of the church is always in utterance and knowledge, so that apart from the truth—which is Christ—there is no giftedness in the church.

Furthermore, being enriched "in utterance" means the church is enriched in the application of that truth to every situation in her life. Just as when *conversation* is used to refer to a person's life and not only to what he says, so *utterance* is used here. A man's whole life speaks and tells who he is. What he says must be the same as what he does. Otherwise, he is a hypocrite who says and does not do. In the church and for the individual believer there is no aspect of life that is not brought under the power of God's grace and enriched by grace. The church is enriched in her institutional life: the preaching of the word, the administration of the sacraments, and the exercise of discipline. She is enriched in her organic life: the study of the scriptures and fellowship one with another. She is enriched in her home life and school life. The grace of God as it is bestowed on the church enriches her in "all utterance," so that by means of the truth her whole life is brought under the power of God's grace.

This enriched utterance proceeds from her enriched knowledge. *Knowledge* refers to true knowledge, the saving knowledge of God in the face of Jesus Christ. It is knowledge by which the church not only has the truth intellectually, but also loves that truth. She knows her God in Jesus Christ as her savior by a true and living faith. She understands spiritual things spiritually. She truly knows herself as the object of the grace of God. She understands that all that she has is bestowed on her by God's grace. She is enriched in *all* knowledge.

In the church alone and by virtue of the grace of God alone there is the saving knowledge of God contrasted with ignorance that exists outside the church. In the church there is the ability to apply the true saving knowledge of God to every situation of life. That is when and where the gift—and all gifts—is used as it is intended: for the church and to the glory of God.

Coming Behind in No Gift

As a result the church "come[s] behind in no gift" (v. 7). This is clear from "so that" at the beginning of verse 7. This means that because the Corinthians have been enriched by the grace of God in all utterance and in all knowledge, they come behind in no gift.

Literally the word translated as "gift" means grace. This indicates what the apostle means by "gift." He does not refer merely to the raw, natural talents of men and women. It is true that men are naturally gifted. This too comes from God. Men have gifts for ruling as mayors, presidents, representatives, and senators. Some have the gift of healing and become doctors and nurses. Others have the gift of business and become successful entrepreneurs. Another may have natural intellectual ability, quick wit, and a ready mind and become a professor or a teacher. In that sense there are gifts in all men.

But those with only gifts are trouble for the church. Examples include women who brag about their gifts but will not use them in the home and instead want to use them in the offices of the church; or the intellectual giant with great ability and profound understanding who leads the church astray into false doctrine.

The apostle speaks of graces. Grace saves the church. Grace

enriches the church. Grace enriched the church of Corinth with many different gifts. Grace that enriches the church in utterance and knowledge then controls all those other gifts so that all the gifts are used for the church. The apostle speaks of the manifold riches of God's grace as everything in the church is brought under the power of his grace and is pressed into the service of the church and therefore to the glory of God. It does not take grace for a man to be successful in business; it takes grace for a man to run his business to the glory of God and to support the kingdom of heaven with his money. It does not take grace to be a mother; it takes grace to be a mother in the church and to do so in faith and for the benefit of God's covenantal seed. It does not take grace to be an intellectual giant; it takes grace to use one's intellect for the advancement of the understanding of the truth, for the salvation of the church, and to the glory of God.

That the Corinthians had gifts was beyond doubt. There may never be a church again in history that has as many gifts as Corinth had. They had gifts of tongues, of healing, and of raising the dead. They had gripping, powerful preachers, such as Apollos, Paul, and Cephas. Besides these pastors and teachers, they had apostles, prophets, and evangelists. They had servants who were dedicated to the church, such as Chloe, Stephanas, Crispus, and Gaius. They had pillars in the church, such as Sosthenes. They had teachers, government, miracle workers, helpers, and healers. And the church was not ignorant but had a thorough understanding of the truth. The Corinthians had gifts!

So it is always true of the church of Jesus Christ in the world. The manifold grace of God enriches the church so she comes behind in no gift. Though a church today may not excel as Corinth did—no one today has the ability to speak in tongues or to raise the dead—she comes behind in no gift. That is, in the life of the church—in her particular situation and time and with her present necessities—she lacks nothing needful for her and has an overflowing of grace to meet every situation.

A Warning about Enrichment

When the apostle teaches that the church is enriched by the manifold grace of God and comes behind in no gift, he wards off several dangers.

First, he combats the idea that the church is pathetically poor in comparison to the supposed giftedness of other institutions in the world. The church is the only place in the world where there are gifts—gifts to meet all the needs of the church in every situation.

This reality about the church is frankly doubted today. That doubt manifests itself particularly in the realm of counseling. When a woman is depressed, she does not seek out the church at all, perhaps will not even inform the church, but goes into the world to a psychiatrist and worldly counselor who has no grace to help her, at best can prescribe some medicine to deal with physical lacks, and fills her with worldly wisdom, about which the apostle has nothing good to say. Perhaps such an approach is even counseled by elders who would rather not deal with the issue or who are looking for a quick fix to an embarrassing problem. When parents have discipline trouble with a young adult, they do not call in the elders, if they do not openly hinder them and frustrate their work, but appeal to counseling centers, psychiatric centers, or medical centers.

What explains the fact that when someone has trouble in his family life, trouble in marriage, or personal trouble, the first instinct is often to seek help elsewhere than the church? It is a lack of faith in the church's giftedness and that the essence of that giftedness is the grace of God in Jesus Christ. It is either a doubt of the power of grace, which is doubt about the power of God, or it is an unwillingness to receive the solution that grace teaches. The rise of biblical counseling centers is a manifestation of just such a lack of faith in the church's giftedness.

In the face of problems perceived as complex and novel, many will seek help everywhere else but the church. They seek especially for the supposed professionals and doctors and disdain the help of the great Physician and Discerner of spirits, who comes through the word and the church, whose word is the power to call out of darkness into God's marvelous light and from the bondage of sin into the glorious liberty of the sons of God, whose word is quick and powerful and sharper than any two-edged sword, and whose essence is the testimony of Christ Jesus and the living voice of God. They do not think highly of the church and her gifts.

The Corinthians had enormous problems, and the apostle commends them all to the grace of God. By the grace of God, which is the power to deliver sinners from sin and to bless the believer in every situation, the enriched church is able to meet every need of her members.

This same doubt about the church's giftedness explains why church members abandon the church to join a mission society that has no right or ability to do missions. In defense of that they speak of all the gifts of that mission society. But that society lacks the one essential gift: the right and power to preach the gospel and to do missions and the promise from God that by means of it he will gather his church. The church alone has that gift.

The apostle denies that the church is a pathetically poor institution in gifts. She has all the gifts necessary for her life and every contingency by the work of the manifold riches of the grace of God. She comes behind in no gift: nothing necessary for her life in the world is lacking in her.

Second, the apostle also wards off the danger of spiritual pride in the giftedness of the church and tempers the church's possession of her gifts when he says that the church possesses the gifts, "waiting for the coming of our Lord Jesus Christ" (v. 7). Paul means the second coming of Jesus Christ. The church does not have perfection, no matter how gifted she may be. Perfection only comes when Christ comes again. That ought to humble everyone and every church in their giftedness. However gloriously gifted she may be, in comparison to perfection she only has in part. When perfection is come, that which is in part will be done away. She is gifted in the present for her present necessity with every sort of grace needful for her.

Third, Paul wards off the most dangerous, or damning, of the spiritual dangers about giftedness, or grace; that is, the view that the church or individual receives those gifts in order that by the use of them the individual and ultimately the whole church merit salvation. This is at its essence Rome's view of giftedness. God gives grace to his church so that the church might cooperate with God and do good works, which good works will form the basis of the church's eternal salvation. This is also the basic doctrine of the contemporary heresy known as the federal vision. By means of grace given in his union with Christ, the believer works good works that will form part of the basis of the believer's justification at the last judgment.

Paul first speaks of the church's "waiting for the coming of our Lord Jesus Christ." If the use of gifts is the ground of one's eternal salvation, "waiting" is hardly the appropriate word. Instead Paul should have said, "Work, indeed work very hard because your salvation depends on it." But he says "waiting," which is the patient expectation of what God promises.

Second, the confirmation of the believer in the final judgment in the day of our Lord Jesus Christ is by "Christ," and the apostle says that he knows that the verdict will be "blameless." If the verdict in the final judgment would depend on the believer's works, Paul could not speak confidently of a blameless verdict. If the verdict in the final judgment were based on works, the actual verdict spoken by Christ could not be known confidently, since it would depend on works that the believer may or may not perform. Because Paul speaks confidently of a blameless verdict in the final judgment, that verdict cannot be based on works performed by the believer. Paul can speak confidently of a blameless verdict because the verdict pronounced over believers in the final judgment will be the confirmation of the verdict of blameless that they already hear in their conscience by faith through the testimony of the gospel. Christ will confirm this verdict publicly and finally in the last judgment. Believers are justified now through the preaching the same way they will be justified by Christ in the judgment: by faith alone without works. Because the verdict that expresses their eternal destinies is based solely on the righteousness of Christ and not on their works, this also guarantees that believers will not be condemned for the use of their gifts, which they in various ways pollute and defile with sin. Rather, believers will be commended by Christ for the cup of cold water given, the visit in prison, or nakedness covered that is done in his name (Matt. 25:44–45).

The Means of Enrichment

The means by which God bestows his grace that enriches his church is expressed in the words "even as the testimony of Christ was confirmed in you" (1 Cor. 1:6). "Even as" in this instance means in proportion to and thus indicates means: in proportion to the confirmation of Christ's testimony in them, so they were enriched in everything by him.

"The testimony of Christ" is the preaching of the gospel according to its essence and power. The preaching in its essence and power is the testimony of Christ. Preaching is about Christ. True preaching is the setting forth of Christ in all the glory of his person, natures, and perfect work. It includes the teaching that at the cross Christ made full satisfaction for the sins of his elect people and merited by his suffering and death perfect righteousness and all the riches of salvation, and that all the riches of grace and salvation are in him. Included in the testimony is the command to repent and to believe in Christ for salvation and the promise that everyone who repents and believes will be saved. The preaching also sharply warns that those who do not repent and believe will perish in their unbelief.

However, Paul means more than that preaching is testimony

about Christ. If the preaching is only some words about Christ, as a book or an article is about Christ, the preaching has no power to save and to bestow the riches and gifts of grace on the church. Rather, in the preaching Christ speaks and bears witness.

This makes the preaching of the gospel a power to "confirm" (v. 8). To confirm means to fix, establish, or bestow. The testimony of Christ is confirmed in the church. The church is built up in and by the gospel and in the assurance of her salvation in Christ. She is established in grace, and she flourishes by grace in and through the preaching. As the preaching flourishes, so the church in proportion flourishes in her giftedness. As the preaching increases, the church is confirmed in the knowledge of her gracious salvation and the assurance of that salvation to the end. This assurance is necessary as the source of her abounding, thankful use of her gifts.

The power to bestow all the riches and gifts is by the preaching. The power to move the church to use her gifts is the preaching. This is true because Christ speaks in and through the preaching everything that is needful for the church and riches besides, great riches for the church so that she is enriched in everything, in utterance and in knowledge, and she comes behind in no gift, so that the whole life of the church is brought more and more under that power. The church does not have the gifts in herself, but she has them as Christ is pleased to speak his powerful word to her and by that powerful word to work in her grace and all kinds of gifts necessary for her life.

God enriches the church because by means of the preaching God effectually calls his elect church into the fellowship of his Son. "For the grace of God which is given you by Jesus Christ" (v. 4) means given you *in* Christ. The church is enriched *in* him. Paul also says that the church is "called unto [into] the fellowship of his Son" (v. 9). The testimony of Christ, confirmed in the church, calls the church into saving fellowship with Jesus Christ.

She is joined with and engrafted into Jesus Christ and united more and more with him.

The riches in Christ flow into the church. As an engrafted branch partakes of the life, sap, and fatness of the tree, so the church partakes of Christ's riches. They are all stored in him. The power of the preaching is to call God's elect church into fellowship with his Son and to enrich her by that fellowship. The church has nothing in herself. Of herself she is naked, poor, and wretched. God gives the church everything she has in Christ.

The grace of God in Christ that enriches the church also saves and preserves the church. This is the apostle's point by the words "who shall also confirm you unto the end, that ye may be blameless in the day of our Lord Jesus Christ" (v. 8). The apostle points to this also when he says, "God is faithful, by whom ye were called" (v. 9). He adds this point because when he speaks of the giftedness of the church, he does not show any confidence in the church. His confidence is in God because God is faithful. God was faithful to bestow grace originally. God is faithful to continue to bestow it. God is faithful to preserve the church in grace. God is faithful to perfect the church in the day of Christ.

Here Paul categorically denies that one engrafted into Christ can fall out of Christ and perish. The church cannot. The individual believer cannot. This must be clear because if one elect member of the church falls, the whole church falls, as we say a building that loses a stone is falling apart. What happens to the parts is imputed to the whole building.

It was necessary for the apostle to say that his confidence rests in God with respect to the church's gifts of grace, because he was about to say to them some things unappealing to their flesh. They had so abused God's gifts that of themselves they deserved to forfeit all of them. Paul's confidence was that the word he had originally brought to Corinth that called them out of darkness into the fellowship of the Son was the same power whereby they would be corrected of their horrible abuse of all those gifts and would be instructed in the right use of them for the church to the glory of God. The power of that word was evident in that they listened, as the epistle of 2 Corinthians makes clear.

The Purpose of Enrichment

In his personal thanksgiving, "I give thanks to God," the apostle leads by example to teach the Corinthians, and the church of Jesus Christ in the world always, what the purpose of all their gifts and riches must be.

He taught that the gifts are not for the one who possessed the gift but for the church, and not even ultimately for the church but for the glory of God in true thanksgiving and worship. Where did all that grace come from? It came from God, the God of grace and the overflowing fountain of all grace, whose grace benefited this people. He is to be thanked; thanked especially in the use of the gift for the church. Thus the gift of grace may return to him by many thanks to him from those who profited from it and from the one who used it.

That is what the Corinthians forgot. They were puffed up. Many were blustering about what they had and what another did not have. Interested only in themselves, they could not give thanks to God. They forgot that what they had received was by grace for the church and for God's glory.

That is the purpose about which Corinth had to be reminded and about which the believer and church always have to be reminded. Everything she has, she has received by grace. In everything she has received, she has been enriched. Being enriched, let her give thanks to God by using everything for his church and to his glory.

CHAPTER 3

THE UNITY
OF THE CHURCH

1 Corinthians 1:10–13

---

10. *Now I beseech you, brethren, by the name of our Lord Jesus Christ, that ye all speak the same thing, and that there be no divisions among you; but that ye be perfectly joined together in the same mind and in the same judgment.*

11. *For it hath been declared unto me of you, my brethren, by them which are of the house of Chloe, that there are contentions among you.*

12. *Now this I say, that every one of you saith, I am of Paul; and I of Apollos; and I of Cephas; and I of Christ.*

13. *Is Christ divided? was Paul crucified for you? or were ye baptized in the name of Paul?*

The church is the fellowship of elect sinners gathered into union with Jesus Christ, God's Son. In that fellowship the church is enriched by his grace so that she comes behind in no gift. That was true of the church in Corinth. That is true of the church of Christ wherever she is found and throughout history.

In verse 3 the apostle also said "peace" to the church. Peace to the church means that in the church the peace of God reigns because God has forgiven the church all her sins by virtue of his forgiving the sins of the believing members of the church. She is at peace with God. That peace follows from the reality that the church is the object of God's grace, and thus the peace of God reigns there.

Being at peace with God, the church also has peace among her members. This is the subject to which the apostle turns in verses 10–13. Peace is synonymous with the church's unity. The apostle is clearly calling Corinth to manifest the unity of the church by "speak[ing] the same thing." The apostle teaches about unity when he calls the church to "be perfectly joined together in the same mind and in the same judgment" (v. 10). To be joined together in mind and judgment is to be unified. The apostle shows that his concern is for the unity of the church when he sharply censures the "divisions" in the church and the "contentions" among the members (vv. 10–11).

The apostle, as a good physician of Jesus Christ, diagnoses the cancer that afflicted the church in Corinth. She did not understand unity. Out of that ignorance arose every sort of contention, division, and schism. Lack of unity is related to the root of Corinth's cancer—her lack of love and refusal to walk in the way of love—because unity is the fruit of love. Love seeks and wherever possible establishes fellowship. In that fellowship of love there is unity. Where there are contentions there is no love. Where there is no agreement there can be no fellowship of love, but only war.

Over against those divisions the apostle says in verse 10, "Now I beseech you, brethren...speak the same thing...be perfectly joined together in the same mind and in the same judgment." The apostle teaches here about the unity of the church of Jesus Christ. He rebukes all divisions: "that there be no divisions among you." In this way he calls the church to walk in the way of love. The way of love includes the fellowship of love among those who are agreed in speech, mind, and judgment. Where that agreement in speech, mind, and judgment is impossible, there is also the impossibility of walking together in the way of love.

What Unity Is

Church unity is a large topic today, as it has always been for the church: unity among Reformed and Presbyterian churches, unity between Reformed churches and Rome, and unity between Rome and the religions of the world. But as unity is talked about by everybody, it is equally apparent that either almost nobody understands in what true unity consists, or there is deliberate departure from scripture's definition of unity in the name of false unity. Just as love is abused and made an excuse for tolerating every kind of evil, so also many calls for unity, the fruit of love, come along with cries that unity requires love, a love that tolerates this or that evil. That appeal to a false love that tolerates evil and departure from the word of God exposes the unity that is its fruit as a false unity. It is not the unity of which the Holy Ghost speaks in this text, the unity that Christ purchased by his cross, or that unity to which the apostle calls the Corinthians, a unity based upon agreement in speech, mind, and judgment.

This false unity is obvious in the case of the Roman Catholics and evangelicals. For the sake of unity with corrupt and apostate Rome, evangelicals deny the gospel of justification by faith alone. This same drive for unity with Rome is also a significant factor, if not the factor, in the corruption of justification in Reformed and Presbyterian churches today through the theology of the federal vision. This heresy teaches that in the final justification in the last judgment, justification will be based on the sinner's works of faith that he performed by grace. This unity cannot be of love, as no unity that tolerates evil can be of love, because love does not rejoice in iniquity but in the truth (13:6).

Less obvious is that a love that tolerates evil is the same basis of unity for many Reformed ecumenical organizations, such as the North American Presbyterian and Reformed Council.[1] That

---

1 The North American Presbyterian and Reformed Council (NAPARC) is an ecumenical organization consisting of thirteen member churches: Associate Reformed Presbyterian Church, Canadian Reformed Churches,

this is true is revealed in the pleas of its movers and supporters for more unity, based not on the truth and a solid discussion of differences, but on the toleration of certain denominational distinctives that others should be willing to overlook. These supposed distinctives include departures in the doctrines of grace, the covenant, creation, and sin. This is a naked appeal to toleration, which appeal reveals the proposed unity as false.

Such an abuse of unity was present in Corinth as well. The church had a misunderstanding about unity. They wanted to have a big tent. In pursuit of that desire the Corinthians demonstrated a willingness to tolerate all kinds of evil in their big tent, to the point that they would not discipline a grossly impenitent sinner, boasted of their toleration of him, and also included heretics who denied the resurrection in their fellowship. The result was that their big tent was a circus tent in which no unity existed. They were rent by discord, strife, and schism.

The apostle calls them to unity. Unity—true, Spirit-wrought, God-glorifying, and church-edifying unity—is the sacred bond of spiritual fellowship and friendship between believers, consisting in their real agreement in true faith that expresses itself in the church's one confession of that faith. The apostle calls them to this unity when he calls them to "be perfectly joined together in the same mind and in the same judgment" (1:10).

By the phrase "perfectly joined together" Paul takes his figure for the unity of the church from the human body. In the body there are a multitude of different parts—hands, feet, arms, legs, and all the organs—that are perfectly joined together in a

---

Reformed Church of Quebec, Free Reformed Churches of North America, Heritage Reformed Congregations, Korean American Presbyterian Church, Korean Presbyterian Church in America (Kosin), Orthodox Presbyterian Church, Presbyterian Church in America, Presbyterian Reformed Church, Reformed Church in the United States, Reformed Presbyterian Church in North America, and United Reformed Churches in North America. Accessed from http://www.naparc.org/member-churches/directories-2/ on November 13, 2017.

wonderful organic unity. In the unity of the body there is a great diversity, and each part has its own unique function. The eyes cannot do what the ears do and neither can the ears do what the eyes do. Yet with all that diversity there is unity, so that the body functions as one. So is the church of Jesus Christ. When the apostle exhorts the church to be "perfectly joined together," he teaches about the organic unity of the church. There is diversity in the church, a diversity of gifts, of sexes, of socio-economic standing, and of many physical characteristics; but in that the church is one. She is perfectly joined together.

With that figure of the body, we understand also how important unity is. If there is a breach of unity in the body, that body is dysfunctional. We know that because we are familiar with autoimmune diseases. If the body attacks itself, the result is death. The body must be joined together.

The apostle teaches the basis of the church's unity when he says, "Be perfectly joined together in the same mind and in the same judgment" (v. 10). This is basically equivalent to saying the church is one in the truth.

"The same mind" refers back to the apostle's figure of the unity of the body. The body's unity flows from the head. The mind controls the body and each part of the body so that the body functions as one. The church's mind is her faith. Faith is spiritual union with Christ, the head. By faith the church's mind is Christ's mind.

The faith that joins with Christ has a certain consistent content. Faith that joins to Christ is not many but one. For instance, faith that joins with Christ does not believe that we are justified by faith alone and that we are justified by faith and good works. Faith that joins to Jesus Christ does not believe that the covenant is conditional and that it is unconditional. Rather, there is unanimity in the church in the content of her faith, so that the unity of the church is nothing less than agreement in the doctrine she knows and believes.

"In the same judgment" refers to the activity of the church to apply that doctrine as the governing principle in all her life as church. She loves the truth and the truth guides and directs her whole life, so that all the judgments she makes about life are made out of the conviction of the truth.

The unity of the church means that there is agreement in doctrine and a consensus on the application of that doctrine. For example, the church knows the doctrine of marriage. She also makes a judgment based on that doctrine regarding life and fellowship. Those who are not in conformity with that doctrine are outside the fellowship of the church. She knows the doctrine of grace and makes a judgment based on that doctrine about those who can be in her fellowship. That is what the apostle means by one mind and one judgment.

The result of that unity is the church's "speak[ing] the same thing" (v. 10). The unified church has one testimony. The apostle speaks of "thing" and not "things." Being of one mind and judgment, she speaks one thing. That thing is the truth. The unity of the church must be manifested and come to expression in her one confession. By "speak the same thing" the apostle does not mean the lowest common doctrinal denominator, usually arrived at by massive concessions in the truth, that can bring the most people together. Rather, he means the truth that the church believes with the heart, on the basis of which she makes all her judgments in the world, which she also confesses publicly with one voice in her official confessions and in all her teaching and preaching. By means of that united confession she manifests her agreement in mind and judgment.

The text speaks of the unity of the local church, Corinth, and thus of every true local church. But whatever diversity can be tolerated in the local church can also be tolerated in a broader application. Whatever cannot be tolerated in the local church cannot be tolerated in the broader application. This gives the lie to any attempt at unity in which the proponents of unity acknowledge that they would not tolerate some doctrine or practice in their churches, but for the sake of unity they can tolerate it in their broader fellowships. That unity is by definition false and misleading. The unity of the local church is the standard and source of all other unity.

At the root it is also the calling of the local church to seek unity. It is her task as well as preaching, sacraments, and discipline. Obedience to this call by local churches results in a denomination of like-minded churches. In this unity the church and churches have peace. Apart from this unity she has only war, strife, and division.

Against All False Unity

The true church of Christ that confesses the truth and loves this unity in the truth can examine any cry for unity by this test. Would this doctrine or practice be tolerated in the local church, so that we would sit at the table of the Lord with those who believe or practice these things? The church must judge any plea for unity by this standard. By this standard she must reject the unity of ecumenical organizations in which there is a plea for unity in diversity, which diversity consists of tolerating false doctrines or practices that would not be tolerated in the local churches.

If a church adopts the unity or tolerates the unity of false ecumenism, even though she may be doctrinally sound herself, she invites in the strife and warfare that comes with that false unity, not to mention the strife and warfare that will come with the influences of false doctrine on her because of that illicit fellowship. Failing to test all cries for unity and to reject what is false, she will entangle herself with those with whom she is not one in mind, judgment, and confession. This entanglement is as disastrous for the church as when a healthy human being climbs into bed with a diseased human being. The result will inevitably be disease and the end, trouble and sorrow. The diseased are quarantined, and so must the true church of Christ do to those with whom she is not one in mind, judgment, and confession by refusing the fellowship.

Remembering the true basis of unity is important when heresy and false doctrine come into the church. When this happens the church fights, sometimes within her membership, to put out the false doctrine and those who teach it. Sometimes, as in the case of the Reformation, such fighting results in new denominations. What must be the view of that new church? What must be the view of the fighting by those defending the truth?

Rome always railed on the reformers: "You rend the bride of Christ!" The reformers took that charge seriously, and they countered it by saying, "No, the bride of Christ is rent by all the false doctrines and errors of Rome. Through teaching the truth, unity is restored."

The same charge, "You are guilty of schism," has been leveled against the reformers of every age. That was charged against Hendrik de Cock, Simon van Velzen, and the *Afscheiding* churches; that was leveled against Abraham Kuyper and the *Doleantie* churches; and that charge was leveled against Herman Hoeksema, Henry Danhof, and George Ophoff in the early 1920s.[2]

If there is an attempt to bring false doctrine into the church, can those who attempt to rid the church of that schismatic doctrine be charged with breaking the unity of the church? Such

---

2 Hendrik de Cock and Simon van Velzen were reformers in the Dutch State Church in 1834, a reformation that is commonly referred to as the *Afscheiding* (Separation). This reformation resulted in the formation of the Christian Reformed Churches in the Netherlands. Abraham Kuyper was a leader in a later reformation in the Dutch State Church known as the *Doleantie* (Grieving). These two groups merged in 1892 to form the Reformed Churches of the Netherlands. Herman Hoeksema, Henry Danhof, and George Ophoff were ministers in the Christian Reformed Church of America in the early 1900s. They were illegally deposed by that denomination for their opposition to the false doctrine of common grace adopted by the Christian Reformed Church in 1924. They maintained that the grace of God is always particular to his elect alone. Their deposition led to the formation of the Protestant Reformed Churches.

fighting within the church is not opposing unity because when the apostle teaches that unity is in the truth, he lays the fault for schism on heresy and false doctrine and on the heretics and false teachers who promote it. Such fighting is not any more censurable than the fighting of the human being against the cancer that has invaded his body. Such fighting is commendable. Those who defend the truth are zealous for the unity of the church. Be zealous for the truth. Be zealous for unity. To be zealous for unity, one must be zealous for the truth.

False doctrine breaks unity. Those who bring in false doctrine are guilty of dividing the church. That has been the universal testimony of the reformers in every age when the church has been afflicted by false doctrine. They felt the lack of unity. That was true of the reformers; of the *Afscheiding* men in 1834, when the church was full of heresy; of Hoeksema, Danhof, and Ophoff in 1924; and of some members of the Protestant Reformed Churches in 1953. When the heretics were expelled and the church was restored again to the same mind, the same judgment, and speaking the same things, the church rejoiced in the unity and the peace brought at last to the churches.

In teaching that the truth is the unity of the church and the confession of the truth is the expression of that unity, the apostle is denying that anything else may be the basis of unity. The unity of the church cannot be based on color, race, socio-economic standing, or cultural battles. The church or a denomination of churches is not one because she has a few theological or practical oddities that serve as her distinctive marks, as some unsightly but familiar warts distinguish one human from another, that may easily be given up and should be given up for the sake of unity. If those distinctive doctrines and practices are not the word of God, are not the truth of the Reformed creeds, and are not the confession of the truth of Jesus Christ, they cannot be the bases for unity and cannot be cause for any division. When one church remains separate from others for the sake of those distinctives, by that fact she is saying that those distinctives are essential matters of the gospel, not merely distinctives but the truth of Christ for which she is willing to remain separate.

There is a great diversity in the church, but there is no diversity in the content of the church's speaking and confessing the truth. There she is unanimous. Neither then may unity be broken for any nonessential matter, so that for the sake of some inconsequential view or practice one church would remain separate from another.

When the apostle makes confession part of the church's unity, he also denies as unity that false unity that pleads only for silence. This plea for unity will not consist in a call to change some doctrine, but for the sake of unity will ask that the offending doctrine not be confessed at some time or place. The sacrifice consists only is remaining silent about the truth for unity's sake.

Unity consists in confession together. If for the sake of unity one party has to remain silent about his confession, significant portions of his confession, or even one article of his confession, and that because his confession necessarily condemns the other's as false, that is no unity at all. To ask a church and believer to be silent about the truth for the sake of unity is the same as asking them to deny the truth for the sake of unity, because the truth then ceases to be their confession. All such attempts at unity are attempts at false unity.

True unity also does not give rise to the peace of the graveyard. False unity can bring a kind of pseudo-peace, a unity in which people can get together but in their gatherings never talk—indeed studiously avoid talking—about differences or about anything important. They do not "speak the same thing," which thing consists in their agreed faith. They talk about the weather or their jobs. To the casual observer there seems to be a convivial atmosphere, but if someone would bring up and confess the truth and condemn the lie, there would be an explosion in such a gathering.

That begs the questions: Are you really unified, then? Is your peace really peace? There is peace in the graveyard, but a peace that clearly indicates that all are united in one thing: death. There is no speaking, but only a deathly silence that is the expression of the reign of death. In unity the church speaks the truth loudly, unanimously, unambiguously, sharply, clearly, and unashamedly. In her speaking she also earnestly contends for the truth once delivered to the saints. The church is at peace when she believes with the heart and confesses with the mouth. "I believed, therefore have I spoken" (Ps. 116:10).

Therein too is a test of unity. Unity that is forced and contrived is not unity. Who has to force the body to be one? This forced and enforced unity is as different from true unity as a barrel of staves bound with an iron ring is different from the natural unity of the human body. All such attempts at unity expose themselves as false by the very fact that they are forced and enforced by the silencing of those who criticize it or say something to offend against it. By being contrived, these attempts demonstrate that they are antithetical to the unity of mind, judgment, and confession in the gospel of Christ. If unity is not based on the truth, there is no unity. That unity will bring not peace but fighting.

No Schism in the Church

The unity and peace of the church are rent not only by false unity, but also by the kind of schismatic contentiousness characteristic of Corinth. In Corinth the members were speaking, but everyone spoke his own opinion and not the truth, and when someone did speak the truth they resisted its force and authority by making it merely a man's opinion. Paul says, "For it hath been declared unto me of you, my brethren, by them which are of the house of Chloe, that there are contentions among you" (1 Cor. 1:11).

Chloe was a woman highly regarded by Paul and a member of the church of Corinth. Some of her household had business in Ephesus, where the apostle was laboring. One by one they brought a consistent report to Paul: "There are contentions in that congregation." To show that he did not easily lend his ear to rumors, Paul mentions many of the household of Chloe. They all said, "That church is divided."

"Contentions" mean fighting among themselves about issues easily resolved by the application of love, some of which Paul will address later in the book. "Divisions" refer to the various parties that formed in the church as a result of those issues. Paul writes, "Now this I say, that every one of you saith, I am of Paul; and I of Apollos; and I of Cephas; and I of Christ" (v. 12). He vividly describes the lay of the congregation. Church life was more like the raucous partisanship of the political process than the blessed fellowship of the church. Everyone had his opinion about this, that, and the other thing in the church. They subjected the gospel and the unity of the church to their own partisan interests.

All the while each faction tried to fly the flag of a certain leading light. We should not take what Paul says about himself, Apollos, and Cephas to mean that those factions actually cared what those men said or thought. It should not be supposed either that any of those men actually led a faction. The warring parties were using those names to lend weight to their factions. They tossed around the name of Apollos, an eloquent Alexandrian who excelled in the pulpit. Cephas is Peter, the apostle and first among equals. Paul was the eminent apostle to the Gentiles. There was even a party of Christ that seemed to stand piously aloof from the contentiousness of the church but was in fact driven by the same spirit, or at least made no effort to correct the schism. While claiming Christ for themselves, they insinuated that the rest lacked him.

The Source of Unity

The apostle beseeches the Corinthians to abandon this party spirit and manifest unity "by the name of our Lord Jesus Christ" (v. 10). This is the ground of his exhortation. In their haste to exalt themselves and to force their thinking on the church, they forgot about Christ, the source of the church's unity. As the body is one in its head, so the church is one in Christ.

By the words "by the name of our Lord Jesus Christ," Paul teaches the Corinthians wherein their unity lay. It lay in Christ as the head, lord, and king of the church. But they made Christ one little party in the church. They did that whether they claimed to be of the party of Christ or of one of the other parties.

The church is one because she has one head. The mind whereby she believes and knows all things is Christ's mind. The judgment whereby she makes judgments is Christ's judgment. The speaking whereby she confesses the same things is Christ's speaking. It is that because "the name of our Lord Jesus Christ," by which the apostle calls them to unity, is the truth of Christ revealed in the sacred scriptures. There in scripture Christ's mind, judgment, and speech are made known and brought to bear on the whole life of the church. Therein the church is one. The truth that she knows is the truth of scripture. The truth by which she judges is the truth of scripture. The truth that she confesses in her confessions and in all her life is the truth of scripture.

Paul also means by "the name of our Lord Jesus Christ" the exclusive authority of Jesus Christ in his church and thus his headship in the church. It is the exclusive right of Christ to speak, rule, and judge every person, every issue, and everything in the church. He does that by means of his truth revealed in scripture. When all things are managed according to the word of God, Christ rules in the church and the church is one. By that means Christ binds the whole church to himself and carries on the whole life of the church and every member of himself and binds them all together. The unity of the church consists of Christ's headship of the church. Whenever the truth is ignored, pushed aside, denied, or silenced, Christ and his headship are denied and unity is compromised.

In this connection Paul asks two powerful rhetorical questions:

"Was Paul crucified for you? Were ye baptized in the name of Paul?" (v. 13). These questions add to his doctrine of Christ's headship and of the unity of the church in Christ her head.

Christ is head because God eternally appointed Christ to be the head and mediator and chose each elect child and thus the whole church of God in Christ. Only as their legal head can he be crucified for them. As head and mediator Christ bought the church by his blood, freed her from the dominion of Satan, calls her by his powerful word out of the world, joins her to his saving fellowship, forgives her sins, imputes to her righteousness, and sanctifies her by his indwelling Spirit. By his cross he purchased unity for the church, a sacred fellowship and bond between the members and Christ and between the members of the church themselves. He broke down the middle wall of partition so that the church of Jesus Christ is the one organism in the whole world where true unity exists.

Baptism is the sign of this unity. Paul brings up baptism in the name of Jesus Christ when he says, "Were ye baptized in the name of Paul?" (v. 13). He implies that they were not, but were baptized in the name of Jesus. They had been baptized in the name of Jesus Christ not because they were baptized on his authority, but because they were baptized into the fellowship of Christ in the church. That was not because the formula used for their baptism was different from our baptisms, but because baptism in the name of the triune God is the sign and seal of union with Christ.

Keeping unity in every age magnifies Christ and honors Christ in his rightful place as the head, lord, and king of the church. That is what the Corinthians forgot. In their divisiveness and with all their fighting, the Corinthians sinned against Christ and God, who appointed Christ to be the head and mediator of the church. To follow men is to deny Christ and to attack unity. To seek one's own interest in the church is to deny Christ and to assault the unity of the church. To corrupt the word of Christ and bring false doctrine into the church is a grave attack on unity by attacking the unity of the church at its fountain and head—Christ. If one has an opinion of how things ought to go in the church, but he will not be regulated by the word of God, is willing to divide and conquer and have factions in the church for the sake of his opinion, puts his opinion in the place of Christ's word, or exalts his ideas over the word of God, that is a serious assault on Christ and unity.

Breaking unity in the church is a deadly serious matter. The real sin—the monstrous iniquity—of every schismatic, false teacher, and those who set aside the truth, plead for tolerance, and on that basis plead for a false unity in the church, is that they rebel against Christ, set aside Christ, and usurp Christ's sole lordship of his church. Breaking unity in any form denies Christ's lordship of the church and casts Christ out of his kingship. It denies God his right to appoint the head and mediator in the church. To assault the unity of the church denies Christ's cross, because by the cross he purchased the church and the unity of the church. To divide the church is to deny the resurrection whereby Jesus became lord of the church, her only lord. To divide the church is gross ingratitude for such a sacred bond and fellowship that he gives to his church.

To divide the church is also to apostatize from Christ. Is Christ divided? That is impossible. Christ and his church are one. This fellowship is the creation of God in Christ Jesus. The church also is not hopelessly divided. The church does not need to be unified. She is one. This is a reality. The fellowship of the church with Christ is sacred and inviolable. It cannot be broken. This unity is as safe and secure in heaven and as untouchable by the vicious party strife of men as is the church's holiness, righteousness, and whole redemption. One either lives in and out of this reality, thereby expressing this unity, or he separates from Christ.

This is the seriousness of unity. So important is unity that the church without it does not have Christ. Proponents of false unity, a unity that involves ungodly toleration of false doctrine, frequently begin their pleas for this unity by noting that the church is badly divided. That observation amounts to accusing the church of being without Christ, since Christ and therefore his church are not divided. Therein is also a warning for every church of Christ: if we descend into contentions and divisions we depart from Christ.

Exhorted to Unity

When the apostle teaches the truth of the unity of the church, he teaches it from the viewpoint of the church's living in that unity. That unity is a reality in Christ. Therefore, it is a calling to the church. That is why the apostle says to the Corinthians, and the word of God says to the church and believers always, "I beseech you, brethren" (v. 10). If believers are not living in unity, for their salvation and for the sake of Christ's church they are called to repent of their schism, to return to Christ, to speak the same thing again, and to be united in one mind and one judgment. So the apostle invokes Christ and says, "If you have the mind and the judgment of Christ because you have the truth—and you do—speak the same thing. Do not give free reign to your wills, desires, and opinions. Let all things be subject to the word of truth. Be on your guard against all schisms, divisions, and threats to the unity of the church. Confess the truth. Flee all false unity, which is no unity but a wicked forsaking of Christ."

Today the church must hear the call to live in this unity in the church. The church may lack unity because carnal contentions reign in her, as in Corinth. The old man in the believer today is as divisive as he was in the Corinthians. It may be that the church lacks unity because many have listened to the well-nigh-irresistible siren song of false unity. She also may lack unity because of a wrong reaction to the rampant abuse of unity to promote ungodly toleration, so that many are turned off by the idea of unity altogether and do not esteem it or practice it as they ought.

The church must hear that unity—true unity—is the precious work of God in the church, is the benefit of the cross of Christ, and is the lively reality of the relationship between Christ and his church and between the members of the church themselves. Then she will esteem unity very highly, seek it ardently, manifest it willingly by agreement in mind, judgment, and confession, and steadfastly resist any and every attempt to corrupt it. The people of God must likewise hear the exhortation to live in the unity of Christ Jesus by being members of a true church of Christ, where he is the head in the truth and his word rules.

This is urgent, lest a church should hear what the Corinthians heard from Christ: "It hath been declared unto me of you, my brethren, that there are contentions among you." Rather, say the same thing.

CHAPTER 4

THE POWERFUL WORD OF THE CROSS

1 Corinthians 1:18

18. *For the preaching of the cross is to them that perish foolishness; but unto us which are saved it is the power of God.*

In the context the apostle introduced the new subject that he will now develop: "the preaching of the cross" of Jesus Christ. In the preceding section Paul exposed Corinth's factiousness and taught the oneness of the church as the body of Jesus Christ that agrees in true faith. The universal, elect body of Jesus Christ becomes visible in her confession. That universal body of Jesus Christ is manifested in the institute agreeing in true faith.

The relationship between these two subjects is that the preaching of the gospel is the means whereby God calls his church out of the world, joins her together as one body, and enriches the body with every grace. The Corinthians had been called and established as a true church of Jesus Christ by the gospel. As a true church of Christ they were enriched by that gospel.

This is why the apostle says, "Christ sent me not to baptize, but to preach the gospel" (v. 17). Paul is not minimizing baptism or contradicting Jesus Christ, who sent the church to preach the gospel and to baptize, but he is exposing the false teachers who were afflicting Corinth with their factions. They boasted of having baptized many and of the many people who followed them. The true teacher of Christ is tested by the gospel he brings and not by how many people he baptizes or how many follow him.

By implication the apostle also teaches about the primacy of preaching as a means of grace. Baptism as a sacrament is dependent on the preaching. Preaching is first. If baptism is subservient to preaching and preaching was Paul's chief work, that is true of every other minister of the gospel. Everything he does is subservient to the preaching. Everything he does must be judged by his preaching. His preaching must be the preaching of Christ. Christ did not send him to baptize but to preach.

Recognizing that preaching is his chief calling, Paul also indicates that Christ sent him to preach the gospel "not with wisdom of words," lest he make the cross of Christ of none effect (v. 17). This does not refer to a complete lack of art or rhetoric in his preaching. The apostle did not lack art in the preaching of the gospel, even though some said his preaching was contemptible. Their evaluation is to be discounted on account of their bad spirit. When men have a bad spirit, they are incapable of properly evaluating the preaching. As with all spiritual things, preaching is foolishness to the carnal mind. If the angel Gabriel came and preached to such men, they would judge it contemptuously.

The phrase "wisdom of words" refers to what was happening in Corinth with the false teachers who baptized many and boasted in their followings. They preached with wisdom of words; they made the gospel palatable and artfully tailored their messages to the tastes of their audiences. That very thing made "the cross of Christ...of none effect" (v. 17). They made it void. The power of their preaching was not the cross of Christ but man's oratory. Therefore, their preaching had no power.

The ultimate expression of the "wisdom of words" is to preach the lie over against the truth and to introduce man's doctrine instead of God's doctrine. That wicked corruption begins with the preacher's tailoring of the message to suit the carnal sensibilities of his hearers. For instance, he knows full well that his congregation is full of those who have among their friends and family divorced and remarried persons, whom they never rebuke and with whom they are closely associated. So the preacher never breathes so much as a word on the subject. If he does come within a country mile of it, he will make sure that the hearer comes away comfortable in his sin. Christ did not send such a one to do such a thing with his word.

In contrast to that faithless—to the gospel and to Christ—preaching, Christ sent Paul to preach the plain, unadorned cross of Jesus Christ. Verse 18 gives the reason: "The preaching of the cross is to them that perish foolishness; but unto us which are saved it is the power of God." The preaching is a power. It is a power because of the word of the cross that it brings. If the preaching does not bring that word but man's word, it is no power.

The Divinity of the Word

"Preaching of the cross" in verse 18 should be translated as "the Word of the cross." The Word of the cross is foolishness to those who perish. The Word of the cross is the power of God unto those who are saved.

That phrase in the text does not refer to Paul's preaching or to any other minister's preaching. Paul brings up the preaching of that Word in verse 23: "We preach Christ crucified. There he insists that his preaching is the Word of the cross. By his preaching then that powerful Word of the cross came to the churches. The phrase "the Word of the cross" teaches about the content of all true gospel preaching and explains the power of that preaching.

Preaching must be the Word of the cross to be true preaching. Otherwise it is just words of man's wisdom. Preaching must be the Word of the cross to be the power of salvation. Every true minister of the gospel and every true church of Jesus Christ must be able to say that their preaching is the Word of the cross; otherwise all their preaching and doctrine are just the impotent words of man's wisdom.

By the Word of the cross Paul refers to the actual power of the preaching. "Word" in verse 18 is the same word used in John 1:1: "In the beginning was the Word, and the Word was with God, and the Word was God." It is the divine Logos, the Word. The Word of God is the speech of God that brings into existence the will of God. In the beginning God said, "Let there be light," and that Word created light. All through the creation God said, "Let there be..." and there was. The Word of God brings into existence what God wills to be. In the following versification of Psalm 29, the Word of God is the voice that effectually carries out God's will:

> The voice of Jehovah, the God of all glory,
> Rolls over the waters, the thunders awake;
> The voice of Jehovah, majestic and mighty,
> Is heard, and the cedars of Lebanon break.
> His voice makes the mountains and deserts to tremble,
> Wild beasts are affrighted, the forests laid bare,
> And thro' all creation, His wonderful temple,
> All things He has fashioned His glory declare.[1]

That Word is also the Word of the cross. Just as God said in the beginning, "Let there be light," and light was, so also two thousand years ago on a hill outside Jerusalem, shaped like a skull, between the crosses of two malefactors, God spoke. He said, "Let there be a cross," and there was a cross. It is the Word that brought about the cross of Jesus Christ.

---

1 No. 76:2–3, in *The Psalter with Doctrinal Standards, Liturgy, Church Order, and added Chorale Section*, reprinted and revised edition of the 1912 United Presbyterian *Psalter* (Grand Rapids, MI: Wm. B. Eerdmans Publishing Co., 1927; rev. ed. 1995).

The Word of the cross refers to that event in its entirety as it was solely the product of God's will and God's doing and involved centrally God's Word. The Word first became flesh. It refers then to Jesus' conception and virgin birth, his lifelong suffering, his betrayal by his supposed friend, his trial before the Sanhedrin and Pontius Pilate, the shouts and sneers of the mob, the vicious blows, the nails, the blood, the spear thrust, the superscription above his head, "This is the king of the Jews," the three terrible hours of darkness, and the agonizing cry of God's forsaken Son out of the depths. The whole event of the cross was brought about by the Word of God: "Let there be a cross," and there was a cross, and all those events took place exactly as he willed it. The subject too of all of that was the Word, God.

The Word of the cross also speaks of the necessity of that cross: sin. There was sin committed against God's most high majesty that had to be punished with extreme punishment. God's justice requires that sin so committed be punished with temporal and eternal punishment. The Word could not be a word of a sword, or beheading, or stoning, or of a Jesus victorious in establishing an earthly kingdom. It is a Word of the *cross*. The cross is the symbol of the curse of God. God said in the law, "Cursed is every one that hangeth on a tree" (Gal. 3:13). The Word of the cross speaks of the perfect justice of God, of the curse of God against the sinner, that God wills the damnation of the sinner, and that God will not allow the sinner to escape. Thus the cross is the instrument to bring that curse of God to the very depths of the soul of Jesus Christ and to make him a curse.

The Word of the cross speaks of the source of that cross deep in the being of God in his love for those sinners who sinned against him. He willed their salvation and manifested love toward them in that while they were yet sinners Christ died for them. Since he died for them, it speaks too of the eternal predestination in love of those for whom Christ died. He died for them because he represented them and stood as their substitute under the wrath of God, and thus he made full satisfaction to God for them.

The Word is not merely God's word about that event. It is not as if the cross took place and afterward God spoke something about that cross. It is the Word of God in that event. It is God's Word that brought that event into reality for the salvation of his people. It is the cross as God conceived of it in eternity and as the creation of Adam, the fall, and all of history leading up to the cross served the cross. God said, "Let there be a cross for the salvation of my people, for the confirmation of the covenant, and for their eternal blessedness in the new heavens and the new earth," and the cross was and the cross did what God willed. It is a divine Word that brought about the divine event of the cross.

When the text emphasizes that the cross is a divine Word, it contrasts the divinity of the Word of the cross with whatever man has to say about the cross and contradicts what appears to man to be the truth of the cross.

The appearance of the cross is that it was man's event. It is true that man was active at the cross. When God came to man in a form in which man could lay hold on God, man showed what he thought about God and expressed his contempt for God by cursing him with the cross. By that the cross exposed man for who he is: a hater of God and his neighbor.

Yet the cross was not in man's power. If the cross were man's in any respect, in that respect it would be impotent and useless for salvation. When Paul says the cross is God's Word, he denies that man was doing or affecting anything by the cross. Man's sin does not overrule the purpose of God, but God uses even man's sin for his own divine purpose.

Furthermore, when Paul makes the cross a divine Word, he rejects whatever man says about the cross in man's wisdom. Whenever man speaks of the cross in his wisdom, he always gets the cross wrong. The cross is always foolishness to the Greek and a stumbling block to the Jew because they do not believe the cross is a divine Word. At best man can look at the cross and say that a good man died for his ideals or that he was an example of courage and sticking to his principles. Or man blasphemes the cross as the foolishness of a vindictive God whom he will not worship. For man the cross is not salvation; the thought is absurd to man. That is why man said at the cross, "If thou be the Son of God, come down from the cross" (Matt. 27:40). Man does not want a savior who died on a cross.

Man was not responsible for the cross. He cannot explain the cross. He cannot contribute to the cross. The cross was not man's word or his event.

Because it was God's Word, it was also God's event. At the cross God carried out his will through the wicked hands of those who took Jesus and slew him. Judas betrayed him. Pontius Pilate and Herod and the leaders of the people were gathered against Christ to destroy him, and they did whatsoever God's hand and counsel determined before to be done (Acts 4:26–28). The cross is not man's word and man's event. It is God's Word and God's event.

The Power of the Word

Because the cross was not man's word but God's, the cross was salvation. God said, "Let there be a cross," and the Word of the cross was the Word of reconciliation, the Word of atonement, the Word of propitiation for sin, the Word of justification, and the Word of perfect salvation. The Word of the cross was, "It is finished." Everything necessary for the salvation of God's people has been accomplished. Because God said, "Let there be a cross," the cross was powerful to accomplish salvation. When God said, "Let there be light," that Word was powerful to bring light into existence; so also when God said, "Let there be a cross," that Word was powerful to bring salvation into existence.

When God said, "Let there be a cross," he accomplished a perfect righteousness, made a perfect satisfaction for sin, satisfied his justice, confirmed the covenant, made the kingdom a reality, and established the only ground of salvation.

By that Word of the cross, death, the grave, and sin lost their power.

By that Word the devil's head was crushed. Just as when God said, "Let light be," darkness was chased away by the light, so God said, "Let the cross be," and salvation was wrought and sin was done away. Being a divine Word, it is a powerful word.

Foolishness to the Perishing

What God did two thousand years ago for his people and their salvation, as the expression of his eternal will for them and their salvation, is foolishness to those who are perishing.

Notice the apostle does not say that the *preaching* of the cross but the *Word* of the cross is foolishness to those who are perishing. That is a more profound point than saying that preaching is foolishness to those who are perishing. The Spirit says that the cross itself, the work of God done by the cross, the Christ of the cross, the salvation accomplished at the cross, the perfect righteousness of the cross, and the God of the cross are foolishness to those who are perishing. If the cross is foolishness, then the salvation of the cross, the covenant of the cross, the kingdom of the cross, the eternal life of the cross, and all the benefits of the cross are all foolishness to the perishing.

A man with all the skills of Demosthenes cannot make the cross attractive or palatable to the natural man. When the natural man looks at the cross, he says, "That man died as an excommunicate. How can he be a savior? A god that would do that to his son is not a good god. How can that be for salvation? A god that wills evil and controls evil, of which the cross is the outstanding example, is not my god." The cross and everything connected with it are ugly and stupid to the natural man. It's a *cross*. Those who die on crosses are criminals, not saviors. If he is a more astute natural man, he may say that the importance of the cross is that it was the Word of God, and the Word of God about the cross is as cursed as he who hangs on the tree. That is what the natural man sees in the cross.

Because the cross is foolish, so also is all of the truth that flows from it and is connected with it. The natural man cannot make sense of it. He cannot make sense of election and reprobation or of the necessity of baptizing all covenantal children while only the elect children receive the promise. He cannot make sense of a promiscuous call of the gospel that calls only the elect and that God gives grace only to his elect. It is all foolishness to him. He cannot make sense of any of it, because the cross is foolishness.

Because the cross is foolishness to the natural man, the *preaching* of the cross is also foolishness to him. When the preaching comes as the Word of the cross, natural man's response is that it is foolish. He does not accept Jesus into his heart or make a decision for Christ. Rather, his response to the preaching is, "That is the silliest thing I have ever heard." If man supposedly makes a decision for Christ or accepts Christ into his heart on the basis of some minister's preaching, that minister is not preaching the Word of the cross. The preaching is foolish to man because its content is foolish to man. The preaching brings the cross concretely before men today, and by that preaching Christ is crucified before them.

Man says that Christ is foolish and that preaching is foolish. When man says they are foolish, he despises them and will not believe. He says about the Christ of the cross, the Word of the cross, and the preaching of the cross that they cannot do anything; they are idiotic and will never amount to anything or accomplish anything in the world; and one certainly cannot build a church, a Christian culture, or an earthly kingdom on them.

This is why God will not have his gospel preached "with wisdom of words" (1 Cor. 1:17). One cannot preach the gospel with the wisdom of words. It is impossible. As soon as a man tries he must deny the gospel, because the content of the gospel cannot be made palatable to man who hates the cross that is the heart of that preaching. If one tries to preach with the wisdom of words, he automatically makes void the cross.

Yet when the apostle says the Word of the cross is foolishness to those who are perishing, he does not refer merely to what natural man does with the cross or to his reaction to the cross. But Paul also means what God does with the Word of the cross and with the preaching of the cross. God operates by that Word of the cross to carry out his eternal will for the perishing of some. "Them that perish" means those who are perishing. The word translated as "perish" is in the present tense and is progressive in meaning. They do not begin to perish when the cross of Christ comes and they reject it and incur guilt for their unbelief and thus perish. They are already perishing before the gospel comes.

They are perishing as the reprobate. They have been perishing since God appointed them to destruction in eternity. He did not appoint them to destruction because he saw what they would do with the gospel, but he appointed them to destruction according to his will. Because of that appointment they are perishing and also reject the gospel. The Word of the cross is not for them. God did not send Christ to die for them. The preaching of the cross is not for them, and it is not grace to them. When the preaching of the cross comes, God uses that preaching to accomplish his purpose of reprobation, so that the perishing perish on account of their unbelief and other sins.

No more than the cross was outside God's purpose and control are the purpose and effect of the preaching of the cross outside God's purpose and control. Preaching the cross comes exactly to destroy man's wisdom, to bring to nothing man's prudence, and to cause the perishing to perish. As the Word of God at the cross was particular, so the preaching of the cross is particular.

The preaching is a mighty power in its foolishness to the perishing. It does not fail when they perish any more than

Christ's cross failed because he did not die for them. As a power the preaching accomplishes God's will as the cross accomplished his will.

Power to Those Being Saved

The Word of the cross is also a power to those being saved. "Us which are saved" are those being saved. This phrase is also in the present tense and is progressive. Those who are being saved are the elect. Before they hear a word of the preaching, they are being saved because God appointed them to salvation in eternity. He did not appoint them to salvation because he saw what they would do with the preaching of the cross, but because he appointed them to salvation they are saved by the preaching of the cross. Because he appointed them to salvation in eternity, he also spoke a Word for their salvation two thousand years ago at Golgotha to bring their salvation into existence, and he brings that salvation of the cross to them through the preaching.

At the cross God said, "Forgive their sins, make them holy, earn for them the Spirit, and establish the covenant." All that was finished at the cross. Now that must come to God's people. It comes in the preaching, so that by means of the preaching all of the salvation God accomplished at Calvary is brought into the possession of his people. God speaks when the Word of the cross comes through the preaching. With a powerful Word God says, "Justify them, forgive their sins, sanctify them, cleanse them with the Spirit, give them to enjoy the benefits of the covenant, and preserve them all through this life to eternal glory." When the Word of the cross comes through the preaching, burdens are lifted, the guilty are justified, the unholy are made holy, the bound are set free, and the burden of the heavy laden is made light. Day by day, week by week, year by year that is the power of the Word of the cross. By that Word they are saved and are being saved.

That is why Christ did not send Paul or any other minister to baptize, but to preach the gospel. That is why the preaching must be central in the church, in the work of the minister, and in the hearts of the people of God. When the preaching comes, the cross comes, the Word of God comes. That Word of God saves. No word of man can do that, no matter how eloquently it may be spoken. If a man tries to preach the Word of the cross with his wisdom, he makes it void.

CHAPTER 5

SALVATION BY THE FOOLISHNESS OF PREACHING

1 Corinthians 1:21–24

---

21. *For after that in the wisdom of God the world by wisdom knew not God, it pleased God by the foolishness of preaching to save them that believe.*
22. *For the Jews require a sign, and the Greeks seek after wisdom:*
23. *But we preach Christ crucified, unto the Jews a stumblingblock, and unto the Greeks foolishness;*
24. *But unto them which are called, both Jews and Greeks, Christ the power of God, and the wisdom of God.*

Certain individuals in the Corinthian congregation divided the church into factions. Those factions each claimed a certain minister for their cause: "I am of Paul; and I of Apollos; and I of Cephas; and I of Christ" (1:12). Those troublers commended themselves to the church on the size of their followings within the congregation. Since each faction had a following, each thought it was worthy of being heard. Those factions preached the wisdom of man. This is the reason Paul speaks of baptizing: "Christ sent me not to baptize, but to preach the gospel" (v. 17).

That preaching is the power to save the church of Jesus Christ, a power on which even the mighty sacrament of baptism is dependent. Preaching of the Word of the cross is the only thing worthy of being heard in the church.

Furthermore, Christ did not send Paul to preach that gospel with the "wisdom of words," lest the cross of Christ be made of none effect (v. 17). By this expression the apostle refers to the way the gospel is preached. The gospel cannot be made appealing to the natural man by artful presentation or rhetoric. The reason is that the Word of the cross is unappealing to man. The Word of the cross is the Word God spoke that brought the cross into being and accomplished salvation by it. That Word is foolishness to the natural man, and therefore the preaching of the cross is foolishness to him too.

In that light the apostle asks, "Hath not God made foolish the wisdom of this world?" (v. 20). If the Word of the cross is the power of God unto salvation, has not God made the wisdom of the world foolish, by which he means worthless for salvation? That was the issue in Corinth. Some were saying, "There is something good to be said for the wisdom of the world. The wisdom of the world must be used to inform the church's preaching. For instance, the wisdom of the world must be used to inform the church's preaching about creation."

It is no different today regarding the church's preaching. Has not God by the cross made foolish the wisdom of the world? God made foolish the wisdom of the world in the interest of his will that his people be saved by the foolishness of preaching. God did something to the world's wisdom so that it cannot be used by the church. If the church tries to use it, she makes vain the cross of Jesus Christ.

This also explains how God makes foolish the wisdom of the world. He makes it foolish by saving his people through the foolishness of preaching and not at all by the wisdom of the world. In verses 21–24 the apostle deals with the issue of salvation by the foolishness of preaching and, by implication, never by the wisdom of the world.

Foolish Preaching

In verse 18 the King James Version translates the Greek as "preaching of the cross" and makes it appear that the subject is the preaching. There, however, the apostle did not speak of the preaching but of the *Word* of the cross. That Word brought about and accomplished salvation for God's elect church at the cross. Now in verses 21–24 Paul speaks of the preaching of the cross: "It pleased God by the foolishness of preaching to save them that believe…We preach Christ crucified" (vv. 21–23). The word translated as "preaching" here is one of the usual words for the preaching.

The preacher referred to in these verses is a herald authorized and qualified to speak on behalf of King Jesus and to declare the word of King Jesus. Note that Paul says "we." He not only refers to himself, but also includes every faithful minister of Jesus Christ then and now. The preacher is simply an ordained minister. Christ must send a preacher just as Christ sent the apostles. Man did not send the apostles, Christ did. Christ sent the apostle Paul to preach. So also today Christ sends preachers through the official call of his church. He uses the church, but Christ sends. He calls preachers and trains them. He gives them a commission, a word to speak, and the authority to speak in his name; and he speaks through them.

Preaching is the official declaration of the cross of Jesus Christ by those ordained ministers. What they preach is the gospel of Christ crucified. They set forth Christ in the fullness of his person, natures, and work. They call all men everywhere to believe in Christ. The apostle indicates that this was part of his message because he says later that the gospel "save[s] them that believe" (v. 21). They promise salvation in Christ's name to those who repent and believe. They threaten the unbeliever with eternal damnation.

The apostle calls preaching folly: "It pleased God by the foolishness of preaching to save them that believe" (v. 21).

He does not call his preaching or the preaching of any minister of Jesus Christ foolish because it actually is foolish, for preaching in and of itself is not foolish. The whole context denies that the preaching is foolish. The preaching of Christ crucified is the God-ordained means to save the church. When Paul says that Christ did not send him to baptize but to preach the gospel, he commends the preaching to the church and to every minister of the gospel as their primary calling and the chief means of grace.

Rather, he makes a concession to opponents of the preaching for the sake of argument. Many unfaithful ministers and their followers in Corinth did not think much of the preaching and in particular of the preaching of Christ crucified. Some thought that for the preaching to be effective it had to be delivered with all the art of the Greek orator. Others thought themselves to be connoisseurs of fine preaching. As a sommelier they sniffed it, swirled it, sipped it, swished it around for a while, spat it out, and graded it. But they never drank it in, believing it to the saving of their souls. Man in general regards the preaching as foolish because he regards the cross of Christ as foolish.

When Paul calls the preaching foolish, he concedes the point for a moment. Anyone who examines the preaching with the eye of man must conclude that it is foolishness. Its foolishness is palpable. The messenger is a mere man. If the archangel Michael would stand on the pulpit and preach, men would be less inclined to speak of the foolishness of preaching. But Christ sends mere men—contemptible men of mean ability with thin voices, ugly faces, and bad fashion—who are nothing in comparison with the gifted and polished orators of the world.

Besides, the content of preaching is foolishness to man because it is the preaching of Christ crucified. "We preach Christ crucified," says the apostle (v. 23). A preacher who preaches something else is unfaithful to Christ who sent him. By describing his preaching as "Christ crucified," the apostle does not mean merely that he preached about the event that happened outside the city walls of Jerusalem on the hill of Golgotha. He means preaching the cross of Christ as the only way of salvation. He preaches Christ crucified as the heart and soul of the whole of Christian doctrine as it is revealed in the entire Bible. He preaches Christ crucified when he preaches the truth as it centers on the cross. Man is hostile toward the cross and its Christ. The preacher has an automatic disadvantage compared to the orator who can sway men to his cause and purpose.

By foolish, Paul also means that in his preaching of Christ crucified he makes all that is of man nothing: all man's works, all of man's will, and anything that man thinks he can contribute to salvation. Thus he makes man nothing. This is not exactly an approached aimed at gaining the good will of the hearer.

Still more, he preached the cross without words of wisdom. The preacher may not preach Christ crucified and the message of the cross with the words of wisdom. It is also impossible. When a preacher attempts to preach the cross with the words of man's wisdom, he makes the cross void.

To preach with words of wisdom means to attempt to make the word palatable, inoffensive, and comfortable for man. For example, about the doctrine of predestination, a preacher says, "God chose those who want to believe, or God rejected those who will not believe." Thus he changes that doctrine and makes it inoffensive, so that man will not be offended and can accept it. Or the gospel is preached but never brought to bear on specific situations and issues afflicting a particular congregation.

When the apostle says, "We preach Christ crucified not with wisdom of words" (vv. 23, 17), he means that the preacher of the word and the church of God through her preachers must plainly, simply, and clearly preach the truth of the word of God—at the heart of which is the cross of Christ—so that it cannot be mistaken, it cannot be taken two ways, there is no gray area, no wiggle room for man, and it is brought to bear on the issues. Christ is presented as the only way of salvation. All men who hear are placed before the command of God to repent and believe. The promise is given that all who repent and believe will be saved. The warning is issued that those who refuse will perish. Without the wisdom of man the preaching has no natural appeal to man.

About such preaching man says, "Folly! That is utter and complete folly, and if you preach that way, you will amount to nothing, and your church will also amount to nothing."

That is what they were saying in the Corinthian church in Paul's day. They were bored with the gospel. Thus they wanted to mix the preaching with Greek rhetoric. Today men tire of the preaching and of preachers too. They long for some new thing. They turn to all kinds of gimmicks. They introduce other new worship forms that especially push aside the preaching for plays, skits, dances, entertainment, and mission presentations. They tire of the preaching and come to church to be amused. They come to church to hear some well-constructed turn of phrase or some inspiring social commentary. If ministers do preach, if it can be called preaching, they take the offense out of it so that any man can listen and say, "Good sermon." They make the cross of none effect too.

Foolish to All Men

When the apostle says that man calls the preaching foolish, he does not refer to some men, perhaps the ruder and more igno-rant sorts, but to all men. The preaching of Christ crucified is "unto the Jews a stumblingblock, and unto the Greeks foolish-ness" (v. 23). Man at his best has this reaction to the preaching.

It is a stumbling block to the Jew. The Jew here is a religious Jew and thus also the religious person, a churchman or church-woman, a professing Christian. When Christ preached to the Jews the way of salvation, they responded by saying, "Give us a sign that thou art the Christ." They wanted a sign when Christ hung on the cross: "Come down from the cross and we will believe that you are the Christ." So the religious person always wants a sign that what is preached is true. "Give us some proof, some outward, visible, and dramatic sign that your preaching is true. If your preaching attracts numbers, we will know it is true. If your preaching gives the church influence in society, we will know it is true. If your preaching gives the church power, we will know it is truth. If your preaching makes the church rich, we will know it is truth." A wicked and adulterous generation it is that seeks a sign! The preaching as such they regard as foolishness.

Because no sign is forthcoming—just as Jesus would not give the Jews a sign except the sign of the prophet Jonah—they stumble at the truth. This means to stumble in unbelief, to break one's spiritual neck, and to perish. That is what the preaching does to the natural man as he is religious. He stumbles. He stumbles because the preaching declares that he and all his religion are not worthy of salvation and that only by faith in the crucified Christ will he be saved. The religious man scoffs at the idea that his religion is of no value to deserve salvation. He is offended that all his works do not merit with God. He declares that the gospel makes men careless and profane if salvation is by faith in Christ and by Christ's work alone. He stumbles, but his stumbling is because he thinks the Christ of preaching is foolish.

To the Greek the preaching of Christ crucified is naked folly. "Greek" means the world at its best. The Greeks were the most sophisticated, artistic, scientific, technical, philosophical, and advanced people the world had ever seen. To the Greek, Christ crucified is folly because the worldly man seeks after wisdom. To seek after wisdom means to look for some visible effect of the preaching on the world. "Show me how your preaching changes the world and makes it a better place." When it does not, he says, "Folly." The Greek is unbelieving man as he analyzes biblical truth by his scientific standards and investigations and concludes that God did not create in six days, the flood was a local event, or the resurrection did not happen; foolishness all.

Both of these reactions were evident in the judgment hall of Pontius Pilate. Two thousand years ago in skeptic unbelief he responded to Jesus Christ, "What is truth?" The Jew was there too, saying, "We have no king but Caesar." The cross is, and the cross always will be, folly to the natural man, whether Jew or Greek. Because the cross is folly, the preaching of the cross will always be folly.

This is the same effect today of preaching Christ crucified. The wisdom of the church world is that you will never amount to anything if you preach the truth. They are right. The wisdom of the church world today is that the cross of Jesus Christ is offensive. They are right. Preach the cross, confess the cross, live the cross, and you will be an offense. You will not attract large crowds. You will never have a megachurch. Many will forsake the preaching of Christ crucified and turn away from Christ and follow him no more. The gospel always brings turmoil, a sword, and division. The gospel will always turn the world upside down. The world will always laugh at the gospel. This arises from the simple fact that when Christ's cross is preached, that cross is folly to man.

The Power of God

The apostle says that foolish preaching is the power of God: "It pleased God by the foolishness of preaching to save them that believe" (v. 21). Whatever man's evaluation of preaching is, preaching is not foolish because by it God saves. As ardently as a man desires the salvation of his soul, let him desire the preaching, for by it God is pleased to save, and without it there is no salvation. The preaching of Christ crucified is powerful, not foolish. It is folly to man, but then it is the folly of God, and the foolishness of God is wiser than men. It is weakness to man, but then it is the weakness of God, and the weakness of God is stronger than men. By his folly and weakness God is pleased to save.

Salvation consists of the satisfaction of man's deepest need, which is to know God by faith. Paul implies this when he says, "The world...knew not God." The whole problem of sinful man can be summarized as his ignorance of God. Man's salvation and eternal life are to know God. Paul says that this knowledge of God is faith: "to save them that believe" (v. 21).

God made man to know him, to love him, and to live with him forever. Just as God made fish to swim in the sea, so he made man to fellowship with God. Just as the fish is miserable apart from the water, so man is miserable apart from God.

When the preaching comes, God gives the sinner the saving knowledge of himself through his Son, Jesus Christ. This is what man needs, although he will not and cannot admit it. This is his salvation. There is nothing in the whole world that he needs besides the knowledge of God.

To know God is not to know him merely intellectually, scientifically, technically, or theologically. It is not to know only that he exists, or merely to know his power and Godhead, or that he is, or that he must be worshiped. To know God is to know him as the God of my salvation in Jesus Christ his Son. It is to know God as the God who spoke in eternity for my salvation, at the cross for my salvation, and by preaching speaks for my salvation. By means of that preaching he comes and speaks to men and causes them to know him. To know God is to know the forgiveness of sins in Christ and to know sanctification, wisdom, righteousness, and redemption. It is also to love, honor, and fear this God.

To know God is life.

To be ignorant of God is death.

By the preaching, God saves, because by preaching he causes men to know him in Christ by faith. Apart from it we perish. Apart from it we are miserable. Apart from it we are ignorant.

It pleased God by the folly of preaching to save those who believe.

The Reason for This

That is also the necessity of preaching. It pleased God so to work. It is the will of God to exert his saving power through preaching.

Preaching Christ crucified is the power to save because by that preaching God is pleased to bring the Word of the cross into the hearts of his elect. That is why Paul brought up the Word of the cross in verse 18. That Word is salvation. God said, "Let there be a cross, and let there be salvation." That Word becomes reality in the heart of an elect when Christ sends out heralds, by means of them Christ speaks that Word, and it powerfully accomplishes salvation in his heart and life.

Further, the preaching brings salvation to the elect because it brings Christ to them. At the cross God stored up all salvation in Christ. The preaching does not then bring merely the benefits of salvation, but it also brings Christ with all his salvation. That is what the apostle means when he says in verse 24, "But unto them which are called…Christ." Christ is the power and wisdom of God. Preaching is Christ to those who are called. When the preaching comes, Christ comes. When Christ comes, God comes. When God comes, he comes with his wisdom and power and applies salvation.

This is why there must be preaching. The preaching is Christ to those who are called. This is why foolish preaching is the power to save.

Still deeper in answering the question why the preaching of Christ crucified is necessary, the apostle says in verse 21, "For after that in the wisdom of God the world by wisdom knew not God." "After that" means because that. So the apostle is saying, "Because that in the wisdom of God the world by its wisdom knew not God," preaching Christ crucified is necessary.

The wisdom of God is God's perfection whereby he is able to order all things so they serve the glory of his name and the exaltation of Christ. In eternity God exhibited his wisdom when he ordered his decrees so everything contained in them served his glory in the highest possible sense. God has the ability to do that because he is a wise God. The wisdom of God therefore is Christ. Christ is whom God decreed so everything would serve his glory. Therefore, everything must serve Christ. Serving Christ, everything must serve God. That is God's wisdom. By saying "the wisdom of God," the apostle in effect says, "for Christ's sake." For Christ's sake the world by its wisdom knew not God.

The world's wisdom has the right to the name *wisdom* because it is a form of wisdom, though it is devoid of all spiritual power to give the knowledge of God. Wisdom is the ability to apply the best means to the highest end. For a carnal man his highest end is the earth and happiness in the earth. It has not escaped the attention of the wise men of the world that the creation is terribly broken. Many have spoken of the so-called problem of evil. The world's wisdom therefore is not only a reference to man's power of intellect, but refers especially to that power of intellect as it attempts self-salvation. That salvation consists in the sinner's attempt to live a blessed life apart from God. Man wants to live apart from God, to live in his sins, and he wants a blessed life too.

The world's wisdom refers to the world at its very best scientifically. It is the world as it investigates the creation to heal diseases and to remedy problems by scientific advances. In psychiatry and psychology man investigates the complexities of the mind to unravel phobias and nervosas. In politics and law the world tries to legislate itself into a utopia. Philosophically the world tries to think itself into salvation.

In the wisdom of God the world at its best—the world as wise—knew not God. God made the wisdom of the world vain and useless to attain to any knowledge of God and salvation: the knowledge of God by faith in Christ Jesus.

That it is impossible for the world to know God by its wisdom is God's wisdom. He so decreed and ordered all things that man cannot know him in any other way than by faith in Christ

Jesus. In Adam all men fell into sin and all the light in man was changed into darkness; his heart became hard and obdurate and filled with enmity against God. God operates in the world blinding man's eyes, shutting his ears, and hardening his heart, so that he does not attain to the knowledge of God. The knowledge of God that he has by means of created things man holds down in unrighteousness; he pollutes and defiles it and brings upon himself the wrath of God more and more.

God does that for Christ's sake because it pleased God by the preaching of Christ crucified to save. "Pleased God" refers to God's decrees. In his council God willed that all his elect people would be brought to salvation by one means: preaching Christ crucified. When God makes all the world's wisdom vain for the knowledge of God, he does so because it pleases God by the preaching of Christ, for the glory of Christ, and for the glory of his own name so to save.

Men, also in the church world, have a lot of good to say about the world's wisdom. Some chastise the church for being anti-intellectual and so embarrassingly naive as to reject the world's investigations of creation and her conclusions about the origin of the world. Speaking good of the world's wisdom lies very near the heart of the error of cultural common grace. According to common grace, by means of a common, non-saving favor God restrains sin in the unregenerate and makes possible good works by them, including some real, retained knowledge of God.

Common grace makes it possible for the world to do much good in its wisdom. God does the very opposite. All that wisdom is worthless to give the one and only good that man needs—the knowledge of God—and indeed that wisdom is so formulated to exclude the knowledge of God. God makes it so. This is his wisdom. For Christ's sake, God in his wisdom made sure that the world by its wisdom will never know him, so that if a man will know him he can only know him through the preaching of Christ crucified.

The church, a minister, a man, submits to that, believes, and is saved; or he rebels against it, seeks his own wisdom, makes void the cross, and perishes. That was the danger in the Corinthian congregation. They were bored with the preaching of Christ crucified. This is always the danger in man's rejection of the preaching of Christ crucified. A man may never pretend to be wiser than God, who will have his people taught by the lively preaching of the word. By his assault on the preaching man threatens his own and the church's knowledge of God and thus salvation. To receive and believe that preaching glorifies Christ, who was crucified for our salvation, and submits to the wisdom of God, whose will it is by the preaching to give us Christ.

For Whom This Is True

If the preaching does not save someone, that is not because the preaching failed. When the preaching is foolish to a man or a church, there is power in that. It is power, because in the preaching Christ comes. The preaching is Christ to those who are called because it brings Christ. It brings Christ before the unbeliever too. This is why the natural man, whether Jew or Greek, rejects the preaching of Christ crucified. The preaching is Christ to them, and apart from the operation of God's grace the natural man rejects Christ. He takes him, tries him, contradicts him, raises false witnesses against him, condemns him, beats him, nails him to a tree, and rails on him. He did that when Christ walked on the earth, and he does that when Christ comes in the preaching.

When preaching hardens men in unbelief, it does exactly what it is supposed to do. By becoming folly to some, as the cross is folly to them, the preaching also becomes the power to bring to naught their wisdom and prudence. Christ must become what God said he would be: a stone of stumbling and rock of offense and a laughingstock of the world. He is that in the preaching of Christ crucified and by means of their conclusion that it is folly.

They judge it folly, criticize it, refuse it, and leave it, and ultimately it too will judge them; or rather Christ will judge them by means of it. This too is God's wisdom and sovereign good pleasure.

When the preaching does not save a man and he stumbles at it, breaks his spiritual neck, and reacts in hysterical laughter and mockery or anger and disgust, the fault is not the preaching's or a defective preacher's. This effect is God's carrying out his will for that preaching. A Christ whom all men love is not Christ. He must become the stone rejected. He must become folly to the Greeks. God does this.

Preaching is always a power according to God's sovereign good pleasure. It pleased God by the foolishness of preaching that some stumble and some laugh. That is implied in verse 21, where the Holy Ghost says, "It pleased God...to save them that believe" by the preaching. This means also that it pleased God by the foolishness of preaching to harden others. The Holy Ghost denies the notion that there is in the preaching a will of God for the salvation of all who hear. Not all men are saved by the preaching. Preaching is a power in this way also.

The apostle also says the preaching is Christ to "them which are called" (v. 24). By the call he refers to the voice of God heard in the preaching, which by means of the preaching comes into the inner being of a man and translates him out of darkness into God's marvelous light. It is as the voice of God that says to the light, "Be." So also in the preaching God says to a man, "Be saved."

That call comes only to God's elect, for by "called" the apostle traces the call to the will of God. Whom he predestinated he also called: calling and election are always inseparably related. Election is the source of the call, and in the call election finds its purpose fulfilled. That call comes by preaching.

Preaching is a power to save those who are called because preaching is Christ to those who are called. They believe, hear the word, and in that word hear Christ and ultimately God himself. That word is powerful to work faith in their hearts, turn them from their folly, grant repentance unto life, forgive their sins, and draw them to Christ. Thus they also come to Jesus Christ, in whom God gives them the saving knowledge of himself, the God of their salvation who decreed their salvation in eternity, spoke their salvation at the cross, and makes them partakers of it in Christ.

By the preaching, God speaks, because when the preaching comes, Christ comes. When Christ comes, God comes. When God comes, he speaks salvation to his people—never man's words of wisdom but always Christ crucified, the power of God to save those who believe.

CHAPTER 6

THE CALLING
OF THE CHURCH

1 Corinthians 1:26–29

---

26. *For ye see your calling, brethren, how that not many wise men after the flesh, not many mighty, not many noble, are called:*
27. *But God hath chosen the foolish things of the world to confound the wise; and God hath chosen the weak things of the world to confound the things which are mighty;*
28. *And base things of the world, and things which are despised, hath God chosen, yea, and things which are not, to bring to nought things that are:*
29. *That no flesh should glory in his presence.*

The church at Corinth was plagued by party strife and division. The factions flew the flags of prominent ministers. The leaders of these factions—false apostles—prided themselves on their artistic, rhetorically brilliant, and worldly wise preaching. Opposed to this the apostle speaks of the calling of a true minister of Jesus Christ to preach the gospel without man's words of wisdom.

In these verses, mocking at the vain pretentions of these light men who dared to divide Christ's church on the basis of their abilities, the apostle writes a rhetorically powerful piece. The Holy Spirit has an art all his own. When he opposes pretentious men, he shows that he too has art. In the Old Testament many of the prophets used ordinary speech, but the Holy Spirit from time to time lifted up a man like Isaiah to angelic eloquence. He does not come behind the Greek orators at all in the presentation and delivery of a message.

At the same time, by this powerful piece of rhetoric, the apostle teaches and adorns the truth. This is the only purpose sacred rhetoric may serve. He does not flatter the Corinthians or any believer with this text. He exalts God. This is the preacher's task. Let God be praised!

God does not need men with their art and wisdom. God saves by the Word of the cross, a Word as plain and rugged as the wood of the cross, a Word that is folly to men. Besides, in the wisdom of God "the world by wisdom knew not God" (v. 20), so that God could save man by the foolishness of preaching.

The apostle concluded in verse 25, "The foolishness of God is wiser than men; and the weakness of God is stronger than men." If man disdainfully calls the preaching foolish, the cross foolish, and Christ foolish, it is God's foolishness, and it is wise. It is also God's weakness, and it is powerful.

To establish that God does not need men, the apostle appeals to the Corinthians' calling. Paul begins verse 26 with "for," which is the same as saying, "In order to establish my doctrine that God saves by foolish means, consider your own calling." Your calling was not a calling of the noble or the wise. This word of the text is the New Testament's equivalent of the Old Testament word of God in Deuteronomy 7:7: "The LORD did not set his love upon you, nor choose you, because ye were more in number than any people; for ye were the fewest of all people."

The apostle addresses the Corinthian church as "brethren," and says, "See your calling." This is not a statement of fact as it appears in the King James translation. But "see" is an imperative.

The Holy Ghost calls the church to consider her calling. This is a call to self-examination in the light of whom God calls and the source and content of her calling. Having examined that calling closely and understanding its meaning, she must come to a definite conclusion that God does everything regarding that calling for his glory. Was it the calling of the mighty, noble, and wise? God saves a lowly lot for his glory. He calls them to let that self-examination and their conclusion have the spiritual, practical effect that no man glories in the presence of God. The implication is that every man thinks of himself soberly and lives soberly in the church in light of that calling and that no one is permitted to do anything through strife or vainglory.

The Idea of the Calling

When the apostle says, "Consider your calling," he does not mean that the church must consider what work she is called to do in the world or how she is to live in the world. Many understand the calling of the church only in the sense of what the church must do or how she must live. For them the calling of the church means exclusively that the church is to be busy in evangelism and missions, busy within the communion of the saints, and busy using her gifts and talents for the mutual edification of the members. If they are deluded by the spirit of the age, they say that the church is to be busy in the service of the world: feed the world's poor, build the world's homes, visit the world's jails, and adopt the world's orphans.

The apostle does not say to the Corinthians, "The remedy for your party strife and division is to consider what you have to do in the world. Get busy!" Some in Corinth thought that. Corinth was a gifted congregation. She wanted to use her gifts, but those desires were selfishly motivated. None were in harmony with the word of God and the principle of love. By their use of gifts the Corinthians had torn the church to shreds. They did not consider their calling in the sense the apostle speaks of it. Because they did not properly consider their calling, all their works were useless, and worse, harmful. A church that does not consider her calling as explained by the Holy Ghost in these verses cannot use her gifts properly and does nothing right in the world. A church that does not believe the truth of her calling as explained by the apostle is useless in the world except for trouble.

The calling the brethren are to consider is the gracious call of God that brings the church into existence in the world and bestows on her all of Christ's riches and gifts. The call of God enriches her with grace for God's glory, not for the glory of the church or of any individual in the church. The calling is the saving call of the gospel mentioned in 1 Corinthians 1:9: "God... [has] called [you] unto the fellowship of his Son." The same calling is mentioned in verse 24: "But unto them which are called, both Jews and Greeks, Christ the power of God, and the wisdom of God." Paul mentions it again in verse 26: "For ye see your calling, brethren." He refers to the saving call of the gospel whereby the church is called out of the sin-cursed world into fellowship with Jesus Christ.

The preaching of the gospel comes with a call, a call that is spoken by Christ, that brings Christ, and that is the power and wisdom of God to those who are called. The calling is the triune God's address of the elect sinner that comes through the preaching, so that by preaching God speaks to the sinner. God addresses the sinner in the depths of his being and calls him out of darkness into God's marvelous light and saves him. In the calling, God speaks, just as God said in the beginning, "Let there be light," and just as God still speaks in creation. "The voice of the LORD is powerful; the voice of the LORD is full of majesty. The voice of the LORD breaketh the cedars of Lebanon. The voice of the LORD divideth the flames of fire. The voice of the LORD shaketh the wilderness" (Ps. 29:4–5, 7–8). So also God calls the sinner and addresses him.

The call comes by means of preaching Christ crucified. The

apostle says in 1 Corinithians 1:23–24 that some are called by the preaching of Christ crucified. In the same context the Holy Spirit denies that the call is synonymous with the preaching of the gospel. The calling comes *by means of* the preaching of the gospel, a gospel that is promiscuously preached. That the calling is not synonymous with the preaching of the gospel is plain in verse 23, where Paul says that Christ in the preaching is "foolishness" to many. If the preaching calls all who hear, in the sense that it is a saving and well-meant call intended to save all, but the preaching is foolish to many, the God of that call is impotent to save everyone he calls. Then man can do with the preaching of the gospel what light was unable to do in the beginning, namely, resist the call of the living God.

In naming the essence of the preaching a calling, the apostle also exposes the patent lie of describing the essence of the preaching as an offer, let alone an offer of salvation intended by God for the salvation of all who hear it. The fact is that those who describe the preaching as well intended by God for the salvation of all who hear do not describe it mainly as a calling, but as an offer. They delight to call it an offer. They cast out of the church those who disagree with them on this point. Those who delight in describing the preaching as an offer corrupt the idea of preaching at its very definition. It comes with the calling of God, not an offer. It is as to its essence a call of God, not an offer of God.

This call, unlike the impotent offer, is saving. This is Paul's burden and the reason he addresses the Corinthians as "brethren." They have been made brethren by the saving call of God. By the call of God those who were aliens from the covenant, kingdom, and church of God and who would have perished in their sin, ignorance, and unbelief have been brought nigh, incorporated into God's family, and saved. The call gives the saving knowledge of God to the ignorant. The call reconciles enemies of God and brings them into his holy family. The call makes known the blessed will of God for the salvation of his people and by that makes them partakers of it. The call of God summons the sinner out of the darkness, ignorance, and death of his fellowship with sin and calls him into the light, knowledge, and life of saving fellowship with Jesus Christ. The call gathers the church out of the world and establishes the church in the world.

Apart from the call of God, man—a man, woman, or child, rich or poor, bond or free, though he or she be the wisest and mightiest, the richest and noblest in the world—perishes. By the call of God men are saved, though they be the most benighted, ignorant, or lowliest of men, or the most inveterate, enraged, and public persecutors of Christ and his church, as Paul was.

Have you been called by the living God? Has he spoken to you in the depths of your being? Has he translated you out of darkness into his marvelous light, so that you know him in Christ; believe in him as the one who justifies you in Christ, forgives all your sins for Christ's sake, declares you worthy of eternal life, and sanctifies you by the Spirit of Christ; and confess him, love him, and cleave unto him? Consider your calling.

Two Conclusions

When the believer considers his calling, there are two outstanding things that he will see.

First, he will see that not everyone is called. The preaching, which is the instrument to bring the call, does not go to everyone. For the greater part of history God confined the preaching to the Jews and "suffered all nations to walk in their own ways" (Acts 14:16). The preaching goes wherever God in his good pleasure sends the preaching. Where God sends it the gospel is preached promiscuously to Jew and Greek, bond and free, rich and poor, wise and foolish; yet even in that preaching the saving call does not come to all who hear. It is particular to God's elect alone.

This is clear in every mention of the call in 1 Corinthians 1. In verse 9 the apostle says, "Ye were called unto the fellowship of his Son." Not everyone was called. "Ye" were called. In verse 24, among those who hear the gospel are Jews and Greeks to whom the gospel is foolish; and there are Jews and Greeks to whom that gospel is Christ. Not everyone is called.

Consider that. It is sobering. Not all are called. Some God addresses powerfully and efficaciously and saves them by that address. Some, who hear the very same preaching that the called hear, he leaves in their sin and unbelief. Indeed, he hardens them in that sin and unbelief, so that they not only reject it, but also blaspheme the gospel, Christ, and God by calling it foolish.

Second, when the believer considers his calling, he sees that those whom God addresses and draws into saving fellowship with his Son are "not many wise…not many mighty, not many noble" (v. 26). He does not call *many* mighty, wise, or noble. The apostle does not say that God does not call *any* mighty, wise, or noble. Sometimes God proves that what is impossible with men—that a camel goes through the eye of a needle—is possible with God. He can bring a rich man to heaven. Sometimes God calls the rich and mighty, but a godly prince is a rare bird, and a genius in earthly things is precious in the church. There is an Augustine here, a Luther there, a Calvin there, but not many. The great men God does not call. The majority of the best men in the world perish in unbelief.

Consider that. If salvation were dependent on what man could do or on his powers, surely those wise men would be saved, and those who are saved, the unwise, would not be saved. This exposes the naked pride incipient in Arminianism and its false doctrine of the calling that God in the preaching of the gospel offers salvation to all who hear, not a calling after all, but an offer. If he offers salvation to all and grace sufficient for all men to accept it, all have likewise an equal opportunity to accept or reject salvation. Then the man who accepts makes himself to differ from another, especially by the exercise of his free will. In the end it would be the wise, the mighty, and the noble who actually are saved. By contrast, considering the truth of the calling that not many mighty, noble, or wise are called—implying that the ones whom God calls are very many foolish, very many weak and helpless, and very many ignoble—abases man.

The lowliness of the called is the spiritual reality of everyone whom God calls, even if he would be pleased to call a mighty man according to the flesh. Regardless of his earthly gifts, that man is weak, helpless, ignoble, and foolish concerning his salvation. He is that first in Adam. Spiritually, according to his fleshly birth he is bad. He is conceived and born in sin, all the light in him is darkness, and he is born under sin, hostile to God and the neighbor. By physical birth man is helpless. He cannot save himself. He does not desire to be saved. He resists God. Besides, he is a fool who would rather perish in his sin than be called to God and be saved. That is whom God saves.

A man will see this if he considers his calling. The church will see this if she considers her calling. She will also be humbled by that consideration.

The Source of the Calling

When a man considers his calling, he must conclude that the calling is to be traced to God and his eternal will. By necessary implication, if the preaching were not a calling of God but an offer from God, by which a man could distinguish himself from his fellows, who also have the same offer, the acceptance of the offer through grace must be traced to man's will. The outcome of that offer has nothing to do with God's will. However, the apostle does not teach an offer but the calling of God. Thereby he directs the church to consider God's will as the source of the calling. The apostle does that when he moves seamlessly from verse 26— where he explains the calling and says that God does not call the mighty, wise, and noble—to verse 27, where he says, "God hath chosen." This refers to God's eternal choice in predestination.

Election is God's eternal choice of certain persons in Christ as the church and his appointment of them to salvation in Christ.

That choice is God's. Because he is a sovereign and independent God, his choice cannot be based on anything in those whom he chooses. God is not dependent on man. To say that God chooses those who respond to the calling is to make God dependent on man and to deny that he is God and election is his. The choice is God's; therefore, it is for God's glory, not man's. God chooses whom he chooses in order to magnify his glory. He does not call the mighty, wise, and noble because he did not choose them. He calls whom he calls, and they receive Christ in the preaching because he chose them for his glory. Election makes the calling of free grace rooted in God's sovereign, free will and eternal good pleasure.

Implied in the truth that election is the source of the calling is the related truth that those whom God does not call were reprobated. God did not choose them. Reprobation is God's eternal passing by of the reprobate with the grace of election and his eternal appointment to damnation of those whom he passed by. That choice is God's. He did not reprobate them because he saw that they would reject Christ in the preaching. That makes God's choice based on man's choice; that makes God dependent on man. A God who is dependent on man is not God. He did not call the mighty, wise, and noble; he did not call all men; he does not call all men in the preaching of the gospel, because he did not choose all men but reprobated many.

That offends many. Believing that in the preaching of the gospel God desires the salvation of all who hear and that God expresses by the preaching his will that all who hear be saved, they cannot make sense of the text. Embarrassed that God teaches in the text that he calls some and does not call others, and especially he does not call the mighty, noble, or wise, they make "chosen" in verse 27 a choice in time or a choice unrelated to salvation as a mere illustration of what God does in salvation. That is an Arminian interpretation of this verse.

God's choice is not in time but in eternity. "Hath chosen" is past tense. God made the choice. Out of it and because of it he calls. That choice is a saving choice because it issues in the calling that saves. Powerfully implied is that the non-choice of some is a damning non-choice, because when the gospel comes to those not chosen, God does not call them with it and Christ in it remains foolishness to them. The relationship between God's choice and his calling in this text is the same as the apostle teaches in Romans 8:30: "Moreover whom he did predestinate, them he also called." By the calling—or non-calling—of all who hear the preaching of the gospel God carries out and executes his decree of predestination.

Thus the calling cannot be an offer. The scriptural word itself denies that calling is an offer. *Calling* and *offer* are not synonyms. But more deeply, since the calling is rooted in God's choice and proceeds from it, the calling cannot be an offer. To make it an offer is a gross denial of election because it automatically implies that the acceptance of Christ in the preaching is in doubt and in the power of man and that man's reception of Christ in the preaching was not already determined by God. Why would God offer what he already determined to do? The calling depends on God's eternal choice. Therefore, it does not depend on man's choice in time.

Such is the logic of verses 26–29 that if the call were God's offer of salvation to all who hear the preaching; if in the calling God were to express a desire to save all who hear; if that were the preaching of the gospel; if that were the call, then a whole different group of people would be saved. If the calling were an offer, in the logic of these verses, of the apostle Paul, and of the Holy Ghost, the calling would save the mighty, the noble, and the wise. It would save those who have the strength—by grace, of course— to accept God's offer. It would save the noble, those who are born with free wills to accept that offer and fulfill the condition of faith. Or it would save the wise, those who can be argued into accepting the truths of the gospel. God does not save many of them, because the preaching is not an offer. If the preaching were an offer, it would not save the lowly, the ignoble, and the weak, and so all men would perish in their sin. It is a call. It is the voice of God in the preaching that effects what God willed in eternity, and so it saves. It saves those whom he chose.

Election as the source of the calling is a choice in love, just as reprobation is a choice in hatred. "God hath chosen" (v. 27) means to choose out for oneself. God picks out for himself the base, weak, despised, and the things that are not. Those words are pregnant with love. God, in his love, in his profound and eternal desire to do good to those whom he picks, chose them out for himself as his own, because he delighted in them and he willed them to be made partakers of the fellowship of his Son and be brought into the family of the triune God. He picked them out of the whole human race. The call does not come to everyone because God did not pick everyone.

If a church will walk in the way of love, she must consider that, and considering it she must believe it. If she does not believe that about the calling, she necessarily believes that she distinguished herself in her love of God. Believing that, she is puffed up. Love is not puffed up. Such a view of the calling makes impossible her walk in the way of love, beginning with her proud walk with God that will inevitably carry over to the relationship with the neighbor. Equally true, if a church and a believer will not walk in the way of love, then regardless of the precision with which they can express the doctrines of predestination and calling, they deny them by their walk. If they consider these doctrines, they will be humbled. Not puffed up, they will walk in love toward God and the neighbor.

The Marvelous Way God Works

Referring to that choice of God's people, the apostle also speaks in verses 27–28 of "things." That is because election is to be understood in the context of God's plan of salvation for the whole world when he created it, including his choice of his people. His whole decree determined the way God would work in time and history for the salvation of people. Election and reprobation are one part of the whole plan of salvation. In the plan of salvation he decreed to work it out by foolish, weak, base, and despicable nothings.

If a man considers his calling, is that not clear? God chose the fall of Adam and of the whole human race as the way of the revelation of his marvelous grace. God chose the way of sin and grace and of death and resurrection. He chose the foolishness of the cross. He chose the foolishness of preaching as the method to bring the cross to his people in history and in their individual situations. When he decided whom he was going to save, he also chose the foolish. He did not choose the man Cain, but the wisp Abel. God loved Jacob, the homebody, and not Esau, the hunter. God did not choose the mighty nations, but Israel, who was the fewest, stiff-necked, and rebellious. He gave Gideon three hundred. God picked a blind Samson to kill more people in his death than in his life. God chose a woman to pound a stake through the general's head. Did God choose Eliab? He picked David and raised him to be king over his people. God counseled Israel not to despise the day of small things.

God always picks the weak things, the despised things, and the base things. He chose the "things which are not" (v. 28). That is man as he is in Adam and as he lies fallen in sin and death and liable to damnation. He is not. He is nothing. He has nothing. He deserves nothing. From among man's race, which is nothing, God chose the very least of all man's children to be God's children. To them he gave power to become his children. That is how he works.

When a man considers the ones God chooses, he cannot find anything in them to explain why they should not have been reprobated. The choice of God is not based on anything in the things chosen, but is itself a gracious choice of the unworthy and worthless. When a man considers his calling, he must ascend finally to

God's election and see that the Spirit in verses 26–29 attributes all of man's salvation to God's choice.

God makes these choices deliberately in order to confound the wise, to shame the mighty, and to make worthless the things that the world counts worthwhile. The apostle says that God has chosen the foolish things of the world "to confound" the wise, or literally "with a purpose." He says the very same thing about the mighty. The ultimate form of this work of God is to choose "things which are not, to bring to nought things that are" (v. 28).

Man says, "See, I have all these things. I have wisdom, might, and power." But God puts it all to shame, confounds them, and brings them to naught because he will not save by those means or on account of those things. A man says, "I have a free will." It is precisely the teaching of the text that if man would have a free will, God would not use it in salvation. Another man says, "I have works." Even if man had works that were worthy of salvation, God would not use them but confound them and those who trust in them.

God always is and forever remains the God who calls the things that are not as though they were and raises the dead. He is and remains the God who takes no delight in man's riches, strength, beauty, ability, or anything at all that man has or delights in. God is and forever will be the God who hides his wisdom from the wise and prudent and reveals it to babes, who gives grace to the humble, resists the proud, makes the poor rich, blesses the meek, feeds the hungry, gives drink to the thirsty, saves the helpless, forgives the guilty sinner, heals the sick, protects the innocent, sets prisoners free, and will by no means clear the guilty. His power is always made perfect in weakness, and out of the mouths of babes and sucklings he ordains strength. By the foolishness of preaching he saves. By the cross he delivers, because the weakness of God is stronger than men and the foolishness of God is wiser than men. His choice, and his calling from that choice, is always man-confounding and man-abasing.

Considering Our Calling

If a man considers his calling, he will conclude that God's choice is always man-abasing and God-glorifying. He will not murmur against the free grace of God's election and the just severity of his reprobation. He will not say that all men must have a chance, or that God offers salvation to everyone, or that man must have a choice. He will adore the God who chooses in this way and works in this way in the preaching. He will love him for that choice and rejoice in it. Rejoicing, he will walk humbly with his God and in the way of love with his neighbor. Let a man consider his calling and see if that is not true. Let him see whether there is one thing at all in him on account of which God chose him and called him. If he says, "Yes, there is," he knows nothing of the calling of God.

If the calling comes to everyone, all are furnished with grace to accept it, and all can equally receive it or reject it, then those who do accept salvation have something about which to boast. They also, at the very beginning, cut themselves off from the possibility of walking in the way of love. This must be obvious: if a man boasts before God, what will keep him from boasting before his neighbor? Such a boasting man cannot walk in the way of love. Charity vaunts not itself and is not puffed up (13:4).

If a man considers his calling and traces it back to election, let that have the practical, spiritual effect in his life of not "glory[ing] in [God's] presence" (1:29). God calls and elects in order that no man "glory in his presence." This means that a man who glories in his wisdom, might, or strength is not going to be in the presence of God. The man who boasts that he decided for Christ, he chose Christ, he accepted the offer, he persevered to the end, or he has works worthy of salvation will not be in the presence of God. God will not have anyone boast in his presence.

Rather, if a man considers his calling, let no man think more highly of himself than he ought to think. What does he have that he has not received? Of what he received, what did he deserve?

Let him glory in the Lord. This is the practical, spiritual purpose of each man's consideration of his calling. Let him abase himself before the Lord, that the Lord might lift him up. Let him glory in God alone in order that God receive all the glory, praise, honor, and thanksgiving for salvation. That man also will walk in love with his neighbor.

CHAPTER 7

SAVING UNION
WITH CHRIST

1 Corinthians 1:30–31

---

30. But of him are ye in Christ Jesus, who of God is made unto us wisdom, and righteousness, and sanctification, and redemption:

31. That, according as it is written, He that glorieth, let him glory in the Lord.

Introduction

In the context the apostle Paul calls the squabbling Corinthians to consider their calling. This is necessary for their walk in the way of love. Walking in the way of love is impossible for a proud man because love does not vaunt itself and is not puffed up. The proudest man is one who boasts of his work in salvation in the presence of God. One who boasts of his works before God will behave unseemly in the church too. Paul especially has this particular form of pride in view when he speaks of "glory[ing]" in verse 29. This he makes clear by his contrast in verses 30–31, where he describes the wholly gracious accomplishment and application of salvation to the elect child of God, so that he may glory in the Lord and not boast in himself.

Considering one's calling by learning the truth about it and believing it is the antidote to pride concerning one's salvation.

The calling the believer is to consider is the saving call of God that comes by means of the preaching of the gospel. By the call God summons the elect church out of spiritual darkness into God's marvelous light. When the elect consider that calling, they will see that God did not call them because of any good or commendable thing in themselves—their power, wisdom, or ability—but solely because of his own gracious choice. They will also see that God did not call everyone, but eternally passing by many, he justly reprobated them. Calling always proceeds from God's election. In his election God chose the foolish, the weak, despised things, and things that are not so that no flesh will glory in his presence. The truth of election and calling is a man-abasing truth.

In verses 30–31 the apostle explains the effect of the calling. By the calling, God brought the elect into saving fellowship with Jesus Christ. This is the connection between these verses and the preceding context. The believer must consider as well the end of his calling, which is saving fellowship with Christ Jesus.

Saving fellowship is also the meaning of baptism, which is a sign and a seal of incorporation into Jesus Christ by true faith. In the context the apostle brought up baptism. He was thankful in the light of the tumultuous state of affairs in Corinth that he had baptized only Crispus, Gaius, and the household of Stephanas (vv. 14–15). Thus the Corinthians could not accuse him of baptizing in his own name and trying to gather a following for himself. Besides, the Lord did not send him to baptize. When Paul said that, he did not denigrate baptism as a sacrament. Rather, he exposed the false teachers who were abusing baptism and boasting of their followings exactly *because* baptism is a sign and seal of union with Christ and God's faithfulness to the believer and his seed. The false teachers took a sign of incorporation into Christ and made it a sign of their power and influence, and so they denied Christ.

In verses 30–31 the apostle speaks of the reality that baptism signifies and seals.

Damning Union with Adam

Verse 30 begins with "but," which signifies a contrast between saving union with Christ Jesus and damning fellowship with Adam. The emphasis is that in Christ "are ye" (v. 30), which contrasts with "things which are not" in verse 28. "Are" and "are not": that is the contrast. When a man considers his calling and ascends from the calling to God's election, he will see that God chose the things that are not. The living God unites "things which are not," we would say nothings and nobodies, in saving union with Jesus Christ.

This is always true of God's works. He creates out of nothing. He always calls the things that are not as though they were (Rom. 4:17). God's work in creation, whether it was the first work of bringing things into existence or creating the massive diversity of the universe, was not his work of superintending an evolutionary process of chance happenings through which the world came to be and is coming to be. Creation is the work of the triune God who calls the things that are not as though they were. He called the entire creation into instantaneous existence out of nothing. By a kind of analogy this is also true of all his works in creation. He called fish and birds out of the water, plants out of dry land, and a host of animals from the dirt, when before there had been none.

What is true of God's creating is true of God's working in salvation. If a man denies that God instantaneously created the world, he cannot understand the greater truth of salvation as God's calling the things that are not. Indeed, if God is the God who does not bring this creation to be, he is not the God who raises the dead in salvation. Denial of creation invariably leads to denial of the resurrection and the whole gospel of gracious salvation. Denial of the truth of creation and denial of the truth of salvation go hand in hand because in creation and salvation God worked in a similar way. It is unsurprising, therefore, that where the truth of salvation by grace is corrupted there is also the corruption of the truth of creation. He always is and always remains the God who calls the things that are not in salvation and in creation.

With the word "but" in 1 Corinthians 1:30 the apostle calls the believer to consider what he was spiritually prior to his union with Christ. Spiritually he *was not*. He was not merely weak, foolish, or despised, but he was not at all. He was a nothing and a nobody. This describes the natural man as he is *in Adam*, as he is regarding his being, shape, and place within God's creation and in history. Spiritually in Adam, he *was not*.

The natural man is in Adam because Adam was his legal head; Adam represented him. Everything Adam did, he did for the whole human race. Furthermore, the natural man is organically connected with Adam so that he comes out of Adam, who is the natural fountain of the whole human race. All men receive their natures from Adam. Adam was the representative of the human race; he was responsible for the entire human race.

In Adam the natural man is also *that which is not* spiritually.

As Adam came from the hands of God he was not *nothing*. God made man glorious, and he was the crown of the creation. God made Adam glorious spiritually. Adam possessed the image of God, so that he resembled God in a creaturely way. That image of God in Adam was his original goodness, which consisted of Adam's knowledge of God, righteousness, and holiness. Adam possessed the righteousness of God, so that Adam was capable of willing according to God's will and of doing what God required, so that he actually did what God required. God expressed his approval of Adam's whole life and of everything he did. God said Adam was perfect. He possessed the holiness of God, so that he was completely consecrated to God and loved God with his whole heart, mind, soul, and strength. Adam loved what God loved and hated what God hated. Adam possessed the knowledge of God, so that in the creation and by God's word to him Adam instantly and spontaneously knew God and loved

God. Spiritually Adam was glorious. He was something, if only a creaturely something.

Adam became *nothing* by the instigation of the devil and through an act of his own willful disobedience. The devil promised Adam everything and left him with nothing. Because of his sin God stripped Adam of everything. God took away the garden. He took Adam's life and stripped him of his spiritual glory by taking away the image of God. All the light in Adam became darkness. His righteousness became unrighteousness. His holiness became unholiness. His knowledge became ignorance. His will became obstinate, rebellious, and obdurate. His mind and heart were full of hatred. He was bound under sin, and his will was corrupted and in bondage to sin. He was judged by God to be worthy of death, and Adam became dead in his trespasses and sins. He was liable to temporal and eternal death. Adam became nothing.

All men became nothing *in Adam*. The contrast in verses 30–31 is not that by their own wicked deeds men became nothing, but in Christ they become something. The contrast is between what men became in Adam and what they become in Christ. The whole human race became nothing in Adam by what Adam did: because Adam sinned in the garden by eating of the forbidden fruit and because God judged Adam, all men became nothing in him. They do not need to commit another sin to be worthy of temporal and eternal death.

This is exactly what the Reformed baptism form teaches in connection with the explanation of the necessity of baptizing the children of believers. "We may not...exclude them from baptism, for...they are without their knowledge partakers of the condemnation in Adam."[1] Our children do not have to know

---

1 Form for the Administration of Baptism, in *The Confessions and the Church Order of the Protestant Reformed Churches* (Grandville, MI: Protestant Reformed Churches in America, 2005), 259.

what baptism means—or know anything at all—in order to be baptized. To understand the Reformed doctrine of baptism and the necessity of baptizing the children of believers, even though they do not know the God in whose name they are baptized, it is necessary to understand how children are partakers of condemnation in Adam. It is not on account of their own sinful deeds or the sinful deeds of their parents, but because of their connection with Adam. Without a consideration of any of their works they are condemned, are judged worthy of condemnation, and become nothing. So also are all men. Union with Adam is condemnation.

Saving Union with Christ Jesus

"But of him are ye in Christ Jesus" (v. 30). Out of that nothingness God joins the elect to Christ Jesus. In Christ he makes those who are nothing to be something spiritually.

"In Christ Jesus" is the main thought of verses 30–31. By these words the apostle teaches the saving union of the child of God with Jesus Christ. First, to be "in Christ Jesus" is to be legally represented by Christ Jesus. He is the representative head, so that he is responsible for all those who are in him. Second, to be "in Christ Jesus" is to be joined with Christ Jesus, to become one with him.

The Bible explains the union of the believer with Christ Jesus in different ways and calls this union *faith*. To be in Christ Jesus is to possess faith. Faith is not first what one knows or believes, but faith is one's union with Christ. The Bible uses the picture of a branch and a tree. As a branch is part of the tree, so believers are in Christ. Because they do not naturally belong to Christ but to Adam, the Bible speaks of their engrafting into Christ. As a horticulturalist takes a branch from one tree and joins it by a living connection with another tree, so the believer is taken out of Adam and joined to Christ. The Bible also refers to this union as analogous to that of the body with the head. Just as the members of one's body are organically united with the head, so believers are united with Christ.

That union with Christ is man's salvation, just as his union with Adam is his condemnation. Describing the saving significance of this union, 1 Corinthians 1:30 says, "are ye." This contrasts with "are not" (v. 28) in Adam. If being nothing in Adam describes the utter spiritual poverty of natural man, "are ye in Christ Jesus" describes the spiritual riches and life that belong to the believer in Christ Jesus. If in Adam man has nothing, by means of his union with Christ Jesus he has everything. Verse 31 describes the salvation that becomes the believer's in union with Christ: "who of God is made unto us wisdom, and righteousness, and sanctification, and redemption."

The first benefit of union with Christ that the apostle mentions is that Christ becomes wisdom from God to us. The phrase should be read as, "Who is made wisdom from God unto us." The words translated "of God" in the King James mean from God. This phrase does not modify the entire description of the saving benefits of our union with Christ, as though the apostle meant to underscore the fact that Christ comes *from* God to us. But he particularly intends to teach that Christ Jesus *becomes wisdom from God* to the one who is united to him.

Christ is not wisdom from God to one who is in Adam. Earlier Paul taught that Christ is foolishness to the natural man. The natural man hears Christ Jesus preached and calls it foolishness. If he is a Greek, he says, "That is stupid. There is wisdom outside of Christ, and I do not need Christ. I can find wisdom somewhere else. I can know how to live my life in the world outside of Christ." So he seeks for wisdom. If he is a Jew, he stumbles at Christ and the folly of the cross. He stumbles at the word that Christ alone is salvation and outside of him there is no salvation. Especially the Jew stumbles at the truth that there is no righteousness in his works of the law, that is, any act of love in obedience to God, and he says, "But what about the law and works!" Despising the righteousness of Christ, he goes about to establish his own righteousness by his works. By that he says that his way of salvation by works is wiser—especially because he supposes it will not make men careless and profane—and by that evil he makes Christ and his cross all foolish. If righteousness is by works, why did God go through all the trouble? The natural man, whether Greek or Jew, says, "Christ is foolish" (vv. 18–23).

When God joins a man to Christ, Christ becomes wisdom from God to that man. The wisdom of God is the perfection of God whereby he is able to decree all things and so to order, arrange, govern, and control what he decrees that all things serve his glory, the exultation of Christ, and the salvation of his elect church.

That Christ becomes wisdom from God to a man means that God so applies and gives Christ to him that Christ is his complete salvation and that man seeks salvation in none other than Christ alone. This means that Christ becomes the way of salvation to that man. When God joins a man to Christ Jesus, God takes everything that is in Christ and adapts it for the salvation of that man and of the whole church. To the one joined to Christ, Christ himself becomes the sweetest, wisest, most glorious reality in the whole world. Because Christ is wisdom from God, that man sees all things in his life and in the world from the viewpoint of Christ Jesus. He especially recognizes that all things serve Christ. He understands all things in a new light and sees all things from the vantage point of eternity and the purpose of God for his own glory in Christ and the salvation of his church. Because Christ is wisdom from God to that man, he stops being offended by Christ or vainly seeking wisdom—salvation—outside of Christ.

Christ becomes wisdom from God to a man in Christ because Christ becomes "righteousness" and "sanctification" to him (v. 31). Paul mentions righteousness and sanctification as the two grand benefits of salvation and as a two-word summary of every benefit of salvation. If Christ is righteousness and sanctification to a man, there is nothing needful for his life and salvation that is not found in Christ.

Righteous is God's judgment that a man is perfect in comparison to the exacting standard of God's law. The one whom God declares righteous he has justified. It is a legal act that changes a man's state from condemned to justified. By "righteousness" here the apostle has in view the work of justification. Sanctification is the other grand benefit of salvation. It consists of the consecration of the sinner to God in love. It is a distinct act from justification. It changes a man's condition and frees him from sin's bondage and pollution. In union with Christ, Christ himself becomes a man's righteousness and his sanctification, so that he is that man's whole salvation.

That Christ is righteousness to the sinner means that the righteousness of Christ is imputed to him freely by faith without works. Since Christ becomes the righteousness of the one who is in him, and being in Christ is faith, Christ becomes the sinner's righteousness by faith only. This is so because God forgives the believer's sins, imputes to the believer Christ's righteousness, and on the basis of Christ's righteousness declares him perfect and worthy of eternal life.

That Christ is the believer's righteousness contrasts with any idea that the believer's works are his righteousness, even and especially the works that he does in love for God and according to the law. He does such works because Christ is a believer's sanctification too. This means that Christ by his Spirit makes the believer a new creature and causes him to walk in all the works that God foreordained for him (Eph. 4:10). But those works are never his righteousness.

These two benefits of salvation are grounded on Christ's work on the cross. This is the reason the apostle adds "redemption." It is as though the apostle said about Christ, "Who is made unto us wisdom from God, that is, salvation, both righteousness and sanctification, because he is our redemption." Redemption is the perfect accomplishment of salvation by Christ at the cross. Redemption is the salvation of the sinner from his guilt and misery and from the dominion of sin. Redemption is what Christ accomplished at the cross by satisfying the justice of God in the place of the guilty sinner and delivering that sinner from his guilt and the dominion of sin by fully paying the debt of his sins and meriting with God perfect righteousness and every benefit of salvation for him. In union with Christ, Christ becomes a man's redemption, which is to say his perfect salvation, by becoming that man's righteousness and sanctification.

Union with Christ is saving. This is the whole burden of the apostle's argument. As union with Adam is condemnation and a man need not do anything more to enter into that condemnation, so union with Christ is saving and a man need not do anything more to achieve that salvation. The point of the text is not so much to define this union precisely, but to emphasize that this union with Christ is salvation.

Union with Christ is not a position into which God brings men, women, and children in order for them to be saved, with the dreadful implication that in that union they must do something to be saved, must fulfill some condition to appropriate salvation or to keep the salvation applied. The text teaches that in union with Christ they *are* saved. That union *is* salvation, and in that union they enjoy Christ and all his saving gifts.

Union and Covenant

To be "in Christ Jesus" also means to be incorporated into the covenant. God personally establishes the covenant with a believer when God unites the believer to Christ. That Paul has the covenant in view when he speaks of the believer's union with Christ is clear from his reference to Jeremiah 9:23–24:

> 23. Thus saith the LORD, Let not the wise man glory in his wisdom, nether let the mighty man glory in his might, let not the rich man glory in his riches;

24. But let him that glorieth glory in this, that he understandeth and knoweth me, that I am the LORD which exercise lovingkindness, judgment, and righteousness, in the earth: for in these things I delight, saith the LORD.

Jeremiah makes a distinction among Israelites who were merely "of Israel" by circumcision and those who really and truly knew Jehovah. There were Israelites who were circumcised, but who did not understand and know Jehovah. By this Jeremiah and the Holy Ghost deny that to be in the covenant simply means that one is circumcised or baptized, or merely a member of the nation of Israel or the church of God in the world. To be in the covenant is to know God, to love him, to be in fellowship with him, to be of his people, and to have Jehovah as one's God. To be in the covenant is to have spiritual fellowship and friendship with Jehovah. "In Christ" then is shorthand for in the covenant of grace. Only those who are in Christ, savingly united with him, and partakers of his salvation are in the covenant.

When the Holy Spirit teaches that union with Christ is the covenant and is salvation, he teaches that membership in the covenant *is* salvation. If union with Christ is the covenant, the covenant is not a way to salvation or a position in which a man is enabled to do something to be saved, but the covenant *is* salvation. If the covenant is union with Christ, it is obvious that the covenant is not an agreement for the purpose of salvation, but in that union believers enjoy salvation. When God joins the elect to Christ, in that union with Christ they enjoy knowing God as their God, love God, and have fellowship with God.

The teaching of a conditional covenant denies this and makes the covenant merely a way or a means to be saved. The basic form of the conditional covenant teaches that God joins an individual to the covenant and in that covenant God gives him a promise, which is conditioned on his doing something, whether his believing the promise, his working some good works, or his covenantal faithfulness. His continuation in the covenant and eternal salvation depend on this condition. It is true that the defenders of the conditional covenant say that these conditions are fulfilled by grace, but the fact remains that in such a covenant salvation depends on what the child does, so that what he does is not the enjoyment of the gift of salvation in the covenant, but the way to salvation and that upon which his salvation depends.

The error is made worse by the teaching that God makes his covenant with every baptized child of believers, elect and reprobate. In the covenant all the baptized children receive a gracious promise from God conditioned on their faith and faithfulness. Such a covenant must necessarily fail in the case of every reprobate with whom it is made.

In the early 1950s the Protestant Reformed Churches fought against such an understanding of the conditional covenant formulated by the liberated Reformed theologian Klaas Schilder. This understanding did not differ in any meaningful way from the conditional covenant theology of Christian Reformed theologian William Heyns and can trace its origin to the conditional covenant of James Arminius. After a massive and tumultuous struggle, the Protestant Reformed Churches excluded that view as a Reformed explanation of the covenant. They made that declaration official by the adoption of an important little document known as the Declaration of Principles.[2] This document demonstrates that the Reformed creeds and the Reformed baptism form exclude as biblical an explanation of the covenant as conditional.

Although condemned by the Protestant Reformed Churches, the conditional covenant view is still alive, well, and flourishing in Reformed and Presbyterian churches. It has also developed and goes by the name of the federal vision. *Federal* in the name

---

2 For the history of the controversy surrounding the adoption of the Declaration of Principles, see David J. Engelsma, *The Battle for Sovereign Grace in the Covenant: The Declaration of Principles* (Jenison, MI: Reformed Free Publishing, 2013), 13–195. For the Declaration of Principles and a brief commentary on it, see ibid., 197–267.

refers to the fact that it is a covenantal doctrine. It is developing the conditional covenant doctrine.

It is developing this doctrine because theologians are beginning to recognize that the covenant is not an agreement or a contract between God and the sinner. They are beginning to recognize that the Bible teaches, in a passage such as 1 Corinthians 1:30–31, that the covenant is union with Christ. So these theologians become loud in their proclamation that the covenant is union with Christ, but they do so in the service of conditional covenant theology that gives the covenant to all the baptized children of believers. When that false doctrine is combined with the idea that the covenant is union with Christ, the result is that Christ is given to all the baptized children of believers, elect and reprobate. All the children of believers on whom the minister sprinkles water are by God incorporated into Christ and are made partakers of his riches and gifts and receive righteousness and sanctification. Their salvation in that union, however, is dependent on their faith and the obedience of faith. The union with Christ—covenant—is a conditional union. That union necessarily fails in the case of every reprobate to whom it is given.

Though they loudly insist that all the baptized children are incorporated into Christ, the teachers of the federal vision in fact deny the apostle's teaching that Christ is righteousness and sanctification to the sinner incorporated into him. Especially they deny that Christ is righteousness to the sinner in the sense that for Christ's sake God forgives the believing sinner all his sins and imputes to him Christ's perfect righteousness for his salvation. Rather, these heretical teachers declare that by union with Christ the sinner is able to do good works, so that by means of this covenantal faithfulness through grace the sinner contributes to his righteousness. The one engrafted into Christ must believe and be faithful—in their mantra, trust and obey—as the condition for his salvation. The sinner by his efforts through grace is his own righteousness.

Although they greatly emphasize the good works of the sinner; yet by their teaching that the good works of the sinner are performed as part of his righteousness before God, they deny that Christ is the sanctification of the sinner. By this teaching they pollute and corrupt those works and destroy the real object of good works, which is thankfulness to the glory of God. For the federal vision, the believer in Christ is not a thankful partaker but a paid mercenary.

For the federal vision, Christ is not redemption to the sinner either. The teachers of the federal vision deny that Christ's cross is the full and complete righteousness of the sinner and that by the cross of Christ the believer is made perfect forever.

Thus they also deny that the covenant—union with Christ—is salvation to those incorporated into Christ. According to these false teachers, there are those who are really and truly joined to Christ who do not avail themselves of the grace of Christ and apostatize out of Christ and perish eternally. The Christ to whom they are joined and the cross—the redemption of that Christ—fails to save them. That Christ and his cross are a failure. These false teachers make void the cross of Christ by their wicked theology. They also have a foolish Christ and God, who went through all the trouble of the incarnation and cross and accomplished nothing for many, and who after engrafting a sinner into Christ does not even know how to save him but lets him perish.

The union with Christ that the federal vision speaks about is a conditional union that ultimately depends on what the sinner does in that union. To assert that in union with Christ the sinner must perform some work that will also be accounted necessary for his salvation is a gross blasphemy and a denial of everything the apostle teaches here about union with Christ. The purpose of the believer's union with Christ is not to bring him to a spiritual point where he can begin to work, however so little, for his salvation. The purpose of union with Christ is to provide the believer with everything necessary for salvation so that he lacks nothing in Christ.

The scriptures teach this when they say, "Ye *are* in Christ." *Are* contrasts with *are not*. Just as the *are not* of the sinner in Adam is condemnation, so also the *are* of the sinner in Christ is his salvation. The union with Christ is salvation. Those so joined with Christ are saved, not because they do something, but because Christ brings with him everything necessary for salvation and applies that unto them. The sinner is not joined to Christ in order to receive grace to enable him to fulfill conditions, but he is joined to Christ to enjoy Christ and the salvation that is in Christ as God's gift to him. If Christ is wisdom from God, both righteousness and sanctification, and redemption, what more does a man need? Indeed, if a man says about his union with Christ that he must do something for his salvation in that union, he denies what Paul says about that union. He also casts aspersions upon God's wisdom in Christ. How wise is a Christ who suffered and died and left something for the sinner to do? That is not a wise Christ, especially in view of the utter inability of man to save himself.

If Christ becomes to believers wisdom from God, God is able to work out in the heart and life of the believer all the benefits of Christ for his salvation. In union with Christ he is saved, without his works, just as in Adam he perished without his works. To teach this is nothing else than the teaching of an unconditional covenant of grace.

Baptism seals the truth of an unconditional covenant. This is the doctrine that must be proclaimed at baptism. Any church can sprinkle water on a baby, but if along with the sprinkling of the water there is not the preaching of the unconditional covenant of God, then the preaching not only is corrupt, but also that preaching corrupts the administration of the sacrament. The sacrament of baptism seals the truth that in Christ and in union with him God makes Christ all things necessary for salvation unto believers and their seed. There is nothing that they or their elect children lack for salvation in Christ. There is nothing they must do for their salvation. Upon nothing that they do is their salvation dependent in any sense. All things are a gracious gift in Christ to them.

The Source of This Union

This saving union—covenant—with Christ has its source in God's eternal decree of predestination. Concerning the source of this saving union, the apostle says that it is "of him [God]" (v. 30). By this the apostle denies that the source of the union is in man or that any benefit of salvation in that union has its cause or explanation in man. When Paul applies this phrase especially to the fact that Christ is become wisdom from God to us, he also implies that all the other benefits of the union and the union itself are of God. That the union and all the benefits of the union are of God is also made plain by the spiritual condition of those whom God joins to Christ. They are the foolish, the weak, the despised, and things that are not (vv. 27–28). Because they are not, they have nothing in themselves. Everything they receive and are, they receive and become in union with Christ.

When the apostle says "of him [God]," he still refers to the contrast between what man became in Adam and what he becomes in Christ. When Paul says that "of him we are in Christ Jesus," he means by contrast that of God in Adam we became *nothing*. That we became nothing in Adam was Adam's fault, but it was "of God." This is the point of verse 21: "In the wisdom of God the world by wisdom knew not God." It was part of God's eternal plan of salvation that the world did not know him.

God did not desire every man to know him. He did not desire that man come to know him in Adam or that man be received into his fellowship and friendship in Adam. It was not God's plan that Adam would obey God and take himself and the entire human race into eternal glory. This is the view of the covenant of works, which explains God's covenant with Adam as a contract between God and Adam in which God promised Adam eternal life on condition that he obeyed. By his obedience Adam could have taken himself and the whole human race—those in him—to heavenly glory. There are many problems with this conception, but one of the most severe criticisms against it is that it makes foolish God's wisdom in Christ and makes Christ nothing more than plan B, and a less inclusive one at that, because what Adam could have done for the whole human race, Christ does for the elect alone.

The apostle reasons very differently. Adam was created to fall. It was of God that Adam fell in order that man would become nothing in Adam. It was of God that man by himself, by his wisdom, and by his works cannot attain unto the knowledge of God, the covenant, and salvation! God made sure of that in Adam for the whole human race.

"But of him [God] are ye in Christ" is the contrast. God brought man to nothing in order that God might save man from nothing. He did that for the sake of the revelation of his marvelous wisdom in Christ. That our union with Christ is "of God" means at the very least that it is accomplished by God, which means that all of our salvation in every single respect is of God.

However, by "of God" the apostle refers not only to God's creating the union, but also to the source of the union. God chooses and determines those whom he joins to Christ Jesus. This refers back to God's choice to call the weak, the despised, and the things that are not. Since the saving call has its source in election, so does the union with Christ that is the fruit of that call. Saving union with Christ has its source in God's will. Those who are joined in saving union with Christ—incorporated into the covenant—are determined by God's will. It is the elect and they only who are joined to Christ. Because union with Christ is the covenant, it is the elect and they only who are members of the covenant.

The Holy Spirit's words "of God" are the pointed denial that all the baptized children of believers are united to Christ and are members of the covenant of grace and that all of them receive grace in Christ and a promise from God. God chooses. The proponent of the conditional covenant says that God incorporated Judas Iscariot and Esau and the other reprobates. The apostle says that God incorporates into Christ and makes members of his covenant only those whom he chooses.

Union unto Eternal Salvation

It should go without saying that when scripture and the Reformed creeds speak about salvation, they mean salvation in heaven. So when the text teaches that the union of the believer with Christ is salvation, it should mean that the union is eternal salvation. But such is the corruption of the truth by the men of the federal vision that salvation does not mean eternal salvation. For them salvation means only that at present the believer is in Christ and enjoys Christ and his benefits, but it is entirely possible that such a one could fall out of Christ and perish. By means of the doctrine of a conditional covenant that consists of a conditional union with Christ, the federal vision denies the preservation of the saints. It denies what the Holy Spirit teaches: that the believer is saved by his union with Christ and that his salvation consists of enjoying Christ now and in eternity.

The apostle teaches the truth that this union is irrevocable and certainly issues in the eternal salvation of the one joined to Christ when he speaks in verse 31 of glorying. Glorying is the activity of the saved sinner in heaven and eternity by which he gives glory to and boasts in God as the God of his salvation. The apostle speaks of glorying now. The believer glories now because he enjoys the beginning of eternal life now, to which Christ's righteousness gives him the right, and which he certainly will enjoy at the end of his life. By speaking of the child of God glorying now, Paul denies the federal vision's insistence that the covenant and Christ can be lost.

One of the main features of the federal vision is that its theologians make a major point out of the apostasy of covenantal members. They take a seeming delight in teaching that apostasy from the covenant means that one who was truly united to Christ falls out of Christ and perishes eternally in hell. The eternal salvation of covenantal members depends on their faithfulness to God, especially by works of obedience, on the basis of which they will be judged in the final judgment. If they do not have these works of obedience, they perish. This is a necessary implication of the teaching that all of the baptized children are incorporated into Christ. The issue of the possibility of a member of Christ falling out of Christ is really settled with the teaching that only the elect are incorporated into Christ, and no one is able to pluck them out of his hand (John 10:28–29).

The apostle speaks of the impossibility of one falling out of Christ when he says that those who are in Christ "glory" now already. This is entirely inappropriate if the issue of their salvation is in fact in doubt and will not be certainly known until the final judgment, when they can be judged on their works—their covenantal faithfulness—as is the teaching of the federal vision. No one tells the runner at the beginning of the race to boast, because the issue of his winning is still in doubt and depends on his running. So the Christian cannot be told to boast now if the issue of his salvation is still in doubt, precisely because it depends yet on his running—covenantal faithfulness. Yet the apostle speaks here of boasting. He speaks of boasting in the Lord now already for those who are in Christ because their salvation, their eternal salvation, is not in doubt but is finished in Christ and depends on Christ alone. Thus it is impossible for that union to fail or to fail to issue in the salvation of those joined to Christ.

The Holy Spirit emphasizes this same point when Paul says that the believers' union with Christ is "of God." Because it is of God, that union with Christ and salvation in that union are perfectly secure unto eternity. What kind of God is it that saves only temporally but does not save eternally? Either union with Christ issues now in our certain eternal salvation, or God is a failure. This is the scriptures' criticism of the conditional covenant. This is the seriousness of the false doctrine of the conditional covenant. If God joins all baptized children to Christ and gives to all of them a promise in Christ; if God gives all of them some grace in Christ, but not all of them are saved; then God, his grace, his promise, his covenant, and his Christ are massive failures in the case of those who are not saved, necessarily so in the case of the reprobate whom he appointed to damnation. In the case of the reprobate, such a God is also foolish, because he promises salvation to those whom he eternally appointed to damnation.

That union with Christ is "of God," and that because it is of God the believer boasts now in God because he will never lose his salvation, also means that the union is absolutely unbreakable by man. This is the promise of baptism to believers and their seed. Baptism is this seal: when God incorporates believers and their elect seed into Christ, he makes an eternal, or unbreakable, covenant of grace, in which he saves them to the uttermost and presents them among the assembly of the elect in life eternal. Either that or he is not God.

If salvation were of man, it is not only possible for the union to fail, but it is also certain to fail. But if salvation is of God, that union cannot fail. Not only is the entirety of the believer's salvation included in his union with Christ, but also that salvation is perfectly secure for him and for his elect children in Christ.

This makes clear the other charge against the heresy of the conditional covenant: it makes God impotent and man strong. A man to whom God gives the promise, "I will be your God," is able to resist God, overcome God, and remove himself from the covenant and salvation. A man to whom God gives Christ is able to do by the grace of God what God was unable to do by his grace, namely, that man is able to become his own righteousness, sanctification, and redemption. In both cases man is made strong and God is made weak.

Because this heresy makes man strong—the decisive factor in his salvation—it allows man to boast in the presence of God. When the federal vision in its development of conditional covenant theology makes the final salvation of the covenantal member contingent on his works—specifically his acts of covenantal faithfulness—and places that decisive verdict in the final judgment, it is carrying the logic of the conditional covenant to its proper conclusion: man may boast in the presence of God. But since God will have no one glory in his presence, that theology also brings all who believe it far from God into hell.

The Purpose of Union with Christ

The purpose of all God's grand, glorious, and gracious work in the sinner in union with Christ is that man glories in the Lord alone.

To glory is to boast. A man boasts in that in which he trusts and in which he rests for life and salvation, for time and eternity. If a man's boast is only in this life, it is a foolish boast, and that man is shallow and wretched. Man must have something beyond this life.

Man must also boast. The apostle does not give man an option not to boast. Man must boast either in himself or in God. Man must boast in the matter of salvation. This is why the haters of the truth often accuse the believer of being proud. He does boast. He must boast. The accuser of him boasts too. The difference is that wherein they boast. The accuser hates the boast of the believer because the believer will only boast in God, which makes man and those who trust in men nothing except robbers of the glory of God and boasters in men. "You are proud," the accuser says, because the believer does not speak of the truth of his salvation as a matter of opinion or something that can be taken or left, but as the absolute truth, which a man must believe if he will be saved. He must have Christ as wisdom from God, righteousness imputed by God to him by faith alone, and sanctification worked in him by the power of the Spirit, and all on the basis of Christ's perfect atoning death in his place, or he has nothing, remains nothing before God, and will thus also be condemned by God. If a man claims to confess the doctrines of salvation by grace without boasting, by that fact he denies the doctrine of salvation, because God saves men in union with Christ in order for them to boast. Those two things—salvation and not boasting—are utterly incongruous.

Besides, it belongs to a man's gracious salvation that he actually does boast. He cannot help himself. So too, if a man professes to teach the doctrine of salvation and then he must warn his pupils not to boast—a kind of feigned humility—on that ground that doctrine of salvation could be condemned as a cleverly disguised self-righteousness. If a man teaches the doctrines of grace and then commands his audience not to boast, he contradicts the apostle and the Spirit, who *command* men to boast. The true doctrine of salvation will both have man boast and have that boasting be in God. The fact that God makes Christ wisdom, righteousness, sanctification, and redemption to a man issues in his boasting in God.

The issue then between truth and lie is not whether man will boast, but what *kind* of boasting man will be doing. He will boast in God, or he will boast in man.

If a man says he will be saved because he has accepted Christ, has done some saving works, has trusted and obeyed, was faithful in the covenant, or has done anything for his salvation however so little, he will be damned. This is man's refusing to become nothing before God. This is man's thinking that he is something apart from Christ. In that pride, which is nothing more than the continuation and development of Adam's original sin in the garden, man will perish. Man must be nothing. God calls the things that are not and raises the dead. Man must be nothing in order

117

that God be everything in making Christ his Son wisdom from God, righteousness, sanctification, and redemption to that man.

He who boasts, and boast he must, let him boast in God. Let his boast first be the confession of the true doctrine of salvation, because any other boast will lead to those warnings about not boasting and will in fact be man's boasting in himself. Second, let his boast in God be, "I and my children were nothing and we are in ourselves nothing, and God saved us graciously, completely, and to the uttermost by union with Christ, who is to us wisdom, righteousness, sanctification, and redemption." Third, let his boast be the joyful reception of salvation as a free gift.

Let that boast in God lead to his complete humility with his brother so that he does not vaunt himself, is not puffed up, and does not behave himself unseemly, but walks in the way of love. That man boasts in God. If a man will not walk in the way of love, he boasts in himself, and God will have no one who boasts in himself in God's presence.

CHAPTER 8

THE MYSTERIOUS WISDOM OF GOD

1 Corinthians 2:6–8

6. *Howbeit we speak wisdom among them that are perfect: yet not the wisdom of this world, nor of the princes of this world, that come to nought:*

7. *But we speak the wisdom of God in a mystery, even the hidden wisdom, which God ordained before the world unto our glory:*

8. *Which none of the princes of this world knew: for had they known it, they would not have crucified the Lord of glory.*

In the preceding context in 1 Corinthians 1, the apostle Paul instructed the Corinthian congregation about the preaching of the gospel. The gospel is the means of grace to bring to the church the powerful Word of the cross (v. 17), so that God's people are saved by the cross. Because God saves his people by that means, and no other, he brings to naught the wisdom of the world by the foolishness of preaching. In that preaching, man and his wisdom are made nothing and God and his wisdom are made everything, so that salvation is nothing of man and all of God (vv. 18–31).

If a minister would teach that about the preaching of the

gospel but not conform his own ministry to that reality, he would be a hypocrite. If he would teach that the preaching is the power of God unto salvation but would attempt to adorn the preaching with the wisdom of man, he would show that he does not believe what he teaches. If he would say that preaching is the power of God but his own ministry consists of virtually everything else except preaching, his confession is only words.

In light of what Paul taught about preaching, he confesses to the Corinthians that he conformed his own ministry to that reality:

1. And I, brethren, when I came to you, came not with excellency of speech or of wisdom, declaring unto you the testimony of God.
2. For I determined not to know any thing among you, save Jesus Christ, and him crucified.
3. And I was with you in weakness, and in fear, and in much trembling.
4. And my speech and my preaching was not with enticing words of man's wisdom, but in demonstration of the Spirit and of power. (2:1–4)

Because Paul did not come with excellency of speech or enticing words of man's wisdom and was with them in weakness, fear, and trembling, the effect of his preaching was demonstrably the work of the Spirit. Because Paul was so demonstrably weak, the effect of his preaching in the formation and development of the Corinthian congregation could only be explained as the work of the Spirit, applying the Word of the cross to God's elect people.

What Paul says about his ministry every faithful minister of the gospel can and must say about his, and every true church of Christ must say about its ordained ministry. By refusing to use man's wisdom in his preaching and to conform his message to the delicate tastes of the audience, the minister of the gospel demonstrates his reliance on and the subjection of himself and his whole ministry to the reality that God is pleased to save his people by the foolishness of preaching.

When the apostle did that and ministers of the word do that, congregations benefit. Certain members of the Corinthian congregation found fault with the apostle's preaching and did not think much of it because he did not preach man's wisdom. The apostle points out that, although he did not preach with excellency of speech, he preached the truth and they were the beneficiaries. A congregation profits when its minister preaches this way and brings this message, because by means of the plain Word of the cross the Holy Ghost causes the faith of the members to stand "in the power of God" (v. 5). The Corinthians wanted something different. If the apostle were to give them something different, that would be harmful because their faith would stand in the wisdom of man, which is useless for salvation. He gave them the pure preaching of the gospel for their benefit.

In verses 6–8 the apostle continues this thought. He says as it were, "When I did so preach, I did speak wisdom." This is the connection between verses 6–8 and the context. In 1:21–24 the apostle granted for the sake of argument that the preaching is foolish, in order to show that even if it were foolish, the foolishness of God is wiser than men, and the weakness of God is stronger than men (v. 25). "Howbeit [but]," when Paul spoke, he did speak wisdom. It was not "the wisdom of this world" but "the wisdom of God in a mystery" (2:6–7). By refusing to speak man's wisdom he was able to speak God's wisdom, just as when a man refuses to speak God's wisdom, all he is left with is man's wisdom, and that is bad for the church.

In verses 6–8, then, the apostle explains the mysterious wisdom of God that he spoke because he refused to speak man's wisdom. This mysterious wisdom of God sounds from the pulpit whenever the gospel is preached. This mysterious wisdom excludes man's wisdom from the preaching. Only this wisdom may sound from the pulpit in the church of Jesus Christ. When and where it is declared, faith stands in the power of God. The faith that stands in the power of God is necessary, because only that faith walks in the way of love. The more faith stands in the power of God, the more faith also seeks and walks in the way of love.

Divine Wisdom in a Mystery

When the apostle says, "We speak the wisdom of God," and "We speak wisdom," he still refers to the preaching of the gospel. This is the declaration by an ordained minister of the truths of God contained in the sacred scriptures, at the heart of which is the truth of God's gracious salvation of his people by the cross of Jesus Christ. The apostle speaks of this as the content of his preaching when he says, "I determined not to know any thing among you, save Jesus Christ, and him crucified" (v. 2). When a minister preaches this he preaches the gospel. When he preaches the gospel he speaks wisdom.

The apostle changes between "I" and "we" because he speaks of his own ministry first. Then he speaks of other faithful ministers of his day in distinction from the false apostles who festooned their preaching with man's wisdom as one adorns a gaudy parade float. Then he joins with himself every true church of Christ with their faithful ministries and ministers of the gospel.

"Wisdom" in verses 6–7 is the wisdom of God, a divine wisdom, which originates in God and is the wisdom according to which God works. The apostle brought up the subject of the wisdom of God in chapter 1:21: "In the wisdom of God the world by wisdom knew not God." The point there was that in God's infinite wisdom, the world by its wisdom could not know God. God made it impossible that the world by its investigation, science, philosophy, and education could know God. God did that to save those who believe by the foolishness of preaching. Here Paul speaks of that same wisdom of God.

Wisdom is the ability to choose the best means to the highest end, and thus wisdom is the best use of knowledge. A fool is one who knows but does not use his knowledge. It is always a terrible thing in the church when the elders come back from a visit and report that some man knows that what he is doing is wrong, but he will not change. That man reveals his folly, his unbelief, and his impenitence. So also in the physical world the farmer who knows that winter is coming but does not lay up in store is a fool. The man who knowingly walks toward the cliff where he will fall off is a fool. A fool sins against knowledge. A wise man uses knowledge. He knows and he applies knowledge to the highest end.

Spiritually, there is no greater goal or higher end than the glory of God. Where God is known and glorified, where God is acknowledged as the only God, where God's name is praised, and where God's word is obeyed, there is wisdom. The natural man shows the terrible corruption of his original wisdom when he shows himself adept at succeeding in earthly life. He makes laws and invents many things, but he turns all that for his pleasure and glory and does nothing for the glory of God. That is a very wicked wisdom that is ultimately no wisdom at all, but damning folly.

God himself is a God of wisdom. He is not only the God who knows with perfect knowledge both himself and all things, but he is also the only wise God. The wisdom of God is his perfection whereby he eternally is able to order his own life and all things in heaven and on earth and in all of history for the purpose of his glory. But the apostle is not speaking of the perfection of God as such, but of the revelation of that perfection of God "in a mystery." About God's wisdom the apostle says, "We speak the wisdom of God in a mystery" (2:7).

"Mystery" does not refer to something difficult to understand. "Mystery" does not refer to the refuge of foolish theology in mystery and paradox. That is, a preacher says both that God offers salvation to all men and that God chooses some men to salvation, and then he defends that nonsense with an appeal to mystery.

"Mystery" is the revelation of the wisdom of God. When Paul says "in a mystery," emphasizing the word "in," he teaches that this mystery is the embodiment of the wisdom of God, so that by means of it God is revealed as the only wise God and he is thus glorified.

The apostle describes the content of the mystery when he says, "which God ordained before the world unto our glory" (v. 7). Paul makes the mystery basically synonymous with God's eternal counsel with the words "ordained before the world." When he calls the counsel "wisdom," he denies that the counsel was arbitrarily decided and teaches that it was ordered by God in wisdom and everything in it was designed to reveal his wisdom. That the counsel was the eternal ordination of God is made clear by the words "before the world." This is scripture's usual way to describe what was done in eternity before the world began and thus also before time began. The apostle has in view not only what God does in time, but also what he does in time *as he planned it from before the foundation of the world.*

By "unto our glory" (v. 7) the apostle teaches that this wisdom of God embodied in a mystery is basically synonymous with the salvation of the church through the cross of Christ. Thus all things that God does in time are carried out according to his eternal decree for those things in order to serve the glory of his church. For instance, creation, Adam, and the fall all serve the glory of the church.

The glory of the church is the salvation of the church from sin and the bringing of the church to heavenly glory. The glory of the church is that she is brought nigh unto God through her union with Christ her Lord, and that she enjoys eternal covenantal fellowship and friendship with God in Christ.

At the heart of the mystery stands the cross of Christ as the eternal will of God and as the means to glorify his church and thus to glorify himself in the salvation of the church. The apostle brings up the centrality of the cross to this mystery when he says that if any of the "princes of this world" had known, "they would not have crucified the Lord of glory" (v. 8). Princes of the world refer to man at his best and to the prince of the world, Satan. Paul does not mean that man merely did not understand that Christ was the wisdom of God, and not understanding, they crucified him. He does not mean that if man as man could have known that Christ was the wisdom of God, he would have embraced him. Man hates God, and behind his hatred stands Christ's inveterate enemy, Satan. Rather, the apostle means that if man and his demonic prince had known that God in his exquisite wisdom would lay the cross of Christ as the means to accomplish his will, merit salvation for his people, and destroy all the works of the devil, then in their hatred of God and Christ they would not have crucified him.

So central is the cross of Christ to this mystery that it is the supreme instance of the wisdom of God that is embodied in all of this mystery, and at the cross the mystery of God and all that was necessary for the realization of it was accomplished.

At the heart of the cross stands the Christ of the cross, "the Lord of glory" (v. 8). He is the very heart of that supreme instance of the wisdom of God. God accomplished his mystery in Christ. God became man in Christ, and God and man were perfectly united in covenant in him. God became man in Christ in order that God in Christ might accomplish the full salvation of his people, so that God in Christ would suffer as a man, and by his suffering God would pay God what God was owed for their sins and reconcile in Christ his elect people to himself. Christ and "the wisdom of God in a mystery" are synonyms (v. 7). Christ is the one in whom the wisdom of God is embodied, and Christ is the one in whom the wisdom of God is fully revealed, so that Christ in his person, natures, and all his work reveals God as the only wise God.

In a few words, the mystery of God is the perfection of God's covenant in Christ.

Mystery Not Hidden but Revealed

"Mystery" also emphasizes not what is hidden, but what God reveals concerning his whole counsel for the salvation of his elect church and the glory of Christ and of all things in the perfection of the covenant. When Adam and Eve fell and were trembling in the garden, God spoke the sweet word that revealed what he had decreed in Christ for his people: the seed of the woman who would crush the head of the serpent. That was the revelation of the mystery of God, the revelation of Christ and his salvation and covenant for the salvation of God's elect church.

That same mystery God declared to his people by the patriarchs and prophets and represented in all of the sacrifices and ceremonies of the Old Testament. Thereby God was revealing Christ and his covenant and salvation.

That mystery revealed, declared, and signified God fulfilled with the coming of Jesus Christ. Christ himself is the mystery: "Great is the mystery of godliness: God was manifest in the flesh, justified in the Spirit, seen of angels, preached unto the Gentiles, believed on in the world, received up into glory" (1 Tim. 3:16). The mystery of God is the whole truth of Jesus Christ, his salvation, his person, his natures, and his works; the whole will of God as it was ordained by God and revealed in the scriptures. When that is spoken the wisdom of God in a mystery comes. That is what the apostle says about his preaching: "We speak the wisdom of God in a mystery" (1 Cor. 2:7). By that phrase he also teaches the main way the mystery of God is revealed: it is through the preaching of that mystery in the preaching of Christ crucified.

What Paul intends to emphasize is that when that mystery is preached, the purpose of God in that mystery—"our glory" (v. 7), that is, the church's possession of the salvation appointed to them in that mystery—becomes theirs. That mystery is made a living reality in the hearts and lives of God's people by the power of God's grace and through the Spirit of Christ when he joins them to Christ by faith. By that speaking—preaching—the eternal will of God for "our glory" when he ordained this mystery is realized. By faith God's people are made one with Christ and indwelt by his Spirit, so that their whole lives are brought under the power of his word and Spirit. Being made one with Christ, they also understand the will of God, believe the word of God, and order their lives according to it for the glory of God, so that the fear of God is the beginning of wisdom in them (Ps. 111:10; Prov. 9:10).

It is a powerful wisdom because it is a divine wisdom, and being such it is also a wisdom that saves. The apostle indicates that when he says, "God ordained [it]…unto our glory." The purpose is the glory of the church. When the gospel comes God carries out that purpose unto the salvation of the church.

The World's Wisdom

Paul contrasts this divine wisdom with the wisdom of the world and of the princes of the world. The wisdom of the world is man's solution to his problems. That man needs salvation and that there is something terribly wrong with the world are obvious even to the natural man. Man addresses those needs with a certain kind of wisdom.

Belonging to man's wisdom is his diagnosis of the problems. Ask a man, what is wrong with the world? He will say that the problem is disease, the breakdown of the family, poverty, wastefulness, no social order, an abuse of resources, or a lack of social justice, education, resources, or good laws.

Belonging to man's wisdom is also his solution to the problems as he has diagnosed them. He applies his knowledge to solve whatever he sees as the issue. He advocates for a better use of the resources, he expends himself to develop medicines or to eradicate diseases, he traverses the globe and space to discover more resources, he proposes more and more laws, and he devotes huge amounts of money to better educate the people.

There is that kind of human wisdom at every level. It appears in politics with every candidate vying to have his or her wisdom and vision for the country adopted. When there is a problem in the church, in the family, or in the life of an individual, man has both a diagnosis and a solution. For example, when some member or former member of the church walks in sin, how many different suggestions are promoted regarding how to deal with that sin? Men stumble over themselves to have their wisdom heard and to suggest what the cause may be, what the solution should be, and what the relationship to that sinner should be to achieve this. But no one asks the question, what is God's wisdom?

As happened in Corinth, frequently God's wisdom is pushed aside in favor of the wisdom of princes. Men say, "He is a leader, a long-established minister, a professor, or well-studied in scripture. He must know what he is talking about," even though he brings not a word of scripture. That wisdom comes to "nought" (1 Cor. 2:6); it accomplishes nothing and is useless for the salvation of men or of the church. Man's wisdom, philosophy, and ideas do nothing and ultimately come to naught in hell.

Hidden Wisdom

Paul says, "But we speak the wisdom of God...even the hidden wisdom" (v. 7). The wisdom spoken and heard in the preaching of the gospel is hidden wisdom, which means that the world and man by nature does not know that wisdom because God hides it.

First, it is hidden in God's decree. It is hidden in the unapproachable and incomprehensible depths of the being of God and in the inaccessible thoughts of God. No man can ascend to heaven and know the will of God or rise up and look into the books of God.

Second, even though the mystery was revealed in the garden of Eden, through the prophets, and in Christ himself, that revealed wisdom was hidden from men, even the very best men. Paul says, "None of the princes of this world knew" (v. 8). When Paul calls some men "princes," he means the best, most distinguished, and most capable of men. None of them knew the will of God or the truth of God by their own wisdom. By their scientific investigations or by their philosophies or their theologies they did not know God's wisdom. This does not mean that they did not understand intellectually, that they could not grasp the basic message of the sermon. Man's not knowing is worse than that. While he understands that the gospel of Christ is the wisdom of God, he will not believe it, embrace it, or love it.

Paul intends to deny that a man can be argued into embracing, knowing, and believing the truth. The truth cannot be so explained and rationalized and its goodness demonstrated that a man by the power of his own intellect will at last see the light and grasp the truth. The princes do not know the truth, and if the princes do not know it, no man knows it.

The proof of that is Christ. If princes could know the wisdom of God by their own intellect and abilities, "they would not have crucified the Lord of glory" (v. 8). The apostle here proves his statement that man of himself cannot know the wisdom of God. When Christ came the wisdom of God came, for Christ is the wisdom of God. Men could touch, handle, and hear the very wisdom of God and could learn by the most exquisite and perfect instruction. They also witnessed regarding Christ's marvelous doctrine and said about him, "No man speaks as this man, who speaks with authority and not as the scribes and Pharisees." They also witnessed the truth of Christ by his many miracles.

What did men do with the wisdom of God? They crucified him!

It was the world's princes who crucified him. Christ did not come to the ignorant but to those who knew the law and the prophets as very few in the history of Israel knew them and as very few in the history of the world would know them. He came to the Jews, those who had the temple, the sacrifices, and the other ceremonies, all of which pointed to Jesus Christ. The Romans were the most educated, sophisticated, and legally competent society in the world—heirs of all the learning of Greece and conquerors of the world. If there was wisdom of princes by which man might know God's wisdom, surely it was found among them.

Yet they crucified the Lord of glory! They did not see under his mean form, his humiliation, and his weakness the Lord of glory. They did not embrace him and kiss the Son because they saw only a man cursed of God. And they did not see because they did not see themselves as those lying in sin and under the curse and whose problem was not earthly and outward but inward and spiritual. They did not see the wisdom of God. They also did not see that God intended to accomplish all his will in the cross of Christ alone. The cross was offensive in the extreme. They all shouted, "If thou be the Christ, save thyself and come down from the cross."

The cross of Christ is the most distinct proof of the utter blindness of man to God's wisdom. If any men could attain unto the wisdom of God in salvation, it would have been the Jews and the Romans. But they crucified Christ.

In that blindness God was operating. God hid his wisdom; he did not reveal it to the wise and the prudent. He hid it in order that Christ would die on the cross to save his people. That is God's wisdom. Hiding it from the wise and prudent and revealing it to his people by the preaching of the gospel, he accomplished their salvation by it. God hid it so that he could shut up the whole world to learning his wisdom through the truth of the gospel.

Spoken Wisdom

That wisdom God speaks to his people in the gospel. The point of the apostle with "we speak wisdom" (v. 6) is that when the gospel comes in its plain and unadorned form, the wisdom of God comes. The preaching of the gospel is not foolishness but the highest wisdom. When we preach Christ crucified, we speak the wisdom of God in a mystery as it was decreed in eternity in Christ and as God made that known in Christ, accomplished that in Christ at the cross, and makes that reality in the hearts and lives of his people. When the minister speaks this wisdom of God, there is a coming of wisdom as concretely as when Christ came in the flesh, and there is the realization of salvation in the hearts and lives of his people that is as real as the cross. It is true; it is not the wisdom of the world or of the princes of the world that comes to naught and accomplishes nothing. This wisdom of God in the preaching accomplishes salvation as it did at the cross.

Now in light of that contrast the question is, from the pulpit in church, what wisdom will be heard? Having ordained it for our glory, God causes it to be spoken for his people's salvation. Having hid it from the princes that they might not attain to it, he gives it to his people by means of the preaching of the gospel.

The apostle meets an objection here. The objection is, "We are being done a disservice when you come to us without excellency of speech and wisdom." Many in Paul's day and many today groan when the gospel is preached, as though it hurts them and they are missing something. The apostle says, as it were, "Are you missing anything when you receive the pure preaching of the gospel? Are you missing anything when the gospel is preached without the impressive learning and wisdom of the world? Are you impoverished thereby? Not at all, for when the gospel is preached, you have the wisdom of God in a mystery. Thus you have everything God ordained that is needful for your faith, life, and salvation."

Explaining this objection, the apostle says, "Howbeit we speak wisdom among them that are perfect" (v. 6). The perfect are God's people to whom he has given faith, on whom the wisdom of God has laid hold, whose minds have been enlightened so they understand the wisdom of God in a mystery, who are justified by faith only and have in them the new life of Christ. When that wisdom comes they say, "Ah, there is wisdom. Not the wisdom of this world that comes to naught, but the wisdom God has ordained for our glory." They judge that the preaching is wise and able to make them wise unto salvation. Judging it to be wise, they embrace it and conform their lives to it.

So also when a man despises the gospel of Jesus Christ, the

truth as it is preached, he shows an utter lack of wisdom and that he is devoid of judgment, senseless, and foolish. He does nothing else than what the princes of the world did when the wisdom of God came to them. If that doctrine is distasteful to some, as it was distasteful in Paul's day, it simply proves that they are imperfect, which is to say unbelieving. That too must be traced to God's work of hiding. Is it any wonder that when the gospel does come, many reject it? Just as when Christ came and very few received him, so the gospel is condemned by many today. God has hidden it from them. That too is his wisdom.

Paul means then that when we speak wisdom, it is open for all to judge. God will judge. The perfect will judge it as the wisdom of God and the only wisdom worth knowing. Love "rejoiceth not in iniquity, but rejoiceth in the truth" (13:6). The unbelieving will judge that wisdom of no worth at all, just as they judged Christ when he came as the wisdom of God.

CHAPTER 9

The Natural Man's Spiritual Inability

1 Corinthians 2:14

---

14. But the natural man receiveth not the things of the Spirit of God: for they are foolishness unto him: neither can he know them, because they are spiritually discerned.

Paul and other faithful preachers in Corinth spoke the wisdom of the Spirit, the wisdom of God in a mystery hidden in the counsel of God, fulfilled in Christ, and revealed in the gospel concerning salvation. Paul did not speak the wisdom of this world. He did not use enticing words or locate the power of his preaching in oratory. His message was not tailored to the preferences of those in his audience. He did not pander to their desires and make his message palatable for them. He did not present man's analysis of man's problem or man's solution to his problems. He taught the wisdom that the Holy Spirit teaches; the wisdom that is able to make men, women, and children wise unto salvation; the wisdom that is the answer to man's deepest problem, which is sin. To have that wisdom is to have the greatest good, that is, to know God as the God of one's salvation in Jesus Christ.

But the natural man does not receive the things of the Spirit, so Paul begins verse 14 with "but" to express a contrast between the fact of the glorious saving wisdom of the gospel and the reality that the natural man does not receive it. The natural man does not receive those things because he cannot receive them, and therefore of himself he perishes in his ignorance. Paul speaks of the spiritual inability of the natural man that makes it impossible for him to receive the wisdom of God.

The contrast in verse 14 can be illustrated. Humans have five senses that receive stimulation from the outside. A man might have a physical disability, such as the inability to hear beautiful music, see the most stunning scenery, smell and taste the most exquisite aroma and flavor of delicious food, or feel the softest surface. Why does this man not hear, see, smell, taste, or feel? Because he is deaf, blind, without taste buds, or all his nerves are dead. He does not perceive those things and does not receive that stimulation because he cannot.

As a man is physically unable to receive sensory stimuli, the natural man is spiritually unable to receive the things of the Spirit. There is in the wisdom of the Spirit the most exquisite sounds, the most glorious and beautiful sights, the most flavorful and tasty food, but the natural man cannot receive these eternal, deep, mysterious, and saving things. It is not merely that he will not, but also he cannot.

The Things of the Spirit

The apostle speaks of the natural man's *spiritual* inability when he says that the natural man does not receive and cannot know "the things of the Spirit."

The Spirit in verse 14 is the third person of the Trinity. He is the Spirit because he is the breath of God. *Spirit* means breath. He is called Breath because unlike the Son who is begotten, the Spirit is breathed, or spirated, from the Father to the Son. The Father breathes out the Spirit, and the Son receives the Spirit and breathes the Spirit back to the Father. Therefore, the Spirit is called *Holy* Spirit because his personal property and his work in the Trinity are to be breathed in and out between Father and

Son as their holy, secret, and deeply intimate fellowship and thus to consecrate Father to Son in the fellowship of the covenantal life of the triune God. In that breathing back and forth of the Breath, there is the closest communion and fellowship between the Father and the Son in the Trinity. The Spirit in the Trinity is the togetherness, the in-ness, the communion and fellowship between the Father and the Son.

This mysterious life of communion within the life of God is the main point of the doctrine of the Trinity. John takes the believer into the triune life of God and describes the communion as "the only begotten Son, which is *in* the bosom of the Father" (John 1:18; emphasis added). The Holy Spirit is the "in" of the text, which translates more literally as "into," and by which the Holy Spirit shows us the Father as embracing his Son by the Spirit and the Son as pressing himself closely into the embrace of the Father in the Spirit.

There in the one being of God, the Spirit among the persons of the Trinity is always searching the deep things of God (1 Cor. 2:10). God is as a mighty deep, a great unfathomable depth. His being is infinite, and in the infiniteness of his being there is the infiniteness of all his perfections and of all his thoughts. Each perfection is an infinite glory, and all of them together are a radiance that no man can approach unto. Each of them is infinite. There is in God all of his decreeing and counseling, all his communion and fellowship, and all his perfection and goodness.

No man knows the things of God but the Spirit. As God, God searches out God: the Spirit is busy in all eternity searching out God, not because he does not know but because that is the most glorious thing a person can do. In that too the Spirit fully knows and comprehends God. The Spirit therefore has "things," from his searching of God's deep things. These "things" the Spirit reveals (v. 14).

Because the Spirit does nothing apart from the word, the things of the Spirit are the word of God. At the heart of the things of the Spirit is the revelation of God in Jesus Christ. God's revelation in Jesus Christ is the content of the sacred scriptures. They are "the things of the Spirit." The scriptures are the great work of the Spirit of God to reveal the things of God, his *magnalia Dei*. The scripture is not man's book; it is the Spirit's book. To attribute errors to scripture is serious; it is an assault on the work of the Spirit and on the Spirit himself. If there are mistakes in scripture, the Spirit is not God. If the Spirit is not God, God is not triune. If God is not triune, the Christian faith is a lie.

Since we confess about the Reformed creeds that they fully agree with the word of God, they are also part of the work of the Spirit. Because they agree with the Bible, the creeds also have authority. Because they speak the truth of the Bible, they belong to the "things of the Spirit." The creeds are the product of the Spirit of Jesus Christ in the church, who guides the church into all truth as revealed in scripture. In that sense the creeds as officially adopted statements of faith hold a special place among the writings of men. No one can despise and denigrate the creeds without despising and denigrating the "things of the Spirit." No one can say that the creeds are unimportant without saying that the work of the Spirit is unimportant or impugning his work and calling him a miserable guide of the church into the truth. Those creeds have only one judge, and that is the Spirit himself through scripture. The creeds may only be tested by scripture and judged by scripture.

The "things of the Spirit" in the context of verse 14 are particularly the wisdom and eternal will of God concerning the redemption of his church and the glorification of all things, those things that "eye hath not seen, nor ear heard, neither have entered into the heart of man" (v. 9). Many stop there, but the scriptures go on. Man does not know these things, but the Spirit knows them and reveals them: "God hath revealed them unto us by his Spirit" (v. 10). We read of the cross of Jesus Christ; the word of God in the cross imputing to Christ all our sins and declaring that it was the perfect work for our salvation, the perfect satisfaction for sin, and the fulfillment of all righteousness; and the word of election and reprobation because God is a God who chooses the weak things, things that are despised, and things that are not (1:28). The things of the Spirit are the truth of "Christ Jesus, who of God is made unto [or for] us wisdom, and righteousness, and sanctification, and redemption" (v. 31). The things of the Spirit are everything that God has freely given to us (2:12), the whole glorious truth of our salvation by grace and the perfection of the whole creation in the new heaven and new earth.

The Spirit's revelation of these things does not refer merely to his revelation of them in scripture. But as the Spirit is the Spirit of faith and illumination, he also makes a man spiritual, grants him faith, and with that faith gives understanding of divine, spiritual, and heavenly things. The apostle makes this clear: "We have received...the spirit which is of God; that we might know the things that are freely given to us of God" (v. 12). Knowing is the particular activity of faith, which a man has only by the work of the Spirit.

Further, concerning those things of the Spirit the apostle says for himself and in himself for the church of all ages through her ordained ministry, "Which things also we speak, not in the words which man's wisdom teacheth, but which the Holy Ghost teacheth; comparing spiritual things with spiritual" (v. 13; see also vv. 6–7). The Spirit does not give those things by secret revelations. The will of God is that now the Spirit works by means of the preaching. Preaching of the truth is the teaching of the Holy Ghost. To despise preaching is to despise his teaching. A man who does such a thing wars with the Spirit of God. By the preaching the Spirit is pleased to make one "know the things that are freely given to us of God" (v. 12).

The church is also a thing of the Spirit. She is formed by preaching and alone is capable of preaching. She cannot be despised without despising the things of the Spirit.

Because they are the things of the Spirit of God, they are perfect. In and of themselves they are perfect and glorious. For a man there is nothing better or more worthwhile in the whole world. To receive the things of the Spirit is to receive divine wisdom. To have the things of the Spirit is to have salvation. To know the things of the Spirit is to know God and Christ Jesus, which is eternal life. They are able to make a man wise unto salvation and make his whole life worthwhile and fruitful.

A Sensual Man

But the "natural" man does not receive the things of the Spirit. The word translated as "natural" in verse 14 is translated in other contexts as "soul." Paul refers to a *soulish* man. The word is used in scripture to refer to Adam as he came forth perfect from the hands of God. As Adam was created without any sin and lived perfectly in the garden, he was a *natural* man. He was of the earth earthy. There was nothing wrong with that, but Adam was about as concerned for heaven as a foot is for learning. If an angel had said to Adam, "There are heaven, salvation, regeneration, redemption, justification, sanctification, and eternal life in glory," he would have been confused. He was not interested in that. He was entirely of the earth. He knew God after an earthly fashion. He had fellowship with God in an earthly way. In this sense he was soulish, or natural.

Because of Adam's naturalness, it is foolish to say that Adam in the garden was laboring for heaven. The thought would never have crossed his mind, because he was natural. If God would have said it to him, Adam would not have known what it meant. Even if Adam had remained perfect, he would have stayed on the earth as an earthly man. Only earth was possible for him to have, because flesh and blood cannot enter the kingdom of God.

This teaches us that if a man has the understanding of the Spirit, although he is flesh and blood, he has more than Adam. He can understand heavenly things and the works of God on the earth. Adam had a natural knowledge. The regenerated believer has a spiritual knowledge. Adam knew God by creation. The believer knows God by redemption.

But Adam did not remain perfect. So "natural" is also used in scripture to refer to man as the natural man Adam departed from God and wholly corrupted himself by sin. It is especially in this sense that Paul uses "natural" in verse 14. He refers to the flesh-and-blood man as fallen into sin and as he now exists under the power of sin.

The apostle mentions some of these natural men in verse 8: "None of the princes of this world knew: for had they known it, they would not have crucified the Lord of glory." That is the kind of natural man Paul refers to: the natural man who, when the things of the Spirit come to him in the form of the Lord of glory, crucifies them. The same word is used in James 3:15: "This wisdom...is earthly, sensual [natural], devilish." Jude uses the same word: there are those who walk after their ungodly lusts. "These be they who separate themselves, sensual [natural], having not the Spirit" (v. 19).

Sensual would be a good translation in 1 Corinthians 2:14: "But the sensual man receiveth not the things of the Spirit." That is man as he fell in Adam, is judged guilty of Adam's sin, and is born totally depraved. That man is sensual in his whole life, in all his thoughts, in all his being. He is only able to receive things that he can perceive with his five senses. He is of the earth. In his life on earth he is devilish, ungodly, and lawless. This natural man is every man by his natural birth: he is conceived and born in sin.

A Spiritual Inability

This man "receiveth not the things of the Spirit...neither can he know them." The apostle says two things about the inability of the natural man: he does not receive and does not know. One could say the two words mean virtually the same thing, so that by a parallelism Paul explains what he means by "receiveth" and "know." Better, the apostle explains two problems with the natural man over against the things of the Spirit.

First, the natural man does not receive them. To receive is to embrace. A husband and wife receive the news that the woman is pregnant and they are happy about that and embrace it. When the child comes they receive and embrace the child, and the child is the center of their lives. The natural man does not receive the things of the Spirit. Regarding these things, the natural man is similar to a woman who receives news of pregnancy and aborts her baby. The natural man does not receive the things of Spirit. When they come to him, he does with them what that wicked woman does with her unwanted baby.

The natural man does not know these things either. The mother who embraces her child does so because she knows that child, knows that the child is hers, and loves her child. The woman who murders her unwanted baby does so because she hates the baby. She can do that because she does not know the baby as her baby but calls it merely a mass of tissue. The natural man does not receive the things of Spirit and aborts them as soon as they come to him because he does not love them. He does not love them because he does not know them. They are as a foreign language to him. They are of an utterly different realm than the one in which he is rooted and lives. He is natural, but they are spiritual.

This is true of the best men. Paul has just spoken of the "princes," that is, man as he has the best education and attains to the highest culture and the most advanced civilization. In all that he is simply a more learned, cultured, and civilized natural man. It refers also to man as he stands in the closest connection with the things of the Spirit and remains a natural man. It is a man born and raised in the church who remains a natural man, unconverted, unrepentant, unbelieving, and who manifests that he is a natural man because he does not receive the things of the Spirit. If baptism only places the child in a more advantageous place to receive and know the promise—a thing of the Spirit—a better position than the heathen in relationship to the things of the Spirit, then in that position the child stands in closest connection to and in the fullest light of the things of the Spirit, so that those things illumine him. If he does not receive them, he increases his guilt and condemnation, and the whole ceremony and all the instruction stand against him.

The natural man—whether in the church or the world—does not receive the things of the Spirit. That is the spiritual inability of the natural man. Since the things of the Spirit are salvation, the natural man perishes in his spiritual inability.

The Reason

The natural man does not receive spiritual things "because they are spiritually discerned" (v. 14).

This is not the ultimate reason a natural man does not receive spiritual things. Some men will never receive the things of the Spirit, even when they come very close to these things and they are most powerfully delivered and illuminated. The ultimate explanation of that is God's reprobation, by which God appointed these men to damnation. Likewise, if there is a natural person who becomes a spiritual man, woman, or child, and he or she receives the things of the Spirit, the ultimate explanation is God's election. He appointed that person to life and salvation. The ultimate explanation of the natural man's failure to receive spiritual things is God's decree of predestination.

But the apostle explains why the natural man as natural man does not receive the things of the Spirit and does not know them: "They are spiritually discerned."

The meaning of *discern* is judge. When the things of the Spirit come and declare the wisdom of God and salvation in Jesus Christ, the glories of the new heavens and new earth, and the wonders of the truth, they are judged. Positively, this means that the things of the Spirit are judged to be of God. They are divine and heavenly mysteries that are able to make one wise unto salvation, that have authority because they are of God, and that must be believed. To discern means to judge them to be perfect, wise, true, right, good, holy, spiritual, and heavenly. A man will judge that there is nothing more precious in the whole world than those things. He will judge.

By "spiritually" discerned the apostle means by the Spirit. The Spirit knows those things, and he reveals them and gives the spiritual power to judge them. Paul does not refer to an innate power and ability that some men have and some men do not have, but he refers to the Spirit himself as he comes and lays hold on a man, changes him in the depths of his being, and causes him to understand spiritual things spiritually. "Spiritually" is the Spirit as he gives to a man power to see, to hear, to understand, to touch, and to feel those spiritual things. "Spiritually" is the Spirit as he makes a naturally dead man alive again; restores to him spiritual powers and faculties, more than even Adam had or could have; makes him a spiritual man who is sensitive to the things of the Spirit; and causes him to know spiritual things with spiritual knowledge and to judge them as true, right, and good. Judging them, he receives them, embraces them, loves them, and lives out of them. He walks in the way of love.

Because the natural man is devoid of the Spirit, he cannot know spiritual things. One cannot argue the natural man into receiving the things of the Spirit. The problem with the natural man is, in a word, his *nature*. In that nature he is devoid of the Spirit. He is dead in trespasses and sins. The problem is not only that the natural man cannot know spiritual things, but also the natural man will not know them because he has a will bound in sin. His will is not free but bound. But the apostle penetrates deeper: the problem with the natural man is that he *cannot*, he lacks the ability to, receive and know the things of the Spirit. As a dead nerve cannot receive stimuli, so the dead, natural man cannot receive those spiritual things. Just as a blind man cannot see, a deaf man cannot hear, and a dead man cannot touch, the natural man cannot receive spiritual things.

The Evidence

There is an unmistakable evidence of the natural man's spiritual inability. The proof is that in his foolishness, pride, and wicked ignorance he assumes the position of judge over spiritual things. The things regarding salvation, that are more precious than gold, and that are divine wisdom he judges as "foolishness unto him" (v. 14).

This judgment of the natural man is the spiritual equivalent of a blind man's judging the relative merits of a Van Gogh and a Rembrandt. He is a completely incompetent judge. The natural man does not judge spiritually, but he judges. His judgment is that the spiritual things are foolish. When the Spirit comes with his things, as the Spirit always comes in the preaching of the gospel of truth, light, life, and salvation, the natural man calls the truth lies, the light darkness, the good bad, and the wise foolish.

That he judges them to be foolish is clear from the natural man's rejection of spiritual things. Some do that quietly. They simply reject them. When spiritual things come, they hear, and they leave. Or when they hear, they forsake those things in which they were born and raised. Although they do this quietly, their rejecting and forsaking are manifestations of a judgment they made about the things of the Spirit. Their judgment is that those things are foolish. "I don't want them in my life, they are not important to me, I don't believe them," they say by their leaving. Others judge loudly. They kick and despise the things of the Spirit and even blaspheme him and his things. They too have made the judgment that the things of the Spirit are foolish.

In that judgment a man exposes that he is natural. If he forsakes, rejects, or blasphemes spiritual things, he simply shows that he is devoid of the Spirit, who infallibly approves of his own things. By that judgment the natural man also shows his wickedness. He is so wicked that he will judge the things of Spirit as foolish. He judges them as the princes of the world judged Christ before they crucified him. He sets up a mock trial, brings in false witnesses, condemns all the things of the Spirit as foolish, and crucifies them. They do not answer to his hopes and his dreams and his way of life as Jesus did not to the princes of the world.

Don't you see the evidence? Go to some street corner and preach and declare the things of the Spirit in the modern-day Corinths of Chicago, Los Angeles, and New York, and you will see what the natural man thinks of them. They are foolishness to him. Try to have some article regarding the things of the Spirit published by the *Wall Street Journal* or the *New York Times*, and you will see what the natural man thinks of the things of the Spirit.

Bring a book about the Trinity, the covenant, or the false doctrines of common grace and the federal vision to the religious book publishers of the day, and you will see what man thinks of the things of the Spirit. Go to some churches and preach the things of the Spirit as they are revealed in the sacred scriptures and set forth in the Reformed creeds, and you will see what religious but natural man thinks of the things of Spirit.

One need not even go that far. The believer's own flesh cannot receive the things of the Spirit. By nature he also rejects, despises, and judges as foolish the things of the Spirit in the gospel.

If a man has heard the things of the Spirit and judged them as divine wisdom, the word of life, above all things most precious, that judgment has only one explanation: the Spirit has laid hold on him. He has given this man spiritual discernment to discern spiritual things. That must be traced even higher. If the things of the Spirit are life to a man, if he embraces them and knows them, that must be traced back to God's eternal will that those things that "eye hath not seen, nor ear heard, neither have entered into the heart of man, the things which God hath prepared for them that love him" be revealed unto him by his Spirit, so that he "might know the things that are freely given to us of God" (vv. 9, 12).

CHAPTER 10

THE CARNAL CHURCH

1 Corinthians 3:1–4

---

1.   And I, brethren, could not speak unto you as unto spiritual, but as unto carnal, even as unto babes in Christ.
2.   I have fed you with milk, and not with meat: for hitherto ye were not able to bear it, neither yet now are ye able.
3.   For ye are yet carnal: for whereas there is among you envying, and strife, and divisions, are ye not carnal, and walk as men?
4.   For while one saith, I am of Paul; and another, I am of Apollos; are ye not carnal?

In the context the apostle contrasted a natural man and a spiritual man. The natural man is man as he comes from his father Adam. The natural man cannot receive the things of the Spirit. He judges those things—the divine wisdom of God—to be foolish, impractical, without bearing on his life, and useless to him. Judging them so, he does not receive them. He passes on and, as the fool, is destroyed.

There is also a spiritual man. He is the elect, regenerated believer in whom the Spirit of Jesus Christ dwells and operates. When the Spirit comes, he takes the natural man and makes him a spiritual man.

As spiritual he judges all things (2:15). By the power of the Spirit he judges the things of the Spirit, which are the truths of sacred scripture. He judges about the things of the Spirit that they are good, holy, and able to make a man wise unto salvation, that there is nothing better in the whole world for him. There is nothing more practical for him than those things. They are as practical and as wise as the salvation of his soul.

The spiritual man judges all things in light of the word of God and by the power of the Spirit. He is able to discern truth from falsehood. He judges himself in the church and in the world. At the end of the world he will judge angels. The spiritual man has the power and authority to judge. He compares spiritual things with spiritual and makes a judgment.

This spiritual man is also "judged of no man" (v. 15). Here the apostle means that the spiritual man is free from the oppressive judgments of men. His conscience and his life are captive only to the word of God. By the word he is judged. To the word alone he is subject, and no man judges him. This is different from judgments by men with the word. Yet even then it is the word that judges him. That is why an Athanasius or a Luther could stand against the whole world alone. They were judged by no man. That is why when a believer errs and strays, the word made powerful by the Spirit brings him back, while a fool passes on and is destroyed.

Paul grounds this reality about the believer in the fact that in Christ the believer also has the mind of Christ: "we have the mind of Christ" (v. 16). God himself, his counsel, and his mind are known of no man and so are not instructed or judged by man. To prove this Paul refers to Isaiah 40:13: "Who hath directed the spirit of the LORD, or being his counsellor hath taught him?" This is also true of Christ and of the believer in Christ.

Paul uses "mind" in 1 Corinthians 2:16 as a synonym for "spirit," as a comparison of the two passages shows. He thereby teaches that this independence of the believer from men's judgments is not by virtue of some innate power of his own, but because in Christ he partakes of the Spirit of Christ, who works in him by the word, so that he receives that word, judges all things by that word, and cannot be judged apart from that word. This is not then a freedom of the believer from all judgment, but his freedom to be judged only by the Lord and that by the word of the Lord. Being judged only by the word of the Lord, the believer is both spiritual and wise. When a man departs from the word of God, he also manifests himself to be carnal and foolish.

In chapter 3:1–4 the apostle applies that specifically to the church. The church in the world is a spiritual body that is supposed to be composed of spiritual believers and their spiritual seed. But the situation in Corinth was different and thus was very grave. The apostle gives a devastating rebuke: "I, brethren, could not speak unto you as unto spiritual, but as unto carnal, even as unto babes in Christ" (v. 1).

Having explained in chapter 2 the heavenly wisdom that belongs to the church by the gift of the Spirit, the apostle in chapter 3 returns to his purpose of exposing the sin he pointed out in chapter 1:11: "It hath been declared unto me of you...that there are contentions among you." He stated the problem. Now he exposes the root of the problem. Where did that contentiousness come from? What was its deep source? Corinth was a carnal church.

The Church As Spiritual

When the apostle says in chapter 3:1, "I, brethren, could not speak unto you as unto spiritual, but as unto carnal," he implies that the church is spiritual. He means to say, "I should be able to speak to you as spiritual, but I cannot." The church is a spiritual body. Her name church—the called-out ones—expresses this reality. She has been called out of the carnal world and gathered into the spiritual body of Jesus Christ. This is the great division in the human race now. It is not between Jew and Gentile, as it was outwardly in the Old Testament, but between church and world. With that distinction there are others: carnal and spiritual,

Christ and Belial, life and death, wise and foolish, justified and condemned, righteous and wicked, and holy and unholy.

The church is not spiritual of herself or in her own power. The members are by nature part of the fallen human race. By nature the church is carnal.

She is spiritual by the power of the Spirit of Christ, who gathered each elect child of God out of the world, regenerated and joined each one to Christ by the spiritual bond of faith, and bestowed wisdom and understanding. The church is spiritual because she is composed of believers who are indwelt by the Spirit, who applies to them the forgiveness of their sins and imputes to them the righteousness of Christ. The Spirit sanctifies them by separating them from the world of impenitent sinners and from sin and consecrating them to Christ in devoted love.

The church is spiritual because the Spirit of Jesus Christ is the source of their spiritual existence—they live out of and by the Spirit. They have a spiritual life that consists of union with Christ by true faith, a life rooted in heaven and that seeks heaven and lives heavenly even in this present evil world.

That she is spiritual means also that she walks according to the Spirit. The apostle implies that when he says, "Ye are yet carnal...and walk as men" (v. 3). The idea is that being carnal, they walked as men walked. By implication the spiritual man and church walk as the Spirit guides. The spiritual church is supposed to walk spiritually, according to the Spirit. That spiritual walk is according to the word. This is the implication of Paul's addressing their lack of receiving the word. This is the implication of his warning ministers to build on the foundation, Jesus Christ, because no other foundation can be laid than is already laid (vv. 10–11).

The spiritual church is directed by the Spirit according to the word. She is governed by the word in her institutional life. The chief mark of a true church is that all things are governed in the church by the pure word of God. A spiritual church is built on the word, hears the word, grows by the word, judges the word by the word, lives by the word, and eats the word. The word is her food, as milk is the food for babies and meat is the food for men. A spiritual church has the pure gospel, eats the pure gospel, and lives by the pure gospel.

That the church is spiritual is also her life and salvation. To be spiritual is to have escaped from death, to be separated from the world, to have overcome the natural, and to possess heavenly wisdom, peace, and comfort.

The Meaning of Carnality

"Now I could not speak unto you as spiritual, but as unto carnal," says the apostle. That is the sharpest rebuke a church could hear. She is opposite of what she is supposed to be. The world is carnal. The church is spiritual once she is called out. Now the church is like the world, returned to its carnality as a dog to its vomit.

To be carnal is to be fleshly. Here carnal refers to the sinful human nature. When God regenerates the believer and makes him spiritual, he does not eradicate the flesh but places the Spirit and the spiritual man in antithesis to the flesh and the carnal man. The Spirit lives in the believer along with the flesh, and the Spirit wars against the flesh. The flesh also wars against the Spirit. The result is that the battle against sin, Satan, and the world begins in the believer.

When Paul calls the church carnal, he does not mean that she is completely devoid of grace and the Spirit. He calls the members "brethren." What he means by carnal he shows immediately afterward when he calls them also "babes in Christ" (v. 1). As babes they were in Christ; they were believers joined to Christ by a true faith. But they were also babes.

In scripture a babe sometimes has a good connotation. The believer is called to desire the sincere milk of the word as a baby desires milk (1 Pet. 2:2). Or as Christ said, "Except ye…become as little children, ye shall not enter into the kingdom of heaven"

(Matt. 18:3). Jesus took babies in his arms and blessed them. The weaned child is a picture of contentment.

When the apostle calls the Corinthians babes, however, he does not compliment them but sharply rebukes them along the lines of his exhortation to the Ephesians: "Be no more children, tossed to and fro, and carried about with every wind of doctrine" (4:14). Here the baby is a picture of carnality: little understanding, rudimentary and confused knowledge of the truth, and hardly any ability to make judgments. As babies' thoughts do not ascend any higher than their meals, their diapers, and their sleep, so the thoughts of the carnal church are sensual and their lives earthly.

When the apostle calls the Corinthians carnal, he tells them they were giving place to the flesh. They were living fleshly as the world. They were allowing their sinful natures to dominate in their lives. The battle against sin was not there. They were seeking earthly things and judging after an earthly manner. Their minds were dominated by earthly concerns. Heaven was the farthest thing from their minds. They were brethren unto whom he had to speak as unto carnal, as unto babes in Christ.

This carnality was fatal to their walking in the way of love. The way of love is the way of life for the spiritual man, just as the way of enmity, hatred, and desire for revenge is the way of life for the carnal man. The way of love is the heavenly, spiritual, and Spirit-wrought way of love toward God and love of the neighbor. The way of petty jealousies, earthly desires, and carnal lusts is the way of the carnal church. As the natural man cannot receive the things of the Spirit of God, so as carnal, it was impossible for the Corinthians to walk in the way of love.

The Evidence of Carnality

The evidence of their carnality was that they had not grown. Twice Paul uses the word "yet." His point is not only that Corinth was a carnal church, but also that she was still carnal. "I...could not speak unto you as unto spiritual, but as unto carnal, even as unto babes in Christ. I have fed you with milk, and not with meat: for hitherto ye were not able to bear it, neither *yet* now are ye able. For ye are *yet* carnal" (1 Cor. 3:1–3; emphasis added). When he came to the Corinthians and first formed them into a church, he found them to be carnal; they were babes in Christ. That is understandable. They had come out of Corinth, the cesspool of the world. They had all kinds of filth clinging to them and all kinds of baggage that went with them.

Finding them as babes and being a good teacher, as a loving mother he fed them milk. When a mother receives her baby, she does not cut big pieces of steak and stuff them in the baby's mouth, but she feeds the baby milk from the breast. This is fitting food for the baby. She also does not speak in full sentences to the baby right away, but she coos at the baby. This is fit for a baby.

Milk is a figure of the apostle's preaching. As milk is a perfect food for a baby, so sound preaching is perfect food for the soul. To feed with milk does not mean a watered-down truth, because that is not the pure milk of the word. It does not mean strategically to cater to the tastes of those in the audience by trimming the message and studiously avoiding their known dislikes, because that is to preach with the wisdom of man's words. Paul gave the whole counsel of God, as he told the Ephesian congregation, and freed himself from the blood of all men (Acts 20:26). He taught the Corinthians all the doctrines of the Christian faith and laid on those new Christians the precepts of the Lord, binding on them the doctrines of marriage, proper labor relations, the Christian in government, and many more things, as will be made clear in the book of 1 Corinthians. He taught them what Christians believe and how that affects their whole lives, so that he gave them the whole truth of God as that on which they could live. The content was not different from any of his other instruction. That it was milk means simply that it was perfectly fitted to the understanding and situation of the hearers.

Ministers do the same thing today. A minister in the catechism room fits the instruction for the children. He tells them stories, but all the while he is teaching profound truths fitted to their capacity. The same thing happens on the mission field. The missionary is a minister who uses milk. It is milk in the sense that the message is fitted to the understanding of the new hearers. Paul first cooed to the Corinthians and fed them at the breasts of the gospel because they were babes. But he neglected nothing needful for their Christian diet and certainly gave them no poison.

Yet they had made no progress! They were like a twenty-year-old who still clamors for milk. They were the disappointing and discouraging teenager who turns from his parents' instruction. Paul rebukes the Corinthians' lack of progress. It was evidence of their carnality.

They flattered themselves that they were spiritual. They flattered themselves especially on their ability to discern good and bad preaching. The apostle cuts it all off and says, "Babyish." "Carnal." "Still!" They were not able to tolerate meat, so he gave them milk, and behold they still choked on milk. They choked on it because they were carnal, their minds were of the earth, and being such, they were babyish. They were not thinking about heaven and spiritual things but were pursuing earthly things. The knowledge of God, which is life itself, was a very light thing to them.

That carnality formed a nearly impenetrable barrier to their growth. That carnality resisted the word of the gospel similarly to a baby who twists and turns and purses her lips to keep out food she does not want.

That attitude toward the word is also the implication of the apostle's teaching that their strife and divisions formed around ministers. Those who said they were of Apollos would hardly give Paul a hearing. Those who said they were of Paul would not listen to Apollos. So they shut out the preached word, as members of a political party will hardly give the member of another party a hearing. The carnal mind is always enmity against God.

Paul is not speaking just to Corinth but to the church everywhere that hears the gospel. If believers are not growing beneath the preaching, there are two, and only two, possible causes. First, the gospel is not being preached, in which case the elders need to work with the minister. Of course, the congregation cannot grow if she is not hearing the gospel. Second, the congregation is yet carnal. If a congregation is hearing the gospel and is not growing, the word of scripture to her is, "Ye are yet carnal."

This applies to the minister in his study. He ought to be building on the foundation Jesus Christ gold, silver, and precious stones. If he is building hay and stubble, he is in trouble, for he is yet carnal (3:12). He is not receiving the word in the study. He is not spiritually working with the word. Why is he not growing? He is yet carnal.

If the minister, an elder, or a member of the congregation comes to you and says, "Are you growing?" and you say, "No, I am not," either the minister is not preaching the gospel or you are carnal. There is a possibility that the minister does not preach the gospel and instead feeds the congregation not baby food or adult food but animal food, hay and stubble. If what is preached is heavenly wisdom, which is the gospel, and to know it is to know God, to understand that is to be spiritual. There is heaven in those words. When that gospel comes and one chokes on it as a baby chokes on a steak, he is carnal.

The Fruit of the Carnality

There is unmistakable fruit in the carnal church. The apostle does not charge the Corinthians out of his own evaluation of them. He does not come to the Corinthians, whom he loved and called brethren, and say merely, "You are carnal." But he proves it. He gives the proof in the form of a question, so that they and every other church of Christ might evaluate themselves.

His proof and questions are the following: "For whereas there is among you envying, and strife, and divisions, are ye not carnal, and walk as men? For while one saith, I am of Paul; and another, I am of Apollos; are ye not carnal?" (vv. 3–4).

Strife and division were the unmistakable proofs of carnality and of the fact that they were not receiving the word. "What do you mean, we are carnal?" The apostle points to their walk, for by their fruits you shall know them. His charge is, "You are carnal." His proof is that they walk like a man, that is, like a carnal man. Literally we read, "according to a man," by which Paul means just as you would expect a carnal man to walk, so they are found to be walking. Their fruits were of the flesh, as the apostle lays out in Galatians 5:19–21: "adultery, fornication, uncleanness, lasciviousness, idolatry, witchcraft, hatred, variance, emulations, wrath, strife, seditions, heresies, envyings, murders, drunkenness, revellings, and such like." They let the world in, and they lived as the world.

Paul points out in particular the strife, divisions, and envyings in the congregation. Just as the unmistakable proof of the Spirit's presence is "love, joy, peace, longsuffering, gentleness, goodness, faith, meekness, temperance," all those against which there is no law (vv. 22–23), the unmistakable work of the flesh is strife and envy. Where strife is the flesh reigns.

This is true personally. If a man has no peace and is plagued by doubts and anxiety, the flesh is reigning. This is true in relationships. In marriage: no peace equals carnality. In the family: no peace equals carnality. In the workplace between boss and employee: no peace equals carnality. If in the church those who are spiritual brethren are at war with one another, the flesh is reigning. They are yet carnal.

Paul gives a concrete example: especially their strife over ministers revealed their carnality. They took the most spiritual thing, the preaching of the word, and turned it into politics. What carnality. "I am of Paul; I am of Apollos," they said. They did not argue over whether one was of Hoeksema or one was of De Wolf,[1] or whether one was of Augustine—defender of sovereign grace—and one was of Pelagius—false teacher of man's free will. Those are controversies between truth and lie. The spiritual church will muster the spiritual courage to rise up, engage in doctrinal controversy, and put out the heretics. The carnal church will allow the heretics to stay and even shelter and defend them.

This point is necessary to understand over against those who censure almost all doctrinal controversy with the rebuke of 1 Corinthians 3:1–4. They chide those who are willing to engage in controversy with false doctrine of dividing the church and of having a bad and party-driven spirit. They plead for unity and toleration on the basis of this text, not a genuine evangelical toleration of those things that are free, to which the apostle will exhort the Corinthians later in the book, but a toleration of false doctrine. If this were the meaning of the apostle and the Holy Ghost, they would be rebuking themselves for what they did when they sharply rebuked the false teachers who earlier had troubled the Galatian churches with the false doctrine of works-righteousness.

Rather, the Corinthians argued whether one was of Herman Hoeksema or one was of Gerrit Vos, one was of Augustine

---

1 In the late 1940s and early 1950s the Protestant Reformed Churches fought a great battle for the truth of the doctrine of the covenant. Rev. Hubert De Wolf and Rev. Hoeksema were two of the ministers who served the large congregation of First Church, which was at the center of the controversy. By preaching heretical statements from the pulpit, Rev. De Wolf thrust himself into the center of the controversy, and those statements became the occasion for a schism in these churches. The controversy was doctrinal in nature, specifically about the question of whether the covenant was conditional or unconditional and ultimately whether election controls the covenant. It was not a controversy mainly about personalities, as many frequently and inaccurately portray it, sometimes in an effort to minimize the seriousness of the false doctrine of the conditional covenant eventually condemned through the controversy.

or one was of Calvin, all faithful ministers who preached the word of God. Those who were supposedly of Paul praised him to the heights and despised Apollos. Those who were supposedly of Apollos had nothing good to say about Paul. That was not because they were competent judges, but because they were carnal.

There is a saying in music: the importance of the musical content renders the concrete mode of expression immaterial. This means that if the music is good enough, it does not matter on what instrument it is played. Take Bach's "Chaconne in D minor." It is exquisite itself, not because of the instrument it is played on. The music enraptures the listener whether it is played on the violin, the organ, the piano, or by a whole orchestra. If that is true of music, it is also true *par excellence* of the heavenly music of the gospel. The gospel transcends the person who brings it, because the gospel is heavenly wisdom. The one who brings it is immaterial as long as the gospel is preached.

Such strife regarding ministers then is not spirituality but carnality. Such strife feigns a great interest in the gospel, but it is the work of the flesh. If it was the work of the Spirit, the Corinthians would have received the gospel and grown thereby. Because their strife was the work of the flesh, they languished and did not develop. Where there is such strife, there is the flesh, and that is deadly.

The apostle rebukes his Corinth sharply because they were being carnal and that threatened their very existence as a church of Jesus Christ. The church is spiritual, but if she will not be spiritual, she is no longer church. That is the issue. That is the deadly seriousness of the issue. The believer is spiritual, and if he will not be spiritual, he is but a man and is carnal.

That is why Paul says to the church and believers who are being carnal, "Brethren, I cannot speak to you as spiritual, but as to carnal." In that there is an implied calling. "Stop being carnal. Stop the strife. Stop the divisions. Stop the envying."

Implied also is the exhortation, "Receive the word that is life and wisdom and that makes all who receive it spiritual and gives spiritual life. Receive the word that you might grow thereby and walk no longer as men, but walk as those who are spiritual, as those who have been called out of the darkness of this world and joined to the church and to Christ, as those whose minds are not on the earth but whose hearts are lifted up to heaven where Christ sits. Be no more carnal, but spiritual." This is the beginning of the walk in the way of love. Love "envieth not...rejoiceth not in iniquity, but rejoiceth in truth...believeth all things" (13:4, 6–7).

CHAPTER 11

THE TEMPLE
OF GOD

1 Corinthians 3:16–17

16. *Know ye not that ye are the temple of God, and that the Spirit of God dwelleth in you?*
17. *If any man defile the temple of God, him shall God destroy; for the temple of God is holy, which temple ye are.*

P reviously the apostle leveled the devastating criticism against Corinth, "Ye are carnal." That was devastating because the church is called out of the carnal world into fellowship with Christ. Indwelt by his Spirit, she is spiritual. As the holy body and bride of Christ she is called to forsake the world, to forsake sin, and to live spiritually in the world.

That was particularly discouraging because the members of the congregation were *yet* carnal (v. 3). Paul pointed particularly to their lack of progress. After all the gospel preaching they had heard, they were still carnal and had made hardly any progress in the Christian life. He also pointed out the unmistakable fruit of their carnality: strife, envy, and divisions, especially as that involved ministers. Who is Apollos, or who is Paul, except ministers given by the Lord to the church to plant and to water? The one who waters is united with the one who plants; they are co-laborers in the vineyard and the building of God (vv. 5–9). If there is any growth, it is God who gives the increase. But the Corinthians were giving place to the flesh, and because of that they were full of all kinds of strife and envy. Where the flesh reigns there is strife.

In verse 16 the apostle gives the antidote to the poison of carnality. He asks, "Know ye not that ye are the temple of God?" The question is rhetorical, intended not to elicit a response from the members in Corinth but to point out a doctrinal truth to them. In pointing that out, Paul also calls them to believe that truth and to live out of it. They knew that they were the temple of God and that the Spirit of God dwelt in them. The issue is not that they did not know, but that they were not living as the temple of God. In their carnality they forgot whose the church is. It is not theirs and does not exist for their sake. It is God's temple.

If the church considers the truth that she is the temple of God, if she knows that truth not merely academically but by faith with the heart and loves that truth with all her being, all her behavior will change. She will give up the church-destroying, God-dishonoring, and Spirit-grieving strife and envy. She will live a church-edifying, God-glorifying, and Spirit-honoring life as his temple.

The Idea of the Temple

When the godly Israelite went from his home in Canaan up to the temple of God, he prayed and sang with his family, "If thou, LORD, shouldest mark iniquities, O Lord, who shall stand? But there is forgiveness with thee, that thou mayest be feared" (Ps. 130:3–4). He prayed that because he was conscious that he was going to the house of God to stand in the very presence of God. On the Day of Atonement, by means of his representative, the high priest, the godly Israelite would stand before the very face of the living God, dwell with him, and fellowship with him in the holy of holies. The Israelite was also conscious that he could stand in the presence of God only because God freely forgave his sins and did not mark his iniquities. He knew that God's purpose in forgiving him was so that he would be holy in the temple and could worship God with his whole heart, cleave unto him, and love him. The apostle would have that spirit live in the hearts and motivate the lives of the members of Corinth.

When the apostle says to the Corinthians, "Know ye not that ye are the temple of God?" he not only addresses them as a true church of Christ, but he also speaks to the church of Jesus Christ wherever she manifests herself in the world.

He speaks to the Corinthian church that is God's by divine election, because God had much people in Corinth (Acts 18:10). Always the church is the elect church. The church is called out of the world by the preaching of the gospel made effectual in the hearts and lives of God's elect people to bring them to faith, repentance, the knowledge of the forgiveness of sin, and a life of holiness.

Furthermore, Paul speaks to the church as she is joined to Jesus Christ and made one with him by faith and as she partakes of Christ's Spirit and of all his wisdom, riches, and gifts. He does not speak of hypocrites, who mix themselves with the church, or of the unbeliever and the nominal church member, who are there because the devil sows his tares in the Lord's field (Matt. 13:25).

He speaks to the church as she always manifests herself in the midst of the world in a true, instituted church of Christ. This institute has officebearers, is the gathering of believers and their seed, and manifests the marks of the true church. Paul speaks to the true church, not to any group that calls itself church or that pretends to be church. That true church in the world shows herself to be true by manifesting the marks of the true church. This is implied when the apostle says the church is "holy" (1 Cor. 3:17).

The outstanding mark of the holiness of the church is that she preaches, maintains, and confesses the truth, a point the apostle has been concerned with for over two chapters. There may be a group where the lives of the people are outwardly unimpeachable, but they despise the gospel. Belonging to the church's holiness is that she properly administers the sacraments, which is closely connected with the exclusion of impenitent sinners from her membership and from the sacraments by church discipline. Belonging to her holiness is spiritual discipline of transgressors. The church is not full of ungodly people who live ungodly lives.

To this church Paul says, "Ye are the temple of God" and "which temple ye are" (vv. 16–17). By "temple" Paul alludes to the Old Testament building constructed on Mount Moriah by Solomon. The whole precinct was the temple. It had an outer court and an altar of burnt offering and a large laver that held thousands of gallons of water. It had a sacred building divided into two parts. There was a holy place, which contained tables of showbread set with dishes and bread, candlesticks with seven lights, a veil, and in front of the veil an altar of incense. Behind the veil was the holy of holies, the second division of the sanctuary. In that room there was the ark set between two cherubim with their outstretched wings. On the ark was a mercy seat, and in the ark was the table of testimony (the law, as the rule of holiness in God's kingdom), Aaron's rod that budded, and a censer full of manna.

Nebuchadnezzar destroyed that temple. Zerubbabel and Jeshua rebuilt it. Herod, the reprobate Edomite, greatly expanded the temple. The temple was there when Jesus walked the earth. It still stood in the apostle Paul's day. The Romans destroyed it in AD 70.

The apostle does not speak of the courtyard but of the sanctuary, the holy place and the holy of holies. There God dwelt. It was his house, but better yet, his palace. In that temple was judgment's royal seat. God sat on the throne between the cherubim. From thence also he ruled in his people and over the whole world.

God did not dwell in that building in the sense that it contained him. At the building's dedication Solomon explicitly denied that: "The heaven and heaven of heavens cannot contain thee; how much less this house that I have builded?" (1 Kings 8:27). God is omnipresent and infinite. Rather, he dwelt in the temple because there he was pleased to give himself in gracious covenantal fellowship with his people. He communed with them on the basis of shed blood. There was the altar. There was also the seat of propitiation on the ark where the blood was sprinkled as the full satisfaction for Israel's sins against the law, and on the basis of which the sins were forgiven and the people were reconciled to God. There God gave himself to be found of his people, and there he took his people into fellowship with himself, especially on the great Day of Atonement. Then the high priest, who bore the names of the Israelites on his shoulders and his breast, carried the people into the most intimate fellowship with God, on the basis of blood and with incense. The temple was God's home and his palace.

That was the glory of the temple. The temple without God was only an empty building with no meaning.

That was the purpose of the temple. It was not built for Solomon or even for Israel. It was built for God to be his house and the place of fellowship with his people.

The Church As the Temple of God

The church is the temple of God. The temple of Solomon was only a little shadow, cast onto the screen of the Old Testament, of what God would do far more gloriously in the New Testament. This fact is made even more pointed in the historical situation of the Corinthian church, because when the apostle called the church the temple of God, the historical temple of God still stood. The church is the real temple of God.

This also makes absurd the idea of premillennial dispensationalism that there will be another brick-and-mortar temple on the pattern of the last chapters of Ezekiel that will be built in the city of Jerusalem at the end of the ages. For the dispensationalist there is no temple of God now, but one must be built again. The dispensationalist denies that the church is the temple of God, just as he denies that the church is the Israel of God and that in the New Testament the types and shadows of the law and the rest of the Old Testament were fulfilled and done away. There the dispensationalist contradicts the apostle Paul and God too. Looking for another building, dispensationalism denies the truth that the church is the building of God, his temple where God dwells.

By this idea dispensationalism also denies the cross of Christ. By insisting on another temple, they must also insist on the reintroduction of bloody sacrifices, to which sacrifices Christ put an end by his own sacrifice, and which must be abolished because his one, perfect sacrifice ended all shedding of blood as atonement for sin. His sacrifice put an end to that building and to all the bloody sacrifices as the way for God's people to have fellowship with him and as belonging to the service of that building. The people of God have fellowship with God not through sacrifices on an altar but through the cross of Christ, so that the church—the local, instituted congregation—is the temple of God.

Paul says to Corinth that the church is the temple of God because "the Spirit of God dwelleth in you" (1 Cor. 3:16). The Spirit of God is God the third person of the Trinity. He is the Spirit about whom the apostle wrote in chapter 2:10, "The Spirit searcheth all things, yea, the deep things of God." He is also the Spirit of Jesus Christ who makes a carnal man spiritual by regenerating him and giving to him spiritual authority, power, and discernment to judge all things and to be judged of no human judgment (v. 15). The Spirit of God inhabits the church. Our houses are ours and we live in them. The church is God's house, indwelt by the Spirit of God.

First, this must be understood of Christ. Christ is personally the temple of God. He is the one man in whom dwells all the fullness of the Godhead bodily (Col. 2:9). Christ said that: "Destroy this temple, and in three days I will raise it up." He spoke not of the earthly temple that Herod had built, "but he spake of the temple of his body" (John 2:19, 21).

Believers are formed into the temple of God as they are joined to Christ and therefore indwelt by the Spirit of Christ. Christ comes to them in the Spirit and takes up his abode with them. They are built and can be built on no other foundation "than that is laid, which is Jesus Christ" (1 Cor. 3:11).

Second, when Christ comes, God comes. God lives in his church. He lives in his church because he lives in each believer. The Spirit forms believers into a building. He establishes them on the only ground and foundation, the chief cornerstone Jesus Christ. By dwelling in each believer he dwells in the church.

We can understand this by an analogy with the Old Testament temple, which was made up of many stones that formed the building in which God dwelt. Now there are no longer stones of rock, but the stones are living, flesh-and-blood people of God, and the temple is a living temple in which the Spirit personally takes up his abode, bringing Christ and God. When the Spirit lays hold on a man, woman, and child, he does not leave them alone as individuals, but he joins them and forms them into a church in a certain location, the institute. In that church God dwells.

Because the church is the temple of God, the outstanding experience of life in the church is fellowship with the living God. The church lives before God's face all the days of her life and in all her activities. When she comes together as church for public worship, she comes to fellowship with God, to worship God, to behold his beauty, and to receive from God grace, the forgiveness of her sins, and all the other blessings of salvation.

This also means that the church must serve God in every aspect of her life.

That the church is God's temple also points out to the believer where he or she must be. If God dwells in his church, that is, in a true instituted church of Jesus Christ, that is where the believer must be. Paul exhorts the believer to be in the church, to live in the church, as in the temple of God. This means also that in the believer's sorrows, tribulations, and afflictions he comes to church to hear God's word and to worship him, as the Israelites said: "One thing have I desired of the LORD, that will I seek after; that I may dwell in the house of the LORD all the days of my life, to behold the beauty of the LORD, and to inquire in his temple" (Ps. 27:4).

At the same time the apostle points out the utter folly of those who forsake membership in a true church of Jesus Christ. That is part of the folly the apostle censors in the context. The Lord takes the wise in their own craftiness; the Lord knows the thoughts of the wise that they are vain (1 Cor. 3:19–20). Those who leave the church always have a reason for leaving and suppose themselves very wise when they leave, but they miss this: God is in the church from which they are leaving, and leaving it they forsake God, Christ, and his Spirit. Even the sparrows and the swallows of the Old Testament rebuke such folly. They had enough sense to build their nests in the temple of God and to raise their young there (Ps. 84:3). Can there be a better and more secure place to build one's nest than in God's house, where there is safety and security and the blessed experience of God's fellowship and friendship?

Besides, many of the free spirits who leave the church have the audacity to complain and to criticize God's house. They do not criticize the house, but the builder of the house and its divine inhabitant. God will take them in their craftiness and with all their excuses. The church is God's because it is his temple.

So much more severe is the rebuke of the man who stays in the church but lives there as though it is his or his little group's church, and thus he divides in that church. The apostle deals specifically with men and members in the church who were living in the church as though the church existed for them. They all wanted the preeminence. They wanted the church to serve them, to recognize their gifts and contributions to the church, and to give them the authority. The church was not theirs or for them, but God's and for him.

"Know ye not that ye are the temple of God" (1 Cor. 3:16)?

The Holiness of the Church

Because the church is the temple of God, she is holy. This outstanding characteristic the apostle emphasizes: "for the temple of God is holy" (v. 17). The connection is this: because she is God's house and God dwells in her, she is holy. Just as the dignity of the owner of a house imparts dignity to his house, so the holy God makes his temple holy.

The church is holy because God dwells in her. The church is not holy because of what she does. That should be clear in the case of Corinth, a church full of unholiness. She did not discipline. The members fought with one another and divided the church. They lived like the world, even getting drunk at the Lord's table. It is astounding that the apostle still calls them holy.

The reason he calls them holy is that the church's holiness is not based on what she does, although that does not excuse the wicked, unholy behavior of some in the church. Rather, the apostle calls the church to consider why she is holy. When God takes up his abode in the church, he makes her holy. It is impossible for a holy God to dwell with an unholy people. Just as he left the Old Testament temple, he can leave an instituted church, so that she becomes false, an empty building. Because the nature of the church, like nature generally, is that she abhors a vacuum, Satan takes up his abode in that false church, and it becomes a synagogue of Satan. Having the name church, it is a habitation of evil spirits.

Holiness is a perfection of God. The holiness of God is his absolute consecration to himself and his glory as the only good. Holiness is an implication of God's perfect goodness. Because he is the only good God, he can be consecrated to no other without denying himself. This entails his absolute separation from sin and his destruction of all that opposes, assaults, or denies his holiness. God is a consuming fire in his holiness.

The holy God abides in the church that by nature is unholy and part of the world. When the holy God takes up his abode in the church, he makes the church holy. He does that by his grace. He is gracious in taking his abode with the church at all, because his presence there has nothing to do with her worth or works but is because he calls the church out of the world, regenerates her, forgives all her sins, separates her from the unholy world, frees her from sin's dominion, and washes her from sin's pollution, so that she is holy not outwardly but inwardly with a real spiritual holiness.

When he makes her holy, God consecrates the church to himself. She is exclusively his. She is his unique creation and not at all man's. She is conceived by God, built by God, inhabited by God, and exists for God. Paul spoke of that in the context. As a wise master builder Paul could lay the foundation, which is Christ, and another man could build on the foundation (vv. 10–11). But except the Lord build the house, the workers labor in vain. To change the metaphor, the apostle could labor in a field and plant, and Apollos could water, but God gave the increase. The church does not belong to any one person or group of persons. It does not exist for a minister, an elder, a deacon, or some prominent member or family. It is not their church. It is God's church.

The church also exists for God's sake. He built it for the purpose that he might dwell in it. It is the same with a man's house. He does not build a house to say, "What a wonderful house," but to live in it. The man does not exist for the house, but the house exists for him, so that he can have a comfortable place to lay his head at night, a pleasant place to eat around a table with his family, a commodious living room in which to have fellowship with family and friends, a place to play with his children, and a yard in which to work and to satisfy man's desire to have his hands in the dirt. The house exists for the one who built it. That is the church. The church exists for God.

Holiness was God's purpose in choosing her. The holiness of the church is the reason God sent his Son to die on the cross to redeem her. Holiness is the work of the Spirit as he abides in the church. She is holy not by what she does, but by what God does in making her holy, as the temple of old became holy when the cloud of glory descended on it and filled the building with God's glory.

A Warning to Desecraters

Because the church is holy, the Spirit says, "If any man defile the temple of God, him shall God destroy" (v. 17). The apostle expresses a principle that follows from the church's holiness. A principle is a universal truth that never changes and holds for all times and in all places. The principle that follows from the church's holiness as God's dwelling place is that God will destroy those who sacrilegiously desecrate his house. Because she is holy, the church is inviolable, which means that God is as committed to destroy those who assault her and her holiness as those who assault him and his holiness. Desecraters of God's temple commit sacrilege, and God destroys the sacrilegious.

That is what happened to Adam when he defiled God's temple in the garden. God destroyed him and brought on Adam and all his posterity a dreadful curse and death. That is what happened in the tabernacle of God to Aaron's sons Nadab and Abihu. God struck them down and destroyed them and forbade Aaron to weep for them. That happened to Hophni and Phinehas when God worked such a work in the family of Eli that God made the ears of everyone who heard it to tingle. That happened to Uzzah, to Ahaz, to Uzziah, to the Old Testament nation of Judah, and ultimately to Jerusalem and the Jews when they destroyed God's temple in Christ and nailed him to the cross. God laid that for the foundation of the revelation of a far more glorious temple and so took the shrewd in their craftiness and made vain the thoughts of those who thought themselves to be wise (vv. 19–20).

Yet the principle holds: the temple is holy because God dwells in the temple, and whoever destroys the temple God will destroy. This happened to the world power Babylon who defiled God's temple and was destroyed by him. It will happen with the world power of antichrist when he will stretch out his hand to defile God's holy temple and will be destroyed by God both personally and as a kingdom.

This addresses those who live in an unholy and unrepentant manner in the church. This addresses those who live in the church as though the church was theirs. This addresses those who were creating division and who still create division in the holy temple of God by their carnal strife, envy, whispering, discouragement, and relentless criticism. They destroy in God's temple, so that the apostle calls them not only schismatics, but also sacrilegious desecraters of God's holy temple. In their carnality in which they demanded that the church serve them, they were defiling God's house. It would be similar to someone who came into your house and trashed the place: turned over all the tables, beat up the walls, tore down the pictures, and slept in your bed. You would be rightly incensed if someone treated your house that way. So God is much more incensed.

Every church member must love this principle that whoever destroys in God's house, him will God destroy, because it means that God destroys your human nature. Our human nature always destroys in God's house, and thankfully God destroys it and frees us from its dominion, frees us from its pollution, and makes us holy. There is salvation in this principle.

This is a word to the church. This principle—that the church is holy and that whoever destroys in God's temple God will destroy—informs the church how she must live in God's house. The church loves sinners, but the church loves God more. When sinners will not turn from sin and by their sins defile God's house, the church will put them out, because God's house is holy.

This is a word to every minister and every officebearer, but especially to a minister to be careful how he builds in God's house. In the Old Testament a man was famous by how he carved in God's house. Then some came into the house and tore down all the carved works and defiled God's house. This is a word to ministers who preach false doctrine in God's house. Those who preach false doctrine in God's house desecrate God's house, and those who destroy in his house will God destroy.

Knowing Herself to Be God's Temple

The church must know herself to be the temple of God and that as such she is holy. She must know that not merely academically, but with the knowledge of faith by the Spirit who inhabits her and makes her holy.

When Paul speaks of wisdom and foolishness (v. 19), he does not speak generically, but applies it to the members of the church. The apostle makes the application that knowing they are the temple of God, that the Spirit of God dwells in them, and that they are holy must become the spiritual wisdom by which members of the church live. That knowledge must control their lives in the church.

First, if anyone destroys in the church, him will God destroy. This is the apostle's word of comfort to the church that she is safe with God and with Christ. This word frees God's people from anxiety about the church.

Second, do not glory in men (v. 21). This applies to each one individually, that he become nothing in the church in his own eyes. One of the worst forms of destroying in God's house is to teach the false doctrine of salvation that allows men to glory in men. Also, who was Paul and who was Apollos? If Paul could say that, every man can say that, and the church says that about every man. The church does not depend on men. The church is God's. Do not glory in men. Do not follow men. Do not seek men. Follow God and seek Christ especially by building on the foundation, Christ, in the truth.

Third, if the church is the temple of God and God dwells in her, how can she live like the world? How can the young people be-bop to the worldly songs and sing the lyrics if they know that they are temples of God? How could a young man or woman, or an old man or woman, defile his or her body by fornication? It is hard to sit in church and to hate the brother if you come into church knowing that you are the temple of God and God dwells in you. It is hard to clamor and complain about the preaching of God's word in the very presence of God. It is hard to live carnally if the church is living out of the principle that she is the temple of God and God dwells in her. It is hard to cheat and steal in the business world for six days if you are the temple of God and God dwells in you.

The apostle intends this principle to affect lives in the church. That is why he says, "Know ye not that ye are the temple of God?" He is not looking for a yes or no answer. That is the equivalent of a command: "Know, believe, and live out of the truths that you are the temple of God, that the Spirit of God dwells in you, and that you are holy!"

Being the temple of God, "all thing are yours" (v. 22). The temple was the center of the whole earth—of the entire universe—and the most important place in the whole world. The things that went on within it were the most important activities in the entire world: God's reconciling his people to himself, forgiving their sins, making them holy, and fellowshiping with them. The whole world served the church, whether that was the heathen nations around or even the wicked within. That is the apostle's application.

If the church knows she is the temple of God, she never has to fear either, for God is with her. Then "all things are yours... and ye are Christ's; and Christ is God's" (vv. 21–23).

CHAPTER 12

THE JUDGMENT OF MINISTERS

1 Corinthians 4:1–5

1. *Let a man so account of us, as of the ministers of Christ, and stewards of the mysteries of God.*
2. *Moreover it is required in stewards, that a man be found faithful.*
3. *But with me it is a very small thing that I should be judged of you, or of man's judgment: yea, I judge not mine own self.*
4. *For I know nothing by myself; yet am I not hereby justified: but he that judgeth me is the Lord.*
5. *Therefore judge nothing before the time, until the Lord come, who both will bring to light the hidden things of darkness, and will make manifest the counsels of the hearts: and then shall every man have praise of God.*

The Corinthians were puffed up with a high estimation of themselves, their abilities, and their place in the kingdom of God. They gloried, but not in God. Along with that they forgot that they had received everything by the grace of God. Paul admonishes them: "For who maketh thee to differ from another? and what hast thou that thou didst not receive? now if thou didst receive it, why dost thou glory, as if thou hadst not received it?"

(4:7). Their pride was at the root of their sins. As pride always does, it led to division, strife, and warfare in the church.

They were especially "puffed up for one against another" (v. 6). This is a reference to the Corinthians' attitude toward ministers in their church. There were ministers—false apostles—who had divided the church into factions. Each faction pushed forward its own theological champion and formed around his name. Those who loved Apollos despised Paul. Those who loved Paul—if there were any—despised Apollos. Those factions had turned the judgment of ministers into a high art form. They practiced it with zeal and were jealous of their supposed prerogative so to judge. They would be offended if anyone would take that judgment from them.

Here the apostle addresses the unlawful judgment of ministers in and by the congregation. This is what he means by "so account of us" (v. 1). In the Corinthians' judgment of ministers there was a definite conclusion to which they had to come. Paul does not forbid any and all judgment of ministers. He says that he is judged of the Lord, and he warns the church not to "judge" before the time comes (vv. 4–5). But he is interested in their unlawful judgment. With him "it is a very small thing that I should be judged of you, or of man's judgment" (v. 3).

When Paul addresses the congregation, "Let a man so account of us" stewards of the mysteries of God, he does not call the man of the world so to think of ministers. What the man of the world thinks of ministers is clear in the context. He regards them as "the offscouring of all things" (v. 13). Rather, Paul calls the members of the congregation to refrain from an unlawful judgment of ministers, and he calls them to a right judgment of ministers as "stewards of the mysteries of God" (v. 1).

He also speaks of the great judgment of ministers, in which every minister will stand. It is the only important judgment of ministers by the only important judge. "He that judgeth me is the Lord" (v. 4). This judgment is the theme of verses 1–5.

The Ministers Who Are Judged

"Us" in verse 1 means the apostle Paul and Apollos. The apostle makes that clear in verse 6: "These things, brethren, I have in a figure transferred to myself and to Apollos for your sakes." Paul was an apostle and Apollos was a minister in the church of Corinth. Apparently Apollos was not the only minister in the large congregation in Corinth, but among the several ministers he was faithful, the most outstanding and gifted, and one around whom one of the factions had formed. Apollos was absent from the congregation, as Paul says in 1 Corinthians 16:12: "As touching our brother Apollos, I greatly desired him to come unto you with the brethren: but his will was not at all to come at this time; but he will come when he shall have convenient time."

Paul puts himself and Apollos on the same plane and speaks of them both as ministers of the gospel. The apostles were ministers too. Paul teaches this in Ephesians 4, where he wrote that the ascended Lord Jesus Christ gave gifts to his church, to some, apostles, and to others, pastors and teachers (v. 11). The apostles were ministers of Christ just as the pastors and teachers whom Christ gives to the church today. A minister is a believing male member of the church who is called by the church and ordained into the ministry of the word and sacraments.

The apostle calls every member of the congregation to account the minister a servant of Christ and a steward of the mysteries of God. A steward is a servant in the house of some great man. The steward has the charge of the house and especially of the treasures that belong to the great man. The minister serving in the church is a steward in the house of the living God, which is his church.

The mysteries of which the minister is the steward are the truths of scripture regarding God, Christ, the plan of salvation, and the consummation of all things. They are the doctrines of the Christian faith, all the truths regarding God's gracious salvation of his elect church in Jesus Christ. They are mysteries because they are hidden in God's counsel. If God does not reveal these things, no man knows them. If a man is ignorant of these mysteries, he is not saved. To know them is salvation. Being mysteries, they are revealed and known by scripture.

The mysteries are treasures of incalculable value because by the preaching of them the elect church comes to the saving knowledge of God. Through the preaching these treasures of eternal life become the possession of God's church and of the individual elect child of God in the church. Their value is no less than eternal salvation for a sinner.

The minister is a steward of these treasures. As a steward he is a servant and has a special office with respect to these mysteries. Not everyone has that office; only a minister has the special office of being a steward of the mysteries of God. In this office he preaches and teaches these treasures. The apostle said that about his own charge: "Christ sent me not to baptize, but to preach the gospel." "We speak the wisdom of God in a mystery" (1 Cor. 1:17; 2:7). There is no more glorious thing than to be sent to speak the wisdom of God embodied in these mysteries.

The judgment the church must make of her minister is that he is a servant in a special office from God regarding the incalculable treasures of the mysteries of God for the church's own salvation. Judging him so, she is to esteem him as a steward and an occupant of the most glorious office a human being can hold.

The Reformed faith expresses this esteem for the office of the minister in the Form for the Installation of Ministers. After explaining that the office of the minister is to preach the mysteries of God, the form says, "From these things may be learned what a glorious work the ministerial office is, since so great things are effected by it; yea, how highly necessary it is for man's salvation, which is also the reason why the Lord will have such an office always to remain."[1] Great things are effected by the min-

---

1 The Form for Ordination of Ministers, in *Confessions and Church Order*, 286.

isterial office. Everything waits on the work of the ministry of the word, because the Lord does not come until all his elect are gathered. The office is necessary for man's salvation because the Lord ordained to save his people by the foolishness of preaching. Because these things are revealed for God's glory, God is glorified in the preaching of them regardless of what men may think of them. The ministerial office is to be esteemed by the members of the church and by the church herself; the ministers who occupy that office are to be esteemed for their position and work in that high office.

This exposes a very insidious assault on the office that oftentimes goes unnoticed: the minister is made busy with everything except preaching and laboring in the mysteries of the truths of God's word. Some of these are good and noble works, but they consume his time and energy and do not allow him as a steward to study and "to bring forth out of his treasure things old and new" (Matt. 13:52). His ministry as a steward of the mysteries of God must be guarded because with it is wrapped up the health, life, and blessedness of the congregation, since everything depends on the preaching.

The church—parents, elders, ministers, and the rest—must communicate to the young men the glory of the ministerial office. Is the message that it is glorious to be a lawyer, a doctor, or a successful businessman, but to be a minister is of no account? Do parents, elders, ministers, and churches press on the young men that the office is a difficult one but forget to tell them that it is a glorious one? Is that what you think of your minister? Here the apostle speaks of the glories of the office and calls the church to esteem it as such.

Holding that great office, the minister remains a servant. He is a servant of Christ. He is never lord in the Lord's house. That he is a servant means that he did not come into the position of the office by his own will, but by Christ's will, and ultimately by God's will.

That he is a servant of Christ also speaks to the esteem in which the congregation must hold the minister. If he were a servant of the richest, most powerful, or most famous man in the world, how would he be treated? In a similar way, what one does to an ambassador of a country, he does to that country; so what one does to a minister he does to Christ.

Judging the Minister's Faithfulness

What is judged in the minister is his faithfulness. "Moreover it is required in stewards, that a man be found faithful" (1 Cor. 4:2). Because he is a steward of the mysteries of God, his office requires him to bring these mysteries in the preaching and nothing else. Doing this, he is a faithful steward. The apostle emphasizes the requirement of faithfulness in verse 5: "The Lord...will bring to light the hidden things of darkness, and will make manifest the counsels of the hearts, and then shall every man have praise of God." For his faithfulness he will have praise of God. The faithfulness that will be judged in the minister has to do with his being a steward of the mysteries of God. Just as the steward of some house is judged by how he managed, used, developed, and preserved the treasures of the house, the steward of God's mysteries must be judged regarding how he handled the mysteries of God.

Faithfulness means that he actually preached and taught the mysteries in the congregation, in the catechism room, and from house to house. Faithfulness means that in his preaching and teaching and in all his labors with the mysteries he scrupulously adhered to the word of God, which is the only source of these mysteries. Because the Belgic Confession, the Heidelberg Catechism, and the Canons of Dordt "do fully agree with the Word of God," faithfulness means also that the minister teaches the doctrines of these Reformed creeds, as he indicated when he signed the Formula of Subscription.[2]

---

2 Formula of Subscription, in ibid., 326.

Faithfulness importantly includes the minister's warnings against heresies, false doctrines, false teachers, and churches that are departing from the truth. Every Reformed steward takes that vow when he signs the Formula of Subscription. He is unfaithful if he does not do that. It is also the command of the Reformed Church Order of Dordt regarding the minister and his ministry: "To ward off false doctrines and errors that multiply exceedingly through heretical writings, the ministers and elders shall use the means of teaching, of refutation or warning, and of admonition, as well in the ministry of the Word as in Christian teaching and family-visiting."[3]

An old Reformed minister said about article 55, "This means that with every text the minister must refute error, warn against heresy, and admonish to faithfulness."[4] If he does not do that "with every text," he is unfaithful. When he does, he is faithful.

A serious threat today to the minister's faithfulness and thus to the congregation's health, life, and salvation is that this aspect of the minister's faithfulness is unappreciated, disliked, or loathed. He is sharply criticized with the intent to shut his mouth because his ministry and his faithfulness as a steward so bring the word that it cuts along the lines of families, friends, and interdenominational friendships where the members themselves should obey the word but do not. The minister must. Every minister must! How faithful would an ambassador of the United States be if he went to the enemy of the United States and upheld all the positive interests of the United States, but when the enemy attacked the interests of the United States he said nothing? He would be recalled. So a minister would be flatly and miserably unfaithful if he would not fight against those who attack his Lord, God's house, and the mysteries he is bound by an oath to defend.

---

3 Church Order of the Protestant Reformed Churches 55, in ibid., 397.
4 Idzerd Van Dellen and Martin Monsma, *The Church Order Commentary* (Grand Rapids, MI: Zondervan Publishing House, 1941), 229.

Faithfulness also means that in his labors with the mysteries of God the minister builds on the foundation of Jesus Christ gold, silver, and precious stones and not wood, hay, and stubble. All of the minister's work will be tested (3:12–13).

Faithfulness means that in his work with the mysteries of God the minister labors hard. A lazy minister is unfaithful.

Faithfulness means too that he labors with the mysteries. Faithfulness is not merely his busyness. A minister can be busy with many things, but if he does not labor with the mysteries, how faithful is he as a steward of God and of his mysteries? If a minister will be so accounted by the congregation and praised by God as a steward of the mysteries of God, he must be faithful in those mysteries and with them. He cannot fault the congregation for their judgment of him if he is unfaithful with that glorious treasure that was committed to him because he does not labor with the mysteries and does not bring them.

Faithfulness means that for the sake of his Lord and for the sake of the mysteries he suffers the loss of his name, interests, and pleasures. How faithful would an ambassador be who, when he was sent to another country, would only play or played so frequently that his work suffered? Faithfulness means that a minister preaches the mysteries regardless of the cost to himself.

That faithfulness begins in the heart. A minister will be judged first regarding his heart. When the Lord comes he "will bring to light the hidden things of darkness, and will make manifest the counsels of the hearts" (4:5). In order for a minister to be faithful, he must be a believer, and all of his work must be done in love for Christ and God who saved him and also gave him that excellent office.

The faithful minister is to be accounted by the congregation as a steward of the mysteries of God and so esteemed. This is a right judgment of ministers.

An Improper Judgment of Ministers

There is an improper judgment of ministers by incompetent judges. This is the improper judgment of ministers that the apostle refers to in verse 3 as a judgment "of you, or of man's judgment." "Of you" means a judgment by the Corinthian congregation. The apostle calls it "man's judgment" because it is a judgment according to a human standard, by humans, for human interests. It is not any and all judgments by the Corinthians that he censures. It is the congregation's improper judgment of him by human standards. Such a judgment is thoroughly carnal.

This judgment may be critical: "Our minister is no good." The judge gives his reasons: his sermons are too doctrinal; all he does is refer to the creeds; he criticizes apostatizing churches and false teachings, especially those churches where my friends and family go, but I want to protect my family and friends who are members in these churches and believe these things; our church is not growing and is even getting smaller. These are some of the critical and carnal judgments of the minister.

Human judgments can also be glowingly positive: "Our minister is a good minister." The judge gives his evaluation: he is well liked; the church is growing by leaps and bounds; he gets along well with the community and lets us get along well too; he is mainly practical and hardly ever doctrinal; he does not criticize false teachers and never applies the word in a way that is painful to me in my particular situation; he is a dynamic speaker. Though positive, these are equally carnal judgments of the minister.

The apostle mentions another human judgment: "Yea, I judge not mine own self. For I know nothing by myself; yet am I not hereby justified" (vv. 3–4). This refers to a minister's own unfair and human judgment of himself. Paul does not forbid a minister to examine his ministry at all, for literally he says, "I know nothing and judge nothing against myself." This implies Paul's judgment of his ministry, in which he could not find anything unfaithful. It is exactly because the minister examines and judges his ministry that Paul warns against the minister's own unfair judgment of himself.

In this improper judgment of his own ministry he applies a human judgment. Because of this he either cripples himself in his ministry or justifies his ministry on poor grounds. The minister concludes, "I am not a good minister," and gives his reasons: I am not like that other minister; I am not popular; I am not voted onto committees; I do not reach overachieving standards I set for myself. The minister may also conclude that his ministry is successful for all sorts of illegitimate reasons: the people praise me, the community gets along with me, I receive all positive reports at family visitations. He remembers not the words of his Lord, "Woe unto you, when all men shall speak well of you! for so did their fathers to the false prophets" (Luke 6:26).

The minister must discount all these judgments. Paul speaks of his own view of these unlawful judgments and tells all ministers to do the same: "With me it is a very small thing that I should be judged of you, or of a man's judgment" (1 Cor. 4:3). This refers to a minister's freedom from those judgments. He can and must ignore them. Indeed, "small" means low. Man's judgments are so low in Paul's estimation that they never get on the list of what is important in his ministry, and he labors in the conviction that what men say of him and his labors is a very small thing.

By implication the apostle also addresses elders who have the oversight of the minister. In their judgment of ministers they may not engage in this unlawful judgment. When the faithful minister suffers from these unlawful judgments from lawless church members, they must comfort him and bring this word to the minister: "It must be a very small thing to you to be judged of man's judgment. You must discount it." They must reinforce with him that the only lawful judgment of him is of his faithfulness and that they so judge him as faithful.

The threat to the minister is that he does not ignore these judgments. Because he does not ignore man's judgments, he becomes unfaithful. No man can serve two masters, and the fear of men is a snare (Matt. 6:24; Prov. 29:25). It is also crippling to the minister in his ministry always to be thinking, "What are they going to think about this sermon, this application, this article, or this speech? How can I say this so as not to offend anyone in the audience?" He must ignore man's judgment.

He must also ignore it because man—the carnal man who issues such a judgment—is an incompetent judge. Man is incompetent because he cannot see the heart. Man cannot "make manifest the hidden things of darkness" and draw out the hidden "counsels of the heart" (1 Cor. 4:5). There are many things regarding the ministry that are never known except to the minister and Christ. There are things about his own ministry that are hidden from the minister himself in this life and will not be revealed until the last judgment.

Besides, man also has no authority to judge the minister by man's standards and for his purposes. The minister is a servant not of men but of Christ. For a man to judge a minister, according to man's judgment, would be similar to one boss judging the servants of another boss, giving them performance evaluations, docking their pay, or firing them. This shows that the unlawful judgment of ministers can only come from a wretched pride that exalts itself above Christ himself and thrusts him out of his lordship.

Another problem with human judgment is that it is always premature. Man judges "before the time" (v. 5). Christ will judge ministers at the proper time.

In the interests of his ministry and faithfulness, every minister must say with the apostle, "With me it is a very small thing that I should be judged…of man's judgment" (v. 3).

The Lord's Judgment of Ministers

The minister's freedom from human judgments does not mean he is free from all judgments. The minister's faithfulness will be judged by a competent judge. "It is required in stewards, that a man be found faithful" (v. 2). "Found" means a judgment pronounced after a careful, detailed examination of his whole ministry, beginning with his heart, extending to all his labors, and culminating in the expression of judgment over that minister and all his labors. The minister will be investigated in a court where he will be studied closely and intensely by a judge. In that court the minister is investigated, a verdict is passed, and a sentence is delivered. Every minister will be judged. No minister escapes that judgment.

The judge is the triune God in Christ: "He that judgeth me is the Lord" (v. 4). He is the minister's Lord and will judge him. Every minister of the gospel will stand in the Lord's court, will be investigated by the Lord, and will hear from the Lord the Lord's verdict over his ministry. The judgment of ministers is the Lord's business. The Lord's standard is faithfulness, faithfulness with the mysteries of God.

Regarding the Lord's judgment of ministers, Paul uses the present tense: "He that judgeth me is the Lord." He was presently judging the apostle, and he judges every minister throughout his ministry. The Lord judges in the minister's conscience. This is what the apostle means in verse 4 by "justified." With that word he speaks of the court of a man's conscience and the judgment of the minister there by the Lord. In the conscience of the minister the Lord praises, "Well done, good and faithful servant." There he also rebukes, "Unfaithful steward with my mysteries." There he graciously judges the minister, forgives his sins, and by praise and by rebuke calls him to greater faithfulness.

That the Lord judges the minister now does not mean he is free from all judgments by men. Implied in these verses is a proper judgment of the minister by humans regarding his faithfulness as a servant of Christ and steward of the mysteries of God. A minister is judged in seminary regarding his doctrine and life. Synod, classis, and consistory judge him by majority vote. The congregation judges him every Sunday whether he faithfully brought the mysteries of God in the particular text. This is not carnal at all but deeply spiritual, and it is done by spiritual men and women according to the spiritual standard of faithfulness. To that judgment a minister must pay attention. That is not man's judgment but the Lord's judgment. The standard of this judgment is the word of God—the mysteries themselves—the Reformed creeds, and the Church Order, not a contrived and artificial list of criterion of good preaching, which is only another form of man's judgment.

The Lord also will judge. "Judge nothing before the time, until the Lord come." This refers to the second coming of Christ and the final judgment. In the final judgment Christ will judge ministers. In that judgment the judge will be Christ and the standard will be faithfulness. In that judgment Christ "will bring to light the hidden things of darkness, and will make manifest the counsels of the hearts" (v. 5).

No minister will escape this judgment. The faithful minister longs for it. The heretics, the hirelings, and the unfaithful ministers fear it, and in it they will be exposed and damned. Even for some elect, believing ministers this judgment is a fearful thing, because in their ministries they did not build on the foundation Christ gold, silver, and precious stones, but wood, hay, and stubble (v. 12). Their aims in their ministries were to be popular, to please men, to make friends, and to offend no one—everything but faithfulness! In their ministries their singular aim was to take a small church and to make it big, and in pursuit of that interest they deliberately brought in those who were not one with the church but were in the church as hay and stubble. In their ministries they accounted the mysteries of God of which they were stewards very light things. They were not busy in them, did not and could not bring them, or if they brought them, strategically trimmed them for the tastes of those in their audiences. They will hear rebuke from the lordly Judge. Their ministries and all their work will be burned with fire, although they will graciously be saved.

The judgment will be gracious. All faithful ministers, even Paul, are not perfect in their ministries. Paul judged his ministry rightly and spiritually and according to a right standard of faithfulness. He says in verse 4, "I know nothing by [literally, against] myself; yet am I not hereby justified." He had nothing against his ministry as far as he was able to judge. According to his judgment he was faithful. But in that judgment he was not justified, because the hidden things of darkness had not yet been made manifest. What hidden things polluted and tainted his ministry? The judgment must be gracious, or all ministers will perish.

The graciousness of the judgment means that God will justify them and their ministries as he justifies all his people in their lives. The apostle implies this when he says, "Yet I am not hereby justified." Ministers stand in their ministries as the believer always stands and is justified before God: on the basis of the perfection of Christ's ministry. He is the officebearer, and he alone was perfect and perfectly faithful. Belonging to that faithfulness was that he laid down his life for his sheep, fully satisfied the demand of God's justice against their sins, and merited for them by his lifelong obedience and atoning death perfect righteousness with God. The minister's salvation will not depend on his faithfulness in the ministry. He will be justified in his ministry the way that all of God's people are justified, namely, by faith alone in Christ. In that justification there will be the public vindication of the faithful minister in all his work on behalf of the mysteries of God and the Christ that he serves.

In that judgment there will be praise: "Then shall every man have praise of God" (v. 5). The idea is not that every single minister will have praise. A heretic will be damned and the hireling will be rebuked. Every faithful minister will have praise. The Lord will not load all of the praise on Augustine, Calvin, or Luther, but each will get a share: "Well done, good and faithful servant. Enter thou into the joy of thy Lord."

Since knowledge of, or belief of (faith), these mysteries is basic to walking in the way of love—love believes all things—it is necessary for a congregation to receive the mysteries of God at the mouth of her minister, so that she accounts him as the minister of Christ and a steward of the mysteries of God. It is walking in the way of love with the minister so to account him.

CHAPTER 13

The Exhibition of the Apostles

1 Corinthians 4:9–16

9. For I think that God hath set forth us the apostles last, as it were appointed to death: for we are made a spectacle unto the world, and to angels, and to men.

10. We are fools for Christ's sake, but ye are wise in Christ; we are weak, but ye are strong; ye are honourable, but we are despised.

11. Even unto this present hour we both hunger, and thirst, and are naked, and are buffeted, and have no certain dwellingplace;

12. And labour, working with our own hands: being reviled, we bless; being persecuted, we suffer it:

13. Being defamed, we entreat: we are made as the filth of the world, and are the offscouring of all things unto this day.

14. I write not these things to shame you, but as my beloved sons I warn you.

15. For though ye have ten thousand instructors in Christ, yet have ye not many fathers: for in Christ Jesus I have begotten you through the gospel.

16. Wherefore I beseech you, be ye followers of me.

In verse 6 the apostle writes, "I have in a figure transferred to myself and to Apollos [these things] for your sakes." Evident is Paul's love for the Corinthians as his "beloved sons" (v. 14). Earlier, when he described their divisions, he spoke of factions that had formed around him and Apollos. Here we learn that there were no factions around Paul and Apollos. The situation was much worse. The congregation was not forming factions around faithful ministers but around false apostles, and she was abandoning her spiritual father and his instruction.

Previously Paul left out of view those who were troubling the congregation and had attached his name to their divisions as if to say that even if the names attached to the factions were those of the most faithful ministers of the gospel and apostles, the schism was intolerable. In this way he taught the people not to glory in men "that no one of you be puffed up for one against another" (v. 6). Such glorying in men contradicted the gospel: "that which is written" (v. 6). This refers to the scriptures that everywhere teach that God is everything and man is nothing. The gospel was at stake not only because the Corinthians gloried in men, but also because the men whom they followed were false apostles who denied the gospel, divided the church, and threatened Corinth's existence as a true church of Christ in the world.

The situation called for hard words, which the apostle uses in verse 8: "I would to God ye did reign, that we also might reign with you." In the epistle on love and himself walking in love, the apostle applies to the church this unprecedented irony. He continues it in verse 10: "Ye are wise in Christ...but ye are strong; ye are honourable." He speaks ironically, with a kind of mockery that a father might use with his foolish son to call him from his folly. By this device the apostle rebukes the Corinthians' folly. This is love.

Love that will not rebuke sin is no love. Love that will rebuke also will use irony such as the apostle uses to expose folly. Love "rejoiceth not in iniquity" (1 Cor. 13:6). Paul's love for his spiritual sons, in which he rebuked them, was real love in distinction from the love of fathers who will not restrain the evil of their sons with even a mild rebuke, let alone hard words. By this the apostle rebukes the thinking that gave rise to their vicious attitudes toward one another and the apostle. They reigned. Reigning, they would put no one before themselves.

Here the apostle also exposes part of the false doctrine of these false apostles. They were teaching a theology of victory, not the proper scriptural theology of victory through strife, suffering, and battle, but victory now. "We reign now; we are full now; we are rich now; we are honorable now," they said. They taught a carnal theology that gave rise to a carnal church. That carnal theology at its heart was the idea that the church's victory would come in this life and that she must strive for victory in this life.

This thinking is present in the church today as well. Who has not confronted this thinking in himself? In the face of suffering for the gospel, who is not attracted to the idea that God does not want his church to suffer? The thinking that the church can be rich now and avoid the sufferings of the gospel is tempting. Who has not confronted this thinking when the minister preaches about the vanity of life and that life is nothing but a continual death? The response verbalized or internalized is, "Why does the minister have to be so depressing?" When he preaches sharp warnings against heresy, which multiply exceedingly, he often hears, "This or that heresy is not a threat to our church," or, "Why do we need to hear about false doctrine all the time?" as though the church is in heaven already. There is also the unbelievably proud response when the Lord brings suffering into someone's life on account of the truth: "The Lord does not want me to suffer but to be happy." In other words, give up the gospel for the sake of a happy life now with a boyfriend or a child or in a marriage or a job. The thinking that we are rich now, full now, and reign as kings now is very much a threat today.

This thinking lies at the heart of the common-grace agenda

to Christianize the world. The church will be victorious in this life in the form of establishing a Christian culture brought about by the church's cooperation with the world. This thinking also lies at the heart of the Jewish dreams of postmillennialism in which the goal of all the church's life and work is an earthly kingdom and that chastises the theology of suffering in this life as defeatist and pessimistic. These are examples of a theology of carnal victory that all equally lead to carnal churches: churches that will not walk in the way of love.

Against this thinking the apostle speaks of God's exhibition of the apostles. This is the meaning of the word "for" that begins 1 Corinthians 4:9. It gives a reason for his ironic statement in verse 8 that he wishes the Corinthians were reigning now so that the apostles might reign with them, because the apostles as leaders of the churches were not reigning but were a spectacle to the world. The Corinthians in their wrong thinking needed a vivid exhibition to draw them back to the kind of life to which God had called them in the gospel. Spiritual children need pictures, so Paul gives them a vividly illustrated picture from the lives of the apostles. By this example he shows them that the way of love in this world is a way of self-denial, especially in suffering for the truth. Love "suffereth long...beareth all things...endureth all things" (13:4–7).

To this example Paul calls them. When Paul says, "Follow me," he does not take back anything he has said about factiousness or following men. When a man follows the apostles in their examples of suffering, he does not follow men, but Christ himself.

Those Who Are Exhibited

The ones who are exhibited for our instruction and thus for imitation by the church and ridicule by the world are the apostles. They were men personally chosen by Jesus Christ to be eyewitnesses to his resurrection glory and were commissioned to preach the gospel of Jesus Christ in the world. When Paul speaks of "apostles," he refers to the word in this technical sense. Sometimes scripture uses technical terms loosely. For example, sometimes the word *deacons* refers to the male officebearers in the church and sometimes to all the saints, male and female, who serve the church by their labors in the church or in some special service of the church. Sometimes the Bible uses the word *apostles* loosely to refer to Paul and all his associates—Timotheus, Silvanus, and others whom he taught to be ministers of the word. Here he means the thirteen men personally chosen by the Lord.

That Paul uses "apostles" in the technical sense is clear because later he distinguishes between himself as an apostle and Timotheus, whom Paul had sent as a minister to the Corinthians to remind the church of Paul's apostolic ways (4:17).

Verse 9 refers to those twelve men whom Jesus chose during his earthly ministry. One of them was a devil, a reprobate who betrayed the Lord and impenitently hung himself. In keeping with the prophecy of the psalms that another would take his office, Jesus Christ by the lot appointed Matthias to replace Judas Iscariot. Last of all there was Paul. Paul refers to himself as "one born out of due time," who was first a persecutor of the church, and one on whom God had grace and whom he made an apostle to the Gentiles (15:8–10).

Those men had the special office in the church of apostle. The name refers to their office as those who were sent by Jesus Christ to be his ambassadors. They bore a message, which Paul calls "the gospel" (4:15). Their office was to be preachers of the gospel. The gospel was not their words or their ideas about Jesus Christ or how the church ought to be run. The gospel is the good news of salvation in Jesus Christ. It is the good news that the triune God had fulfilled his promise revealed to Adam in the garden, published by the patriarchs and prophets, and signified by all the ceremonies and laws of the Old Testament. It is the good news that God had accomplished all of salvation in Jesus Christ. The gospel points out Jesus Christ as the savior in the fullness of his person, natures, and works. The gospel points out faith in Jesus Christ as the only way of salvation.

With that gospel the apostles commanded all men everywhere who heard the gospel to believe in Christ. With that gospel they gave the precious promise that those who repent and believe in Christ will be saved and find mercy. With that gospel they issued the warning that all who do not believe will be damned. The gospel is the doctrine of Jesus Christ as it forms the whole confession of the church that is gathered by the gospel. The gospel is the teachings of Jesus Christ as the Lord of his church, as they regulate the whole life and conduct of the church.

As apostles their office consisted in proclaiming the gospel faithfully. This must be emphasized. They did not hedge. They did not soften the gospel. They did not change it or adapt it to the tastes of their audiences. They preached the gospel faithfully.

As apostles their office was special because they were the fathers of the church: "For though ye have ten thousand instructors in Christ, yet have ye not many fathers: for in Christ Jesus I have begotten you through the gospel" (v. 15). Here Paul does not call himself a father in the absolute sense of the word, but in an instrumental sense. The gospel was the power to beget the church. Christ was the begetter of the church, and he worked through the apostles as instruments.

This is the same idea as when we refer to Athanasius and Augustine as church fathers, because by means of the development and preaching of the truth, they as it were brought forth the church. There are also fathers of the Reformation, Luther and Calvin. There are the fathers of Dordt, whose voice speaks to us in the creeds yet today to teach us what they believed and what we as their spiritual children must believe. There are the fathers of the Secession, Hendrik de Cock and Simon van Velzen, and Abraham Kuyper, the father of the *Doleantie*. There were the fathers of 1924 and 1953 in the Protestant Reformed Churches, Herman Hoeksema and George Ophoff. They are fathers in an instrumental sense, because they begat in the truth. The apostles are preeminently the fathers of every true church. The others are fathers only because they brought the church back to their fathers, the apostles.

In this sense Paul also speaks in verse 17 of "my ways," as the ways of a faithful Christian father are all the instruction he gives his children in fulfillment of his baptismal vow. As a father he also has the power of discipline: "What will ye? shall I come unto you with a rod, or in love, in the spirit of meekness?" (v. 21).

The apostles are the fathers of every true church of Jesus Christ because they preached the gospel. The power of the gospel is to beget the church of Jesus Christ by calling the individual elect children of God out of the darkness of this world into the light of Jesus Christ, separating them from the world and joining them to Christ and his body, the church, forgiving their sins, sanctifying their lives, and preserving them in the gospel. It is the power of the gospel to bring about a sharp antithesis between the church and the world and to do what it has done since the garden of Eden: to place enmity between the Seed of the woman and the seed of the serpent. In short, the gospel is the power to save the church. Those who have been begotten by the gospel are saved by it.

Since the apostles are the spiritual fathers of the church, they must be honored, obeyed, and imitated by believers as sons must honor, obey, and imitate their fathers. That was true of the apostle regarding Corinth. He was in a most esteemed position in the church. This is true of every church of Jesus Christ in the world. The church is truly apostolic when she has been begotten by the power of the apostolic gospel. Every time the church experiences a reformation, she is begotten again by the apostolic gospel. The apostles are the fathers of the church, and they have the highest position in the church. Jesus said about them that they will sit on thrones to reign with him, judging the twelve tribes of Israel (Luke 22:30).

Made a Spectacle before the World

Those men who have begotten the church by the gospel and must be highly esteemed by the church are exhibited. "Set forth" in 1 Corinthians 4:9 means exhibited. They are made a vivid picture in the world. Are they reigning in the world? "God hath set forth us the apostles...as it were appointed to death." Paul refers to the ancient practice of publicly and ostentatiously parading a condemned criminal through the streets so everyone could see him, the crowds could jeer at him, and the children could scorn him, and by that means the government gave a vivid lesson to all.

The apostles were so exhibited. They were exhibited "unto the world," by which Paul means the whole universe, including devils as fallen angels. They were also exhibited "to angels, and to men." The angels are the elect angels, who are ministering servants of the church and are concerned with everything that happens in the church. God also exhibited the apostles to men, both ungodly and righteous.

As a consequence the apostles were made "a spectacle." A spectacle is a theater. The apostles were the main prop.

10. We are fools for Christ's sake...we are weak...we are despised.
11. Even unto this present hour we both hunger, and thirst, and are naked, and are buffeted, and have no certain dwellingplace;
12. And labour, working with our own hands: being reviled, we bless; being persecuted, we suffer it:
13. Being defamed, we entreat: we are made as the filth of the world, and are the offscouring of all things unto this day.

What an exhibition God made of those fathers of the church! They suffered for the gospel. They suffered the loss of food and drink, honor and standing, their proper wages, health and freedom, and eventually their lives.

They were made "as the filth of the world, and are the offscouring of all things" (v. 13). "Filth" and "offscouring" refer to the practice of keeping a criminal at public expense so that when something went wrong the criminal went to the flames. The criminal was a scapegoat. So were the apostles: if something went wrong the apostles went to the flames.

They were not the first to endure that vile treatment. Paul says that God exhibited the apostles "last" (v. 9). Jesus told his disciples that the prophets were first in this honor, "For so persecuted they the prophets which were before you" (Matt. 5:12): the prophet Abel, whom Cain slew; Enoch, whom they hunted but God translated; Noah, whom they mocked; all the way to Zacharias son of Barachias, whom they slew between the temple and the altar (23:35). Christ himself said, "The foxes have holes, and the birds of the air have nests; but the Son of man hath not where to lay his head" (Matt. 8:20; Luke 9:58). Pilate paraded Christ in a purple robe and a fake scepter for the Roman soldiers and the mob, and the high priest said that it was expedient that one should die for the people. That same Christ they paraded from Gabbatha to Golgotha to the hoots and sneers and general delight of the passing crowds. So also the apostles: God has exhibited the apostles last.

The Reason They Are Exhibited

What explains the world's vile treatment of the apostles, who have the highest honor in the church and "are fools for Christ's sake" (1 Cor. 4:10)? "For Christ's sake" literally means on account of Christ. On account of Christ is the reason the world thought so little of the apostles and treated them so vilely. The word "fools" summarizes the world's evil view of the apostles.

This means, first, that the apostles were believers and apostles only because Christ had mercy and grace on them. Not even they would have believed the gospel apart from Christ. Christ set his love on them and had mercy on them. Who was Paul? He was a persecutor of the church, a man in the grip of the false doctrine of salvation by works and mad with hatred toward Christ and his church. The Lord had mercy on Paul "as one born out of due time" (15:8). What had Paul that he had not received? He and the other apostles had received only because the Lord took them out of their error and unbelief, because the Lord gave them faith and joined them to his church, and because the Lord made them apostles. They did not make themselves to differ from the world, but Christ did.

Second, because of the Lord they also suffered. When Paul says that they are accounted as fools for Christ's sake, he refers to the gospel of Christ, the doctrine of Christ, and the life that the doctrine of Jesus Christ teaches to and demands of the disciples of Jesus Christ. Because of that doctrine and the preaching of it, the apostles were hated of all men. Paul did not say, "I have some good ideas for you," but he came with the gospel as gospel. The word was authoritative, declaring believe this and live, reject this and perish, so that one could not take it or leave it.

The cause of the suffering was especially the apostles' application of the word, which calls the church to suffer for Christ's sake in the world—what he calls "my ways which be in Christ, as I teach every where in every church" (4:17). No one is offended only by doctrine. No one is offended by election and reprobation and the antithesis, except when these doctrines are sharply applied. They are so applied not as mere ideas, but as the way of life demanded by the gospel, so that departing from them, one departs from Christ and his gospel. It is Christ in those doctrines as they require the church and the individual believer to conform themselves and their whole lives to Christ that brings about a sharp antithesis and enmity between church and world.

For Christ's sake is not the deepest reason for the exhibition of the apostles. The apostle expresses the deepest cause when he says, "For I think that God hath set forth us the apostles last" (v. 9). It was God's will that his apostles so existed in the world.

It was God's will that they be an exhibition for the whole church. God provided in the apostles a condemnation of the world because the world condemns the most honorable men in the church; God condemns the world because the world condemns Christ as he is present in the apostles and their doctrine.

God also provides an example of his grace and the effect of the gospel on a man's life in the world. It was God's will that the most honorable men be the most despised. It was his will that the apostles—in their high office and possessing the truth—not reign now, be full now, or be rich now, but that they be despised now in the world for the truth's sake, that they might be exalted in due time.

Following the Apostles

In his teaching that the exhibition of the apostles was for Christ's sake—the truth—and according to the will of God, the apostle also sharply admonishes the Corinthians' thinking that they reign now. In that they were not following either Christ or the will of God. "I write not these things to shame you, but as my beloved sons I warn you" (v. 14). This warning the apostle expresses in the biting and unprecedented irony in verses 9–10: "We are fools for Christ's sake…God has set forth us…last. But ye are wise in Christ."

When Paul calls the Corinthians "wise," he does not commend them. "Wise" means shrewd. When he says "in Christ," he refers to the truth, the doctrines, and their application. "You are shrewd, Corinthians, in the doctrines." Because they were shrewd they were rich, full, and reigned now as kings.

The apostle says, "Corinthians, in your confession of the truth and of Christ you display an unbecoming judiciousness and shrewdness. In your confession of the truth you carefully guard your standing, honor, and position in the world. In your confession of the truth you protect your bellies, backs, bank accounts, and businesses. You will suffer the loss of nothing for Christ's sake and incur no damage to yourselves for the sake of the truth. You know what to say and when to say it or not to say it, so that you deftly avoid all persecution for the truth's sake, and all the while you studiously appear to remain in Christ. It is not that you do not know the truth, but you are shrewd with the truth with an unbecoming and gospel-denying shrewdness. For you the presentation of the truth, that is, the garb and words with which you dress it up, are more important than the truth itself. You are extremely concerned about tone and not very concerned about the content at all. In that you depart from Christ and the example of your spiritual father."

In that too Paul addresses the thinking that they reign and are full now. Their unwillingness to suffer for Christ's sake was because they wanted comfortable lives in the world. They did not want to be rejected by the world. They did not want to be alone, where Israel's safety always lies. They wanted to enjoy the things and the relationships the world has to offer. They had lost sight of heaven and were living like the world. What is wrong with the union? If I don't join, I will not be able to feed my family. What is wrong with a little Sunday work, if it gets me a better-paying job? Why do I have to suffer such things in my family for this truth?

Although such thinking and behavior are shameful, Paul did not write those things to shame them, but to warn them. It was a shameful forsaking of Christ. It was shameful adorning of the tombs of the prophets by lip service to their words without following their examples of suffering. It was a shameful departure from the clearly revealed will of God.

Rather, Paul warns all the brethren against such a confession of the truth that they must say in the judgment, "Lord, I was wise in Christ. I was taught the truth, knew the truth, but refused to suffer the loss of a nickel for it. When the truth required me to give up my honor, standing, family, and friends, I hedged and was shrewd. When the truth required me to give up my business, job, food, and drink, I was shrewd. When the truth required me to give up my life, I was shrewd. When the truth required us as churches to stand alone and be the offscouring of the earth, we carefully crafted our statements to offend none and to be accepted of all." Let no man who is shrewd in Christ and in the confession of the truth think that he has not departed from the gospel, although he may in an official kind of way still confess it.

Over against that judicious, studied, and shrewd confession of Christ, Paul says, "Be ye followers of me" as one of the apostles whom God exhibited so that you might follow me (v. 16). Follow Paul's method, which is prominent in this book on love. In his warning to his beloved church he uses sarcasm and irony. That is astounding! The apostle would be harshly criticized today for his tone. He would be called unloving. The Holy Spirit honors Paul's method as love and employs it in his book on love: "As my beloved sons I warn you" (v. 14). His motivation for all his warnings, sharpness, and rebuke was love. That is a testimony to the church that she may not buy into the thinking that a sharp rebuke and irony and sarcasm are out of harmony with love.

What is true of the church's father is true of believing fathers. Let fathers and mothers take notice. If their sons walk in folly or in worldliness, or make a shrewd confession of the truth, a sharp rebuke in irony is appropriate and loving. Love means that a father is willing to do that. Failure so to warn and to call back from such a dangerous confession is not love, but hatred.

Follow the apostles in their doctrine. They are fathers in their doctrine. They have begotten every true church in the gospel. To be apostolic that church must follow the apostles' doctrine, which is the doctrine of the Reformed faith.

Follow the apostles in the confession of their doctrine, which was such a confession that they were willing to suffer for it. When Paul says, "God exhibited us last" and says, "Follow me," he teaches the believer and true church of Christ that they cannot have the truth without suffering. It is impossible. They cannot have the truth and a judicious confession of it, a confession of convenience, a confession that spares food and drink, standing, honor, and place in the world and among men. To follow the apostles means to follow them in their doctrine and their suffering for that doctrine.

To follow the apostles, then, means that for the sake of the truth we are willing to give up everything, even our lives. For the sake of the truth we are willing to give up our good names, to be reviled, to be hated, and to give up our food and drink. To walk in the way of love one must first have the love of the truth, which is one's love for God and for Christ revealed in the love of the truth. Here Paul speaks especially to the officebearer who must follow him in his singular fidelity and indefatigable zeal for the truth and proclamation of the gospel. Paul was an officebearer who called out his opponents who wanted to be held in great esteem in the church, but who studiously avoided suffering for Christ's sake and taught others the same.

The idea that the Christian church will Christianize the world, so that at the very least she can have a standing in the world—not to mention the Jewish dreams of those who would rule the whole planet—is absurd on the apostolic example. Those who strive after it do not strive after anything either apostolic or Christian, but anti-Christian. If anyone would have Christianized the world it would have been Paul, who labored more abundantly than all and besides could raise the dead! But which of the apostles died peacefully in his bed? Which of them was not beheaded like James and Paul, or crucified upside down like Peter? John died an old man, but in exile as one appointed to death.

Indeed, to have the apostolic truth means that the church and believer will likewise suffer for it because God will set her forth and make her a spectacle in the world and to angels and men, to be esteemed as fools for Christ's sake. That is the lesson and the warning to all the beloved brethren of the exhibition of the apostles.

By this lesson the apostle heads off the thinking that can afflict the church that she has arrived, that the battle for the truth is finished, that she can live on borrowed capital, and that she does not need to hear this or that because it is not a threat to her; or that she is rich and full as though she were already in heaven. Then she must remember the exhibition of the apostles. Remembering, she must be warned. Warned, she must heed Paul's exhortation, "I beseech you, be ye followers of me." Confess the truth boldly. Live it faithfully. Suffer for it willingly.

CHAPTER 14

THE EXERCISE OF
CHRISTIAN DISCIPLINE

1 Corinthians 5:1–5

1. *It is reported commonly that there is fornication among you, and such fornication as is not so much as named among the Gentiles, that one should have his father's wife.*
2. *And ye are puffed up, and have not rather mourned, that he that hath done this deed might be taken away from among you.*
3. *For I verily, as absent in body, but present in spirit, have judged already, as though I were present, concerning him that hath so done this deed,*
4. *In the name of our Lord Jesus Christ, when ye are gathered together, and my spirit, with the power of our Lord Jesus Christ,*
5. *To deliver such an one unto Satan for the destruction of the flesh, that the spirit may be saved in the day of the Lord Jesus.*

The apostle begins a new section in the book of 1 Corinthians in which he addresses specific situations that have troubled the church at Corinth. He ended the previous section with these words: "For the kingdom of God is not in word, but in power"

(4:20). By the contrast between "word" and "power" he does not mean preaching and power. Preaching of the cross of Christ is the power of God to save those who believe. Rather, he contrasts the vain and showy preaching of the false apostles and the Corinthians' shrewd confession with the infallible efficacy of the word of God preached by one who is his servant. Not being the gospel, the speech of the false apostles had no power. The proof of that was the current condition of the church of Corinth.

Paul already treated the preaching as an aspect of the kingdom and of its power. The preaching is a power of God to the church. It is the power to save and to communicate to ignorant and foolish men the wisdom of God. It is the power to forgive sins. It is the power to build up the church of Jesus Christ on the foundation of the apostles. It is the power to sanctify unholy men and women to be the holy temple of the triune God and his Spirit. It is the power to uphold them in suffering.

That power stands in sharp contrast with the fleshly pragmatism of the Corinthian ministers and the members of the congregation, to whom every text was a calculation, taking into account what they wanted to hear and discarding what they did not, a kind of preaching with man's wisdom and by man's words. Although that was attractive to them and appealed to their flesh, it was mere words, and that preaching led to a confession of the truth that was mere words too. The kingdom of God is not in word but in power, the power of faithful preaching.

In the last verse of chapter 4, the apostle refers to another power of the church of Jesus Christ: the power to discipline. Paul begins by asserting his authority and will to discipline: "What will ye? shall I come unto you with a rod, or in love, and in the spirit of meekness?" (v. 21). By "rod" he refers to church discipline. When Paul contrasts coming "with a rod" and coming "in love and the spirit of meekness," he does not say that his coming with the rod is out of hatred. The whole point of including this section on church discipline in the book on love is to establish that although it is a disagreeable necessity for the church, exercising discipline is walking in the way of love. Rather, by this contrast Paul means that his love toward the Corinthians, out of which he would discipline them if necessary, is more evident if he comes mildly to a repentant congregation. What father—which he was of the Corinthians in Christ—would rather show his love with the rod and would not much prefer to show his love during a pleasant time at the dinner table?

Verse 21, then, should be the first verse of chapter 5 and begin the section on discipline in the church. In this verse Paul establishes that he has the authority to discipline. Discipline is apostolic in the New Testament church. Christ, who called him, committed to him a rod with which to come to the refractory congregation. When he comes with a rod, he also has the will to discipline, so that if need be he will exercise that rod.

The apostle's will to discipline stands in sharp contrast to the Corinthians' lack of will to discipline. Evidence of the sorry state of affairs in Corinth, as it is always the evidence of a sorry state of affairs in the church, is that in Corinth discipline had ceased to function. Even for the grossest of sinners discipline had ceased to function.

That was serious because the exercise of Christian discipline is one of the marks of the church, whereby the true church is distinguished from the false. Paul points out the seriousness of the situation in verse 6: "Know ye not that a little leaven leaveneth the whole lump?" By her refusal to discipline, Corinth was threatening to fill herself with the same wickedness and was threatening her very status in the world as a true church of Jesus Christ. That is because discipline and the preaching are not only badges worn by the church, but they are also the means whereby the church is preserved as a true church of Jesus Christ in the world. The church that refuses to discipline is threatened by Christ, that he will come and take away her candlestick. He will remove her as true church of Christ (Rev. 2:5, 20). Paul calls the Corinthians to exercise this power of the kingdom of God "to deliver such an one unto Satan…that the spirit may be saved in the day of the Lord Jesus" (1 Cor. 5:5).

It cannot be overlooked that the call of the church to exercise discipline occurs in the book on love. That discipline, which many call unloving, view as unloving, and fail to exercise, the apostle calls love. He demands that in order to walk in the way of love the church must discipline. Refusing to discipline, the Corinthians showed that they had no love. The way of love and walking in the way of love by a true church of Jesus Christ, and by implication her members, is the exercise of Christian discipline. Exercising Christian discipline is the call of the apostle to Corinth and therefore to every true church of Jesus Christ in the world.

The Object of Christian Discipline

The object of Christian discipline is the church member. This is clear because the apostle speaks of a current member of the church whom the Corinthians would not put away from themselves. In verse 12 the apostle distinguishes the work of the church in discipline from his non-judgment of the world: "What have I to do to judge them also that are without?" The fact that Christian discipline can be exercised against the member of the church is explicit in every Reformed confession of faith when the believer promises to submit to church government. Included in that is the promise to submit to discipline.

This indicates the gravity of the sin committed by the church member who will not sit for discipline but asks for his membership papers and leaves. If anyone commits a sin and walks impenitently in that and discipline is exercised against him, the word of the apostle here is, "Sit for the discipline." If he does not, he aggravates his sin by a gross violation of and an impenitent trampling on the name of God that he took on his lips when he confessed his faith and promised to submit to church discipline.

One who refuses to sit for discipline has not excommunicated himself, since excommunication is an act of church discipline. Rather, his situation is worse. Sick and dying, he will not take the remedy. He leaves the church and adds to his sin that was the occasion of discipline. He is like a cancer patient to whom the doctor wants to apply the extreme remedy of chemotherapy, but the patient says, "No, I will not take it." Implied in the exercise of discipline is that the member must sit for the discipline.

This indicates the sin of the church that takes such a wicked person into her communion. By taking a noxious cancer into her communion, she declares that the disciplining church is no church and sets herself in proud opposition to the Lord himself, who works through the disciplining church.

Church discipline is not exercised against any member, or even a member who has fallen into gross sin but immediately repents. Rather, church discipline is exercised against the member who has fallen into sin and walks impenitently in that sin. In Corinth the man had committed "fornication as is not so much as named among the Gentiles, that one should have his father's wife" (v. 1). The member had violated the seventh commandment by sexual relations with his father's wife, not his biological mother but his stepmother, his father's second wife. That man not only did that once, but the language of text is that he was still involved sexually with his father's wife. He sinned grossly and impenitently lived in it.

The apostle shows that he does not mean to limit discipline just to the man in Corinth and to his particularly vile sin of fornication. Paul intends these principles of discipline to be applied broadly, because later he speaks of fornicators, covetous, extortioners, idolaters, drunkards, and railers (v. 11). Committing any sin and impenitently walking in that sin make a member of the church the object of church discipline.

It was not the fact that the Corinthians had among them a man who would actually commit that particularly gross form of fornication that called for the apostle's rebuke. Rather, the cause for the rebuke was the man's walking impenitently in the sin and the church's refusal to discipline that sinner. The refusal to discipline was rank because the sin was vile. This is what the apostle means by "ye...have not...mourned" (v. 2). The man was a member of the church and had fallen into gross sin. He walked in that sin impenitently, but the church had not mourned. The church did not mourn herself, and the members did not call the man to mourn, that is, to repent.

The man's gross, impenitent sin had become public: "It is reported commonly...among you" (v. 1). The object of Christian discipline is a member of the church who falls into sin and who by his impenitence makes it public. It is both the sin and the impenitence in that sin that makes one the object of discipline.

The Nature of Christian Discipline

Against that impenitent and now public sinner the apostle calls the church to exercise discipline. That discipline consists in the excommunication of the sinner by barring him from the supper of the Lord and from church membership. This is clear because Paul speaks of the church's removing him, of "tak[ing him] away from among you" (v. 2) and of "deliver[ing] such an one unto Satan for the destruction of the flesh" (v. 5). Both are references to church discipline. Furthermore, Paul speaks in verse 3 of a judgment, "I...have judged already," which is also a reference to discipline. By taking away and judgment, the apostle refers to the official decision of the church in which she judges a man who has fallen into sin to be impenitent and refuses that man the sacraments, the means of grace, and thus excludes him from the fellowship of the church. The church cuts him off from being a member in Christ's church.

The important question is, when does that take place? The apostle in these verses and later in the epistle makes clear that discipline takes place when the impenitent sinner is refused the sacraments. In chapter 11 the apostle brings up the matter of discipline again and speaks of the refusal of the Corinthian congregation to judge themselves, that is, to judge themselves regarding their coming to the table of the Lord (v. 31). That refusal to judge themselves involved their refusal to cut off from the fellowship of the table sinners who were well known. In chapter 5 this is powerfully implied in Paul's grounding of his doctrine of Christian discipline in the Old Testament feast of unleavened bread, a feast closely connected with the celebration of the passover and without which the passover was profaned, a point no Jew in the Corinthian congregation could miss (vv. 6–8).

That is also the answer of the Reformed faith. When is a person cut off? The Reformed faith says when he is refused the sacraments. Not final excommunication but the refusal of the sacraments is to cut a person off from the church, from fellowship with Christ, and from the means of grace. This is the teaching of Lord's Day 31, which in explaining the keys of the kingdom of heaven says that when sinners are "forbidden the use of the sacraments...they are excluded from the Christian church, and by God Himself from the kingdom of Christ."[1] Excommuni-

---

1 I follow the translation of answer 85 of the Heidelberg Catechism in *Confessions and Church Order*, 119. The translation in the more scholarly work of the church historian Philip Schaff is weak here: "are by them [the officers of the church] excluded from the holy Sacraments and the Christian communion, and by God himself from the kingdom of Christ." Schaff's translation makes the Catechism say that the exclusion from the sacraments is one step alongside exclusion from the Christian church, or excommunication. Schaff's translation obscures the important point made in the Catechism that the impenitent sinner is excluded from the church at the point of being excluded from the sacraments. This point is clear in the original German: "*von ihnen durch Verbietung der heiligen Sacramente aus der Christlichen Gemeine und von Gott selbst aus dem Reiche Christi werden ausgeschlossen*" (Philip Schaff, ed., *The Creeds of Christendom with a History and Critical Notes*, 6th ed., 3 vols. [New York: Harper & Row, 1931; repr., Grand Rapids, MI: Baker Books, 2007], 3:338). The official Dutch translation made by the Synod of Dordrecht says the same thing: "*van henlieden door het verbieden der Sacramenten uit de Christelijke gemeente, en van God zelven uit he Rijk van Christus gesloten worden*" (F. L. Rutgers, *De Berijmde Psalmen, met eenige Gezangen*, 1913 [New Delhi: Isha Books, 2013], 27).

cation comes as the final seal on the exclusion of those sinners from the church of Jesus Christ.

This point has two practical applications. First, regarding a member of the church who has been placed under discipline and refused the sacraments, he may leave and the church will grant him his papers, but he stands outside the kingdom of heaven. Second, it speaks to the attitude of the church and of the individual members of the church toward those who have been so set outside the kingdom of heaven but ask for their membership papers. Those cases will never proceed to excommunication, but the church and the members of the church may not have the attitude, "Since he has not been excommunicated, we may fellowship with him." He has been refused the sacraments and stands outside the kingdom. Therefore, the attitude of the church and church members must be that they have no fellowship with him. If that matter is known only in the consistory and such a person asks for his papers and leaves the church, the consistory has the duty to make it known to the congregation for its benefit. The congregation must know that such a person has been set outside the kingdom of heaven, so that the members may know how to treat such a person.

Christian discipline exercised against the impenitent sinner is the power of the church to exclude someone from her membership, to exclude one also from the sacraments and from the means of grace, and to remove one from the kingdom of heaven. He or she is no longer a member of the church. That also is instructive to us regarding a member who leaves while under discipline or has been excommunicated. Whether he leaves after having been officially refused the sacraments, or whether he leaves after having been excommunicated, he may take his papers and another church may wickedly receive him into its fellowship, but the judgment stands. He is not a member of Christ's church. He cannot be. Discipline has excluded him.

That this is the nature of Christian discipline also makes

Christian discipline spiritual and distinguishes it from the corporal punishments of the state.

The Power of Christian Discipline

Because discipline sets the impenitent sinner outside the church, he is delivered unto Satan for the destruction of the flesh. The work of Satan is to destroy flesh. If a man is a hypocrite, he is only flesh and will be destroyed eternally. If he is a child of God, his flesh will be destroyed, but his spirit will be saved through his repentance. This is the other side of discipline and also its power. Delivering one judicially and officially in the name of Christ over to the power of Satan, discipline is the instrument for the destruction of the sinner's flesh. By destroying his flesh, discipline serves the purpose that his "spirit may be saved in the day of the Lord Jesus" (v. 5). One is either a member of Christ's church—not hypocrites, who are only ever members outwardly and spiritually belong to Satan—or one has been delivered to Satan. If a man is set outside the church, he is delivered into the hands of that malignant spirit and becomes his toy, as a cat plays with his captured mouse.

Outside the kingdom of heaven, outside the church, Satan rules with an iron fist. He is the god of this world. Read the front page of the newspaper, turn on the television, or listen to the radio, and you will understand that Satan is the god of this world. This refers to the power God gave him over human beings when Adam fell in the garden. God delivered the whole human race over to Satan, and he may ride man as a wild man rides a beast. He drives man, holds men in this or that sin at his pleasure, and ruins him in those sins.

In his church Christ delivers his people from that. To be members of the church and to be regenerated and sanctified is to be free from Satan's dominion. To have access to the preaching and the sacraments as members of the church is the means of grace by which God preserves his people in the world.

Discipline hands a man over to Satan. One's deliverance over to Satan is "for the destruction of the flesh" (v. 5). This refers to God's giving a sinner over to his sin. Sometimes this is very visible. It is not uncommon even to see a change in the person's face and demeanor. There are other visible signs. If he is a drug addict, he fries his brain. If he is an alcoholic, he destroys his body. If he is a man given to sex, he contracts a sexually transmitted disease or ruins himself in some other way by his fornication. This is a very literal destruction of the flesh.

The flesh is also destroyed spiritually. When the church delivers one over to Satan, the flesh that is destroyed is his old man. In his sin and impenitence his old man was ruling and was running his life. Discipline—handing him over to Satan—will be the instrument to ruin and break the old man of sin.

This means, first, that when the church disciplines she must not be under any illusions about what she is doing. She is giving one of her members officially and judicially into the hands of that evil spirit. That is what discipline does. When a man is set outside the kingdom of God, there is no other place for him to go except to the kingdom of darkness. The ruler there is Satan. That sinner will be very miserable indeed.

Second, when the church hands a sinner over to Satan, she should not be surprised when she sees unbelievable hardness in the disciplined sinner as Satan latches on to him and drives him in his sin. This does not mean that prior to the official sentence of the church that hands the sinner over to Satan he was not already in Satan's power. He was because Satan dominated in his life. However, the ecclesiastical sentence that officially hands one over to Satan has a salutary purpose.

Third, the church must believe that God is sovereign in that discipline and over its effect. Here we see the grace of God in the discipline of the elect but in himself impenitent sinner. Satan destroys flesh and soul of the reprobate. With his elect people God gives Satan the right only to destroy the flesh. The sovereign in discipline is God. Satan is an instrument in his hand.

Because of this reality, excommunication must be seen as a remedy. This is the apostle's point. Discipline uses the destruction of the flesh by Satan for the salvation of the sinner's soul. This can easily be understood. If a man has cancer, there are many remedies, and the doctors use them. But if the cancer does not respond, the doctors come to the extreme remedy, the most potent of drugs, and the one they had been saving for just such an occasion. The drug itself is dangerous, and if it does not work, the cancer will kill the person. Discipline is a remedy, the last one.

The sinner who professes to know and to learn from Jesus Christ, to hear his word and to have his wisdom, shows by his impenitent sin that he is not learning from the word. The preaching and the sacraments are the usual medicine God uses to work in us faith and repentance. But this man despises the admonitions and all the word of God. The church must hand him to Satan.

This addresses a certain misunderstanding regarding discipline. The misunderstanding is that the church can carry out the judgment of excommunication, refusing the sacraments and finally setting one outside the church, and then encourage the man to sit in the back of church. This is not the same as the man in hardness flaunting the church's discipline and coming to church to show his hardness. The church service is a public gathering. The congregation can be warned in that instance. Rather, the church says to the excommunicated sinner, "Having now set you outside the church, we tell you to come back to church and sit in the back." It is like a king who sets a subject outside the kingdom for rebellion and then says, "You may sit in my gates." The apostle says, "Take that wicked person away from among you." By discipline the church takes him away from the church and delivers him to Satan. That is also how he will be helped: not by hearing a good sermon, a good many of which he has already refused to hear, but by Satan's destroying his flesh.

"The kingdom of heaven is not in word, but in power" (4:20). That is some power that God has given to the church: the church may make a judgment over a man and say about him, "You have no part in this church, in the kingdom of God, or in heaven so long as you remain impenitent." As a power, discipline is effectual. The flesh will be destroyed by Satan. If a man is a reprobate, he will be destroyed body and soul, but if he is one of God's elect, the flesh only will be destroyed, that the soul be saved in the day of Christ.

Discipline Is the Church's Work

That power is not the power of any individual but of the church. The apostle indicates that when he says, "When ye are gathered together" (5:4). He has already judged, and he calls the Corinthians to judge as the church and to begin this work. It is given by Christ to believers and their seed as a church of Jesus Christ. They have the right to judge. They alone have the Spirit by which that judgment is made.

The church exercises judgment through a consistory. "Gathered together" does not refer to doing discipline in the public assembly for worship in the church. Paul has his eye specifically on the consistory, the gathering of two or three or more to carry out the will of Jesus Christ. The consistory, men duly elected and installed by believers into their office, has the right and the power to make a judgment.

Yet discipline does not begin with the consistory, and it is not done exclusive of congregational involvement. The apostle makes this clear when he addresses not only the consistory but the church, and he makes a pointed application to the congregation about fellowshiping with the impenitent sinner.

The Reformed faith honors this when announcements about discipline are made, when the congregation is exhorted to pray for and admonish the brother, and when the form for excommunication is read. Discipline is always carried out by the congregation. Discipline is not strictly a consistorial business. The apostle will not let us say that discipline begins with the consistory but puts the responsibility on the individual church member. He says that discipline begins with the members of the church when he says, "Ye…have not rather mourned" (v. 2).

First, he refers to the spiritual attitude of the members of the church toward sin, any sin, and by implication toward the sin of the man who needed to be disciplined. Their spiritual attitude was all wrong. They had lost sight of sin and of how serious sin is in the sight of God. So they did not mourn over their own sins. They were living unrepentantly. They did not daily ask for forgiveness.

This heads off a charge against a church that will discipline, that she is proud and thinks she is better than everyone else. The will to discipline stems from deep mourning, deepest humility, and a deep knowledge of a God who is highly offended by sin and of the greatness of his wrath against sin. Mourning over sin—all sin, but the believer's sin in particular—is love toward God whom we have offended and must be called love inasmuch as sin is a manifestation of hatred toward God. Discipline in the church begins in the heart of the spiritual man or woman who mourns for sin. This is the essential thing for the church's discipline. The church must be spiritual and full of the glory of the Lord and deeply concerned for his honor.

If the church is proud, she will not discipline. Pride is the very opposite of mourning for sin. Pride is not taking sin seriously, excusing it, or calling it by a hundred other names except *sin*. If a church categorizes sin as excusable, a bad habit, a syndrome, a disorder, a mental problem, or a lack of intelligence, she will never discipline. This is what the apostle says: "Ye are puffed up" (v. 2). He refers to the pride of the Corinthians in which they did not mourn, were carnal, and were interested more in their own earthly well-being and the earthly well-being of their families and their friends than for the honor and glory of God. The man or church who will not discipline the impenitent is proud.

In their pride they did not discipline, and they also congratulated themselves on their tolerance. The apostle speaks of this in verse 6: "Your glorying is not good." They said, "We are very loving, because we allow sin in the church and are sympathetic to sinners."

Second, their lack of mourning showed that they had no love for the impenitent sinner. The apostle accuses them of a lack of love for the sinner, for the church, and for Christ. Discipline begins with the proper relationship of love between fellow members of the church who are willing to mourn for one another and, walking in love, to admonish one another. The poor sinner is a sheep whom the roaring lion has snatched. He is living a wicked life, by which he is already outside the kingdom. The Corinthians would not mourn. They congratulated themselves on how tolerant they were. They walked with him arm in arm toward the cliff, at the bottom of which yawned hell. It was an utter failure to walk in love, which "is not puffed up" and "rejoiceth not in iniquity" (13:4, 6). Discipline begins with the members' mourning for one another and their love for one another in which they exercise the power God gave them to admonish and at last to bring a man to the church and to deliver him over to Satan for the destruction of his flesh in order to save his spirit in the day of Christ. Anything less than that is not love, but hatred.

Paul says to the Corinthians, "Ye have not mourned, and that is why you will not discipline." If discipline becomes the exclusive work of the elders, there will be no discipline in the church. That is because sins are being hidden within marriages, homes, families, or groups of friends. That is also because these unspiritual people elect equally unspiritual elders who will not discipline. That is also because when the church does muster the spiritual courage to discipline and lay hold on some notorious sinner, the unmourning and unloving family and friends try to protect the impenitent sinner and in various ways cover him and frustrate the work of the church.

If a man's attitude toward a family member who walks in impenitent sin is that it is a consistorial matter, discipline as a function of the church has effectively ceased in that church. That attitude is fundamentally no different than Corinth's. It knowingly and grossly tolerates wickedness in the church that has not become public knowledge. Along with that toleration will be the insane glorying of Corinth about toleration and love, which is not love because it rejoices in iniquity. Discipline cannot begin with the consistory. It must begin with the members of the church. When it does and we do our duties regarding one another, the sinner is taken to the church, and the church carries out its judgment.

The Spirituality of Discipline

Discipline so carried out is the work of Christ in his church by his Spirit. The apostle draws attention to the spirituality of discipline by the phrases "present in spirit" (5:3), "my spirit, with the power of our Lord Jesus Christ," and "in the name of our Lord Jesus Christ" (v. 4). These phrases refer to the power behind discipline, the Spirit of the risen Lord, the one who motivates and works discipline in the church.

The Spirit is present where Christ is present, and Christ is present where the truth is present. "The name of our Lord Jesus Christ" refers to Christ's truth as it demands the discipline of the impenitent sinner. The toleration of impenitent sinners in the fellowship of the church denies the truth of Christ. Christ and impenitent sinners cannot coexist in the same church. If they are allowed, Christ must be cast out. If they are allowed, Christ will be cast out. Christ in his church by his Spirit motivates discipline. Christ is resolved on discipline, and where he is present, there the church will discipline.

"In the name of our Lord Jesus Christ" also refers to the right of the church to discipline in Christ's name. Although the discipline is done by the church, it is not the church that disciplines, and although she wields that power, she does so instrumentally:

"in the name of our Lord Jesus Christ." This is why discipline is a power. What the church binds on earth is bound in heaven. What the church looses on earth is loosed in heaven. Christ carries on discipline in his church.

Christ does that by his Spirit. "The power of the Lord Jesus Christ" refers to the Spirit of Christ as the power in and behind discipline, which means that discipline is a spiritual activity. Only spiritual men will discipline. This is the meaning of "my spirit." That same Spirit was present in the church of Corinth. The will to discipline came from the Spirit of God, the Spirit that a spiritual man alone has.

Discipline is spiritual because only a spiritual church will do it. Moved by the Spirit to mourn for sin and for the sinner, a spiritual church will also in love discipline him. This is the opposite of the very unspiritual reaction to sin and the sinner, "We all sin every day." This view regarding sin reveals a palpable lack of the Spirit, and where that view is present no discipline will be carried out even for the grossest sins. The spiritual church understands the power of the grace of God to forgive sins, to turn from sins, and to change lives by the Spirit.

Discipline is also spiritual because the one who stands behind it is the Spirit. Why does that judgment of the church—you stand outside the kingdom—have such power? What explains the power to cut off from the church, the power to deliver over to Satan, the power to destroy flesh, the power to exclude from the kingdom? The Spirit of Christ ratifies the sentence. He binds on the conscience of the sinner that he is cut off from the church and the hope of salvation and has been delivered over to Satan and the destruction of the flesh except he repents. Furthermore, the Spirit alone can work repentance by discipline. This is his remedy to grant repentance unto salvation to his elect people. Because God never takes his Holy Spirit from his elect people even in their deep and melancholy falls by which they grieve the Holy Spirit, discipline is a remedy.

The Purpose of Christian Discipline

Discipline has a salutary purpose. It is not done by a disagreeable church. It cannot be done by a proud church. It is done by a spiritual church of spiritual men and women walking in love to save a sinner. That is what Paul says: "That [in order that or for the purpose that] the spirit may be saved in the day of the Lord Jesus" (v. 5).

This is not the only purpose of discipline. Discipline is also for the church because it removes a rotten and incurable member. That is the apostle's point when he brings up "leaven" in verse 6. The reference is to the passover and to the feast of unleavened bread that followed it, during which the Israelites were to have no leaven in their bread. Paul applies that to the church's discipline. The sinner whom the church proudly refuses to discipline is as leaven that spreads through the whole lump until it is all leavened. The warning to the church that proudly will not discipline and congratulates herself on her tolerance is that your church will be leavened by the sin. It will spread throughout your church and will eventually destroy your church until Christ comes and removes his candlestick and you become a false church wholly hostile to the gospel, devoid of the Spirit's saving presence, and turning the instrument of discipline into oppressive inquisition against the godly who rebuke you for your covetousness and idolatry. That same warning can be issued against the family that will not put out the leaven from among them: that impenitent sinner will work you until he destroys your family.

Thus when Paul says, "In order that the soul may be saved," he does not teach that everyone who comes under discipline will be saved. Regarding the hypocrite who is exposed by discipline and who dies excommunicated or with the sentence of the church refusing him the sacraments, he dies outside the kingdom of heaven. If discipline means anything at all, it means that Christ does discipline through his church on earth and he does not undo it after death. Christ does that to rid the church of a rotten and incurable member who was cancer in his church.

This reality is the reason only a spiritual church can discipline. That thought is intolerably disagreeable to any other church. The Lord is not pleased by discipline to work repentance in everyone who comes under discipline. In this case the church may rest content that she has done the Lord's will to exclude the sinner. Discipline is not general in its saving effect, any more than the preaching or the sacraments are general. Discipline is particular, and its saving effect does not depend on the will of man, but depends on the grace and will of God alone.

Because discipline is done in the name of our Lord Jesus Christ, that is, on the authority of Jesus Christ and exercising the power of Jesus Christ, discipline honors Jesus Christ. Since it is done in Christ's name, it honors God. The impenitent sinner violates the law of God by his wicked life and obstinacy. In love for Christ and God the church disciplines. The church that refuses to discipline dishonors Christ. Any man or member who stands in the way of or attempts to frustrate or undermine discipline stands in the way of Christ, his Spirit, and God, and by that he reveals that he is so unspiritual, proud, and unloving that he will oppose God himself.

Besides, by both his impenitence and the church's refusal to discipline him they blaspheme the name of God. The apostle implies this when he speaks of the church's refusal to discipline for a sin that is "not so much as named among the Gentiles" (v. 1). When the world sees that sin is tolerated in the church, what do people say? "Look what grace has the power to do. It makes people worse than us," and they blaspheme God. The church that disciplines gives no ground for that blasphemy.

Discipline is also for the benefit of the sinner. Oftentimes, the charge against the church that disciplines is that she is terribly unloving toward sinners.

In response the church may ask with a little irony, "How

loving is it to allow in the church the sin and confusion that a man has his father's wife, at which sin even the world blushes?" Expanding the example, she may ask, "How loving it is to allow the obscenity of divorce and remarriage to run rampant in the church, so that a man kicks his wife of twenty years to the back pew and ostentatiously sits in the front pew with his new wife, while the minister preaches about love and they cover the altar of God with tears? How loving is it to allow the extortionate and covetous member of the union—who intimidates, murders, destroys, pickets, threatens, and drives away business from the child of God on Monday through Friday, rebelling against God's authority—to sit in your pew and your elder's bench on Sunday and claim the grace of God as cover for his maliciousness? How loving is it to allow a man to destroy his family by his drunkenness, while no one says anything for twenty years? How loving is it to allow a sinner to go on supposing he is in the kingdom of God, about whom God says, 'If you walk in that way and die in that way, you are going to hell'? How loving is it to place our arms around him, invite him into our fellowship or make him a member of our church, and congratulate ourselves on our tolerance while God is against him?" That is about as loving as hikers who see another hiker running toward a cliff but never warn him of his impending fall. That is no love at all, but a malicious hatred.

The church that will not discipline cannot claim love for sinners. That church hates the sinner, because discipline is a remedy for sinners to destroy their flesh that their spirit may be saved in the day of Christ. The church that will not discipline and those individuals who interfere with the church's discipline have that sinner's blood on their heads.

The church that loves sinners disciplines, so that their spirits might be saved in the day of Christ. That is another charge against those who will not discipline: they are shortsighted and ignorant. For the sake of a few days of earthly pleasure or for the sake of a few days of earthly fellowship with a man, they are willing that he spend eternity in hell. Not only is their failure to discipline no love at all, but it is selfish besides.

It is walking in the way of love to exercise discipline: for the glory of God in Christ, for the purity of his church, and for the salvation of sinners taken captive by Satan.

CHAPTER 15

PURGING OUT THE OLD LEAVEN

1 Corinthians 5:6–8; Leviticus 23:6–8

---

6. *Your glorying is not good. Know ye not that a little leaven leaveneth the whole lump?*
7. *Purge out therefore the old leaven, that ye may be a new lump, as ye are unleavened. For even Christ our passover is sacrificed for us:*
8. *Therefore let us keep the feast, not with old leaven, neither with the leaven of malice and wickedness; but with the unleavened bread of sincerity and truth.*

6. *And on the fifteenth day of the same month is the feast of unleavened bread unto the Lord: seven days ye must eat unleavened bread.*
7. *In the first day ye shall have an holy convocation: ye shall do no servile work therein.*
8. *But ye shall offer an offering made by fire unto the Lord seven days: in the seventh day is an holy convocation: ye shall do no servile work therein.*

To impress on the Corinthians—the church—the necessity of Christian discipline as the way of love and the badness of glorying in their false love and ungodly toleration, the apostle calls the Corinthians to keep the feast of unleavened bread: "Therefore

let us keep the feast" (1 Cor. 5:8). The reference is to the Old Testament feast of unleavened bread, one of the seven major feasts
that Israel celebrated every year. The details of these feasts are
found in Leviticus 23. The city of Corinth had a very large Jewish
population, and the church of Corinth probably had many Jews
in it. The apostle's reference to an Old Testament feast would have
been easily understandable to the Jews in his audience and easily explainable to the rest. This call to keep the feast is not a call
to purge out actual leaven and to make unleavened cakes and eat
them, but to keep the fulfillment of that feast in the exercise of
Christian discipline by purging out impenitent sinners.

The apostle also brings up the feast of passover, another of
the seven annual feasts. That is because there was an inseparable
connection in the Old Testament between passover and the feast
of unleavened bread. The one could not be celebrated without the
other, the celebration of the one involved the celebration of the
other, and defiling one defiled the other. There could be no feast
of unleavened bread without the feast of passover. Because there
was passover there must also be a feast of unleavened bread.

The indispensable connection between those two feasts
teaches that there is an inseparable connection between redemption in the cross of Jesus Christ and holiness guided by the law of
God. Holiness—consecration to God in all good works and separation from all uncleanness—is the fruit of Christ's redemption
and is inseparably connected with the forgiveness of sins. The
redeemed church is holy. This is because the cross of Christ is the
power to make holy. The power of Christ's cross makes an unholy
people walk in holiness.

It is this close connection that the apostle draws attention to
when he grounds the call to keep the feast of unleavened bread
in the sacrifice of Christ our passover. The holiness purchased by
the cross of Christ and applied to the people of God was typi-
fied by the feast of unleavened bread. The apostle shows too that
this is his main interest when his exhortation is, "Let us keep the

feast...with the unleavened bread of sincerity and truth" (1 Cor. 5:8). God commanded the Israelites to eat unleavened bread for seven days during the feast of unleavened bread. Because they had been delivered from Egypt and into fellowship with God by the blood of the lamb, their entire lives were to be holy, not merely one day.

One aspect of keeping the feast of unleavened bread was the calling of every Israelite to purge out the old leaven. It is this aspect of the feast to which the apostle especially points in his stirring call to exercise church discipline.

The Feast of Unleavened Bread

The feasts of unleavened bread and passover were both instituted by God for the Old Testament church of Israel in remembrance of their deliverance from Egypt. They were distinct feasts, each with its own significance, but also closely and inseparably related. From the beginning God commanded the celebration of the feast of unleavened bread as part of the passover celebration. It was not merely an historical coincidence that the same night the Israelites celebrated the first passover in Egypt, they were driven out with such haste that their bread was unleavened and consequently they had to eat the passover with unleavened bread. Unleavened bread was required for the celebration of the passover by the law of God from the institution of the feast and ever after, as Exodus 12:15 makes clear: "Seven days shall ye eat unleavened bread."

The institution of the feast of unleavened bread was repeated in Leviticus 23 as one of seven annual feasts of the nation of Israel. The institution of the feast was repeated again by Moses in Deuteronomy 16. The Bible records the celebration of the feast by the returning exiles in Ezra 6:22.

Understanding the symbolism of leaven is central to understanding the typology and significance of the feast of unleavened bread.[1] Leaven was a lump of old dough that had fermented and soured. Today we would call it a yeast sponge. It is a living, breathing organism that must be fed daily and cared for, so that when the baker makes dough he can add a small piece of the old leaven to his batch of new dough. The leaven works through the dough until the lump is thoroughly leavened.

To keep the feast of unleavened bread it was necessary for Israel to purge out leaven. About keeping the feast God says in Exodus 12:15, 19–20: "Even in the first day ye shall put away leaven out of your houses...Seven days shall there be no leaven found in your houses...Ye shall eat nothing leavened; in all your habitations shall ye eat unleavened bread." Verse 20 is not a repetition of verse 19, which instructs regarding Israel's houses. The word "habitations" in verse 20 should be translated as "assemblies," that is, the public gatherings of the Israelites throughout the feast of unleavened bread. Deuteronomy 16:4 makes the command more comprehensive: "There shall be no leavened bread seen with thee in all thy coast seven days." The Israelites had to purge out leaven from their houses, their assemblies, and all their coasts, so that the land was free of leaven for seven days. It was an individual, a family, and a corporate duty of the nation of Israel.

The New Testament Reality of Leaven

Leaven is an Old Testament type of sin.

The scriptures are full of references to sin as leaven in the church. Jesus warned his disciples in Matthew 16:6, "Take heed and beware of the leaven of the Pharisees and of the Sadducees." In Mark 8:15 he added, "and of the leaven of Herod." Matthew 16:12

---

1 Typology is the study of the things that God ordained in the old dispensation to be shadows of later new-dispensational realities. God's covenant is one and unchangeable, and his dealings with his people are the same in both the old and new dispensations. In the old dispensation, before the coming of Christ and his Spirit and the church's spiritual maturity in the new dispensation, God dealt with his people as children and thus with pictures.

explains that Jesus spoke "of the doctrine of the Pharisees and of the Sadducees."

The false doctrine of the Pharisees—works-righteousness— was leaven. That doctrine is present wherever salvation by sovereign grace is denied and salvation by the work or the will of the sinner is approved. Tolerate that false doctrine in any form and leaven is allowed into the church.

The leaven of the Sadducees was their antinomian, worldly, and unbelieving lives. Those wicked lives were the direct result of their Epicurean doctrine that denied heaven, hell, spirits, the resurrection of the dead, and the final judgment. That carnal doctrine led to carnal lives. The Sadducees' error was antinomianism in all its forms, which teaches that believers are saved by grace to do wickedness, that the church is delivered to sin, and that she may sin in order that grace may abound. This is rife today in the church world, and I give only one example of this thinking. It is present when the church tells the adulterous member who has divorced his wife and married another to confess his sin to the church, but his confession does not include ending the adulterous marriage. The excuse for that wickedness is that there is grace and forgiveness. Grace is used to excuse and to tolerate sin, sin that is gross as it was in Corinth, so that the church in fact says, "We are delivered to do this wickedness." That church also prides itself—is puffed up—with its ungodly toleration. Included in the leaven of the Sadducees was also their theological liberalism that denied all the cardinal truths of scripture.

The leaven of Herod was that of the ungodly reprobate in the sphere of the church. Herod was petty, vain, and vindictive. Caesar—no schoolboy himself—famously said that it was better to be Herod's pig than his son. One had a better chance of living in that arrangement. Among his sins was his divorce of his wife and remarriage to the wife of his brother Philip. John the Baptist rebuked Herod, and Herod killed John.

The apostle calls leaven "the leaven of malice and wickedness" (1 Cor. 5:8). In the church malice and wickedness take two basic forms. There is the leaven of false doctrine, which is maintaining doctrines contrary to the Christian faith. There is also the leaven of a wicked and impenitent life, which is maintaining practices contrary to the Christian faith.

Paul calls leaven "malice" because he refers to the old man of sin whose principle sin is hatred of God and the neighbor and who resides yet in the believer after his regeneration and always threatens his holiness. Leaven is called "wickedness" because the old man is the source of nothing good but only of evil, so that as an evil root the old man gives rise to the weeds of wickedness in the life of the believer. This is the opposite of what believers become in Christ: "ye are unleavened" and "a new lump" (v. 7). In this verse the believer is also called "old leaven," because he still has the old man from the original lump in Adam. He is yet in his flesh what he was before being incorporated into Christ. The leaven is his old man of sin, his evil lusts, and his works.

Further, he says this in connection with the situation in Corinth of the man who was living in fornication with his father's wife. The church did not discipline him for living in that gross fornication but allowed him to be a member, and the people fellowshiped with him and defended him. In this they gloried. Paul says, "Your glorying is not good" (v. 6). The apostle means that the leaven of sin so puffed them up that they viewed their unrighteous toleration of that sinner as holy and loving. Paul means also that *the man* as he lived in sin is leaven. The impenitent sinner is leaven. Those who take wicked and impenitent persons into or refuse to put them away from their church and their company or companionship will find to their great hurt that they are leaven. Therefore, the Spirit says, "Put away from among yourselves that wicked person" (v. 13).

Purging Out Leaven

The church therefore is called to put away leaven (v. 8). The reality of purging out leaven is putting away sin and impenitent sinners from the fellowship and company of the church through discipline and refusing to fellowship with them in one's life. Basic to this is that believers do this personally in their own hearts, lives, houses, and fellowship. This is why in calling the church to discipline and so to put leaven in the form of the impenitent sinner from her assembly and fellowship, Paul makes a general calling to church members to do this in their own lives. The church member who is so unspiritual as to refuse to put away leaven in the form of sin and impenitent sinners from his or her own heart, life, and fellowship will never muster the spiritual strength to do that in the church proper. The corollary is also true: if the church in her members is full of associations with sin and impenitent sinners, the church will also be that way. Even more, by virtue of those ungodly associations the church is leavened in the leavening of her membership.

To put away leaven is first a personal call to the believer. Some try to evade the meaning and calling of the apostle in the whole chapter to discipline and thus attempt to overturn and undermine the work of discipline in the church by making an illegitimate and unfounded distinction between what the church does officially in discipline and what a believer does in his own life. Paul makes clear in the chapter that he not only calls the church to discipline, but also calls the individual member "not to keep company" with the impenitent sinner, "no not to eat," and to "put away from among yourselves [not merely the church institute] that wicked person" (vv. 11, 13).

That calling to the believer involves his purging out the leaven in his own heart. Purging "out...the old leaven...of malice and wickedness" (vv. 7–8) is the same as crucifying the old man of sin, his lusts, and his works. The believer is called to be spiritually sensitive to sin, to its ugliness and hatefulness to God. It is the call to recognize sin in his life, the call to know himself as he really is—holy—and thus also to be sorry for sins and lusts, to repent of the sins, and daily to flee to the cross of Jesus Christ for forgiveness. It is the careful guarding of his life against the influences of the world.

That calling to the believer also involves his purging out wicked persons from his life, associations, and fellowship. The apostle makes this clear when he makes leaven not merely impenitent sinners but malice and wickedness in the heart. There will be no purging in the church through discipline if leaven is not first purged in the hearts and lives of the children of God. How can the church discipline an adulterer if the church members hang out with him, or other adulterers, every week at their gatherings? How will the church warn the impenitent adulterer of his impending doom if the members invite him, or other adulterers, to sit around the dinner table and say nothing to him, or to them, of their sin, the wickedness of their lives, and God's judgment to come? Then added to the wickedness of the association is the wicked excuse that the associations are all under the name of grace, love, and forgiveness, as if such wickedness has anything at all to do with God's grace, love, and forgiveness.

Second, when God commanded in Deuteronomy 16:4, "There shall be no leavened bread seen with thee in all thy coast seven days," the Old Testament type indicated that the call to purge out leaven also includes the organic life of the church. The calling is to keep out sin and impenitent sinners from her life as church not only institutionally, but also organically, not only in her church membership rolls, but also in her societies, schools, boards, and from all that belongs to her life as God's church in the world. For instance, there could be no excuse for the admittance of a labor union member to the school society or enrollment in the school on the ground that his church does not recognize that sin as sin. By virtue of his impenitent continuance in the rebellion, murder, idolatry, profanity, and covetousness of his labor union membership, he is leaven and must not be permitted in the church institute, in the school association, or in the school enrollment.

The call to purge out leaven is to the instituted church of Jesus Christ, each member and through her elders to the whole church, officially to exercise discipline by purging out the leaven of false doctrine and impenitent sinners. That was clear in the Old Testament type when the law required purging leaven from Israel's "habitations," or the assemblies (Ex. 12:20). It is also clear in the apostle's pointed application of the calling to keep the feast of unleavened bread specifically to the situation of Corinth and her failure to discipline. Church discipline, arising organically out of the spiritual church and exercised according to the command of Christ, is keeping the feast of unleavened bread. Failure to discipline, organically and institutionally, is blatant violation of the law of God, a great failure to love the Lord with all our heart, mind, soul, and strength, and failure to keep the feast. Paul grounds discipline in the law and thus makes it a matter of love, as Christ himself said: "If ye love me, keep my commandments" (John 14:15).

To keep the feast of unleavened bread the church must put away the leaven of the impenitent sinner. Put him away officially by discipline. Put him away organically in the life of the congregation. Do not let him come to the gatherings. Do not have him over for dinner. The impenitent sinner is leaven in the church, and he must be put away by discipline. Purge out the old leaven and keep the feast of unleavened bread.

The Reasons for Purging Leaven

The apostle gives two powerful reasons for purging out the old leaven.

First, sin and impenitent sinners—leaven—must be put away because of the nature of leaven. Leaven stands for sin as a defiling power that thoroughly corrupts. The apostle makes this point in

1 Corinthians 5:6 with a rhetorical question: "Know ye not that a little leaven leaveneth the whole lump?" This is a proverb taken from the fact that a tiny piece of leaven placed in a lump of dough works itself through until the whole lump of dough is thoroughly leavened. Similar are the proverbs, "Bad company corrupts good manners"; "A rotten apple spoils the whole bushel"; and "The principle thoroughly works itself through." The point of the proverb is that leaven is a power that works itself through the whole lump into which it is placed.

Sin is a power of corruption and a principle that establishes itself and works through in all of its implications. False doctrine starts very small, but soon all the implications of it are worked out and worked out in the entire church. This is why some man cannot believably defend his membership in a church that teaches false doctrine by saying, "But I do not believe those things." He is the dough, the false doctrine is the leaven, and it is working slowly but inextricably on that church, that man, and his family. Unholiness starts small but works itself through the whole church.

Leaven in whatever form it takes, whether false doctrine or sin, corrupts and corrupts thoroughly. If the church lets one divorced and remarried person sit in her pews and with the members at their tables and by that speaks comfortably to him and grants him easy access to heaven, then the church will be full of that in a short while and with more violations of the seventh commandment besides. Any preaching about that wickedness will be easily suffocated to death.

This proverbial nature of leaven is true of the believer's associations, friends, and fellowships. Leaven present in his family and associations in the form of sin and impenitent sinners, who if they were members in his church would be under discipline, is leaven that also comes into the church through that disobedient member who will not purge out the old leaven. It comes into the church in the form of powerful, personal, and relentless pressures on the minister and the elders not to preach or speak about specific false doctrines or sins of life. If my family is full of union members with whom I am on good, friendly terms over their union membership, I will become angry and cause trouble when the minister preaches against that wickedness. If my family is full of divorced and remarried members with whom I am on good, comfortable terms regardless of and perhaps because of their wickedness, I will be highly offended when the minister preaches against that.

That leaven leavens the whole lump was obvious in Corinth. The fornicator was already having his effect, and Paul pointed that out. The church would not discipline the impenitent sinner, and Paul says that the members were "puffed up" as a lump of dough (v. 2). That puffing up was the effect of that leavening sinner, and it took the form of their "glorying" (v. 6). That is a reference to their unrighteous forgiveness, unholy toleration, and faux love. It was not good. They were being threatened as a true church of Christ. Therefore, he calls them to put away that wicked person!

The Old Testament type called Israel to remember the power of leaven. In Deuteronomy 16:3 God said to Israel, "Seven days shalt thou eat unleavened bread therewith, even the bread of affliction…that thou mayest remember the day when thou camest forth out of the land of Egypt all the days of thy life." This means that when they ate unleavened bread they were to remember their history and the day God brought them out of Egypt, when God delivered them from the bondage and corrupting power of Egypt as the land of sin and affliction. It is as though God said, "When you eat the unleavened bread of the truth, eat it as the bread of affliction and remember your history when the Lord brought you out from the world, from sin and death, and delivered you from doctrinal errors. Remember that a little leaven leavens the whole lump."

Church history stands as a continual case study of the failure to purge out leaven. There was one decision involving three points of common grace, but this doctrine leavened a whole denomination. Many viewed it as no large deal. Many today still attempt to minimize the whole history and the deliverance that God made from that leaven. They refuse to see it as leaven and are thus blind to the fact that that leaven has thoroughly worked itself through. In the face of the preaching of sovereign, particular grace, a church said, "We want the world." God gave them the world and will give them the world. Beware of leaven!

A church that will not discipline for divorce and remarriage will be full of sins at which the world would blush. Soon there will be fornication, sodomy, lesbianism, and more. Beware of leaven. "Know ye not that a little leaven leaveneth the whole lump?"

In 1 Corinthians 5:7 the apostle gives the second reason to purge out leaven: "For even Christ our passover is sacrificed for us." Deuteronomy 16:3 makes the same point with the curious instruction, "Thou shalt eat no leavened bread *with it*; seven days shalt thou eat unleavened bread *therewith*" (emphasis added). In the two phrases "with it" and "therewith" are expressed the close connection of the feast of unleavened bread and the feast of passover. The night of the passover the Israelite roasted a lamb and set it before his family. With one hand they took a piece of lamb and with the other hand they held a piece of unleavened bread. God said they should eat "therewith," that is, with the lamb eat unleavened bread. The law extended the commandment to the whole keeping of the feast of unleavened bread for the following seven days. All the unleavened bread they ate that whole week of the feast of unleavened bread was eaten with passover lamb that they had consumed on Friday. Eating leavened bread during the week that followed the passover was inconsistent with eating the passover lamb and defiled that eating.

The lamb, Jesus Christ, delivered the church from sin, the world, death, and the guilt and bondage of sin by his blood. It is as the apostle says, "Ye are unleavened" (1 Cor. 5:7). He describes the church of God and the believer according to the work of Christ at the cross. The church was unleavened at the cross. She was freed from the guilt and pollution of sin, both original and actual, so that she is perfect through the perfect work of the cross. The church is called, then, to purge out leaven in order to be a new lump in harmony with and by the power of the cross of Christ. You are unleavened. Be unleavened. The holy life of sorrowing for sin, flying to the cross for forgiveness, fighting against the old man of sin, obeying God's law, and separating from sin and impenitent sinners is the only life consistent with the cross of Christ, the passover. It is impossible to eat Christ Jesus and leavened bread. It is impossible to eat Christ Jesus and to fellowship with sin and impenitent sinners.

It is also impossible to keep the feast of unleavened bread—the holy life called for by Christ's redemption and that is the fruit and effect of Christ's redemption—and refuse to purge out leaven. The apostle says, "Therefore let us keep the feast, not with old leaven…but with the unleavened bread of sincerity and truth" (v. 8). Purging out leaven is in the interest of keeping the feast. He means there the feast of unleavened bread that follows on the feast of passover. The feast of unleavened bread represented the entire holy life of the Israelite in the covenant of God and land of Canaan that was purchased by the passover lamb. That feast could not be kept with leavened bread.

This means that lives of holiness for the church and believers are impossible while they refuse to put away sin and impenitent sinners. They cannot walk in the way of love—which is the way of holiness—while they maintain fellowship with sin and impenitent sinners. Besides, by so doing the church makes vain her confession to have eaten the passover lamb, Christ Jesus, for he cannot be eaten with leaven. "Purge out, therefore, the old leaven, that ye may be a new lump."

The Urgency of Purging Leaven

The urgency of the call for discipline in particular is expressed by the apostle when he says, "Therefore let us keep the feast." That calls to mind the warning of God in the instructions for the feast: "Whosoever eateth that which is leavened, even that soul shall be cut off from the congregation of Israel, whether he be a stranger, or born in the land" (Ex. 12:19). That same serious warning is repeated by Jesus: "Beware of the leaven of the Pharisees and of the Sadducees and of Herod" (Matt. 16:6; Mark 8:15). It is expressed by the apostle in the rhetorical question whether the Corinthians understand the power of leaven, and thus the corrupting influence of the impenitent sinner whom they insisted on parading as a trophy of their loveless tolerance.

Leaven makes it impossible to eat Christ the passover.

Leaven makes it impossible to live a holy life and so to keep the feast of unleavened bread.

Leaven in the end does not just leaven, but it brings a cutting off: "that soul shall be cut off." Paul accuses those who will not discipline and refuse to cut off the impenitent sinner not just of refusing to purge leaven, but of actually profanely eating leaven when they should be eating unleavened bread and thus profaning not only their holy lives, but also their whole confession of Christ Jesus. The soul that eats leaven shall be cut off. Refusing to cut off the sinner and put away that wicked person, they bring cutting off into their lives, families, and congregations. God is not mocked. That leaven will work through until God cuts off members of that family, members of that congregation or that church who are influenced by and defiled with that leaven.

Do not believers have love: love for sinners who will be cut off; love for the church and all those who will be influenced by that leavening sinner? Purge out the old leaven.

In the way of purging out leaven the church can also be a new lump and keep the feast "with the unleavened bread of sincerity and truth" (1 Cor. 5:8). Notice: sincerity and truth. This means the truth that is genuine, without any mixture of the false, wickedness, or maliciousness. The life of holiness consists in feasting on the pure, unleavened bread of sincerity and truth. This is the truth of Jesus Christ and his redemption as revealed to us in the scriptures and preached in the gospel. This is the truth of Jesus Christ and his redemption as summarized in the Reformed creeds. This is the truth of the life consecrated to God in holiness, a life governed by the truth of the word of God.

Eating unleavened bread, then, is the appropriation by faith of the unsullied truth of Jesus Christ in the preaching of the gospel and by faith living by it in our daily lives in love. The painful and difficult way of purging out leaven is the way to partake of and fellowship with the crucified body and the shed blood of Jesus Christ and to experience fellowship and salvation purchased by the Lamb. Without holiness no man shall see the Lord.

CHAPTER 16

THE CHURCH'S CALLING TOWARD THE IMPENITENT

1 Corinthians 5:9–13

---

9. I wrote unto you in an epistle not to company with fornicators:
10. Yet not altogether with the fornicators of this world, or with the covetous, or extortioners, or with idolaters; for then must ye needs go out of the world.
11. But now I have written unto you not to keep company, if any man that is called a brother be a fornicator, or covetous, or an idolater, or a railer, or a drunkard, or an extortioner; with such an one no not to eat.
12. For what have I to do to judge them also that are without? do not ye judge them that are within?
13. But them that are without God judgeth. Therefore put away from among yourselves that wicked person.

In these verses the apostle is still dealing with the subject of Christian discipline. Discipline is the power of the church to exclude impenitent sinners from her fellowship and the sacraments and thus from the kingdom of heaven. That is likewise her calling. Failing to discipline, she is liable to the judgment of God.

The mandate to discipline is the command of the apostle Paul from the Lord. Paul in verses 6–8 grounds the call to discipline in the Old Testament scripture and the feast of unleavened bread.

Continuing to explain the subject of Christian discipline in verses 9–13, the apostle addresses the calling of the individual church member toward the impenitent sinner. He begins by bringing up a previous letter on the subject: "I wrote unto you in an epistle not to company with fornicators" (v. 9). That letter has occasioned all kinds of unprofitable speculation. The explanation of the letter is easy. The inspired book of 1 Corinthians is not the first letter Paul wrote to the church at Corinth. Earlier he had written a letter addressing the same matter of keeping company with impenitent sinners. In that letter he dealt especially with fornicators, a fact unsurprising in a city infamous for fornication even among the licentious Romans.

In verse 9 Paul mentions the content of the letter: "not to keep company with fornicators." In verse 10 he explains what that letter could not mean: "yet not altogether with the fornicators of this world…for then must ye needs go out of the world." In verse 11 he says as it were, "But I even told you in that letter what I meant, for I wrote that if any man who is called a brother be a fornicator…do not keep company with such a one, no not to eat." By bringing up the previous letter, he is telling the Corinthians that he is not now teaching them anything new, but he is teaching what he always taught and also what he wrote to them before. In verses 12–13 Paul gives the ground for his teaching about not keeping company with impenitent sinners. Finally, he specifically applies his general doctrine to the case of the wicked person in Corinth whom the congregation had refused to discipline and instead wickedly tolerated and embraced with evil love (v. 13).

The fact that the apostle brings up this previous instruction about not keeping company with impenitent sinners to the Corinthians is important.

First, he takes away any excuse of ignorance on the part of

the Corinthians regarding their fellowship with impenitent sinners. Many use ignorance—feigned or otherwise—as an excuse for their continued fellowship with wicked persons, especially their own blood relatives and close friends, as though this matter of not keeping company with the impenitent is an unclear matter in scripture or the principles of scripture are unclear in application to their particular situation.

Second, he heads off any attempt to inoculate against his instruction by misrepresenting it and making it appear absurd or foolish. Apparently some in Corinth attempted to apply the apostle's instruction to only an ill-defined "world." Loud in their talk about the antithesis and not fellowshiping with the world, they were hypocritical because of their fellowship with their impenitent brothers and sisters. The apostle unmasks that tactic, exposes the absurdity of that interpretation, and in so doing adds another passage on the subject of not keeping company with impenitent sinners, so that he clearly sets down the doctrine in the scriptures.

After such instruction, continued refusal to separate from the impenitent can no longer believably be defended as ignorance but is revealed to be obstinacy in the face of the Spirit's clarity. Paul did write, as Peter said, "some things hard to be understood" (2 Pet. 3:16). The matter of the church's and the believer's calling toward the impenitent is not one of them. At stake is nothing less than the honor and glory of God. At stake is the faithfulness of the church toward her head and lord, Jesus Christ. At stake is the holiness of the church, a holiness that she threatens if she will not put away wicked persons from her fellowship. At stake is the antithetical life of the church that she sullies by her illicit and unholy fellowship with impenitent sinners. At stake is the very existence of the church as a true church of Jesus Christ in the world, because a little leaven leavens the whole lump. The Holy Spirit in memorable and unmistakable language explains the church's calling toward impenitent sinners.

A Broad Application of a Concrete Case

The apostle pointedly applies his doctrine of church discipline to the concrete case in Corinth in which a man sexually had his father's wife, his stepmother. This man is the specific subject of the apostle's closing exhortation in verse 13: "Therefore put away from among yourselves that wicked person."

With that language the apostle also exposes what lies very near to the heart of a person's refusal to cut off fellowship with the impenitent sinner. The refusal to put away a wicked person is a refusal to judge the impenitent sinner, usually a dear family member or close friend, as a wicked person. If the church is spiritual enough to see that the man who maintains false doctrine or wicked practices is in fact wicked in the eyes of God, Christ, the Spirit, and the holy angels, she will put him away as wicked in her eyes. The refusal so to judge exposes the carnality of the church and Christian who will not judge wickedness as wickedness. Either that or it exposes their lawlessness: they know it is sin, yet they refuse to require the repentance of the sinner but cover his sin with a wicked grace and an unholy forgiveness.

In the closest connection with the matter of official church discipline, the apostle teaches a general principle that must be applied in the case of an excommunicate and also has a much broader application to impenitent sinners generally. The broader application is clear, because the apostle brings up the church's relationship to the impenitent world, and because the man whom he calls them to put away was not yet excommunicated but was an impenitent in need of excommunication. To say that Paul refers only to excommunication in these verses is absurd. When Paul brings up the world, he brings up the whole matter of the church's calling toward impenitent fornicators, extortioners, and covetous of the world, as well as those same impenitent who are called brothers. In the case of the brother, he does not call him an excommunicate or some similar designation but refers to his impenitence: a brother who is also called a fornicator, an extortioner, or some other kind of sinner because he lives in that sin.

That Paul is interested more generally in the impenitent comes out with the word "judge" in verse 12. The idea is not a general judgment, or even the specific judgment of excommunication—which many impenitent sinners conveniently but wickedly avoid either by their membership in some church that tolerates their wickedness or by leaving the church when discipline is administered—but a judgment regarding a man's penitence or impenitence. When a member of the church lives impenitently in his sin and becomes the object of the church's discipline by his impenitence, yet wickedly he will not sit for discipline, that does not free the church members from the necessity of making a judgment about that person. His leaving and sinful refusing to sit for his discipline does not change his spiritual condition and the calling of the church toward him. His insistence, often, on fellowshiping with the members of the church, his family and his friends, calls the believer to make a judgment, because he insists on being called a brother, a believer, and a fellow Christian and demands to be included in the fellowship of the church and in the lives of the members, while he lives a wicked life doctrinally and practically.

There is no one bolder in this regard than the impenitent sinner. Having brazenly defied God by his sin and impenitence, he seemingly takes a wicked delight in spoiling the fellowship of the church and family of God by his corrupting presence; especially if he is able to create division in the family between those who will and will not cut him off. Such a division is a loud word from God about the leavening effect of the impenitent sinner and a powerful reason to cast him out.

Two Kinds of Impenitent

The apostle refers to the impenitent in two circumstances. There are the impenitent whom he calls "this world" and "them...that are without." There are also the impenitent whom he calls "a brother" and "them that are within" (vv. 10–12).

There are the impenitent "of this world" and "them...that are without," those who are fornicators, covetous, extortioners, or idolaters of this world. "World" refers to the world of sinful men fallen in Adam and under the spiritual power of Satan by God's just judgment. In that world all men are conceived and born in sin. In that world they are incapable of any good and inclined to all wickedness. In that world there is only impenitence.

That is the great difference between the church and the world: in the church there is penitence. In the church, God by his grace softens the hearts of his elect people and calls them out of their impenitence, out of the world and into the life of the kingdom of Jesus Christ. That life consists of daily sorrow for sin and rejoicing in God as the God of their salvation. The church is populated by true believers, truly sorrowing for their sins, turning from that sin, all expecting their salvation from Christ alone, and all justified by faith alone.

Penitence also distinguishes the proper partakers of the Lord's supper from improper partakers. The improper partaker is the impenitent, whether his impenitence is known only to himself or also known to the church. The proper partaker of the Lord's table is the penitent. The Reformed Form for the Administration of the Lord's Supper speaks of that. First it warns those who are defiled by certain sins and impenitently continue in such sins to abstain from the meat and drink of the Lord's table. Then the form encourages the hearts of God's people: "This is not designed...to deject the contrite hearts of the faithful, as if none might come to the Supper of the Lord but those who are without sin." The form points out that the believers' coming to the table is not a testimony that they are perfect and righteous in themselves, but is a testimony of their sorrow for sin and true faith in

Jesus Christ, that their righteousness is in him, and that they are resolved to live in holiness.[1]

Penitence is the constant, daily sorrow for sin and faith in Christ for righteousness. The impenitent lives in sin and does not turn away from it. The apostle says, "If any man be"; that is, he commits and keeps on committing that sin and does not turn from it, is not sorry for it, and does not hate it. He may express from time to time some regret, disappointment, and trouble that his sin brings to him. But the superficiality and insincerity of his confessions are evident because he never breaks with and turns from that sin.

The other impenitent is the one whom the apostle calls "a brother" and "them that are within." The brother is one who by confession belongs to the sphere of the church. He has been baptized and instructed. He sits in church for a certain period of his life. He makes a certain kind of confession of faith in Jesus Christ. He may insist that he is a Christian, a believer, and a righteous man. He has a certain claim on that basis to the fellowship of the church.

The apostle's language recognizes two kinds of impenitent brothers. There is one who is excommunicated. This is clear from the concrete case of the man in Corinth, whom the apostle insists should be disciplined and put out of the church. There is also more generally the man who is called a brother who is "a fornicator, or covetous, or an idolater, or a railer, or a drunkard, or an extortioner" (v. 11). This man lives impenitently even though he does not come under the official discipline of the church and perhaps never will. He is not sorry for his sin and continues to live in it. He also insists that he is to be regarded as a Christian man and a believer.

---

1 Form for the Administration of the Lord's Supper, in *Confessions and Church Order*, 269.

A fornicator is an impenitent violator of the seventh commandment. He may be a young person who engages in premarital sex and is not sorry and even apparently gets away with it. He may be a person who impenitently views pornography on the Internet. The fornicator is certainly the sodomite, the woman or man who is sexually attracted to the same sex, whether or not one engages in same-sex relationships. The fornicator is the married person who divorces his or her spouse for reasons other than fornication. The fornicator is the divorced person who marries another while the first spouse is living. That person—regardless that he is called a brother or insists that he is a Christian man—if he lives impenitently in that sin, is a fornicator.

There are two words in scripture for the covetous. One refers more generally to covetousness and is used in the tenth commandment. Related to that word is another that refers more specifically to covetousness for things. Although covetousness is a heart matter, the heart exposes itself in a person's life. This inclusion of covetousness is for the safety of the church that judges. Often the retort to the church that engages in discipline or to those who will not keep fellowship with impenitent sinners is, "You cannot judge the heart." The apostle includes covetousness, which is a heart matter.

How does the church judge if a man is covetous? His life exposes his heart. By its fruits a man can know a tree. The covetous person makes himself known by his massive debts that he has no intention of paying back. He takes what is not his own, and he will not return it. He borrows oft, as the wicked, because he is never satisfied and does not pay back. The covetous man is contentious, angry because his schemes for earthly advantage and wealth are frustrated. The covetous man lacks contentment with such things that he has, especially with simple food and raiment. The covetous man is exposed by his union membership. Covetousness, the love of money, is the root of a host of evils.

The idolater is one who worships other gods. By this the

apostle refers to those who break both tables of the law of God. The apostle brings in the whole first table of the law, which deals with the worship of God, and makes that a ground for not fellowshiping with an impenitent sinner. A man's life may be squeaky clean and even recognized as exemplary, but his doctrine is Satan's. Besides engaging in the gross forms of idolatry, such as the black arts, the idolater impenitently believes false doctrine. Included in that is one who engages in false worship, violates his oaths, and does not keep the Lord's day holy.

The railer is a slanderer or impenitent violator of the ninth commandment. He is a gossip, a tale bearer, a backbiter, and he does not love the truth. He does these things against God's people, his church, and his truth. A railer believes in and propagates false doctrine and especially engages in wicked scorning, slandering, and opposing the true doctrine.

A drunkard is one who drinks alchoholic beverages to excess. He is filled with wine, and by implication he is not filled with the Spirit. A drunkard is a spiritually vacuous person. In this day we may add the impenitent drug abuser and illegal drug user, which amount to the same thing.

An extortioner breaks the eighth commandment. The Greek word translated as "extortioner" is the same word that in literature refers to the mythical Harpies.[2] An extortioner is a harpy in financial matters, a spendthrift, a miser, and a union man too. A member of a union, so long as he continues impenitently in that sin, is an extortioner. He extorts from his employer and fellow men by violence or the threat of violence and intimidation. He is that whether he engages in that activity himself or by virtue of union membership through the ones appointed by the union to

---

2 The Harpies, whose name means snatcher, personify the demonic force of storms and are always represented as half eagle and half women. In Greek mythology they were sent by the gods to snatch away people and things from the earth. Sudden, mysterious disappearances were often attributed to the Harpies.

carry out its devious works. Even if the union would never once strike, a member is still an extortioner because he is pledged to it or some other form of extortion from the employer. Behind his extortion stands the threat to ruin the employer by the strike. Equally extortionate is the employer who takes advantage of his customers and employees. Especially he exploits the needs of his employee, even the practical reality that his employee cannot just quit, or evilly keeps back his wages by fraud and deceit.

The apostle's concern is "with such," that is, with all these specifically and all those like them who are called brothers and who live impenitently in their sin.

A Calling Not to Keep Company

The believer is called "not to keep company…with such an one no not to eat" (v. 11). "To keep company with" is the translation of the mildest Greek word used in scripture for fellowship. It means to have a familiar acquaintance with someone. With the impenitent sinner called a brother do not have a general friendship.

By forbidding that mild form of fellowship, the apostle also forbids more intimate fellowship. He does not leave this to implications but states it explicitly: "no not to eat." "To eat" refers to the intimate fellowship of friends. The believer's friends are in the church, and part of membership in the church is friendship among the church members, which includes eating and drinking together in a holy fellowship. Believing families do that. Believing friends do that with each other. That reality of friendship and fellowship comes to the ultimate culmination in the public worship of the church and especially at the table of the Lord, where believers sit down together as those who have been called out of the world, called out of impenitent sin, and saved by grace. Together they eat and drink at the table with the Lord and other penitent sinners. With the impenitent they may not eat.

When the apostle forbids eating with the impenitent, he forbids having that fellowship not only at the Lord's table, but also at any believer's table: in his home, at his Christmas and other parties, or at the restaurants for a dinner date.

The apostle denies that his prohibition of keeping company applies "altogether with the fornicators of this world" (v. 10). There is a certain kind of thinking that the text forbids. The apostle wrote a previous letter forbidding the members of Corinth to keep company with fornicators. Apparently there were those who said, "We do not fellowship with the world," yet they had fellowship with those who were called brothers who were fornicators or lived like the world in some other way. In defense of their fellowship with the wicked brother they said, "The apostle wants us to live like hermits in isolation," by which they attempted to make his teaching look stupid. Paul defends his earlier letter: "[When] I wrote unto you in an epistle not to [keep] company with fornicators," I did not mean "altogether with the fornicators of this world" (vv. 9–10). He makes absurd the thinking that a man obeys the apostle's command if he does not keep company with fornicators of this world and defends against any attempt to make this teaching look foolish: "Not altogether with the fornicators of this world...for then must ye needs go out of the world" (v. 10). He does not deny that the church is called to live in antithetical separation from the world, but only denies that it is "altogether."

If the teaching of scripture and the Spirit that believers may not keep company with or eat with the impenitent means exclusively those in the world, we would have to go out of the world. Is that not obvious? Who has not given money at the grocery store to a clerk who is fornicating with her third husband? Who has not engaged in business with an extortionate businessman? Who has not been in the same restaurant with a coveting world? Who has not in the course of his business dealings sat down at a business luncheon with a thoroughly worldly man or entertained him at one's shop?

When Paul says "not to keep company," he does not mean "altogether with the fornicators of this world." He does not deny that the antithesis and its requirement of spiritual separation apply to the world. No one can use this text to excuse friendship with a worldly person. Rather the apostle's emphasis is on "altogether." When Paul says, "not altogether with the fornicators of this world," he does not teach that we may fellowship with the fornicators of this world. Rather, he teaches that his prohibition not to keep company with fornicators and such like is not exhausted by applying it to the ungodly world, so that if you do not fellowship and eat with impenitent sinners of the world, you are free to keep company with the wicked brother. He also teaches that the strictness of his prohibition not to keep company, which includes eating with a man, cannot be applied to the world as one can apply it to a brother.

When Paul denies that his meaning is not altogether with the fornicators of this world, he implies that he does mean "altogether" with the fornicator or other impenitent sinner called a brother. To make this point very sharp and to point out the folly of many interpretations, the apostle teaches that the calling of the church toward the impenitent brother is more than her calling toward the impenitent world. What would make the church's life in the world impossible if she did it with the impenitent of the world is exactly what she is called to do over against the impenitent brother.

Paul also forbids the kind of thinking in which a Christian supposes that because he does not have friendships with worldly persons—go to bars and movie theaters, ski with them or sit at the beach with them and have them for friends—he obeys the commandment of the apostle not to keep company with fornicators. Yet all the while he scrupulously avoids fellowship with the "world," he indulges in friendship and close fellowship with the man who is called a brother who lives in impenitent sin. He has no problem inviting this man to his house, to family parties, going to dinner with him, going to his house, and carrying on familiar conversations with him when they meet at this or that public gathering. Paul demolishes that pretention to an antithetical life in those cases and applies the calling not to keep company particularly to those situations: "When I wrote not to keep company with fornicators, I did not mean altogether with the fornicators of this world, but when a man is called a brother, keep no company with him—no not to eat."

Thus if a man is eating and drinking and carrying on familiar conversations with an impenitent one who is called a brother, he is doing exactly what the Spirit forbids here. In a certain sense not going to a bar or movie theater or listening to worldly music is the easy side of the antithesis, the separation between Christ and Belial, church and world, temple of God and the synagogue of Satan. When applied to a brother, the sword that Jesus spoke of—"I came not to send peace, but a sword" (Matt. 10:34)—becomes very real and discipleship very sharp because it separates between those who are called brothers.

A Necessary Judgment

The calling of the believer toward the impenitent begins with his judgment of the impenitent. This is the apostle's point in verses 12–13: "For what have I to do to judge them also that are without? do not ye judge them that are within? But them that are without God judgeth."

When he speaks of his own judgment, Paul makes judging the responsibility of the believer and not only of the church officially through her elders. Discipline is the responsibility of the believer and thus of the whole church. The apostle speaks of his nonjudgment of the world and by implication of judgment of those who are within, a judgment that he also calls believers to make. Those who are without God judges. He judges their penitence or impenitence, executes his sentence, and deals with them accordingly. Because God judges we do not need to judge. But the believer and church are called to judge those who "are within," that is, the man who insists on being called a brother, a Christian, a believer, and especially a member of one's own church, while he lives in sin. This exposes the excuse of many for not making a judgment, that the apostle is only talking about those who come under official church discipline.

The judgment involves the man's penitence or lack of it. The apostle explains in verses 12–13. "Judge" means the judgment that a man is living wickedly and impenitently. When one judges that a man is impenitent, he warns the man of his wicked ways. Included in this, but not exhausting it, would be official church discipline, which eventually will result in excommunication.

This judgment and consequent warning are made impossible by fellowship with impenitent sinners. This exposes the continued fellowship with impenitent brothers for what it is— fellowship that tries to fly under the flag of warning and rebuke. If one judges a man to be impenitent and then rebukes him and warns him, at that point fellowship is impossible. Furthermore, a distinct part of one's judgment and warning is the calling not to keep company with that impenitent sinner. By so judging and subsequently separating from the impenitent sinner, one frees himself from the blood of the impenitent person.

God judges those who are without. He reveals his wrath every day against the ungodliness and unrighteousness of men. He shows a man in his conscience that he is displeased with him and his life. He warns him, and that man knows he is walking impenitently in sin. The believer is not under the same obligation toward the world as toward the brother. Paul says, "What have I to do to judge them also that are without?" (v. 12). God judges them. The idea is that when I am in the world carrying on my life and giving money to a fornicating clerk and doing business with a wicked extortioner, I am not responsible for them. Is their blood on my head if I do not warn them? The apostle says, "No." God judges those who are without.

But Paul says, "Do not ye judge them that are within?" (v. 12). If there is a man who is called a brother, who says that he believes in Christ, insists that he is a Christian, even boldly lays claim to fellowship with the church, yet walks in impenitent sin, and a believer does not judge him and tell him that his way of life is sinful, he is responsible for that man's sin. By the believer's failure to judge and to act according to that judgment he is responsible for that man. The life that that impenitent sinner lives is the broad way to hell. On that way God's wrath rests on him. If he dies in his sin he will go to hell. By the failure to judge, the believer leaves the sinner under the impression—not only by lack of words, but also by fellowship—that he is right with God, that together they are good Christian brothers, and that they may fellowship because there is nothing wrong in his life.

The apostle points out an absurdity in those who will judge the world but cannot do the same for a brother. In the light of the word of God, who cannot judge the world and say about the world that it is under the wrath of God? The believer can apply the word and see that because of its way of life the wrath of God rests on it. But the same believer will not judge those within. He cannot apply that same word of God to a brother who lives wickedly—whether in doctrine or life—and for his eternal good judge him and warn him.

When Paul calls believers to judge and not to fellowship with the impenitent, he also charges all those who fellowship with the impenitent brother with unrighteousness and unjust judgment. They are corrupt judges every one. Imagine a courtroom into which comes an extortioner, a murderer, a drunkard, a wife beater, or a child abuser, and on clear evidence the judge condemns him. Then another fornicator comes into his court, and the judge examines him and knows full well that he is guilty, but because he is a friend, the judge lets the fornicator go. That is an unjust judge. Such is also the unjust judgment of those who are able to condemn the world but not their friends, brothers, or acquaintances.

Then add to that scenario that the wicked man whom the

unjust judge released goes and commits his crime again. Whose fault is that? That is the force of the apostle's question: "Do not we judge them that are within?" If we as believers know of a brother who is walking in impenitent sin and still keep company with him, eat and drink with him, invite him to parties, and have close fellowship with him, and the brother dies in his sin and God sends him to hell, where do we stand? What will be the charge of the great Judge who will judge in the judgment day? Do not we judge those who are within?

The Urgency of This Calling

By calling unjust those who are capable of judging the wickedness of the world but not of their brother, the apostle also accuses them of a lack of love. There is no love in unrighteousness, and there is no love in the unrighteous judgment according to which the church and believer refuse to judge a wicked man as such and thus also refuse to put away that wicked person from them, but on the contrary fellowship with him and even eat and drink with him so that he dies unwarned in his sin. The way of love and walking in the way of love demands a righteous judgment according to which the church judges an impenitent as such and according to which judgment she puts away that wicked person, refusing to fellowship with him, no not to eat.

Seeing this connection between a righteous judgment and love, the text also exposes as false and wholly ineffective the oft-cited reason for fellowshiping with the impenitent brother: to show him love. Will the church walk in the way of love over against the impenitent brother? Then let them keep no company, no not to eat.

There is urgency in the apostle's instruction in verse 13: "Therefore put away from among yourselves that wicked person." Literally he says, "You shall put away..." The text is not only expressing urgency in the command to the church regarding the impenitent, but also is expressing some confidence that his word will have an effect on a spiritual people. Before they did not listen, and he instructs them again, and now they will listen. "You shall put away that wicked person." Unless the church faithfully engages in this calling, she is not faithfully engaged in discipline.

Discipline is not only the actual sentence over a man or woman to bar from the table and to excommunicate from the church, but it is also a daily reality of not keeping company with the impenitent. The church might officially engage in discipline, but if the membership will not put away from themselves those wicked persons, the church is not engaging in discipline, and that discipline is undermined. This applies especially in the case of those impenitent who insist on being called brothers and claim the fellowship of the church as their right, but who lead impenitent lives doctrinally or practically and on whom the discipline of the church officially cannot come, because they are members of churches that tolerate or approve their sins. If the lives of the members are full of such people, there will be no will to discipline in the church. They are keeping company with those whom the church would discipline. Those whom the church would bar from the Lord's table, and whom the Lord himself bars from his table and fellowship, the members will have at their tables.

That relationship between the members' fellowship and the church's discipline is important. The idea of "therefore" in verse 13 is that if members will not "put away from among themselves" a wicked person, what becomes of church discipline? The failure of the church to discipline sinners and the failure to separate from sinners leads to changing the church's doctrinal positions. Many no longer blush at homosexuality. That did not come as a bolt out of the blue but is the fruit of the church's ineffectual hand wringing and ultimate failure to discipline and to separate from those who are wickedly divorced and remarried. If my friend who is dear to me, or my son or daughter who is dear to me, walks in sin and I refuse to put him away but continue to eat and drink with him, it will not be long before there is severe pressure on the pulpit to shut its mouth. "Stop preaching that. Be more tolerant. Show some love." Soon the church will keep the key of discipline in her pocket, where it will rust for lack of use.

Furthermore, the urgency is this. If the believer has an impenitent sinner, who is a brother or sister or close friend, a member of the family or inner circle, in his fellowship and at his table and will not put that wicked person away from him, he is disobedient to the apostle, to scripture, and to the Holy Ghost. Refusal now is obstinacy.

If the believer has by the grace of God put away from himself that dear but wicked person who is living in impenitent sin, even in the face of vigorous and slanderous opposition, he can be encouraged that it is the will and word of God. He is obedient to the apostle, scripture, and the Holy Ghost. The Spirit commends that as righteous and loving. It is not unloving but loving. That action is not judgmental but the fruit of righteous judging. That action is not venomous. It is brotherly and obedient.

As with church discipline, the believer may comfort himself in the way of obedience that, doing the will of God, the outcome is in God's hands. As with discipline, of which this is a part, it is a remedy by God's grace, a remedy for the destruction of the flesh that the spirit may be saved in the day of Christ.

CHAPTER 17

SETTLING DISPUTES AMONG SAINTS

1 Corinthians 6:1–8

---

1. Dare any of you, having a matter against another, go to law before the unjust, and not before the saints?
2. Do ye not know that the saints shall judge the world? and if the world shall be judged by you, are ye unworthy to judge the smallest matters?
3. Know ye not that we shall judge angels? how much more things that pertain to this life?
4. If then ye have judgments of things pertaining to his life, set them to judge who are least esteemed in the church.
5. I speak to your shame. Is it so, that there is not a wise man among you? no, not one that shall be able to judge between his brethren?
6. But brother goeth to law with brother, and that before the unbelievers.
7. Now therefore there is utterly a fault among you, because ye go to law one with another. Why do ye not rather take wrong? why do ye not rather suffer yourselves to be defrauded?
8. Nay, ye do wrong, and defraud, and that your brethren.

The apostle Paul begins a new subject with these verses. He has finished the matter of the Corinthians' failure to walk in the way of love demonstrated by their refusal to put a wicked person out of the church. Church discipline belongs to the marks of the church. When and where it is exercised according to the word of God and the command of Christ, there we can be certain that Jesus Christ is ruling and reigning by his Spirit, executing his judgments in the church. Where it is lacking, there is an unspiritual and carnal church.

The apostle also addressed the companion problem that members of the church fellowshiped with impenitent sinners. That always goes along with man's despising Christ's discipline. Indeed, the beginning of the church's failure to discipline is the members' failure to cut off impenitent sinners from their fellowship.

By disciplining and cutting off impenitent sinners, the church walks in the way of love. She shows that love does not delight in iniquity. She shows her love for God and for Jesus Christ and his word. She shows her love for sinners by doing good to them.

Now the apostle treats another aspect of the walk of the church that calls for love: settling disputes. Love is the believer's esteem of the other as precious and dear and the determination of the believer to do good to the other. This other the Bible calls the neighbor. That neighbor is also that same person as he demands of my time, energy, money, honor, reputation, and many other things.

In the church there are many neighbors living together in one body, and there are bound to be disputes. In these disputes the Corinthians showed an utter lack of love. The members hated one another. In pursuit of their rights they audaciously sued one another in the courts of law over every problem and trouble. Paul, describing the situation, exhorts them to settle the disputes in the church amicably, equitably, and wisely.

But Paul is not finished when he says, "You have to settle your disputes." The apostle, the scriptures, and the Holy Spirit are never satisfied with a little practical advice. They penetrate to the spiritual root of the problem and lay bare the spiritual failing that caused the disputes, and therefore the spiritual principle out of which the Holy Spirit will have us live as neighbors in the church: love.

Squabbles over Earthly Things

The basic question of 1 Corinthians 6:1–8 is, what are these disputes? Although the King James Version does not use the word *disputes*, this English word captures the substance of the Greek word translated in the King James as "a matter" in verse 1. The word *pragmatic* or *practical* originates from that Greek word. Technically the word refers to a dispute in court, a suit, or a tort settled in court between two parties. Therefore, it refers generally to a dispute between two parties. By "a matter" Paul refers to a dispute between two parties in the church.

In verse 4 he refers to these same disputes with the word "judgments," which means disputes that need to be settled in court. Besides, in these verses the apostle clearly refers to legal disputes between members of the Corinthian congregation, because they went to the secular courts of law to settle their disputes.

Those disputes the apostle further defines as "things that pertain to this life" and "things pertaining to this life" (vv. 3–4). The Corinthians disputed over worldly things, not about doctrine, theology, and eternal life. They were so concerned about worldly things because doctrine, theology, and eternal life did not interest them much. They concentrated on food, property, business cases, money borrowed and loaned, wills and inheritances, and the like. Just as when someone came to Jesus and said, "Master, speak to my brother, that he divide the inheritance with me," and Jesus responded, "Man, who made me a judge or a divider over you" (Luke 12:13–14), so they squabbled about anything and everything that pertains to this life.

They disputed against one another, brother with brother, and defrauded the brother. By "brother" (1 Cor. 6:6) the apostle does not refer to a blood relative, although he does not exclude that. There may be those who are brothers by blood who are also spiritual brothers in the church. But the most important and fundamental relationship between two human beings is the spiritual relationship. It supersedes any blood relationship, so that humans who are not related by blood can be spiritual brothers because both are members of the one household of God, the church. In this church Christ is the elder brother and the elect are the other brothers and sisters in the church.

The apostle recognizes that there may have been wrongs committed in the disputes, as he says, "Why do ye not rather take wrong? why do ye not rather suffer yourselves to be defrauded?" (v. 7).

Settling the Disputes

Paul does not condemn the settling of disputes when he condemns going to the worldly courts. Rather, he insists that disputes between brothers be settled. This insistence is clear from the words "and not before the saints" (v. 1). He asks the Corinthians, "Why do you go before the worldly courts to settle your disputes and not before the saints?" Further, Paul insists on the settlement of their disputes when he says, "If then ye have judgments of things pertaining to this life, set them to judge" (v. 4). The idea is that if brothers have a dispute about earthly things that needs to be settled, "set them to judge," that is, for the settlement of the dispute.

The settlement involves a judgment. Set to hear and to decide the case those "who are least esteemed in the church" (v. 4). In that judgment the evidence is laid out, pleading takes place one side against another, a verdict is rendered by a competent judge, and by that verdict an end is made of the dispute between brothers as legally and as finally as a judgment rendered by a worldly judge.

Paul also means that they must settle the dispute regardless if one would actually take his brother to court. Perhaps today it may be more injurious to one's business and reputation to take his brother to court, so he does not do it. But his refraining from suing the brother in court is not done out of principle, besides in his heart he nurses a grudge against the brother. If he could he would take his brother to court. Paul says, "If you have judgments, settle your disputes."

Although the apostolic command to settle disputes about earthly things should be enough for believers, the apostle gives additional reasons why the disputes can and should be settled. The apostle calls disputes about earthly matters the "smallest" (v. 2). They are "the smallest matters" from the viewpoint of eternity and importance. The apostle takes a very dim view of disputes about money and earthly things. They are little. They are not quite nothing, but they are of almost no importance.

This is a very different view than believers often take of these earthly disputes. Believers dispute about them because they make them big and the most important things in their lives. Thus they consume the believer's thinking, time, and energy. The apostle says they are smallest, the most unimportant, and frivolous things about which to dispute.

Because they are smallest they must be settled. Because they are smallest they can be settled very easily. They are not hopelessly complicated. Because they are smallest they should be settled. Just as a burr under the saddle can cripple the horse, and it is not the mountain ahead that wears you out but the grain of sand in your shoe, so the smallest matters if left unattended and unsettled cause the biggest problems.

Besides, the disputes should be settled because they are matters of brother against brother. It is a sin against one's brother not to settle a dispute. Settle the disputes about matters pertaining to earthly things, whether that is between wives and husbands, brothers, cousins, nephews, uncles, fellow believers, or business associates.

The Judgment of Saints

"If then ye have judgments of things pertaining to this life, set them to judge who are least esteemed in the church" (v. 4). Here the apostle refers to the disputing parties' choosing an arbiter. The idea of "set...to judge" is to set someone to hear the case and to make a judgment that will end the matter between the two parties.

The judge must be a fellow member "in the church" and one who is "least esteemed." In the settlement of earthly disputes, the Spirit will not have members of the church choose the mighty and esteemed in the church, the leaders, the elders, or the minister. They must choose the least esteemed. The apostle abases the pride of the disputers and deflates the inflated sense of the importance of their disputes. They are unimportant; they are the smallest. To prove that point, Paul says to them, "Set those who are least esteemed in the church to judge."

This does not mean that the chosen person is a fool, for the apostle says, "Is it so, that there is not a wise man among you... one that shall be able to judge between his brethren?" (v. 5). Although the chosen one may not have the greatest financial acumen and the most business experience or be the most powerful, popular, and influential man in the community, he is wise and able to judge because he is a believer enlightened by the Spirit of Jesus Christ and by the wisdom of the gospel.

The apostle says to the saints, "If you have a dispute with a brother in the church over earthly things, settle the dispute. If you cannot settle it by yourselves, then set one in the church who is least esteemed, a wise man, as judge to arbitrate the dispute, and let his judgment be final and prevail between the two brothers as really as a judgment of a worldly judge would prevail."

One person may say, "That is silly and naïve. The dispute involves my business and large amounts of money." The point is that even if the dispute involves a billion dollars, the least esteemed in the church can decide it. Another may say, "Well, this matter with the brother is way too complicated. No saint can possibly handle it and unravel it." Paul means that even if it is as complicated as the Gordian knot, a saint can make a judgment, and probably as easily as Alexander untied that tangled braid. Someone else may say, "The judgment needed involves the very existence of my business, my inheritance, or my will. It is way too important. The saints are incompetent to judge my dispute." A man might not say that out loud, but he will say it in his heart, so that he does not do what the apostle says. He may even take his brother into a worldly court. He at least will nurse his grudge.

The apostle anticipates all these objections and many more and commends the least saint as a competent judge in the greatest of the saints' disputes about these smallest matters—earthly things—when he says, "Do ye not know that the saints shall judge the world?…are ye unworthy to judge the smallest matters? Know ye not that we shall judge angels? how much more things that pertain to this life?" (vv. 2–3).

In these disputes the saints are the most competent and worthy judges in the whole world. No better judge can be found than among the saints because the saints will judge the greatest matters. They will judge the entire universe. No matter can be bigger than that. The saints are competent and worthy to judge because they are going to judge the greatest personages in the entire universe: Satan, Michael, Gabriel, and all the serried ranks of angels. All will come in review before the judgment of saints. The apostle refers to the participation of the saints in the judgment of Jesus Christ at the end of the ages. They can make judgments about earthly things, the smallest matters, because they will judge the cosmos and angels.

The saints are competent to judge in these matters because they have wisdom. The apostle asks if there is a wise man among the Corinthians. Indeed, among the saints is wisdom. They can apply spiritual principles in small earthly matters so that they are settled to the glory of God, the glory of Jesus Christ, the honor of the gospel, and the spiritual welfare of the disputants. They are the best judges because they can remind their fellow saints that earthly matters are the smallest. They can admonish fellow saints to correct their views about these earthly things and call the saints back in their disputing to the more excellent way of love.

Not the Courts of Law

The apostle says that disputes must be settled by the judgment of saints, not by the judgment of the courts. "Dare any of you, having a matter against another, go to law before the unjust?" (v. 1). "Go to law" refers to a legal case in a secular court. The Corinthians were involving the secular authorities, specifically the courts, in their disputes over worldly things.

This verse cannot be used as a blanket prohibition against saints' ever going to law. For instance, the apostle says nothing about the saint's going to law with the unbeliever and the unrighteous in earthly matters. The courts are for this purpose. This verse should have some importance for a Protestant Reformed church member because this verse was hurled into the face of the Protestant Reformed Churches when they sued for their properties and name in a court of law.

The answer to that charge is simple. First, the churches were not dealing with brothers, but with schismatic rebels. Second, there had been attempts to settle the matter out of court, but it became apparent in those attempts that the churches were not dealing with those who were honest. Third, it was not a personal matter, a matter of brother against brother, but of a particular consistory's claiming the right of protection from the civil authorities against those who would disrupt the church's property, the peace of her meetings, and her ability to assemble freely for worship. The church has that right. Without ever allowing the crown rights of King Jesus to be infringed on, a consistory may, if circumstances demand it, go to law to claim the protection of the authorities for her property, her name, and her peace.[1]

Further, when the apostle says that believers may not go before the unrighteous and unbelieving judges with their disputes about worldly things, he does not teach a negative view of the earthly magistrate as a magistrate or intend to dishonor him in any way. Paul's view of the magistrate the Spirit expresses in Romans 13: "Let every soul be subject unto the higher powers. For there is no power but of God: the powers that be are ordained of God...he is the minister of God to thee for good" (vv. 1, 4). The magistrate in settling worldly matters strictly according to the law is competent to judge. If the dispute is disrupting the peace of society, he will judge and punish the evildoer and reward the good.

Neither is the apostle sanctioning thievery and corruption, as though the church is a band of crooks. He forbids brother to go to law against brother to settle an earthly matter that could be easily settled between the brothers or by a judgment of the saints. He condemns their readiness to defend their property to the last penny. He censures their litigiousness and willingness to interrupt brotherly fellowship, friendship, harmony, and peace in the church, so that they will not lose a single earthly possession, a single bit of honor, or a single bit of face. That willingness the apostle forbids and calls audacious: "Dare any of you?" (v. 1). Yes, they did. They were so bold that they dared to interrupt the fellowship of brother with brother for the sake of a few pennies or thousands of dollars. Over the smallest of matters they dared.

---

1   The Reformed faith speaks of this right of the consistory in article 28 of the Church Order: "The consistory shall take care that the churches, for the possession of their property and the peace and order of their meetings, can claim the protection of the authorities." The article also recognizes the "smallness" of these matters when it warns, "It should be well understood, however, that for the sake of peace and material possession they may never suffer the royal government of Christ over His church to be in the least infringed upon" (*Confessions and Church Order*, 389).

They were that bold in their contempt for brotherly love and in their shabby treatment of the brother. They were so bold that they were willing to make the smallest matters the greatest.

Paul calls it not only audacious, but also shameful: "I speak to your shame" (v. 5). It was shameful because while professing themselves to be wise, to know the truth, to have the gospel, and to be one with their brother in Jesus Christ, they shamefully dragged the brothers before a court of law. It was shameful because professing themselves to be wise, they acted like fools.

A Failure to Love

Therein was utter failure. "Now therefore there is utterly a fault among you" (v. 7). The apostle gives his conclusion to this matter. He penetrates to the spiritual root of the disputes. Before a man went to law, before his brother defrauded him of a single penny, before the brother did any wrong, there was already a fault with them. The problem was not the lawsuit as such. The problem was not even the brother's defrauding of a brother or his doing the brother wrong. Those lawsuits and those disputes simply brought out the problem.

The apostle defines the problem. "You do not rather suffer wrong. You will not rather be defrauded. But you do wrong and do defraud and that your brother." There is the apostle's penetrating spiritual analysis of disputes about earthly things between brothers.

The spiritual failure that lay at the root of involving the civil authorities in their disputes was an utter failure of love. They were brothers, that is, they were all alike the objects of the love of God that made them accepted in Jesus Christ by the redemption of them from the guilt and dominion of their sins and forgiveness of all their debts, so that for those who had defrauded, God restored what they had taken away. They had been washed as brothers and as the objects of the grace and mercy of God from all their filth, vileness, sins, and pollutions. Being brothers, they had been joined in a bond of sacred fellowship with Jesus Christ. Joined in that sacred bond, they were alike members of the one household of God. But, being brothers, they squabbled like enemies, antagonistically, audaciously, and shamefully treating their brothers without love by involving the civil authorities and dragging their brothers before a court of law.

As brothers they were both pilgrims and strangers on the earth, but where was the spirit of the pilgrim and stranger in their disputes with brothers over earthly things? Where was the spirit of Abraham in his dispute with Lot over earthly things when their servants squabbled over grazing land and water? Where was the spirit of Abraham, who took his brother onto the mountain and said, "Look over the whole land. If you go east, I'll go west. If you go north, I'll go south. I will suffer myself to be defrauded of what is mine"? The land was Abraham's, not Lot's, but when the matter was earthly, Lot had the first pick. While professing to be a pilgrim and stranger on an earth where he had no abiding place, Lot made earthly things the greatest as though there was nothing else.

What an utter fault was evident in Corinth. They made pennies principles. Paul says, "Ye do wrong, and defraud, and that your brethren" (v. 8). How did they harm their brothers? Of what did they defraud their brothers? Of love. It is possible that they were crooks in the disputes, but that is not the apostle's point. They did not pay their love debt in their disputes. Love is our greatest debt (Rom. 13:8). This love is an abiding debt that we never finish paying.

If you or I have a dispute with a brother about earthly things, and if we will not settle it, or if we settle it by dragging our brother before the earthly authorities, the source is an utter failure of love. We defraud our brother of the greatest debt we owe to him. By defrauding him of our love, we injure him in the greatest way we can injure him.

Because love is our debt to our brothers, we need the judgment of saints in our disputes with the brothers and not the judgment of an earthly judge. The earthly judge in these matters cannot render the one judgment the saints need to hear. He might be able to render a strictly legal judgment. But the apostle's way forward fits with the spiritual principle. The saints are the most competent judges in the world because they are wise. They are not wise with the wisdom that understands the ins and outs of earthly litigation, torts, and business law, but wise with the wisdom of heaven, of Jesus Christ, and of the Spirit of God, and they are able to judge all things. Wisdom is the spiritual virtue to adapt all things to the glory of God and the welfare of the brother. The wise judges in disputes between brothers can point the brother to his debt of love. The wise judges can point to the need to suffer wrong and to be defrauded if that is what it takes for the good of the brother.

These wise saints can point us to the judgment to come. The apostle brings that up as part of the wisdom of saints and part of their judgment. Not only does that speak to the competence of saints to judge, but it also speaks to what saints tell their fellow saints when they have to suffer. They point them to the final judgment, when Christ will judge. He will right every wrong and reward every suffering. The saints will say, "Now, brothers, have patience."

The saints can point their fellow saints to the proper view of earthly things. In our lives as pilgrims and strangers, earthly things are not the biggest, but they are staffs to help the saints on our way to heaven. If the love of the brother demands that we give up our thousands or millions or billions, so be it. The saints can remind each other to view earthly things as the smallest. The saints will also be governed in their judgments by the only principle that can govern a judgment between brothers: love. The saints call each other to walk in love for the advantage and salvation of the brother. The saints can settle disputes for the glory of God and for the church's good and peace.

The scriptures tell the saints, "If you have a dispute with a brother about earthly things, settle it by the judgment of saints and pay your debt of love to the brother."

CHAPTER 18

THE UNRIGHTEOUS EXCLUDED

1 Corinthians 6:9–11

9. *Know ye not that the unrighteous shall not inherit the kingdom of God? Be not deceived: neither fornicators, nor idolaters, nor adulterers, nor effeminate, nor abusers of themselves with mankind,*
10. *Nor thieves, nor covetous, nor drunkards, nor revilers, nor extortioners, shall inherit the kingdom of God.*
11. *And such were some of you: but ye are washed, but ye are sanctified, but ye are justified in the name of the Lord Jesus, and by the Spirit of our God.*

Often heard as an attempt to blunt the force of the truth of the preaching is the retort, "But that is not a salvation issue." The scriptures do teach that some things are not salvation issues. These things belong to the Christian's liberty in Jesus Christ. This is why the apostle says, "Meats for the belly, and the belly for meats: but God shall destroy both it and them" (v. 13). There Paul rebukes those who would trouble the church by their non-salvation issues, argue endlessly about them, and attempt to bring the church into bondage to man's commandments and to externals. The response of the church is, "Meats for the belly, and the belly for meats."

There are also issues the Bible makes salvation issues that

many men would prefer not to be salvation issues. These are matters of doctrine and way of life that the gospel condemns as false and unrighteous, but which man refuses to recognize as such. In reply and in an attempt to blunt the force of scripture's condemnation of that false doctrine or evil life, man replies, "But that is not a salvation issue."

This is not a legitimate reply to biblical teaching regarding one's doctrine and life. It is, however, an admission that there is no repentance in the face of the clear biblical teaching regarding the doctrine and life that God's word demands.

The apostle answers this kind of thinking in these verses. He condemned the Corinthians' litigiousness in disputes about earthly things. With that instruction in view the apostle anticipates the objection that it is not a salvation issue: "Know ye not that the unrighteous shall not inherit the kingdom of God?" (v. 9). This principle governs whether something is a salvation issue, even something so apparently harmless as a lawsuit.

The apostle warns the church not to be deceived regarding that principle. The way of love is not the way of toleration of sin. The way of love is as broad and as narrow as the commandments of God. There is no wedge that can be driven by profane men between love and the commandments.

Paul also applies the principle to the church: "Such were some of you: but ye are washed, but ye are sanctified, but ye are justified" (v. 11). The apostle applies the principle to draw out of the church her gratitude that calls for love, a lack of which was the source of the Corinthians' atrocious treatment of one another. They had forgotten the principle that the unrighteous are shut out. They had forgotten that their salvation was gracious. They also forgot to love.

It is frequently the case that the approach of the apostle to sin—naming sin as sin, pointing out that such impenitent sinners are excluded from the kingdom of God, and actually excluding them by discipline and removing them from the church's

fellowship—is not acknowledged to be loving. It is harshly criticized as unloving. The apostle, though, in exhorting the church
to walk in the way of love, takes the lead by pointedly warning
the unrighteous that they shall not inherit the kingdom. That is
love. It is motivated by a deep love for the righteousness of God,
love for the holiness of the church, and love for the unrighteous
sinner, who can only be saved in the way of his repentance.

From What the Unrighteous Are Excluded

Paul states the theme of the text twice. In verse 9 he says, "Know
ye not that the unrighteous shall not inherit the kingdom of
God?" Again in verse 10 he writes, "[Such] shall [not] inherit the
kingdom of God." This is the gospel's powerful negative declaration that always accompanies the gospel's positive declaration
that the righteous shall inherit the kingdom of God. The gospel
says that all the righteous and only the righteous shall inherit the
kingdom of God. The righteous are all those who with sincere
faith believe the promise of the gospel, repent of their sins, and
receive the forgiveness of sins by faith only. All who do not sin-
cerely turn from their sins—repent and believe—shall not inherit
the kingdom of God and stand exposed to the wrath of God as
long as they continue unconverted. This negative declaration of
the gospel always accompanies the positive.

This is how the gospel preaching is a key of the kingdom:
according to that testimony God actually judges men. That testimony of the gospel is also the basis for Christian discipline.
By his impenitence a man shows himself to be unbelieving
and unconverted, and he must be excluded from the church by
Christian discipline. This testimony is part of every true church's
administration of the sacrament of the Lord's supper.

The unrighteous are excluded from the kingdom of God.
The kingdom of God is another name for what scripture else-
where calls the kingdom of heaven and the kingdom of Christ.
All of these names are synonyms for one reality: the gracious

rule of the triune God by Jesus Christ in the hearts and lives of his people.

It is called the kingdom of heaven in scripture because its origin is heavenly and its nature is spiritual. It is not an earthly kingdom or a kingdom whose benefits consist in the abundance of earthly things. It is a kingdom whose benefits are spiritual, the benefits of salvation. "The kingdom of God is not meat and drink; but righteousness, and peace, and joy in the Holy Ghost" (Rom. 14:17). Its origin is heavenly. Christ said, "My kingdom is not of this world: if my kingdom were of this world, then would my servants fight, that I should not be delivered to the Jews: but now is my kingdom not from hence" (John 18:36). The kingdom was conceived in eternity in God's counsel. Concerning the rule of God's king, Christ Jesus, David said, "I will declare the decree: the LORD hath said unto me, Thou art my Son; this day have I begotten thee" (Ps. 2:7). Jesus said about his kingdom, "I appoint unto you a kingdom, as my Father hath appointed unto me" (Luke 22:29). It is the kingdom God appointed to Christ and in him to his elect people. It is a kingdom of Christ because he is the God-appointed king who rules in the name of the triune God and for his glory.

It is called the kingdom of God because in the most comprehensive sense it is his—he conceived it, he established its unmovable foundation in the cross of Jesus Christ, he appointed the Mediator and King of the kingdom, he chose the citizens, and he perfects the kingdom. The goal of the kingdom is God. His word is law in the kingdom, his grace is the power of the kingdom, and his love is the way of life in that kingdom.

To inherit that kingdom is salvation. To receive that kingdom is the gift of salvation! In that kingdom the elect receive by gracious imputation the righteousness of Jesus Christ by faith only and apart from all works. In that kingdom they are transformed according to the image of Jesus Christ, so that they have already in this life a small beginning of the new obedience. In the kingdom they are made sorry for their sins. There they are brought under the saving rule of the triune God in Christ Jesus.

The righteous inherit. This is the positive implication of the apostle's statement that the unrighteous are excluded. All the righteous inherit. Only the righteous inherit.

No unrighteous shall inherit. "Know ye not that the unrighteous shall not inherit the kingdom of God?" The unrighteous are those who break the law of God. The apostle's examples are of those who break the law of God. It is not a matter of merely breaking a commandment or several commandments outwardly, but in breaking commandments one breaks the spirit of the law, which is to love God and the neighbor.

The apostle also teaches that the unrighteous are impenitent. He teaches that by implication when he says, "Such were some of you" (1 Cor. 6:11). A change had taken place in the Corinthians. That change was their repentance. They were sorry for their sins, which included turning from sin and stopping sin. The apostle can say about them "were," not that they are yet such while vainly mouthing some words about sorrow for their sins and talking about love for sinners and grace. They "were" because by God's grace they confessed their sins, turned from them, and lived new holy lives.

That is not because repentance merits with God or because repentance is a condition to enter the kingdom, but because true sorrow for sin is the certain gift from God to the citizens of the kingdom of heaven. Repentance is the unmistakable characteristic of the faith that justifies. The impenitent reveals by his impenitence that he is unbelieving and ungodly and that he stands outside the kingdom. His impenitence is a statement.

The impenitent one is not acquitted in the judgment. God makes the judgment, and he never says about the impenitent one that he is righteous, but declares that he is unrighteous and guilty. Being unrighteous, he does not inherit the kingdom. To be excluded is to be damned. Unrighteousness, all unrighteousness, is a salvation issue.

The Apostle's Concrete Cases

The apostle makes his doctrine specific. In the light of verses 1–8 the unrighteous were those who sued their brothers in court. To sue a brother in court and to involve the civil authorities in an earthly dispute that can be settled without them or by the judgment of saints is an enormous transgression of love, violation of the law of God—failing to seek the brother's advantage in every instance I can or may—and a salvation issue.

Paul also uses the occasion to make pointed applications to other violators of the law: fornicators, idolaters, adulterers, effeminate, abusers of themselves with mankind, thieves, covetous, drunkards, revilers, and extortioners shall not inherit the kingdom of God. Just as the society of Corinth took all those things for granted as liberty, so does modern society. The apostle's list is read with hardly a thought about what he makes salvation issues.

No fornicator shall inherit the kingdom of God. The Corinthian society certainly did not see fornication as evil. The proverb of the apostle about food, "Meats for the belly and the belly for meats," the whole city of Corinth said about sex: "The body for sex and sex for the body." The world today takes for granted that a man may visit a strip club, view pornography, and engage in all kinds of perverse sexual practices. The world takes for granted that boyfriends and girlfriends may have sex together and live together. The world takes for granted that two unmarried people may live together as though they were married, sleeping in the same bed and sharing the same house.

Included in fornication is dancing. Some will say in defense of their gyrations that David danced. I suppose if someone would dance to a lovely psalm, praising God with all his being, not too many people would fault him. If that kind of music was played and that kind of dance was suggested at the weddings and on the dance floors, it would be the social equivalent of a wet blanket on a cold night. That dancing of the Old Testament is a world—and a kingdom—away from the dancing that is done in imitation of the world, to the world's music, and that belongs to the kingdom of darkness. Dancing is worldly. If it were only worldly, it would be enough to condemn the practice. But dancing is fornication in the same way that enticing a man or a woman is fornication. It is a prelude to fornication as it was for Israel in the wilderness. As such it is a violation of the seventh commandment. It is a salvation issue. Dancing is a serious matter. That is why, if need be, the church will discipline for it.

Idolaters shall not inherit the kingdom of God. An idolater is someone who places his trust in something besides God. He is a superstitious man. He places his trust in his business acumen, money, health, bodily strength, and anything and everything besides the one true God. He does not trust God. Belonging to idolatry is impenitent false doctrine, inasmuch as a man creates by his false doctrine an idol of the true God. If a man says God loves all men, but the Bible says, "Jacob have I loved and Esau have I hated" (Rom. 9:13), that universalism is idolatry, and the man who teaches it is an idolater as surely as Ahab was with his Baal.

No adulterer shall inherit the kingdom of God. Adultery is sin against the marriage bond by sex with another person outside marriage. This includes all unbiblical divorce—divorce for any cause besides fornication—as well as the wickedness of remarriage, also of the so-called innocent party. The doctrinal error that allows for divorce for reasons other than adultery and for the remarriage of divorced parties is not a minor matter. Inasmuch as it is adultery, it is also a salvation issue. It may not be minimized and tolerated. No adulterer shall inherit the kingdom of God.

Singled out by the apostle as a specific violation of the seventh commandment and as unrighteousness is sodomy. The "effeminate" and "the abusers of themselves with mankind" (1 Cor. 6:9) both refer to the homosexual. The effeminate man is the more female in the obscene relationship, and the abuser is the more masculine in that relationship. These words also refer to all of the perversions that go along with the sin of homosexuality, such as crossdressing, transgenderism, and bisexuality, and would include the sin of lesbianism. The world—and with it many professing Christians—takes for granted that a man can have sexual relations with a man, a woman with a woman, or humans with animals, or everyone all mixed together. The Bible here condemns homosexuality and all such perversions as sin.

Because the apostle included covetousness, he also makes homosexual thoughts, desires, and tendencies sin as well. The sin is not merely in the act, but in the desires. As Jesus said about fornication generally that the man who looks at a woman to lust after her commits fornication with her (Matt. 5:28), so also a man who looks on a man to lust after him, or a woman who lusts after another woman, commits fornication.

Furthermore, it must be noted that the Holy Ghost condemns sodomy and other such sins right along with adultery and fornication. Today many are loud in expressing their disgust and opposition to homosexuality—they will not make a wedding cake for homosexuals—and they are bold to say that it is a salvation issue and a man must repent of his homosexuality. But they tolerate the adulterer, especially the divorced and remarried who cause hardly a ripple on the ecclesiastical pond, especially because some of the leading turtles in these ponds are themselves defiled by that unrighteousness. Many have no qualms about making them cakes. The judgment of God on those who tolerate the adulterer will be that soon they will have to deal with homosexuality.

No thieves nor covetous—the corrupt man in his earthly possessions, the miser or the spendthrift, the crook or the thief, and the man who sues his brother in court—shall inherit the kingdom of God.

Likewise the drunkard shall not inherit. He is the man given to the sin of drinking too much alcohol. He drinks it to the point of inebriation. Here also the drug user is condemned, inasmuch as his drug use impairs him and destroys him as alcohol affects the drunkard. It is a sin. No drunkard—or drug user—shall inherit the kingdom of God.

A reviler is a blasphemer of the truth, of the church, and of holy things. A reviler likewise shall not inherit.

An extortioner is not merely the loan shark, but also the union member. This is a salvation issue, for he likewise shall not inherit the kingdom.

The apostle says, "And such were some of you." This is a twist. Here he confronts the believer, the justified man and citizen of the kingdom, with his original condition. Paul says "some" because some church members are born into an outwardly upright environment. Some are called out of an outwardly wicked and gross environment. However, by "some" he does not intend to exclude any person from a natural depravity. Such were we all by nature. We were in those sins, and we were guilty of them. Further, our natures are still prone to those sins. All of us as unrighteous were excluded from the kingdom by nature.

When the apostle says "such were some of you" and "the unrighteous shall not inherit the kingdom of God," he does not mean that they are excluded from the kingdom because they committed particular sins, and thus for them there is no hope. This is part of the retort raised against preaching that the unrighteous are excluded: "But it is not a salvation issue. Are you saying, then, that they cannot go to heaven?" This is not what the apostle teaches. When he says that some of them were called from that mess, he also cuts off that interpretation. The kingdom saves also from those depths of sin. Paul means that the impenitent, the unrighteous, who show themselves to be unrighteous because of their impenitence and persist in that impenitence, so long as they remain unconverted to God are excluded. They are shut out of the kingdom.

Why are they shut out? They are shut out because they are unrighteous. The kingdom of God is a kingdom of the righteous.

It is not a kingdom of the unrighteous. Being a kingdom of the righteous, it is a kingdom of the repentant. The unrighteous are impenitent. It is a kingdom of the righteous who are righteous because they "are washed," "sanctified," and "justified in the name of the Lord Jesus, and by the Spirit of our God" (1 Cor. 6:11), and who are that because they have received the kingdom as a gracious inheritance from God.

A Gracious Inheritance

The kingdom of God is a kingdom of grace for sinners unrighteous by nature. In this kingdom righteousness is given to the unrighteous. This kingdom is inherited.

An inheritance is the substance of a father that he leaves to his children at his death. They receive that inheritance out of the good will of their father and at the death of their father. God triune is the Father, and his inheritance is his kingdom. When Paul calls it an inheritance, he indicates as well that this comes to the heirs by the death of the testator, so that God who promised this, in Christ, brought the inheritance into force by his death on the cross.

The inheritance is inherited by the work of God. God causes the righteous to inherit by washing them. Like a mother washes her dirty child, God washes the citizens of his kingdom. He washes them thoroughly. "Ye are washed...ye are sanctified... ye are justified." There is the thorough washing of naturally unrighteous men, women, and children from their sins and unrighteousness that excluded them from the kingdom.

The washing includes their sanctification. Sanctification is the power and work of the God of the kingdom when he establishes the gracious and saving rule of Christ in the hearts of men, women, and children to overcome the power of sin in their hearts and lives, to deliver them from that power, and to cleanse them from the pollution of sin. Not sin but Jesus Christ rules. That rule is the very gift of the kingdom. It is sanctification that issues in an actual turning from sin in deep sorrow and a godly life in principle, so that the believer begins to keep not only some but all the commandments of God. It is such a sanctifying power that Paul says that the Corinthians were these kinds of sinners before and implies that they are not that now. The inheritance of the kingdom gives them the power to overcome sin, to turn from sin, and to hate sin.

Included in that gracious inheritance is the justification of the heirs of the kingdom: "Ye are justified." The relationship between these twin benefits of the kingdom—justification and sanctification—is that they are sanctified because they have been justified. The justification of the unrighteous is the foundation of their salvation in the kingdom. Their unrighteousness excludes them. Their justification saves them and is the ground for every other benefit and blessing of the kingdom. That justification consists in God's forgiveness of their sins and his imputation of the righteousness of the King of the kingdom, on the basis of which God declares them to be righteous and heirs of his kingdom. That justification is by faith alone. That justification is not the justification of good people but very obviously and pointedly in this text is the justification of the ungodly, as it always is. God declares the ungodly and guilty (in himself) believer worthy of eternal life in the kingdom.

When the apostle says in verse 11, "In the name of the Lord Jesus, and by the Spirit of our God," he makes the application of salvation all God's work. That it is done "in the name of the Lord Jesus" means on the basis of the work of Jesus Christ. The work of Jesus Christ is his death on the cross, his payment of the sinner's guilt, and his earning for the unrighteous sinner the Spirit of Jesus Christ. The work of Jesus Christ accomplished on the cross is the salvation of the sinner. By Christ's work on the cross he accomplished the salvation that he applies in the kingdom. The work of Christ on the cross, the Word of God spoken at the cross, is the actual power to sanctify from the pollution of sin and to justify the sinner from the guilt of his sin.

When Paul adds in verse 11 "by the Spirit," he means that the gift of the kingdom is also God's work in the heart of the sinner. The Spirit of God is the third person of the Trinity as he is given to Christ to be the worker of salvation in the hearts of his people. The Spirit of God lays hold on the sinner and in his consciousness justifies him by faith only. The Spirit operates in his heart, breaking sin's power, working to turn the sinner from his sin, and giving to him faith and repentance, so he is thoroughly cleansed from all his sins.

This is the work "of our God" (v. 11). When the apostle says that, he traces the inheritance of the kingdom as a gift of grace by the work of Jesus Christ through his Spirit all the way back to God, to the God who was our God before he washed us while we were still in our sins. The God who is ours is not our God because we loved him, chose him, and turned in repentance to him, but the God who first loved us, picked us, and appointed to us a kingdom and salvation.

In summary, that the kingdom of God is inherited means that the kingdom is the gift of grace. God gives it. He gives it to those who by nature are unrighteous and undeserving. He gives it to those who are all by nature like some of them were as to their actual condition in life—the fornicator, idolater, adulterer, effeminate, abuser, thief, covetous, drunkard, reviler, and extortioner. The one who becomes righteous—legally and actually—and inherits the kingdom is the unrighteous by nature.

But the unrighteous are excluded. Their unrighteousness and their impenitence indicate that they are not justified and sanctified, are devoid of Christ and the Spirit, and are strangers to the grace of God.

Knowing This

The apostle teaches this doctrine, the church must teach this doctrine, and believers must believe this doctrine in order always to remember about the kingdom itself and about their own reception of the kingdom that these are gracious gifts. Because the unrighteous are excluded, all are equally unworthy of the kingdom because all are unrighteous. There is no principle difference between the invisible unrighteousness of the covetous and the openly vile unrighteousness of the homosexual. If the unrighteous are excluded, all are excluded by nature.

The apostle will have the church remember this in order not to be deceived (v. 9). The deception is that the unrighteous shall inherit. This is a very wicked deception because if the unrighteous shall inherit, by that fact the righteous shall *not* inherit. The unrighteous will always cast out the righteous. That is why when the church carves out a place for the unrighteous in her membership, the end result is that that church will eventually persecute the righteous and cast them out and that church will become a false church and a synagogue of Satan.

This deception is common and comes in many different forms. It ensnares those who forget about the gracious inheritance of the kingdom.

The deception that the unrighteous shall inherit comes in the form of the false doctrine of salvation by the sinner's works, either wholly or in part. The kingdom of God can be only a gift of grace, an inheritance, not a reward to unworthy and unrighteous sinners, certainly not a reward for any works of the sinner, whether the sinner who extorts from his fellow man or the sinner who attempts to extort from God his glory by going about to establish his own righteousness by his deeds of love. Since those deeds are unrighteous and imperfect—and not even the most vigorous proponent of works-righteousness would contend otherwise—they cannot be the basis of inheriting the kingdom, or the unrighteous inherit. When the apostle states that the kingdom includes righteousness, he excludes from the kingdom all who seek another righteousness in addition to Christ's.

The theology that teaches a general grace of God gives to the unrighteous the favor of God—the grand benefit of the kingdom.

If that theology lodges in a church, the favored wicked will cast out the righteous from the kingdom. Indeed, any form of conditional theology, a theology that teaches salvation dependent on man's decision to accept Christ into his heart, or faith as man's work, or man's good works of love and obedience, is the same in that it denies that the kingdom of heaven is an inheritance and teaches that the kingdom of heaven is the reward for man's work. It also by that teaches that the unrighteous inherit the kingdom of God because God must accept what is imperfect as perfect.

Do not be deceived; the unrighteous shall not inherit the kingdom of God.

This deception, that the unrighteous shall inherit, comes when justification and sanctification are divorced from one another. By this both are corrupted. A justification without its twin is no justification, and sanctification apart from justification is nothing more than self-righteousness. The apostle distinguishes them and yet joins them together: "Ye are washed...ye are sanctified...ye are justified" (v. 11).

When the grace of God is used as a cover for a licentious life, they are separated. When the grace of God is used as an excuse for failure to discipline sinners, they are separated. When the thinking is adopted: he is a really nice guy and I like him, or he is my son and I am attached to him, although he lives a wicked life, and I will defend him and his place in the church or in my fellowship, then justification and sanctification are separated, and this deception that the unrighteous shall inherit the kingdom has been adopted.

There is the deception that the unrighteous can inherit the kingdom of heaven when a church member knows full well that another member of the church is living an ungodly life and does nothing about it. There is the undermining of the discipline of the church by opposing it, obstructing it, or not obeying it when it is actually carried out. Why? Someone supposes that the unrighteous can inherit the kingdom of God. For one of these things is true: either that man is not going to heaven and my failure to warn him and discipline him reveals a total failure of love, or I believe that he is in fact going to go to heaven impenitent and unrighteous.

Sorrow for sin must issue in turning from it. The justified believer is at the same time and according to the work of the same God, the same Spirit, and on the ground of the same cross the sanctified believer. Such is the power and grace of the kingdom that the unrighteous are declared righteous by the imputation of Christ's righteousness, and the unrighteous are made righteous, so that they hate their sins and turn from them and walk in a new and holy life.

There is the notion, which the old man embraces wholeheartedly, that one can go on in his sin and still inherit the kingdom of God. Note well, it is not that the child of God does not sin. There always remains in him a vicious root of sin. There are infirmities that remain against his will—those besetting sins, those such-were-some-of-you sins. The child of God does not continue in his sins but sorrows because of them, turns from them, and hates them, and if he could he would eradicate his old man entirely.

That common deception that one can continue in sin and still inherit the kingdom was also the theological root of the Corinthians' atrocious treatment of one another. They were deceived that their unrighteousness—no love and suing the brother in court—would not keep them out of heaven, because that was not a salvation issue. The apostle says that is a deception (v. 9).

Know that salvation is a gracious gift to the unrighteous. "Know ye not that...such were some of you?" Here the apostle pointedly applies the principle that the unrighteous do not inherit and teaches personally that the believer's salvation is a gracious gift.

If salvation is a gracious gift from God, every believer has only one debt, an ever-abiding debt to love the neighbor as himself. The apostle lays his finger on the Corinthians' terrible treatment of one another. When they insisted on their rights, they forgot their origin. He points them to their origin. As the prophet of the Old Testament did, Paul calls the Corinthians to look at the rock whence they were hewn and the pit from whence they were dug (Isa. 51:1). In order to live in true thankfulness, they must first know their misery and gracious deliverance.

Where that is known, there is also gratitude, and where gratitude is, there is love of the neighbor. Where there is no love for the neighbor, there is unrighteousness, and the unrighteous shall not inherit the kingdom of God. Remembering that, love one another as those who have been so washed.

CHAPTER 19

A PECULIARLY CHRISTIAN SEXUAL ETHIC

1 Corinthians 6:13–20

---

13. *Meats for the belly, and the belly for meats: but God shall destroy both it and them. Now the body is not for fornication, but for the Lord; and the Lord for the body.*

14. *And God hath both raised up the Lord, and will also raise up us by his own power.*

15. *Know ye not that your bodies are the members of Christ? shall I then take the members of Christ, and make them the members of an harlot? God forbid.*

16. *What? know ye not that he which is joined to an harlot is one body? for two, saith he, shall be one flesh.*

17. *But he that is joined unto the Lord is one spirit.*

18. *Flee fornication. Every sin that a man doeth is without the body; but he that committeth fornication sinneth against his own body.*

19. *What? know ye not that your body is the temple of the Holy Ghost which is in you, which ye have of God, and ye are not your own?*

20. *For ye are bought with a price: therefore glorify God in your body, and in your spirit, which are God's.*

In these verses the apostle does for the congregation of Corinth what the wise father of Proverbs did for his son and what every wise father should do for his sons: he explains the peculiarly Christian sexual ethic. Ethics is a branch of study that treats conduct in a particular field. There is medical ethics, which treats the conduct of nurses and doctors and other practitioners in the medical profession. There is a sports ethic, a teaching ethic, a business ethic, and many others. The Christian has a peculiar ethic for every area of life. This ethic governs their conduct in every area of their lives, whether in the home, school, society, or business. The Heidelberg Catechism treats this ethic in its explanation of the ten commandments. At the heart of that ethic stands the command of God to love the neighbor as yourself, which is the fulfillment of the whole law.

Belonging to Christian ethics is the Christian sexual ethic, which treats the subject of proper Christian behavior in the realm of sex. The world has its sexual ethic: in it almost nothing is forbidden. As with other areas of life, Christians have a peculiarly Christian sexual ethic. That ethic is not the result of their sexual prudishness, but it is from God and clearly revealed in the sacred scriptures, the only rule of faith and every area of life. That ethic is received by the regenerated heart and lived by the power of the Spirit of Jesus Christ, who rules that heart and controls it according to the word of God.

The difference between the Christian and the world in the realm of sexual ethics is not that the Christian and the church do not talk about sex and the world does. The Bible teaches about sex. The wise father in Proverbs taught his son about sex, the apostle teaches it to Corinth, and before that God taught his people through Moses in the law about a sexual ethic that was diametrically opposed to that of the Canaanites, Egyptians, and other heathens. The difference between the church and the world is that the world's sexual ethic corrupts the gift of sex, and the church lives according to the word of God and uses sex rightly.

The difference is that the world lusts, while Christians love in their sexual relations.

That Christian sexual ethic, the behavior of Christians regarding sex, is peculiar. *Peculiar* has to do with one's property. What is peculiar to you is what you own. That belongs to the Christian's sexual ethic. The Christian is owned by someone. He is owned by Christ. He was "bought with a [fair, goodly] price" (v. 20). He was not bought cheaply. He was bought with blood. Having been bought, he is owned body and soul by Jesus Christ, who is then lord of his body. The Christian behaves in a certain way with respect to his body because he is owned by someone. He lives in the peculiarly Christian ethic according to the word of his Lord and because it is the word of his Lord.

When he does that, he will also be peculiar. *Peculiar* also means strange, an odd duck, or weird. The Christian who lives according to this word of God will be peculiar in that sense. He will be an odd duck, weird, and strange in the world, because this ethic is antithetical to the way in which the world lives regarding sex.

The apostle begins his treatment of the Christians' sexual ethic by contrasting it with things indifferent. There are many things regarding our bodily lives that are indifferent. A Christian may eat pork, drink wine, smoke a cigarette, enjoy a fine cigar or a good pipe, wear wool and linen together, use doctors and medicines and vaccines, and eat meat on whatever day he pleases. These things are indifferent. The Corinthians understood that too. They said, "All things are lawful unto me" (v. 12). They are lawful in the sense that the Christian's liberty in things indifferent is within the law, not outside or beside the law.

The apostle must address the subject that all things are lawful, "but all things are not expedient" (v. 12). The Christian's liberty is not controlled by what pleases him, but by expediency. *Expediency* means profitable to him and to his neighbor. What rightly belongs to my liberty might not be profitable to me and to my neighbor.

Besides, that something is indifferent to me means that I may not be brought under its power. If it is to remain indifferent, I cannot be controlled by that thing. It is a special kind of slavery to be controlled by something that is indifferent. The drunkard is a slave to what ought to be indifferent. That slavery conflicts with liberty. The apostle applies that to meat and food. There are things that belong to your liberty: what you eat, drink, and put on. "Meats for the belly, and the belly for meats: but God shall destroy both it and them" (v. 13).

But the body is not for fornication. What also controls the Christian in his liberty is the purpose of God with his creation of a thing. There is a purpose of God with the belly. God gave bellies for the purpose of eating and enjoying food. God also made meat for those bellies. The purpose of the meat is so that a man can eat it and enjoy it. But God did not make bodies for fornication. Neither did he make the Lord Jesus Christ in order that bodies can be pressed into the service of fornication. He made the body for the Lord, and he made the Lord for the body.

That is not how the Corinthians—the world's sexual ethic—viewed fornication. Sex was no different than eating and drinking. The term *Corinthian* in the ancient world was a synonym for a fornicator and sexual deviant. A Corinthian male woke up, dressed, ate, drank, fornicated—with men or women made no difference—and went to sleep. They were all equally allowed. So also our society: one can do what he wants, when he wants, with whomever or whatever he wants, as long as he wants.

But the body is not for fornication: there is a peculiarly Christian sexual ethic.

The Command Governing Sex

The Christian sexual ethic begins with a particular view of sex and fornication. Implied in what the apostle teaches about sex is that sex is good. Sex is a good creation of God, given in the beginning and enjoyed even by Adam and Eve in paradise. They were both naked, and they were not ashamed. Sex is not a sin. It is not dirty. The sin is fornication, the corruption of sex by sinful and depraved man.

That view of sex is governed by the law of God. There is a particular Christian view of sex because of the law of God. Christian behavior generally and Christian behavior regarding sex are not governed by societal norms, lusts, customs, superstitions, taboos, or fear. They are governed by the law. Sin is transgression of the law.

The command of God's law that governs sex is the seventh commandment, in which the law uses the word "adultery." *Adultery* is the specific term for sexual sin against the spouse in marriage. Paul describes sexual sin generally and uses the word "fornication." *Fornication* is a term that covers all sexual sins: the acts that lead up to sex, the enticements, the thoughts, and the acts themselves. Both adultery and fornication are implied and thus forbidden in the seventh commandment.

The world also has its view of fornication. The word *fornication* was originally a euphemism. The root of the word means the arch of a bridge. It was a euphemism for where the prostitutes pedaled themselves to the men. The world still speaks euphemistically about fornication. If the world has to define fornication, it gives very benign definitions. Fornication is "voluntary sexual intercourse between two unmarried persons or two persons not married to each other."[1] Or fornication is "voluntary sexual intercourse outside marriage."[2] This sounds almost as harmless as two people going out for dinner.

The apostle calls fornication sin. Speaking of fornication, he says, "Every sin," including fornication (v. 18). Fornication is not merely sexual intercourse outside marriage, but fornication is sexual uncleanness. Fornication is transgression of the law of

---

1 http://www.dictionary.com/browse/fornication.
2 https://www.thefreedictionary.com/Sex+before+marriage.

God in the seventh commandment. This is the point the apostle makes in the text: fornication is a sin, a sin that renders a man guilty before God, a sin that rendering him guilty before God makes that man liable to God's judgment, and a sin that pollutes him and defiles him. In his just judgment God can give a man over to that sin. If one continues in it unrepentantly, God will send that sinner to hell. The fornicator and adulterer and abuser of himself with mankind shall not inherit the kingdom of God.

Do not trivialize sin by making things sin that are not sin. The apostle warns about that when he teaches in the context that there are indifferent things. Making indifferent things sin is just as bad as making sinful things indifferent. Do not use this passage to make things sin that are not sin. Not only is that a false interpretation and use of the passage—which is an injustice perpetrated against the word of God and the brother against whom it is used as a club—an offense against the believer's liberty to use those indifferent things, and a lack of love, but also such a use trivializes sin.

Trivializing sin leads man to absurdities. A man chastises another for the "sin" of smoking, while his daughter is living in a third marriage, about which he says nothing. Or while it is practically a crime to eat a cheeseburger dripping with bacon fat, it is not seen as much of a problem for two teenagers to fornicate as long as they use protection.

Such a trivializing of sin also removes the focus from the particular sin the apostle treats here. The passage is not about smoking or eating greasy cheeseburgers, but fornication. Fornication is sin.

What is fornication? Specific examples must be given of acts that are fornication. Why? Because many things that are fornication are placed in the realm of liberty.

In addition to what was said in 1 Corinthians 5, there is Jesus' word, "Whosoever looketh on a woman to lust after her hath committed adultery with her already in his heart" (Matt. 5:28).

Pornography, whether in books, in magazines, or on the Internet, is fornication. Included in that is dress. There may be women who are not harlots by trade, but they dress like them. The Heidelberg Catechism reminds us that "whatever can entice men thereto" is fornication.[3] No Christian woman may dress like a harlot, wearing skirts that barely cover their bottoms and low-cut dresses and blouses that barely cover their bosoms. Even more atrocious and inexcusable is when they come to church dressed that way.

Fornication is not liberty but sin. The Corinthians counted it among their liberties. That is still the view of the world. A man may eat and drink whatever he wants and fornicate too. The world has more problems with what a man eats and drinks than what he does with his body. How many thou-shalt-not-fornicate commercials are seen on television as opposed to the spots that tell the horrors of smoking? If a man is fat, the world wants to make him thin, but if a man fornicates, the world wants him to have his liberty. Whether fornication is sin is not a matter of culture, preference, feelings, time, or circumstances, but of God's law, which does not change and says for all ages that fornication is sin.

Fornication's Uniqueness As Sin

Fornication is a unique sin. The apostle indicates this in verse 18: "Flee fornication. Every sin that a man doeth is without the body; but he that committeth fornication sinneth against his own body." Fornication's uniqueness is not that it is the unpardonable sin. It is gross sin, but it is not unpardonable. David teaches that there is redemption, forgiveness, washing, cleansing, and deliverance from that sin, and so likewise does Christ, Paul, and the Holy Ghost. Fornication is unique because there is no other sin by which a man can so sin against his own body. It pollutes and defiles the body in a way that no other sin can.

---

3 Heidelberg Catechism A 109, in Schaff, *Creeds of Christendom*, 3:347.

This is what Paul says: "Every sin that a man doeth is without the body." He does not mean, for example, that a murderer does not defile his hands by his murder or that the liar does not pollute his tongue by falsehood. Rather, those sins are committed as it were outside the body, but by fornication man sins in his body. Literally Paul says that fornication is the sin "into" a body. Fornication penetrates into and defiles the human body like no other sin can.

With that unique view of fornication, there is also a unique command to man. The word of God to young and old, to married and single, and to men and women is, "Flee fornication!" The only other sin that the Bible says to flee from is idolatry. But if one understands that idolatry is spiritual fornication, there is only one sin the Bible tells man to flee from: fornication. Run from it. Do not get as close as you can. Do not experiment and play around with it. Run from it! Can a man take fire into his bosom and not be burned? So also run from fornication. Run from it as you would run from a forest fire.

For the single person this means absolutely no sexual relations before marriage. For the married person this means holiness in marriage and the proper use of sex in marriage. This means that a husband can enjoy his wife, and a wife can enjoy her husband, but in that they flee from fornication, especially into the arms of each other.

By contrast, do not stand and fight fornication. She has slain many a mighty man. Her lips are sweet as honey and smooth as oil, but her feet go down to hell and lay hold on death, and her end is bitter as wormwood. She allures, but she is loud and stubborn, and this whore has a brazen forehead. Once she lays hold on a man she leads him to death, as a farmer leads his cattle to the slaughter house. Flee from fornication (Prov. 5:3–6; 6:24–25; 7:10–21; 9:13–18).

If we fall into it, fleeing from fornication means to repent quickly and seek forgiveness and cleansing in the cross of Jesus Christ. Flee fornication!

The Reason to Flee Fornication

The Christian man or woman does not flee fornication for the reasons that the world may give when it speaks of abstinence. The world may speak disparagingly of certain kinds of sexual relations and may even say to a young person or a married person, "Do not have sexual relations before marriage or outside marriage." The world also has its reasons. A man might catch a sexually transmitted disease and ruin his health or impregnate the woman and ruin his life and reputation. The world says to the young woman regarding abstinence, "You will get pregnant too soon in your life. You will not be able to finish high school, college, or even grade school." The world says to the ambitious man, "You will get a blot on your name. You will ruin your chances in the business world or in the political world or in the community." But if you can protect yourself from disease, keep from getting caught, stop yourself from getting pregnant, then go ahead and commit fornication. The world preaches abstinence, but only because of the repeated failures of protection. That is the world's ethic.

That is not the Christian's ethic. He has a particular view of fornication, a particular command about fornication, and particular reasons to flee fornication.

The reasons the apostle gives in these verses are not the only reasons. Proverbs also has reasons to avoid fornication: you give your honor and wealth to strangers, by means of a whorish woman a man is brought to a piece of bread, he is grievously wounded physically and spiritually with deep scars, and he consumes his flesh (5:9–11; 6:26; 7:26–27). The Bible recognizes some of these practical things. But these are not the only or the main reasons the believer must flee fornication.

The reasons in 1 Corinthians 6 are peculiar—peculiarly Christian and distinctly theological. Doctrine and life are inseparable. The word of the church when there is apostasy of life must be that it comes from bad doctrine. Life flows out of doctrine.

First, flee fornication because the body will be raised. The

Corinthians misunderstood the resurrection, so the apostle spends the whole of chapter 15 explaining the resurrection. The Corinthians took the words "God shall destroy both it and them" (6:13) to mean that they could do whatever they wanted to their bodies, because God will destroy their bodies. That is not true. The apostle means that the *physical life* of the body will be destroyed and the physical purpose of the body will be destroyed, but the *body* will not be destroyed. The purpose of the belly to eat meat will be done away, but the body and the belly will not. It is true, we live as new creatures now in mortal flesh that is dead, but the body will be raised. It will be raised by the same power whereby God raised the body of Jesus Christ. In eternity the body will be the instrument for the believer's life to the glory to God. He will praise God in a glorified resurrection body. Thus in this life the body that will be raised must be the instrument to glorify God. This means no fornication.

Second, flee fornication because the believer in his body is already a member of Jesus Christ. The believer is not a member of Jesus Christ merely in his soul, but also in his body: his hands, your hands; his feet, your feet; his head, your head. By fornication the believer takes the member of Jesus Christ and joins it to a filthy harlot. The harlot is not merely the woman who sells herself for sex, but also the woman who engages in any sexual activity outside marriage, whether for money, for social or economic advancement, or for gratification of lust. The apostle speaks only of the harlot, but his application is not limited to women or even to women who sell their bodies, but includes all fornicators. By fornication the believer takes the sanctified and cleansed body that is a member in Christ and joins it to a filthy harlot and defiles his body with fornication.

The apostle grounds that in God's original creation. When God made Adam and Eve in the beginning and joined them together and said, "They shall be one flesh" (Gen. 2:24), he included in that union the sexual relationship. In fornication there is a dark, demonic parody of and assault on marriage. Not merely homosexuality and the desire of homosexuals to marry attack marriage, but also fornication in all its forms assault marriage. In fornication, because of the nature of the sexual relationship, the believer joins his body to the harlot; but because the believer is joined to Christ, he defiles by that act the members of Christ.

The Bible points out the great sin of that sinful union: "He that is joined unto the Lord is one spirit" (1 Cor. 6:17). The apostle makes a comparison: if a man in marriage cannot commit adultery without great sin because he is one flesh with his wife, so much more the believer who is married to Christ commits a great sin by fornication. In marriage two are one flesh; in marriage to Christ two are "one spirit." The believer sins against that when he commits fornication.

Third, flee fornication because "your body is the temple of the Holy Ghost, which is in you" (v. 19). The believer is indwelt by the Spirit of Jesus Christ. From heaven Christ sends his Spirit, who abides in the believer as in a temple or a palace. By the Spirit, Christ gives the believer saving communion with him. Because fornication sins against the body as no other sin can, by fornication the believer defiles the temple of the Holy Spirit. A man cannot defile his temple like that with any other sin or earthly activity. Smoking and eating too many cheeseburgers do not defile your temple. Even if those things were sin, they cannot defile the temple of the Holy Ghost like fornication does.

Only fornication defiles the temple, so that the fornicator is as a man who walks into Solomon's temple with an ax, overthrows the laver, hacks at the altar, overturns the table of showbread, kicks over the golden candlestick, slashes the curtain, lights a fire with the wood of the ark, and sacrifices a pig in the holy of holies. That is what a fornicator does with his body. What does the Spirit think of such a sacrilegious desecrator of his temple? Flee fornication!

Furthermore, the believer is not his own, not in body or soul. How the world tries to impress the opposite on the believer! Those loud, stubborn, brazen-headed whores say, "I am my own, and I can do with my body what I want." The lusty man says that he is his own and can do what he wants with his body.

The believer confesses, "I am not my own. I was bought with a good price." That phrase makes one think of Hosea, who had to buy back his wife, the whore, with a good price (Hos. 3:2–3), or of Ezekiel's touching description of God, finding the blood-soaked, abandoned little baby girl in the field and having compassion on her and adorning her with his beauty (Ezek. 16). God bought his church with a good price to make her the wife of his Son, washing her from her sins, forgiving those sins and cleansing her from them, beautifying her with salvation, and even taking up his abode with her by his Spirit. We are not our own; we belong to him as our husband, our lord, and our bodies belong to him. He may use our bodies as he pleases, and we must use them as he pleases, "for ye are bought with a price" (1 Cor. 6:20).

That is God's word to the believer who falls into fornication. "Ye are bought with a price." Flee fornication to his cross and find forgiveness for the sin of defiling your body, release from the shame of that, and cleansing from the pollution and dominion of that sin. You are bought with a price. Flee fornication!

The Purpose for the Christian Sexual Ethic

Fleeing fornication, the calling of the believer is to glorify God in the body. "Now the body is not for fornication, but for the Lord; and the Lord for the body" (v. 13). This is a remarkable statement, in which the apostle says that in a similar way as God made meats for the belly and the belly for meats so they can be eaten and enjoyed, so God made the body for the Lord and the Lord for the body. He exalted and glorified Christ Jesus to be lord and made him lord also of the believer's body.

Glorify, then, the Lord in the body. For the young person this means by holiness and abstaining from all sexual relations until marriage, by holiness in dress, conversation, and language. For married persons this means that husbands give themselves to their wives and wives to their husbands. That glorifies God in our bodies. Sex is not the sin; fornication is the sin. Flee fornication and glorify God in your bodies!

CHAPTER 20

Sex in Marriage

1 Corinthians 7:2–5

---

2. *Nevertheless, to avoid fornication, let every man have his own wife, and let every woman have her own husband.*

3. *Let the husband render unto the wife due benevolence: and likewise also the wife unto the husband.*

4. *The wife hath not power of her own body, but the husband: and likewise also the husband hath not power of his own body, but the wife.*

5. *Defraud ye not one the other, except it be with consent for a time, that ye may give yourselves to fasting and prayer; and come together again, that Satan tempt you not for your incontinency.*

The apostle Paul begins chapter 7 with "Now concerning the things whereof ye wrote unto me," which indicates that he begins a new section in the epistle in which he answers certain questions of the Corinthians. Evidently the Corinthians had sent to Paul a series of questions about various issues in the congregation. He could not deal with them right away because more pressing and fundamental issues had to be handled. The apostle has dealt with those issues; now he can answer their questions about other matters.

The fact that a church sent questions to the apostle is instructive. That is an important way to learn; asking questions prompts learning and instruction. The questions were not from individuals in the congregation but were officially from the church. That still happens today. A church at every classis has the opportunity to ask questions of the classis. Church Order article 41 treats this.[1] The Corinthians' questions were about sex, love, marriage, and singleness. It is important that at this point the apostle deals with these matters.

He has cursed all sexual uncleanness as fornication. That fornication was evidence of the Corinthian society's worship of sex as a god. The same can be said of our society, which brazenly parades its debasing and abuse of God's good gift of sex. It uses sex to sell products. It glorifies fornication and peddles it in magazines, books, billboards, and Internet pages. The apostle damned all that and sharply warned the church to flee fornication.

Sex is not the sin; fornication is the sin. Sex is a good gift of God. Here the scriptures speak frankly about this subject. That directness contrasts sharply with our frequent embarrassment and torturous circumlocution. Scripture's plain speech is a weapon against the bawdy excesses of the world. The scriptures deal openly and frequently with this subject. So does the holy apostle. He was not embarrassed about it and did not consider such a question beneath his apostolic dignity. The elders of Corinth were not embarrassed to ask the apostle. The Holy Spirit was not embarrassed by their questions but inspired these words for their and our instruction and as a bulwark against the lasciviousness that characterizes the world's sexual relationships.

The Goodness of Sex

The sexual relationship is the subject of verses 1–5. The word of God about that relationship is that it is good. This is the word of God that underlies the whole of 1 Corinthians 7.

The text and context point out the goodness of sex in several

---

1 Church Order 41, in *Confessions and Church Order*, 393.

respects. When the apostle says regarding the unmarried that it is good that a man not touch a woman, he implies the opposite. In marriage it is good that a man touch a woman and by implication that a woman touch a man. The apostle teaches the goodness of the sexual relationship when he calls the satisfaction of the sexual need of husband and wife paying of a debt—a debt the husband owes to his wife and the wife owes to her husband. Paying a debt is a good thing. The love of the neighbor is an abiding debt. Belonging to the love debt that husband and wife pay one another is sex. Paul also calls this relationship good when he says that the proper relationship between husband and wife is a bulwark against the temptations of Satan. The husband and wife may be apart for a time by consent, but they must come together again so Satan will not tempt them.

That sex is good is taught explicitly by Paul in verse 9: "it is better to marry than to burn," that is, it is better to marry and to enjoy sex in marriage than to burn in lust and fornication outside marriage. He does not teach the goodness of sex outside marriage, so that it is good to have sex outside marriage, but it is better in marriage. Rather, he teaches the badness of sex outside marriage and the goodness of sex in marriage. He uses the word "better" in the way we might say it is better to go to heaven than to go to hell.

Sex is not inherently sinful, animalistic, base, or shameful. It is good. Some may think that it is evil as such, that it was necessitated by the fall, or that it is redeemed by having children. This is not the scriptural view. Scripture in these verses speaks of the sexual relationship in marriage as such. It is good. Indeed, it was good before the fall. This is the word of God regarding Adam and Eve in the beginning. "They were both naked, the man and his wife, and were not ashamed" (Gen. 2:25). There is God's word about the goodness of the sexual relationship between Adam and Eve before the fall in the garden. It belonged to the intimate communion of their marriage in the beginning.

This view the church must have. This is the view that believing husbands and wives must also have.

Sex within Marriage Only

The apostle teaches that sex is good only in marriage: "Let every man have his own wife, and let every woman have her own husband" (1 Cor. 7:2). Our criticism of the world's treatment of the subject of sex is that the world defiles and corrupts that good relationship by its sins, perversions, fornication, adulteries, sodomies, scandalous clothing, pictures, movies, and peddling products by means of sex. The world's defiling of the sexual relationship is part of its assault on the marriage relationship to which sex properly belongs and in which alone it is good.

The grace of God to believing husbands and wives restores a proper attitude and behavior in the sexual relationship in marriage. It is good; it is good in marriage; it is good only in marriage.

The apostle speaks to the unmarried in verse 1: "It is good for a man not to touch a woman." This is God's word that the sexual relationship is reserved exclusively for a married man and woman. "Touch" is an important word. The Spirit in his instruction here is deliberate. There are translations of this passage that may appear on the surface to be more forceful but are in fact misleading. The New International Version paraphrases it as "It is good not to marry." That is not what the Holy Spirit says. In fact, the context denies that, for the apostle says that it is better to marry than to burn. In addition to the evil of paraphrasing the word of God, it is not even an accurate paraphrase. The English Standard Version has, "It is not good to have sexual relations." This too is not what the Spirit says, although it is certainly implied in his instruction to the unmarried.

The Spirit said "touch," which literally means to set ablaze. The Spirit calls attention again to his warning to flee fornication, because a man cannot take fire into his bosom and not be burned (Prov. 6:27). The Spirit says to the unmarried, "Do not touch a woman; do not touch a man," by which he means touch sexually. By this word the Bible is realistic in its warnings to the single about sexual relationships. Sexual relationships do not come out of nowhere. When two unmarried young people finally get into bed together, that does not come as a bolt out of the blue, but it is the end of a development that began with their illicit and passionate touching of one another. The beginning of that was the lust about which James wrote, "When lust hath conceived, it bringeth forth sin" (1:15). In the word "touch" is also the church's ground for its prohibition against dancing. There is touching in that activity that leads to and is the prelude to fornication. Sex is not good for the unmarried man and woman. It is good for them that they not touch a woman or a man.

Sex is for the married, and for them alone sex is good. The unmarried man and woman must keep that word in mind. It is not good for me in the unmarried state, but it is good for me in the married state. The young man therefore keeps his strength for his wife, and the young woman keeps her virginity for her husband. They flee especially from the touching that leads to fornication. Sex is not good for the unmarried. It is good for the married.

Avoiding Fornication

Having taught the goodness of the sexual relationship for the married, Paul also teaches its necessity in marriage. That is the word of the Holy Spirit: "To avoid fornication, let every man have his own wife, and let every woman have her own husband" (1 Cor. 7:2). He says again that it is necessary when he commands a husband and wife not to be separate, that is, they may not abstain from sex, except it be by consent for time, and then they come together again (v. 5).

Sex in marriage is necessary, first, for avoiding fornication.

On the one hand the apostle has in view the unmarried person. To avoid fornication the unmarried must keep marriage in mind: "It is better to marry than to burn" (v. 9). The Holy Spirit teaches that the remedy for fornication among the unmarried is sex in marriage. This ought to be a powerful reason for a dating young man and woman not to put off their marriage. Delaying marriage until college is finished, a career is established, or the world is traveled is part of our culture today that grants sexual relationships to the unmarried. They can and they do put off marriage for that long because they are already having sex together, fornicating. To avoid such fornication let every man have his own wife, and let every woman have her own husband in marriage.

A man and woman burn in lust and put themselves through tortures, and the remedy is right before their eyes: get married to avoid fornication. Carefully the unmarried make sure not to marry only for the sake of the physical and make that a foundation of sand for their marriage. To avoid fornication is not the main reason to marry, but it is a reason. It is a reason for two believing young people, who are one in the Lord, to marry. It is a reason for two believing young people who know they are going to get married not to put off the marriage.

On the other hand it is also true for the married that to avoid fornication, let a man have his wife, and let a wife have her husband. That is not only good, but also necessary.

A Debt in Marriage

Within marriage the sexual relationship is necessary because it is the payment of the abiding love debt that husband and wife have as the nearest neighbors to each other. By "defraud" in verse 5 the apostle refers to sex in marriage as a debt.

With this word he teaches that among believers and in marriage sex is very different from fornication. In fornication one seeks his or her own pleasure and gratification and in so doing hates his neighbor. In fornication sex is the god. For the natural man, also in marriage, the sexual partner is merely a tool for base self-gratification. Not so for the believer. He can and does actually love his wife and in the sexual relationship consciously pays a love debt to her. The same is true for the Christian wife. Christian love is to seek the good of the other, and that extends all the way through a believer's life to sex in marriage. In love the husband pays his debt to his wife and seeks her good, and the wife pays her debt to her husband and seeks his good. The main concern of the husband is not what can he get out of this, but what is his duty toward his wife and how does he love his wife. The main concern of the wife is not what she can get out of this, but what is her duty toward her husband and how does she love her husband. There is nothing selfish in the relationship, but it is full of Christian love and concern. It is very different from the beastly intercourse of the world.

When the apostle calls sex a debt in marriage, he also teaches its necessity. Paying debts is necessary, and so paying this aspect of the love debt to the spouse is necessary. He calls the failure to pay this debt fraud: "Defraud ye not one the other, except it be with consent for a time, that ye may give yourselves to fasting and prayer; and come together again, that Satan tempt you not for your incontinency" (v. 5). In this very practical instruction to married couples the apostle makes a remarkable statement. So necessary is that relationship that the apostle also subjects prayer to it. Prayer as the chief part of our thankfulness is the most important spiritual exercise. While the apostle permits Christians to "defraud" one another "for a time," it must be "by consent," only "for a time," and only for "fasting and prayer." And he requires that they "come together again." The spiritual need for prayer fulfilled in a time of prayer and fasting does not rule out satisfaction of the physical need for sex. Spiritual believers who are healthy in their prayer life will also recognize their physical need for sex and find satisfaction of that need within marriage.

The married couple may, according to the apostle, for the sake of the affliction of the flesh and for the sake of a special time of prayer, abstain from sex for a time. On this he puts two strict limits. It must be by mutual consent and only for a time. When the apostle says "with consent," he indicates that there is communication between husband and wife about this aspect of their marriage. When he says "for a time," he makes this temporary. Such a situation is entirely conceivable: a special time of devotion to the church, or an especially difficult time in one's life where there is affliction of the flesh and a time of deep prayer. Then they come together again, so that Satan does not tempt them.

Satan's Attack on Marriage

The sexual relationship in marriage is necessary so that Satan does not tempt the married couple. All other reasons for a lack of sex in marriage—fake or over-righteous spirituality, anger, dissent, unresolved problems, all of which the apostle exposes with the word "incontinency" (v. 5)—neatly play into the devil's hand in his relentless assaults on marriage. Sex is an integral, God-ordained part of the marriage relationship. It is that for both the man and the woman, not just the man, which the apostle indicates. The man or woman who ignores that reality opens himself or herself to the temptation of Satan and consequently exposes his marriage to ruin. Satan will use sexual temptation as a powerful weapon against the married believer. The believer drives that temptation away by his right use of sex.

Sex is not only good, but also in marriage it is necessary to avoid the temptations of Satan and to pay the love debts husbands and wives owe to each other.

Behind the apostle's instruction on the goodness and necessity of sex in marriage stands the Bible's lofty doctrine of marriage. Scripture's doctrine is that marriage is the earthly symbol of the intimate relationship between the elect church and Jesus Christ. In marriage God gave this sexual relationship to husbands and wives as part of the earthly symbol to symbolize the closeness and intimacy of the relationship between the church and Christ. It is not a sickly, superficial relationship, but a deep relationship of intimate communion and fellowship between Christ and his church, a relationship that the believer experiences by faith with Christ, in which there are secrets between the believer and Christ and in which there is the expression of the deep need of the church for communion with Jesus Christ. We need Jesus Christ and do not want to be separate from him. We want him near to us, and we draw near to him. There is also in that relationship the fiery jealousy that stands behind the instruction "let every man have his own wife" (v. 2).

The world today makes sex a god. The church thoroughly condemns this. The main thing in his life is not sex, but the believer's union with Christ Jesus by faith. Sex is not God, God is God.

If believers have issues in their marriages, let them begin with their views of their marriages. If a couple comes to the minister and says, "We have a problem in our marriage: we are not sleeping together," the problem is not first that they are not sleeping together, but that they are not loving each other in Christ. If they were, it would hardly be necessary for the minister to say, "You need to have sex together." Rather the minister says, "You are not living out of the reality of your marriage as a symbol of the marriage relationship between Christ and his church, but you are being selfish in your marriage." The apostle's practical instruction about sex to married couples is rooted in his doctrine of marriage.

Teaching about Sex

There is a grave danger that the church does not do as the apostle does. There is a danger that the church is not frank and open in her instruction. There is a danger that the church only says, "Flee fornication," but does not explain as the wise father of Proverbs did. "Be satisfied with your wife; be ravished with her love. Enjoy marriage" (5:19). The Holy Spirit says to married men and women, "The sexual relationship is good." He says to unmarried men and woman, "At present it is not good, and to avoid fornication, get married." The world glories in its shame, but that must not be an excuse for the church's reticence.

The church must teach regarding sex as part of the glorious doctrine of marriage. Parents should teach it too. The church should teach it publicly. If she does not teach it, the world will teach the children its view of sex by television shows, billboards, and Internet sites.

Listen to the wise father of Proverbs:

> My son, attend unto my wisdom, and bow thine ear to my understanding…The lips of a strange woman drop as an honeycomb, and her mouth is smoother than oil: but her end is bitter as wormwood, sharp as a twoedged sword…Remove thy way far from her, and come not nigh the door of her house…Let thy fountain be blessed: and rejoice with the wife of thy youth. Let her be as a loving hind and a pleasant roe; let her breasts satisfy thee at all times; and be thou ravished always with her love. (5:1–19)

When is the last time a father so instructed his son? "Remember, she may become your wife or the wife of some other man in the church. Be chaste and holy." When is the last time a father so instructed his daughter? "You are not wearing that to church; you are not wearing that on a date. It tempts men." Do parents, as the wise proverbist, without embarrassment teach their children the right use of the sexual relationship in marriage?

We must teach it frankly and openly. We must warn our sons and daughters and ourselves too, because they have our flesh, "Flee fornication. It is not good for a man to touch a woman." Explain to them, "Now to avoid fornication, marry, and in marriage let every man have his own wife and every woman have her own husband." That is what the Spirit says. Let parents and the church teach it.

CHAPTER 21

MAINTAINING
A MIXED MARRIAGE

1 Corinthians 7:12–17

---

12. But to the rest speak I, not the Lord: If any brother hath a wife that believeth not, and she be pleased to dwell with him, let him not put her away.
13. And the woman which hath an husband that believeth not, and if he be pleased to dwell with her, let her not leave him.
14. For the unbelieving husband is sanctified by the wife, and the unbelieving wife is sanctified by the husband: else were your children unclean; but now are they holy.
15. But if the unbelieving depart, let him depart. A brother or a sister is not under bondage in such cases: but God hath called us to peace.
16. For what knowest thou, O wife, whether thou shalt save thy husband? or how knowest thou, O man, whether thou shalt save thy wife?
17. But as God hath distributed to every man, as the Lord hath called every one, so let him walk. And so ordain I in all churches.

In chapter 7 the apostle begins to answer questions that the Corinthians sent to him by official letter. I maintain that this is what the Reformed churches do, following the apostolic practice, when they allow the consistory to submit questions to the classis by means of the credentials of her delegates, or when they ask at every classis meeting, "Does your church need the help of classis for the government of your church?" Here opportunity is given to the consistory to ask questions of the classis. Paul had received from the Corinthians questions for which they needed answers for the proper government of the church. Those were pressing matters about the lives of the individual members of the church. Those matters had to do with marriage, the single life, and sex. The apostle authoritatively and bindingly addresses these matters.

The apostle already taught that it is good that married persons use sex in marriage. By contrast he has insisted that it is not good for the unmarried to use the sexual relationship. If they cannot contain, it is better for them to marry (vv. 1–5, 9).

Continuing his instruction, the apostle alludes briefly to the teaching of Jesus Christ about marriage: "Unto the married I command, yet not I, but the Lord" (v. 10). Regarding marriage and certain situations in marriage, what Paul is going to teach the Corinthian church and the church of Jesus Christ everywhere and for all times, the Lord already taught. Paul will review it for them and apply that teaching to their situations.

Jesus taught the unbreakable bond of marriage. The permanence of the marriage bond was the outstanding feature of Jesus' teaching on marriage. That was the Lord's teaching in Matthew 19:4–12, when he answered the Pharisees' tempting question, "Is it lawful for a man to put away his wife for every cause?" (v. 3).

First Corinthians 7:10–17 is the divine commentary on the Matthew 19 passage, in which Jesus prohibited divorce and remarriage and the remarriage of the so-called innocent party. Some do not believe that; some in Corinth did not believe that and thought that Jesus allowed the remarriage of the innocent party. Paul says no. His no is not his but the Lord's, who taught the unbreakable bond of marriage. If there is a divorce—only for fornication—Paul makes crystal clear that Jesus' teaching in Matthew 19 prohibited the remarriage of the innocent party— the one against whom adultery was committed. "Let her remain unmarried, or be reconciled to her husband" (1 Cor. 7:11). There are two options and only two options for legitimately divorced people in the church: they may remain unmarried, or they must be reconciled to their spouses. They may not remarry. In light of this passage it is indefensible to appeal to Matthew 19 in support of the false doctrine of the remarriage of the innocent party.

From that Paul continues to instruct about another marriage situation that Jesus did not address: a mixed marriage. What is the biblical instruction regarding a marriage between a believer and an unbeliever, or where there is a difference between a husband and wife on doctrine and religion? The apostle says that the Lord did not address that: "But to the rest speak I, not the Lord" (v. 12). Paul means that Jesus did not concretely address this situation and now Paul must. There are certain situations relating to marriage about which Paul will give instruction. The first situation is the mixed marriage.

The Mixed Marriage

That the apostle addresses the situation of a mixed marriage is clear in verses 12–16. He refers to "any brother [who] hath a wife that believeth not" (v. 12). The brother is the believing fellow saint in the church. He is married to a woman who does not believe. Paul continues and speaks of the believing woman in the church who "hath an husband that believeth not" (v. 13). A mixed marriage is a marriage between a believer and an unbeliever. Being married, these two are united in the closest possible relationship that can exist between two human beings, a relationship in which they are one flesh.

Between these two people so united there is also the deepest possible division that can exist between two human beings, a great spiritual and antithetical divide in which spiritually they are totally at odds with one another. The one loves Jesus Christ; the other hates him. The one cleaves to the one, true God; the other opposes him. The one believes; the other does not. The one is born from above; the other is born from below. The one is spiritual; the other is carnal.

What makes Paul's instruction urgent is the marriage between these two people. If they were not married, the issue would be simple. There would be a real and physical separation between them, and they would not be married. But in marriage they are joined by God himself in the closest possible union that can exist between two people. They are no more twain, but one flesh. Indeed, they possess between themselves the unbreakable bond of marriage that God establishes and not man. This is the unbreakable bond of marriage that the apostle has just taught in verses 9–10, and on the basis of which he forbids divorce and remarriage in verse 11.

How did the mixed marriage come about so that two human beings who are so antithetically divided have been joined together in marriage?

No believer may willingly marry an unbeliever. This is the apostle's word in verse 39 regarding the widow, who "is at liberty to be married to whom she will; only in the Lord." What the apostle teaches about the widow applies to all of the people of God. To marry in the Lord is the marriage of two who are spiritually one in Christ, who believe the same doctrine, are governed in their conduct by the word of God, and are members of a church that is one in these areas. It is the marriage of two who are of the same religious convictions. This is one of the basic applications of the antithesis. The holy people of God may not be unequally yoked together with filthy unbelievers (2 Cor. 6:14). This applies to the marriages of believers. No believer may marry someone who does not believe the way that he or she believes.

It is possible that a believing man or woman lives in sin for a while and sinfully disobeys this word of God to marry in the

Lord. Then he or she marries an unbeliever and later is sorry for that.

The apostle also explains the possibility of a mixed marriage by the call of God: "The Lord hath called every one" (1 Cor. 7:17). The gospel calls one spouse according to God's sovereign good pleasure, and also according to God's sovereign good pleasure may leave the other spouse in sin. No doubt that is what had happened in Corinth. The church had been founded not long before the apostle wrote this passage, so that the call of the gospel itself established the antithetical divide between two married people. The Lord sovereignly makes that decision.

A mixed marriage can be the result of hypocrisy on the part of a man or woman. One spouse marries another in good faith. Both are members of the church of Jesus Christ and both confess the same truth; but one is a hypocrite.

A mixed marriage can be the result of a believing spouse's living temporarily like an unbeliever in unrepentant sin. The hardness divides them spiritually.

All of these are examples of what Paul means when he says, "If any brother hath a wife that believeth not...and the woman which hath an husband that believeth not" (vv. 12–13).

The Calling to Maintain

If the believer finds himself in such a mixed marriage or knows of someone in such a marriage, the word of God to the believer in that situation is to maintain the marriage. Paul teaches this when he says, "Let him not put her away...[and] let her not leave him" (vv. 12–13). These phrases are not a general prohibition of divorce, but a prohibition of divorce on account of the spouse's unbelief. By that prohibition of divorce the apostle commands the believing spouse to maintain the marriage.

The qualification on that command to maintain the marriage is the willingness of the unbelieving spouse to live with the believer: if "she be pleased to dwell with him," and "if he be pleased to dwell with her" (vv. 12–13). It is possible that the unbelieving spouse is not pleased to dwell with a believing spouse. Then the apostle's word to the believer is, "Let him depart. A brother or a sister is not under bondage in such cases: but God hath called us to peace" (v. 15). Here Paul recognizes the possibility that the unbeliever is not pleased to dwell with a believer. The unbeliever sinfully and cruelly abandons the believer on account of his or her faith. It is a form of persecution for righteousness' sake. The believer may let the unbeliever depart; the believer is not under bondage to follow and to seek to maintain the marriage in such cases.

Two special applications of this rule deserve mention. One instance where this is applicable is in the case of abuse. There is a permissible leaving by the believer from that unbelieving spouse who manifests both his unwillingness to live with the spouse and his unbelief by his abuse of the spouse. The abuser does not strictly depart, but he is surely unwilling to live with the believing spouse.

Another instance involves church membership. The unbeliever is not pleased to dwell with the believer when the believer insists on the necessity of membership in a true church that requires relocation. The unbeliever is unwilling to move and thus unwilling to dwell with the believer in the place to which God called the believer.

In both cases the believer is not under bondage to maintain the marriage. The believer does not dissolve the marriage bond, but is not under the bondage of the debt of love to maintain the marriage and one's responsibilities in it.

The apostle here does not give a new reason for divorce. That was John Calvin's position. He said that Paul was allowing a new reason for divorce and consequently also for remarriage, because the believing spouse was not under bondage. Calvin's interpretation of "not under bondage" was that one so abandoned may remarry. After explaining it so, Calvin also said that

Paul's teaching was "at variance"[1] with the Lord's teaching and with what Paul had just written in the preceding context: "let her remain unmarried, or be reconciled to her husband." It is, however, exactly Paul's—and the Holy Ghost's—point that in this instruction about marriage and its application to special situations the apostle is not at variance with the Lord, but applies the Lord's teaching about the unbreakable bond of marriage to this situation.

Rather, "not under bondage" means that the abandoned spouse is to be at peace if his or her unbelieving spouse wickedly and cruelly leaves. Be at peace and let the unbeliever go. One is not under bondage in such cases. The marriage bond is not broken by those wicked actions of the unbelieving spouse any more than it is by adultery, but one is not under bondage so that the deserted spouse must follow the unbeliever and try to maintain the marriage. Let the unbeliever go and be at peace, because it is God's will for one's life that he or she rests in the good will of the sovereign God. Have peace in the goodness of God in that difficult and humanly impossible situation. Have peace in God's calling to faithfulness in that situation and to live as a eunuch for the sake of the kingdom of heaven. Since this peace is the fruit of God's gracious calling, the believer who finds himself in such a situation is also able to live at peace by the powerful and sustaining grace of God.

Also live at peace in the church. There should be no stigma that attaches to this individual, so that the believer finds in the church the family and fellowship that is denied to him or her because the unbelieving spouse has left.

God has called to peace. That has to ring in the souls, ears, and hearts of those who endure that difficult situation. Even

---

1 John Calvin, *Commentary on the Epistles of Paul the Apostle to the Corinthians*, trans. John Pringle (Grand Rapids,MI: Baker Book House, repr., 1979), 1:240.

then, they maintain their marriages by not remarrying. They are faithful even though their spouses are unfaithful. That is love. That is the love of God that he shares with believers by faith.

If the unbelieving spouse is pleased to dwell with the believer, maintain the marriage. That is the apostle's criterion for maintaining the marriage: "She be pleased to dwell with him...[and] he be pleased to dwell with her" (vv. 12–13). "Pleased" indicates a clear knowledge of and consent to the life of a Christian to which God has called the believing spouse. It is a decision of clear knowledge and consent because the believer makes clear what is involved in his life as a Christian according to God's calling. The believer lives antithetically in the marriage, even though there is the closest relationship possible between the spouses. The believer makes known his faith, his convictions from God, the requirements of God on his life, and the calling of God to him.

For example, the believer makes known the calling of God to join a true church of Jesus Christ and that he will join that true church wherever that takes him. The believer insists that the children of that marriage are baptized and catechized in the doctrine of the church and sent to the good Christian schools. The believer insists on a godly atmosphere in the home with good music, Bible reading, church attendance every worship service, and prayer. The unbeliever is "pleased," consents, to dwell in such an environment. This is made known by the unbeliever's not leaving the spouse and continuing to live in the marriage bond. The unbeliever maintains the marriage.

With such an unbelieving spouse the believer maintains the mixed marriage. Unbeliever and believer live freely in their marriage. God has called them to peace in that too. They have children together, and that involves the sexual relationship in the mixed marriage. The apostle says "dwell with," which is to live openly and freely in the same house together, so that the unbelieving husband is the head of his believing wife, and the unbelieving wife is still the help to her believing husband.

Maintain the marriage, says the apostle. Anything short of the unbeliever's leaving or making the Christian life of the spouse impossible requires the believer to maintain the marriage.

The Ground for Maintaining

The apostle gives the ground in verse 14: "For the unbelieving husband is sanctified by the wife, and the unbelieving wife is sanctified by the husband: else were your children unclean; but now are they holy." This verse is familiar to any Reformed person, because it is closely connected with the Reformed doctrine of baptism. In the questions to the parents in the Reformed baptism form there is a footnote referencing the statement that the children of believers are sanctified in Christ. That footnote grounds the baptism form's statement about the children's sanctification in 1 Corinthians 7:14. That is a mistake. The original form does not have that footnote.

No matter what role this verse may have played in the controversy surrounding the issue of sanctification of the baptized infant children of believers, this is not the main scriptural proof for that statement in the baptism form about the sanctification of the children of believers in Christ.[2] Better proof is a phrase found

---

2 Every Reformed parent must answer this question at the baptism of their children: "Whether you acknowledge that although our children are conceived and born in sin, and therefore are subject to all miseries, yea to condemnation itself, yet that they are sanctified in Christ, and therefore, as members of his church, ought to be baptized?" The English translation then references 1 Corinthians 7:14 (*Confessions and Church Order*, 260). This reference is not found in the Dutch text as found in the liturgy of the Dutch Reformed churches (GKN, Dr. A. Kuyper's churches). See F. L. Rutgers, H. Bavinck, and A. Kuyper, *De Berijmde Psalmen Met Eenige Gezangen, in Gebruik Bij De Gereformeerde Kerken in Nederland* (Maasluis: Uitgevers-Genootschap, 1913), 68. Furthermore, in his excellent commentary on the baptism form, Dutch Reformed minister Bastiaan Wielenga shows that this text was frequently quoted by the opponents of the phrase "sanctified in Christ" in the baptism form to show that it meant merely an external setting apart of baptized children, an interpretation he later points out leads to a doctrine of the covenant "held by Socinians and Anabaptists

in 1 Corinthians 1:2, which says that we are sanctified in Christ Jesus, which refers also to the children of believers. It is not even the purpose of 1 Corinthians 7:14 to prove that the children of believers are members of Christ and his covenant and ought to be baptized, although this verse has important implications for the baptism of infant children of believers.

To understand the phrase "else were your children unclean; but now are they holy," one must start with the first phrase stating that the unbelieving spouse is sanctified by the believing spouse. The translation "by" in that phrase is a mistake. A literal rendering is better in this case: "The unbelieving spouse is sanctified *in* the believing spouse." There is no sanctifying activity of God on the unbeliever. There is no sanctifying activity of the believing spouse on the unbelieving spouse. There is an antithesis between them.

The passage teaches that there is a sanctifying activity of God by his grace and Holy Spirit in that mixed marriage on the believing spouse and his or her children born into that mixed marriage. Sanctification is the work of God to cleanse his people from sin, consecrate them to himself in devoted love, and establish an antithesis between church and world and between believer and unbeliever. There is an activity of God in that mixed marriage so that God powerfully strains out the contagion, the sin and the wickedness, that would otherwise infect the believing spouse and the children. God protects them. Ordinarily, it would be spiritual suicide for a believer to come into that kind of close contact with an unbeliever and to live so close to the world. In this mixed marriage by his grace God causes the believing spouse to maintain the marriage and to maintain it in such a way that there is the closest bond possible between two humans and yet there remains a spiritual separation between the two.

---

and later by the Remonstrants and rationalists" (B. Wielenga, *The Reformed Baptism Form: A Commentary*, trans. Annemie Godbehere, ed. David J. Engelsma [Jenison, MI: Reformed Free Publishing Association, 2016], 317).

The apostle proves that from the effect: "Else were your children unclean; but now are they holy." What explains that holy children can be born from such a marriage? God's activity explains that. It is God's activity alone that the believing spouse hears this word and maintains the mixed marriage. There is a promise to that believing spouse from God, "I will be active in that marriage for your sake and for the sake of your covenantal children to sanctify you and your children and to maintain my covenant." The apostle in the statement "else were your children unclean; but now are they holy" is not contradicting the teaching of scripture that only the elect children of believers are holy. He does not say that all the children born of a mixed marriage are holy, but he proves the promise of God by its effect, that even a mixed marriage can issue in holy children because God sanctifies and preserves the holiness of the believing spouse and the believing spouse's children.

The purpose is to give the believing spouse encouragement and assurance. God takes away the anxiety of the believer at the thought of maintaining a mixed marriage, especially this thought: What will happen to my children? Will the unbelieving spouse influence those children?

God says maintain the marriage, and he grounds his command in his own sanctifying work and covenantal promise to the believer spouse. He turns even that extraordinarily difficult situation for the profit of his people. It seems so contrary to the word of God that there is an antithesis between believers and unbelievers, and then that God commands the believer to maintain the marriage to an unbeliever. It is not contrary but is based on the truth of the unbreakable bond of marriage that he spoke in the beginning, so that what God joined together let no man put asunder. So unbreakable is the bond that even the spouse's unbelief or abandonment of the believer cannot destroy the bond. In faithfulness to marriage, in obedience to the word of God, believing his calling us to peace, and trusting his promise in such a situation, the believer maintains a mixed marriage. If the unbelieving spouse abandons, the believer lets the spouse go, for God has called the believer to peace. The believer maintains the marriage also by not remarrying.

The Hope in Maintaining

In that too God gives the believer hope. This is not the only hope of the believer, but it is part, a significant part, of his hope in maintaining the marriage. It is one reason that the abandoned spouse does not remarry and maintains the marriage: "For what knowest thou, O wife, whether thou shalt save thy husband? or how knowest thou, O man, whether thou shalt save thy wife?" (v. 15).

The word of God to the believing spouse is to maintain the marriage, because in the maintenance of the marriage the unbelieving spouse may be saved. The word to the abandoned spouse is do not remarry, because in your not remarrying the unbelieving spouse may be saved. It may please God in the way of the believer's obedience to gather another of his elect children. In the way of obedience, regardless of the conversion of the unbelieving spouse, God gives peace to his people. They will not always see that in the beginning, but they will see that. It is God's promise. He gives them peace from the depression, despair, and doubt.

This is a powerful reason derived from Christian love. First Corinthians is the book on Christian love. It is a love of God that obeys and a love of the neighbor that suffers long and much. With love always goes the hope that the unbelieving spouse will be converted. Out of love the believer maintains the mixed marriage.

CHAPTER 22

ABIDING IN YOUR CALLING

1 Corinthians 7:17–24

---

17. *But as God hath distributed to every man, as the Lord hath called every one, so let him walk. And so ordain I in all churches.*
18. *Is any man called being circumcised? let him not become uncircumcised. Is any called in uncircumcision? let him not be circumcised.*
19. *Circumcision is nothing, and uncircumcision is nothing, but the keeping of the commandments of God.*
20. *Let every man abide in the same calling wherein he was called.*
21. *Art thou called being a servant? care not for it: but if thou mayest be made free, use it rather.*
22. *For he that is called in the Lord, being a servant, is the Lord's freeman: likewise also he that is called, being free, is Christ's servant.*
23. *Ye are bought with a price; be not ye the servants of men.*
24. *Brethren, let every man, wherein he is called, therein abide with God.*

Throughout chapter 7 Paul addresses various issues in the church regarding singleness and marriage. He also calls those in mixed marriages to maintain them. God promises his grace to the believer in a mixed marriage, grace that consists in God's sanctifying the believing spouse and the children of the believing spouse in that difficult situation.

Paul makes a broader application of his instruction concerning the calling of the believer in a mixed marriage. This is the implication of the word "but" in verse 17. "But" is not an adversative; it does not introduce a contrast. The idea is that if the situation of a mixed marriage does not apply to you, nevertheless the principle behind the apostle's instruction on the believer's calling to maintain his or her mixed marriage applies to everyone. The principle that he ordains in all churches (v. 17) is "let every man abide in the same calling wherein he was called" (v. 20).

When God addresses believers in mixed marriages, calling them to abide, the believer should not say, "Well, that does not apply to me." Rather, the believer should hear a principle that applies to every believer: let every man abide in his calling and let every man, woman, and child, called of God, renounce their own wills and will God's will. The calling to maintain a mixed marriage is simply one particular form of the Christian life, and the principle that governs the believer in that difficult situation applies to all believers in every situation. The Christian life calls everyone to renounce his own will and without murmuring to follow the will of God. In this abiding, love shows that it "doth not behave itself unseemly, seeketh not her own, is not easily provoked, thinketh no evil; rejoiceth not in iniquity, but rejoiceth in the truth; beareth all things, believeth all things, hopeth all things, endureth all things" (13:5–7). This is what the apostle ordains in all the churches.

The Calling Wherein We Were Called

When scripture uses the Greek word translated as "calling" and "called" in chapter 7:20, it uses it in two distinct but closely related senses. "Calling" refers to a person's life situation: "Let every man abide in the same calling." "Called" in the phrase "wherein he was called" refers to the saving call of the gospel. The idea is let every man abide in the station in life in which he was when the call found him, or in which he finds himself when the gospel comes to him throughout his life.

The basic exhortation of the text is for believers to abide in those life situations.

Paul illustrates this teaching with two examples. A man may be called by the gospel in circumcision. The gospel comes to him as a Jew by nature, or we might say that the gospel finds him as one who was born of believing parents, who never knew a time when he did not know God in Jesus Christ, who always had known the law, who was brought up in a good Christian school, and who was taught catechism as a child. The gospel can also find one in uncircumcision. He is a Gentile, or we would say that he was converted in adulthood. He knows a time when he did not know God and lived profanely, and the gospel called him out of that ignorance and saved him.

Abide in your calling.

The apostle makes the same point by the example of the gospel's calling a slave or a free man. The gospel finds a man, woman, or child in freedom. In today's terms we would say that the gospel finds a man as a self-sufficient and successful businessman. In his economic situation he does not answer to anyone else. The gospel can also find a man as a slave, a servant of another, who in his economic situation answers to someone else.

Abide in your calling.

This calling is what God has distributed to every man. Paul does not refer merely to what God distributes to church members, but also to the Lord's sovereign and providential distribution to every man, woman, and child. Paul told the Athenian philosophers on the Areopagus, "God that made the world and all things therein...giveth to all life, and breath, and all things"

(Acts 17:19, 24–25). The life situation of every man, woman, and child is from God—whether as a Jew or Gentile, male or female, bond or free, rich or poor, born in the church or converted in adulthood—all is from God. Whether God gives many gifts or only a few, whether God gives marriage or singleness, whether God gives authority or places under authority, to every man there is a distribution from God.

Because it is from God, there is a word from God to everyone. With the distribution God says, "Serve me. In your calling renounce your will and will my will." If the calling is from God, it must be used to God, unto God, or for God in the sense that it serves God.

Your life situation then is not the result of happenstance or of your own skills, efforts, or intelligence. It is a distribution from God. When one loses sight of the truth that absolutely everything he has is from God, his life is off the rails. This is the fact of life that no wicked person will admit. God gives to the wicked their life, breath, and all things, but they will not serve God with them. They will not say, "I received this from God. I have a calling from God with these things." This is their inexcusable unthankfulness. They will not be subject to God; they will not serve him and worship him.

One's calling is not difficult to understand, for that calling is made known in his life situation in harmony with the word of God. In the situation in which one finds himself God makes his voice loudly heard. A married woman to whom God has given children does not need a degree in rocket science to understand God's calling to her. It is not to work in a factory. Her calling is to raise her children. God makes that known in her situation. He makes that known in his word. The calling of a married man with a wife and children is not hard to understand. It is not to play after work, to be out with friends, to spend money on himself, but to be with his wife and to teach his children the fear of God and support the causes of the kingdom of heaven. His very life situation makes known his calling.

WALKING IN THE WAY OF LOVE

The Meaning of "Abide"

In that calling the word of God is "abide" (v. 20).

The apostle first explains the meaning of "abide" by the phrase "so let him walk" (v. 17). When he says "walk," he rejects the notion that abiding in your calling means laziness, whether physical or spiritual.

Second, to abide in your calling means that the calling is not a part of your life but it *is* your life. A man does not lay bricks; he is a bricklayer. A woman does not merely take care of children; she is a mother. That calling is one's life.

Third, to abide in your calling means to walk in that calling "as God hath distributed" (v. 17). This means to keep in the boundaries of God's distribution. God has not given to everyone everything; he distributes to each some particular things. To some he gives intellectual accomplishments, and to some he gives strong bodies with which to work while perhaps they do not have many intellectual gifts.

Fourth, to abide in your calling means to be content in your calling. This is obvious from the word "abide," which means to remain and contrasts with the birdlike flitting about of the discontented person, who does not remain but chases this or that. The grass is always greener on the other side of the fence. There are men who cannot stay at a job and consequently throw their families into turmoil. Remain in the sense that you are content. This also comes out in one of the apostle's examples. He says to the servant, "Care not for it" (v. 20). To be free from worry and anxiety is part of the peace of contentment. It is as scripture says in Hebrews 13:5: "Be content with such things as ye have." Covetousness disturbs the peace to which God calls his people.

Fifth, to abide in your calling means to keep God's commandments. The apostle teaches this when he says, "Circumcision is nothing...but the keeping of the commandments of God" (1 Cor. 7:19). Abiding in one's calling is not merely being busy. A woman who makes herself busy with unnecessary things cannot say that she is remaining in her calling. She is just being busy. A man who makes himself busy with unnecessary things cannot say that he is remaining in his calling. He is just being busy. The heart and soul of remaining in your calling is keeping God's commandments.

The keeping of God's commandments in your calling means that your calling must be lawful. A man cannot abide in an unlawful life situation. The calling in which the gospel finds you and in which you are to remain must be lawful. If the gospel finds you in a job where you are working on Sundays, you have to leave your job. Leaving that job is abiding in your calling. If the gospel finds you in a labor union, you must leave the labor union.

This condemns as disobedience many callings to which men say they are called by God. For example, God calls you to leave your church and family to live far away from them in another part of the world. No! Do not disgrace the glorious description of the life of the Christian as a calling of God by that wickedness. It is far better to admit that you do not care at all about the will of God than to call that a calling from God. A calling from God keeps the commandments.

The keeping of the commandments that is pleasing to God is that which is done out of faith, faith that refuses to depend on your own works for righteousness. It is a keeping of the commandments in love for God and as the practice of thankfulness, while recognizing that when you have done all that is your duty to do, you are an unprofitable servant.

This points out that the heart of abiding in your calling is the service of God. It is not doing something *for* God. God does not need you to do anything for him, because he is independent. This service of God is the willing renunciation of your will and the willing of God's will in your whole life, your whole life situation, with all the gifts and talents God has given in every lawful situation in which you find yourself. It is as the Heidelberg Catechism so succinctly puts it: "That so every one may fulfill his office and calling as willingly and truly as the angels do in heaven."[1]

When the apostle says about the free man that he "is Christ's servant" (v. 22), he does not intend to be limited to that man only, but he intends that all believers understand that in their callings they are the Lord's servants and are called to serve him. This is why the unbeliever, although he stays at his post for fifty years and outwardly does his job well, does not abide in his calling, because in everything he does he does not serve and worship God. Believers in their callings are the Lord's servants. They receive everything from God, and everything is unto God. He is the master; they are the slaves. His will is everything; their wills are nothing. His glory is everything; their glory is nothing. That is abiding in their callings.

For the believer this is his liberty. When Paul comforts the Christian slave with the truth that in his servitude "he is the Lord's freeman" (v. 22), this applies to all believers. To be Christ's slave, to keep his commandments, to serve him with everything I am and with everything I have is liberty. To serve self, to seek self, to be worried about what other men think, or to serve men's whims is oppressive bondage. To serve Christ, to serve God, and to abide in your calling, regardless of the difficulties, is liberty.

Because abiding in your calling is the service of the Lord, you have the liberty that the Lord grants to you. He says to the servant, "If thou mayest be made free, use it rather" (v. 21). Here the apostle and the Spirit by the apostle grants to the believer liberty in abiding in his calling. If he finds a job that is more advantageous for himself, his family, the church, and the schools, he may use it rather. Then also abide in your calling.

Called Therein by the Gospel

"Let every man abide in the same calling wherein he was called" (v. 20). The ground of this exhortation is the saving call of the

---

1 Heidelberg Catechism A 124, in Schaff, *Creeds of Christendom*, 3:353.

gospel. The saving call of the gospel is the living voice of the triune God through the preaching of the gospel, whereby he addresses the elect sinner in the heart of his being, calls him out of darkness and sin, and brings him within and establishes him in the kingdom of God's dear Son. The saving call of the gospel comes to those who are laboring and heavy laden, to the elect people of God in the world.

Whenever you bring up the saving call you must bring up election, because they are so tightly joined together and cannot be separated. The call proceeds from election. God does not call everyone. He distributes to everyone, and in that distribution and by means of it there is a command from God to serve him. Although the gospel is proclaimed promiscuously, by it God calls only his people.

The relationship between the two uses of the Greek word translated as "calling" and "called" is that the saving call of the gospel is the ground for the command to believers to abide in their callings.

This is true, first, because the saving call of the gospel makes circumcision and uncircumcision and bond and free nothing. The gospel call means that it does not matter for salvation if a man is circumcised or uncircumcised. Therefore, a man's works, his merits or demerits, and his station in life do not matter for salvation. What matters is the eternal good pleasure of God. He calls that one, regardless of his life situation, with the powerful gospel call and saves him, and he does not call the other one.

This makes abiding in your calling a matter of thankfulness. The reason to abide is not to do something for God or to merit salvation by works in that calling. If the motivation is any other than thankfulness in all of your work in your calling, all that work is wickedness and unfaithfulness in your calling.

Second, the call of the gospel is the ground of abiding in your calling because the gospel is the power of abiding in your calling. The gospel makes of slaves the Lord's free men, and the gospel makes of free men the Lord's slaves. The gospel liberates a spiritual slave, who is bound in iron and woe and perishing in the guilt of sin, because of which he was bound under the power of sin and only could sin and serve himself. The calling liberates him by making him Christ's slave.

This is the transforming power of the gospel call. That call transforms a man's whole life situation this way: whereas before the call his life was dominated by sin, after the call his life is dominated by Jesus Christ. The gospel call does not make a circumcised man uncircumcised or an uncircumcised man circumcised. The gospel call does not make a physically weak person strong or an intellectually weak person to be strong intellectually. This is not the transforming power of the gospel. The gospel call takes a man in his entire being and in his whole life situation and places him under the power of the grace of God. In this way it transforms his life situation and makes the whole life situation of the believer a calling from the God of his salvation. The believer's calling is not only a distribution from God his creator, but also an office from God his redeemer.

The most important questions in his life are not, what do I want to do? What is convenient for me? What is easy? What is advantageous for me? What will improve my lot and make me happy? If these are his questions, that man is thinking wrongly. Yet the believer in a difficult life situation is often told, "God does not call you to suffer. God wants you to be happy." The important question is rather, what is the will of the one who gave me everything I have and made me what I am not only by creation, but also by redemption in Jesus Christ?

The gospel call places your life under the commandments of God and the power of grace.

The power of that call is the truth of your redemption: "Ye are bought with a price" (v. 23). Slaves made free, free men bound, and circumcision and uncircumcision made nothing are rooted in the saving blood of Jesus Christ. The gospel calls and saves because it is the gospel of the redemption of Jesus Christ. It is a power to cleanse from sin, to free from guilt, to liberate from bondage, and to bring a life and everything in that life under the power of grace.

You have been redeemed and bought with a fair price, not a cheap price. You were not stolen, you were bought by the blood of God's dear Son, so "be not ye the servants of men" (v. 23). To serve men is a denial of the cross. To serve your lusts and desires, to will your will instead of God's, is a denial of the cross of Christ. That is how serious it is not to abide in your calling.

Only the power of the blood of Christ's redemption is powerful to forgive your sin of willing your own will when you do not abide in your calling. The power of that redemption of Christ makes you thankful to abide in your calling. This is the power of your abiding because by the saving call of the gospel God takes the blood of Christ and by its power washes you, cleanses you, frees you, and places your whole life under the power of his grace.

Abide in your calling.

The Purpose of So Abiding

The most important question in your life, then, regardless of your situation, is not what do I want, but what does God will? God wills ultimately his glory. That is it. He wills to save you. He wills to bless you. He wills you to be happy in heaven. He wills your entire life situation. He wills all for his glory. This is what Paul means by "therein abide with God" (v. 24). The purpose of abiding in your calling is the purpose of God's willing your salvation, earning that salvation on the cross, and calling you: his glory.

This idea comes out in a literal translation of verse 24: "Abide in the presence of God." There are wicked and miserable workers who do a good job when the boss is looking, but when he is not looking they are lazy, complaining, and backbiting thieves. This kind of worker Paul condemns as men-pleasing. This type of life is wicked too. A man or woman who lives for self is like that worker who does a good job when the boss is around, but for the rest he or she seeks self.

The thought that must govern your life is abide with God, that is, through the cross of Jesus Christ and on the ground of his righteousness your whole life is lived in the presence of God. God is always there wherever you go and whatever you do. When you lose sight of that, you seek yourself and not the glory of God.

When you abide before God, you do everything for the glory of God. This is the purpose. So a believer also walks in the way of love for the God who called him, by seeking God's glory and not his own. Let every man abide in his calling before God. So it has been ordained in all the churches.

CHAPTER 23

CONCERNING THE SINGLE LIFE

1 Corinthians 7:25–28, 32–40

25. *Now concerning virgins I have no commandment of the Lord: yet I give my judgment, as one that hath obtained mercy of the Lord to be faithful.*

26. *I suppose therefore that this is good for the present distress, I say, that it is good for a man so to be.*

27. *Art thou bound unto a wife? seek not to be loosed. Art thou loosed from a wife? seek not a wife.*

28. *But and if thou marry, thou hast not sinned; and if a virgin marry, she hath not sinned. Nevertheless such shall have trouble in the flesh: but I spare you.*

32. *But I would have you without carefulness. He that is unmarried careth for the things that belong to the Lord, how he may please the Lord:*

33. *But he that is married careth for the things that are of the world, how he may please his wife.*

34. *There is difference also between a wife and a virgin. The unmarried woman careth for the things of the Lord, that she may be holy both in body and in spirit: but she that is married careth for the things of the world, how she may please her husband.*

35. *And this I speak for your own profit; not that I may cast a snare on you, but for that which is comely, and that ye may attend upon the Lord without distraction.*

36. *But if any man think that he behaveth himself uncomely toward his virgin, if she pass the flower of her age, and need so require, let him do what he will, he sinneth not: let them marry.*

37. *Nevertheless he that standeth stedfast in his heart, having no necessity, but hath power over his own will, and hath so decreed in his heart that he will keep his virgin, doeth well.*

38. *So then he that giveth her in marriage doeth well; but he that giveth her not in marriage doeth better.*

39. *The wife is bound by the law as long as her husband liveth; but if her husband be dead, she is at liberty to be married to whom she will; only in the Lord.*

40. *But she is happier if she so abide, after my judgment: and I think also that I have the Spirit of God.*

There are two states of man regarding the opposite sex: marriage and the single life. The word of God addresses the believer in both states. Paul has addressed the calling of the believer in marriage in light of the goodness of sex in marriage. The sexual relationship between a husband and a wife is good and wholesome. It is good for the married to use the sexual relationship (7:2–5). By contrast Paul briefly addressed the single and said that it is not good for a single man or woman to touch one another (v. 1). In his discourse on the married state, the apostle directs the single person who burns to the remedy in marriage (v. 9).

Now the apostle turns in earnest to the believer and the single state. This is what he means in verse 25: "Now concerning virgins I have no commandment of the Lord." Singles are what he means by "virgins." He speaks to the church regarding the instruction the church must give to the single people, and he speaks to single people themselves.

His instruction is absolutely antithetical to the world's instruction to single people. The world also has a word about the single state. If there is not in the world a kind of despair regarding singleness that leads to a self-centered self-indulgence, there is in the world a pleasure-madness in the single state. The single state is widely regarded as a better state than marriage not because single persons can be devoted to the Lord, but because they can indulge themselves. The world says to the single person, "Singleness is for selfishness, for self-centeredness, to use your time for yourself, to work for yourself, to do what you want when you want and how you want." This explains why man, now freed culturally and socially from the constraints to marry, never bothers to marry at all but remains single, all the while indulging his lust, including his sexual appetite. Singleness, the world says, is for self.

"Not so," says the apostle. First, he takes away all despair regarding singleness. "It is good," he says (v. 26). Second, he gives sound instruction about the calling of the single person before God. In connection with the previous verses, singleness is a calling. Singleness is not selfishness, but for the Lord.

The Meaning of Singleness

The apostle uses two terms for single persons: "virgins" and "unmarried" (vv. 25, 28, 32, 34, 36–37). The meaning of "unmarried" is clear. The meaning of "virgins" is not so clear. The Greek word translated as "virgins" is in the feminine gender. It is translated in verse 25 as though the feminine word refers exclusively to females. But the word refers neither exclusively to females nor to a special class of individuals in the ancient church who took a vow of celibacy, a practice that can find no support in this text. It is obvious from a plain reading of the passage that "virgins" is a synonym for the unmarried. This is clear because in verse 25, where the subject is "virgins," the apostle calls himself a virgin when he says, "As one that hath obtained mercy of the Lord to be faithful" that is, faithful in his virginity. Additionally, throughout the text the apostle uses masculine possessive pronouns and verbal forms with the feminine term "virgins." It would be better to translate the Greek word used throughout the passage as "virginity." The word is feminine but refers to male and female members of the church who have never been married. They are a special class of the group of unmarried about whom the text is speaking.

In verses 25–28 and 32–40 there are references to various forms of the single life. First, there is that group of singles in the church that Paul addresses in verses 39–40: the widows and widowers. There he does not introduce another subject but addresses a form of the single life after one's spouse has died.

Accordingly, it is important to notice some features about the apostle's description of the widow and widower in the church. He does not put in the category of the single the divorced person. The divorced are not single. They are married but divorced. This is the teaching of the words "the wife is bound by the law as long as her husband liveth: but if her husband be dead, she is at liberty to be married to whom she will" (v. 39). The apostle says that she is not single, though she is divorced, as long as her husband lives. The divorced are not single, but their state is a special form of the married state. Their marriage bonds are not broken, and they are called to be eunuchs for the sake of the kingdom of heaven.

Regarding those who are legitimately divorced because of the fornication of their spouses, the apostle addresses the erroneous argument that many use to justify their remarriages after divorce while their spouses are still alive. The ground of the erroneous argument is that Paul said, "If her husband be dead, she is free from that law; so that she is no adulteress, though she be married to another man" (Rom. 7:3). This is interpreted to mean not physically dead but spiritually dead. Paul addresses this spurious argument for the remarriage of divorced persons by the word "dead" (1 Cor. 7:39). The word translated as "dead" in this passage is not the normal Greek word for *dead* but is the Greek word that means sleep. Literally, Paul says, "If her husband sleepeth, she is at liberty to be married." This means "dead" in the sense of sleeping in the grave. This makes the argument about the spiritual death of the husband absurd. How strange is it to say that every time the husband goes to sleep, the wife is free to divorce? When Jesus said that marriage is only broken by death, he meant real, physical death, a point that Paul drives home by using the word "dead" or sleep. Death alone makes a married person a widow or a widower. This is one form of singleness in the church. Being a widow or widower, he or she is free to remarry.

Another form of the single state belongs to those who have never married. They are the young people, the children of believers, and the unmarried who have passed from adolescence into adulthood. Paul indicates in verse 36 by the words "[has passed] the flower of…age" that he refers to both the young unmarried and the older single people in the church The apostle also calls these unmarried in the church "virgins," which refers not only to females, but also to males, and indicates one who has not experienced the sexual relationship.

More importantly, the question is, why does the apostle call the unmarried males and females "virgins"? Why not refer to them simply as the unmarried? First, by referring to both sexes the apostle makes clear to the church and the single person that virginity is not a concept that applies only to women. It is most physically conspicuous in the case of women, but the men have virginity too. They have virginity that must be guarded and treated with comeliness, as the apostle says, as carefully as the women's virginity. The men are not allowed to live as they please before marriage.

Second, when Paul speaks of virginity in the Greek language and in the English translation, as can be expected, virginity is virtually personified. This virginity can be guarded, kept, treated dishonorably, given in marriage, and received in marriage. Paul makes virginity not only a physical feature, which in the case of a male is lacking, but also and at bottom is a matter of the heart. This is his point in verse 37 when he speaks of "virgin." He does not tell parents how to treat a daughter, but he speaks to the single person about virginity and makes it a matter of the heart and not an exclusively physical matter. "He that standeth stedfast in his heart, having no necessity, but hath power over his own will, and hath so decreed in his heart that he will keep his virgin[ity]."

Virginity begins in the sanctified heart. It is spiritual; it is the chasteness of the believer's thoughts and heart that governs his outward behavior. This virgin or virginity for the believer involves power over his will. "No necessity" means he does not have the overwhelming desire for sex, so that he dominates his sexual desires and passions. When he burns, it is better to marry. He is free to marry. No shame attaches to his marrying. The man or woman who stands steadfast in his or her heart keeps his or her virgin.

Concerning those two forms of the single state—the unmarried and virgins, and the widows and widowers—the apostle says, "I have no commandment of the Lord" (v. 25). The Lord Jesus Christ in his earthly ministry never gave specific instructions regarding the unmarried and the single in the church. The Lord addressed the married, but Paul now gives his judgment. It is the judgment of one who was single. He speaks by experience. The Lord distributed that to him in order that he might so speak to the churches. It is the judgment of an apostle who has the authority of Jesus Christ to instruct in the church.

Lest we think that the apostle's instruction is only from a man, Paul says, "I think...that I have the Spirit of God" (v. 40). Thereby he makes his instruction that of the Spirit. There is a word in the Bible to the single about his or her singleness. It is instruction that the apostle and so by emulation that parents of the single and the churches of the single must give.

The Goodness of Singleness

The Spirit's first word to the single is that singleness is good. Paul says that to the widows and to the unmarried and virgins: "I suppose therefore that this is good for the present distress…it is good for a man so to be" (v. 26).

The goodness of the single state is not that it is more holy than the married state. This is the apostle's point in verses 27–28, where he guards the goodness of the unmarried state against a misunderstanding that it is more holy. "Art thou bound unto a wife? seek not to be loosed. Art thou loosed from a wife? seek not a wife. But and if thou marry, thou hast not sinned; and if a virgin marry, she hath not sinned."

On the basis of these verses and the rest of 1 Corinthians 7, it is impossible to maintain that singleness is more holy than marriage. This is the thinking behind the wicked Roman Catholic doctrine of celibacy. That is also the doctrine of devils that forbids marriage on the ground that there is something unholy about the married state (1 Tim. 4:1, 3). This is the wicked thinking that God judges by means of the scandalous Roman Catholic buggery. Throughout 1 Corinthians 7 the apostle teaches the goodness and holiness of marriage and the sexual relationship in it. He does not contradict himself.

Paul also denies that the goodness of singleness consists of the freedom to do what one wants, whereas marriage is bondage. He teaches that in verse 32 when he says that the unmarried person is bound to seek the will of the Lord, "how he may please the Lord." The contrast between marriage and singleness in verses 32–33 is not that the married person is worldly because he seeks the pleasure of his spouse and the single person seeks the pleasure of the Lord. But the contrast is that the married person seeks to do the will of the Lord by seeking the pleasure of his spouse. A single person seeks the will of the Lord in his single state.

Singleness is good as such because it is a good state from God. He makes singleness. Singleness is also good because it is honorable. Paul teaches this aspect of singleness in verse 35 in the word "comely," which means honorable. Singleness is honorable in the church because one can serve God and Jesus Christ.

The goodness of the single state is also that it is a special gift of God's grace. Paul states this in verse 7: "I would that all men were even as I myself. But every man hath his proper gift of God." The word translated as "gift" means grace. Singleness is a grace from God. It is not a grace to everyone, but only to his people. God distributes in his church graces from the fullness of Jesus Christ, and one of the graces is singleness, so that the single person in the church has the grace from God to live in that state in holiness and as pleasing to God.

This speaks to the single person who may be tempted to be discontented with his gift and to suppose that God in Jesus Christ deals stingily with him in not giving him a spouse. By that thinking he fails to recognize that singleness itself is a gift. One's singleness is not the result of the inevitable circumstances of life, but it is a gift from God as much as marriage is a gift from God. Just as God brings to every man his wife and to every woman her husband, so he brings to the single their singleness. The state itself is a gift.

Since this state is a gift of God's grace, there is grace to the single person to use singleness for God's glory. This is what Paul means when he speaks about a man and his virgin in verses 36–37 and defines the gift of singleness as standing "stedfast in his heart, having no necessity, but hath power over his own will, and hath so decreed in his heart that he will keep his virgin." That is some gift. It is the power of the grace of God that gifts the single person with singleness. It is the power to stand steadfast in the heart and to have no necessity to marry and have the sexual relationship. It is power over the will, the passions, and the desires. In verse 9 Paul calls this gift continence, or "contain." Singleness is good because it is a gift from God. God does not deal stingily with single persons, but he showers his grace on them.

Singleness is also good because the single person obtains mercy from God. The apostle teaches this in verse 25: "I give my judgment, as one that hath obtained mercy of the Lord to be faithful." The reference is to the mercy of the Lord in singleness to be faithful to his virgin. The single person must be faithful to someone, just as the married person must be faithful to his spouse. The calling of the single and the married does not differ in that essential calling for faithfulness. The singles are faithful to their virgin because they obtain mercy from God. This is the mercy of God, just as the grace of God that saves single persons and grants them a place in God's church.

This addresses the temptation of single persons to despair that God has forgotten them. He has not forgotten them, for they have obtained mercy from God to be faithful.

This also addresses the temptation to think that their state is miserable. It is not a miserable state, for the mercy of God takes pity on the miserable and delivers them from misery. In giving them mercy, God has delivered them from the misery of their sins, guilt, and pollution, as he delivers every other believer, and has given them a grand gift in the state of singleness.

They also obtain mercy in the sense that God knows their particular trials, temptations, and troubles that attend singleness, and he has mercy on them. In his mercy, for instance, God delivers them from their own selfishness in singleness. By nature single persons would always serve themselves. God gives them mercy to be faithful to their virgins and to God.

There is a sense in which that good state of singleness is even better than marriage. This is the remarkable teaching of the apostle. For all of the scriptures' high doctrine of marriage, the apostle says it is better to be single. This is not for every man. God said of Adam and in him to the majority of men and women, "It is not good that the man should be alone" (Gen. 2:18). But for some it is good. It is good for the "present distress" (1 Cor. 7:26). The same thought underlies the apostle's teaching to the widow, who "is at liberty to be married to whom she will; only in the Lord" (v. 39). "But she is happier" if she remains single (v. 40).

It is better for the present necessity because the married person has "trouble in the flesh" (v. 28). There are particular troubles in this life that attend marriage. This addresses the temptation of a single person to look at the married and to say, "They have everything, and I have nothing." God says, "No." Those who are married will have trouble in the flesh. Is that not true? The trouble is not with marriage. The trouble is the two sinful people in the marriage. The trouble is the kind of children that two sinful people bring forth in their marriage. There is the trouble of seeking to please the spouse, who is not always kind and grateful in return. Yes, there is trouble in marriage, including the extraordinary trouble that may come to marriage in the form of an unbelieving spouse, a spouse who abandons, or a spouse who lives in sin for a time. Marriage is good; marriage is a blessing; but with two sinful people in marriage there is trouble. It is better to be single. It is better if they are as the apostle to "spare" (v. 28) them that trouble.

The Calling to the Single

To the singles in their good and honorable state, there is a calling. That is the second word of the Holy Spirit to the singles and to the church regarding them. This is important because it addresses the temptation to single persons to suppose that they are useless in the church and have no place or calling there. This addresses the calling of the single person not to wallow in self-pity at the lack of a spouse. Let every man abide in his calling.

There is a calling to single persons. The calling is not to please themselves. This is the apostle's teaching in verse 32: "I would have you without carefulness. He that is unmarried careth for the things that belong to the Lord, how he many please the Lord." Implied is that one who is unmarried may not care for the things of himself or herself in place of caring for the things of the Lord. This is the negative side of the calling. In every sphere of life one's calling reveals the sin to which one is tempted. For a worker the calling is to be faithful; the temptation is to be unfaithful. The calling of a husband is to love his wife and to dwell with her; the temptation is to live independently of his wife. The calling of the wife is to submit to her husband; the temptation is to rebel against him. So it is with the single. The calling to attend on the Lord reveals the temptation of the single to attend to himself or herself.

The calling of singles is to care "for the things that belong to the Lord, how he may please the Lord" (v. 32). "The unmarried woman careth for the things of the Lord, that she may be holy both in body and in spirit" (v. 34). Care for the things of the Lord is the calling. Attend without distraction on the Lord.

Paul does not leave that calling general, but in the description of the calling of the single person he is specific. What are the things of the Lord? His church, schools, covenant, kingdom, people of God, the doctrine, the holy life, and the truth are the things of the Lord.

The first calling of the single person is to be holy in his body. He attends on and is faithful to his virgin.

This extends to holiness in an antithetical life. Singleness is not an opportunity to be involved in bars, clubs, dance halls, and movie theaters. The single are called to holiness. A young person may not think he may live as he pleases. The word of God to the single is, be ye holy in singleness.

Holiness in attending on the Lord means also that the work and the causes of the kingdom of heaven must be dear to the single person. I wonder sometimes if the complaint that one has no place in the church is not the fruit of one's own withdrawing and not being involved in and concerned with the things of the Lord. For the single person, your work is not your own; your money is not yours either; neither is your time. They are the Lord's, who gave you grace and mercy to be faithful and to use your time for the church, to give of your economic increase for the schools and the causes of the kingdom of heaven. How incongruous and strange it is that one who has no monetary burdens to the extent that a married couple with many children has can only squeak out a few dollars for the school offering. This is not attending on the things of the Lord. This is not attending on the Lord honorably and without distraction.

What is distracting from attending on the church, the schools, and the covenant? Is it oneself? The calling to the single and to every other member of the church is to be church-minded, school-minded, covenant-minded, and kingdom-minded believers and members in God's church.

That was the judgment of the apostle Paul. He was single, and he said to all the single and to all believers, "I would that all men were even as I myself" (v. 7). He is an example not only to the single, but also to all believers in his absolute devotion to the cause of the church of God. No one labored more abundantly than he did. There was no man whom God used more for the furtherance of the gospel. He sought to please the Lord. Follow Paul.

Speaking of the goodness of the single state and of the calling of God to single persons, the apostle says, "I speak for your own profit; not that I may cast a snare upon you" (v. 35). No minister of the gospel says things to cast a snare on the people of God, that is, says things to compel them to do what he wants. Every minister's desire is that the people of God will be convicted by the word and Spirit. Paul does not cast a snare but speaks for their profit in attending on the Lord without distractions.

Singleness is not bondage. It is a gift, the fruit of God's grace and mercy. It is in fact deliverance, as the fruit of grace and mercy, from bondage in one of its worse forms. The believing single person is delivered from the bondage to which every man is prone: to serve himself. This is the word of God and of the Spirit and the judgment of the apostle for the single.

CHAPTER 24

THE PRINCIPLE OF CHRISTIAN LIBERTY

1 Corinthians 8:3

---

3. *But if any man love God, the same is known of him.*

In chapter 8 the apostle Paul begins to treat the new subject of "things offered unto idols," about which the Corinthians had questioned the apostle. That they had asked about the subject is evident from verse 1, where Paul says, "We know that we all have knowledge." The apostle does not refer here to general knowledge, whether doctrinal or otherwise, but to knowledge concerning the whole matter of things offered unto idols. Therefore, an appeal to this passage to disparage doctrinal knowledge and the importance of it is an abuse of the passage. Rather, "knowledge" refers to the Corinthians' familiarity with the issues surrounding the subject of things offered unto idols and their opinions regarding it. When the Corinthians asked the apostle concerning the subject, they undoubtedly also expressed their opinions on the matter. Otherwise, how could he ascribe knowledge to them?

In the Corinthians' day meat was commonly offered to idols and then bought and sold. Such meat was virtually the only meat that could be purchased. Besides, the temple where the meat was sold functioned as a civic gathering place for the residents of the town or village. One could hardly carry on business there without coming into such forums and eating meat offered to idols. The Corinthians questioned that practice.

It is necessary to understand the entirely mundane character of eating things offered unto idols. That mundane character can be grasped if the issue is put in today's terms. Eating meat offered to idols was similar to buying something made by a union shop, shopping at a store that is open on Sundays, or buying the products made by a corporation that publicly supports the "marriages" of homosexuals.

In today's parlance, the wickedness of the union and of membership in it are not in dispute in the Protestant Reformed Churches as they were not in Reformed churches generally long ago. The issue is whether a Christian may with a clean conscience buy something made in a union workplace by those who wickedly have joined the union. Again, the wickedness of doing business on Sunday is not in dispute among true Christians, but may a Christian shop any other day at a store that keeps its doors open on Sunday? Or the vileness of the sin of homosexuality is not in question among believers, but may a Christian buy the products sold by the corporation that supports homosexuality?

About these matters the apostle says, "We all have knowledge." We all know and agree that idolatry is a sin, just as all Christians agree that union membership is sin, doing business on Sunday is a sin, and supporting homosexuality is a sin. But if you buy a car made by union members, shop at a store that is open on Sundays, or buy a product made by a corporation that openly supports homosexuality, have you not defiled yourself and compromised your confession about the sinfulness of these activities?

Some members in the Corinthian church, whose consciences were weak, thought such thoughts and should not have bought meat offered to idols. There were equally some in the church whose consciences were not weak and who vigorously contended that it was their liberty to eat things offered to idols. To impress their point on the others, they ate boldly and publicly to the grievous injury of the weak in the church. What were the Corinthians to do?

In verse 3 the apostle puts aside the specific question because he must first teach the principle that governs the whole sanctified life of the believer, including the believer's liberty. The principle specifically governs the believer's use of his liberty regarding a weak brother. The apostle brings the whole matter of meat offered to idols back to its proper starting point: "If any man love God, the same is known of him." This is the principle of Christian liberty that unravels the tangled web of questions concerning the believer's liberty, his use of liberty, and how to deal with the weak brother whose conscience cannot use liberty.

What the Principle Is

While treating the matter of things offered to idols, Paul speaks in verse 9 of "this liberty of yours." Chapter 8 is not confined to this specific subject of eating things offered to idols, but teaches broadly of the justified believer's liberty in Christ Jesus.

In the history of the church this liberty has been called adiaphora, things indifferent, and Christian liberty. Calvin called it "intermediate things,"[1] by which he meant things between what God either specifically commands the believer to do or forbids the believer from doing.

All of these names refer to the liberty of the believer in Jesus Christ. That is, the believer in the New Testament church, in distinction from the believer in the Old Testament church, is no longer under law but under grace. The apostle speaks to this distinction in Galatians 3:23–25:

> 23. But before faith came, we were kept under the law, shut up unto the faith which should afterwards be revealed.

---

1 Calvin, *Commentary on the Epistles of Paul the Apostle to the Corinthians,* 1:272.

24. Wherefore the law was our schoolmaster to bring us unto Christ, that we might be justified by faith.
25. But after that faith is come, we are no longer under a schoolmaster.

In the Old Testament the life of a believer in the church was minutely regulated by the laws of God, which addressed every nook and cranny of a person's life. The purpose of the law was not to propose a new way of salvation, but to teach Jesus Christ to the believer, so that the believer in the Old Testament was also justified by faith. The purpose of the law was to shut up the believer unto the faith that afterward would be revealed, that is, faith that could function without that minute regulation of life by the law.

This difference between the Old Testament and New Testament can be easily understood. If you give a small child a job, you cannot simply tell the child to do the job. You must tell the child exactly how to do it. When you explain the directions, you cannot overload the child with large leaps in instruction, but must divide the directions into many short increments. Even then you have to keep a close watch on the child to be sure that he does everything you asked him to do. This is how to deal with the child according to his capacity. But you can simply tell an adult to do a job. He does not need all the minute details directing him how to do it.

In the Old Testament the church of God was a child, and God dealt with her as a child. In the New Testament the church has grown up. The church is no longer under law but under grace. Under grace there is a liberty for the church, a point that both Peter and Paul made at different occasions. Peter, speaking of the life of the church under the law, said to the synod of Jerusalem, "Now therefore why tempt ye God, to put a yoke on the neck of the disciples, which neither our fathers nor we were able to bear?" (Acts 15:10). Paul, needing to rebuke Peter for dissembling on this point, said, "If thou, being a Jew, livest after the manner of Gentiles, and not as do the Jews, why compellest thou the Gentiles to live as do the Jews?" (Gal. 2:14).

There was a serious dispute in the Corinthian church about one application regarding liberty—eating meat offered unto idols. There was no dispute in Corinth, as in Galatia, about the existence and exact definition of Christian liberty. The issue in Corinth was an *application* of the truth of Christian liberty. Some were weak and thought it was improper to eat meat that had been offered to idols. Some were bold with their liberty and clamored for the use of their liberty.

The Starting Point Regarding Christian Liberty

But the starting point in the dispute was all wrong. Have you ever had a dispute with someone who started wrongly? In the dispute they keep asking, "What is wrong with it?" Or they say, "But that is my right." You can observe that in children, not because they are the only ones who do that, but because they have not yet learned to disguise their selfishness with a thin veneer of piety. One brother has a toy, but he is not playing with it. Another brother starts to play with the toy. The toy's owner suddenly is interested, grabs the toy, whaps his brother, and a fight erupts. How do you deal with the two brothers? The toy's owner keeps saying, "But it is my toy!" You say, "We all know it is your toy, but the dispute erupted because it was your toy and that is all you were thinking about."

This is what Paul means when he says in 1 Corinthians 8:1, "We know that we all have knowledge." This knowledge includes the fact of Christian liberty, its ground in the believer's justification by faith alone, and the truth that some activities belong to the Christian's liberty and are not sinful. If you start with knowledge in the matter of Christian liberty, you start wrongly. Knowledge puffs up. The one who begins with his knowledge in Christian liberty will be so puffed up that he will sin when he uses his liberty. His sin is not the activity itself—as the Corinthians' eating meat offered to idols—but the sin is his use of liberty without love and thus sinning against love by callously wounding his brother's weak conscience. The starting point with Christian liberty is not knowledge.

The starting point for Christian liberty is this: does a man love God? The apostle teaches this in the words "but if any man love God." The apostle's purpose is not to deny the importance of the knowledge of Christian liberty, but to teach that this knowledge apart from love is not true knowledge of Christian liberty at all because it lacks love, its chief part.

Love is a delight in another person as precious and dear. Love is what makes a little child beam in the presence of his mother. He delights in her as the most precious person in the world.

Love is also the determination to do good to that one who is precious and dear to you. Love is what makes a mother care for her children. She is determined to do good to them. Love is not seated in feelings. Love is seated in the will. When God regenerates his people and infuses new qualities into them and quickens their wills, he also makes them love.

Love seeks fellowship with the beloved. The end of love is a covenant. Love and covenant are related as cause and effect. Love embraces the beloved with a covenantal embrace of the most intimate fellowship and friendship.

For understanding the application of Christian liberty, the starting point is, does a man love God? The God whom man is to love is the only true, triune God, who lives in himself in blessed covenantal fellowship, whom to know in Christ Jesus is life eternal, who himself is good and only does good, and who is the overflowing fountain of all good. The God whom man is to love is the God about whom Paul said on the Areopagus, "In him we live, and move, and have our being" (Acts 17:28), the God of heaven and earth who made all things for himself, who has no need of anything, who is perfect and perfectly self-sufficient in himself. The God whom man is to love is the God about whom Paul says, "There is but one God, the Father, of whom are all things and we in him" (1 Cor. 8:6).

Paul here does not ask mankind in general, "Do you love God?" He speaks to the church and says, "If any man love God." This is the church about whom he says, "There is…one Lord Jesus Christ, by whom are all things, and we by him" (v. 6). The God whom believers are to love is the God of their salvation who revealed himself in Christ Jesus. The God whom they are to love is the God who sent Jesus Christ to be the sacrifice for the sins of his people, who raised him from the dead, who has freed his people from the cruel bondage of sin, and who on the basis of the death of Jesus Christ earned for his people the right to love him.

The love of God is the heart of the whole law. Behind all those rules and regulations that Moses gave to Israel was one, unchanging, eternal principle: "Hear, O Israel: The LORD our God is one LORD: And thou shalt love the LORD thy God with all thine heart, and with all thy soul, and with all thy might" (Deut. 6:4–5).

That is what Jesus said when the Pharisees tempted him and asked him to choose the "great" commandment among the ten in the law (Matt. 22:36). Summarizing the whole law, Jesus said, "Thou shalt love the Lord thy God with all thy heart, and with all thy soul, and with all thy mind. This is the first and great commandment" (vv. 37–38). The love of God fulfills the whole law.

The love of God is not first of all what a man does. The love of God is a matter of man's nature. Man must be a lover of God. The man who loves God has a regenerated heart that loves God. That heart is the spiritual center of his life, and out of his heart are all the issues of his life. Because his heart is dominated by the love of God, everything he does is dominated by the love of God. A man loves God, or he hates God.

If a man loves God, the love of God fills his soul. God is not a part of his life, but his whole life is regulated by the love of God. God is first and everything in his life. To love God is to cleave to

God; to love him with all your heart, mind, soul, and strength; and to fear, honor, and glorify God. It means to seek God only, to subject everything in your life to the will of God, and to serve God with your whole being. Out of love for God a man does everything.

This does not involve perfection in this life, but the outstanding example of the love of God is sorrow for sin. A man who loves God becomes a sinner before him. He knows himself in the light of God and the requirement of God's law and is humble before him as a sinner and receives from him by faith Christ's righteousness.

This is the principle of Christian liberty. If any man loves God, he is free. Perfect freedom is to love God with everything that you are and in everything that you think, say, and do.

This is the principle that clears up the struggle over things offered to idols or any question of Christian liberty. If we will talk about man's liberty, let us begin with the principle that a believer is free now to love God. The apostle brings the whole matter of liberty back to the proper starting point: The love of God.

The Source of Christian Liberty

"If any man love God, the same is known of him" (1 Cor. 8:3). By this statement the apostle denies that the source of Christian liberty—the love of God—and thus the liberty itself are the work of man. No man by nature loves God; he hates God and loathes him with his whole being. Lacking love for God, his whole life is wrong. Lacking love for God, he cannot use anything right, because he has no right to use it and cannot use it in love.

The lack of love for God was vividly displayed in the Corinthians. They insisted on their knowledge of liberty, while they used their liberty to destroy their brethren, casting spiritual stumbling blocks in front of them and scandalizing their weak consciences. Why? Because they did not love God, they did not love their brethren.

The Greek word translated as "known of him" is in the perfect tense. If a man loves God, the same has been known by God. "Known" is a synonym for love. "Known" is not to be understood in the Arminian sense that God looked into the future to see who would love him, and then God chose those people. The biblical meaning of "known" is loved. Knowledge and love are one in God. You cannot distinguish between knowledge and charity in God. Whom God knows he loves; whom he loves he knows. He knows them with his love, and loving them, he knows them.

Being loved and known of God refers to the eternal love of God. God delights in his people as precious and dear to him. God determines to do good to them, and that good consists of their salvation. Loving them, God establishes a relationship of fellowship and friendship with them.

This points to the deepest source of their love as rooted in the love of God himself. If you love God, where does that love come from? Not from yourself, for by nature you do not love God. No man whom God has not known and loved from all eternity can or will ever love God. The deepest source of that love is God's own love, for love always begins in God.

Love in God is his delight in himself as the highest good and his seeking his own blessedness. The Father seeks the Son and the Son seeks the Father in the Spirit. God in himself is love. He did not need his creatures in order to love. God has love for his creatures too. In that love he delights in them, and he seeks their blessedness in him.

The text proves that God loved only some men, not all men. If God loved all men, all men would love him, for that is the power of God's love. He loves certain men, sinful men, men whom he made good and able to love him in Adam, but who in their father Adam sinned and rebelled against God, hated him, and became his enemies. These same men who are dead in their sins are also entangled in every sort of evil. Their condition the apostle vividly describes as unrighteous, fornicators, idolaters, adulterers, effeminate, and abusers of themselves with mankind, and about them he pointedly reminded the Corinthians, "and such were some of you" (6:11). That is whom God loved. His love cannot have any cause in those who are loved because of their own vileness.

That God loved only certain men, that he knew them, means that he delighted in them and appointed them to salvation in Jesus Christ. That God knew them means that God in his commendation of his love for them sent Christ to die for them while they were still enemies of God. God was not their enemy, for God loved them. It means that God in his love sought them and sent the preaching of the gospel to call them out of their darkness into God's marvelous light. It means that by the power of his love, God regenerated their hearts and changed them from being hating hearts to loving hearts. It means that God in his love, for the sake of Jesus Christ's perfect satisfaction, righteousness, and holiness accomplished at the cross, forgives their sins and counts them righteous—those who love God perfectly—and worthy of eternal life. It means that God puts his love in their hearts, so that they live their whole lives—with a small beginning of the new obedience—out of love for the God who saved them. If these men love God, the same are known of God.

How the Love of God Is So

The love of God for his people, by which he makes them love, is the principle of Christian liberty. First, there is only one God. Man is not God and neither are his rights and liberty God, but God is God. The neighbor is not God either, so that his weakness controls another. God is God. This speaks to one's liberty, because liberty is ruled by God and no one else: not yourself, not your neighbor.

Second, the love of God is the principle of your liberty because only the one loved by God is free from the guilt of his sin—justified—and has the right to love God. Those whom God has not loved do not have the right to love God, because Christ has not died for them and they remain in their sins.

Third, the love of God is the principle of Christian liberty because only those whom God loves actually love their neighbors. The love of God in a man's heart means that he loves his neighbor as himself. That is what Jesus said: "The second [commandment] is like unto [the first], Thou shalt love thy neighbour as thyself" (Matt. 22:39). The first and great commandment is to love God. The second is like unto it. The one commandment has two great parts: God is first, and if a man loves God, knows him as the God of his salvation, believes in him, and trusts, glorifies, and fears him, he will love his neighbor. No man whom God has not loved will love his neighbor.

Further, where does your love come from? Your love of the brother is God's own love for that brother that he shares with you. God does not love you more because you eat meat or love the brother less because he does not eat meat. God set his love on the brother because God so willed and for no other reason.

Before asking, therefore, about liberty, about meat offered to idols, about insurance, shopping at this store or that one, buying products made by union members, or any other matter of liberty, you first must ask, "Do I love God?" "If any man love God, the same is known of him."

If we understand this principle, we can begin to address the matter of Christian liberty in Jesus Christ. "We all have knowledge," says the apostle (1 Cor. 8:1). The apostle here does not extol ignorance. There is nothing so puffed up as ignorance. Neither is the apostle denigrating knowledge. No doubt there were some in Corinth, as there are some today, who laid the blame for every problem in the church on knowledge. "If we would not have so much knowledge [doctrine], we would not have so much strife. What we need is more love," they say. Then they try to find support for that ignorant babble in the apostle. The apostle does not blame knowledge. It is not the fault of knowledge that man uses his liberty to assault his brother.

Paul keeps together what God keeps together: knowledge and love, and he regulates them one with the other. Knowledge is regulated by love, and love is informed by knowledge. He teaches that knowledge—any knowledge—apart from the regenerated heart that loves God and the neighbor is nothing but conceit and ignorance. This is true of Christian liberty in the same way that the doctrine of justification by faith alone is not the reason that men are careless and profane and live malicious and wicked lives. The doctrine is not the problem, but the men who abuse it. So here.

The apostle teaches that the principle of Christian liberty is that there can be no liberty apart from God's regeneration of a man's heart. Apart from God's rule by sovereign grace in a man's heart there is no liberty. Liberty begins with God's love for a man. If he does not have God's love in his heart, he will be puffed up by whatever knowledge he has. Knowledge can only affect the unregenerated heart that way. Knowledge only makes a sinner a bigger sinner. You know some facts, but not very well. You do not know as you "ought to know" (v. 2), that is, to know that all love begins in God's love for man.

More seriously, such a way of knowing—to know apart from the love of God—is destructive. It is destructive first for the one who has that kind of knowledge. He is puffed up, and being puffed up he stands outside the kingdom of heaven. Second, that kind of knowledge destroys the brother. One who has that kind of knowledge smites his brother with liberty, and smiting his brother, he sins against Christ and God.

If a man loves God, the same has been known by God. That is where you must begin. Your liberty begins in your gracious salvation from God. It begins with God by the power of his love changing your heart. If you will talk about Christian liberty, you must start in that new heart in which the *will*, the *can*, and the *must* of the law are all one and everything is regulated by the love of God.

The apostle also regulates all things in your life by love. If knowledge—the very best attainment of a man—is regulated by love, the man's whole life is so regulated. Then too the apostle defines Christian liberty. It is not to do what you please. Your liberty is not even to do what you have the right to do. True liberty is to do everything in love for God. If a man loves God, the same has been known by God, and then his whole life will be properly regulated. This is the principle of Christian liberty.

CHAPTER 25

THE LIMITATION ON THE EXERCISE OF CHRISTIAN LIBERTY

1 Corinthians 8:9–13

9. But take heed lest by any means this liberty of yours become a stumblingblock to them that are weak.

10. For if any man see thee which hast knowledge sit at meat in the idol's temple, shall not the conscience of him which is weak be emboldened to eat those things which are offered to idols;

11. And through thy knowledge shall the weak brother perish, for whom Christ died?

12. But when ye sin so against the brethren, and wound their weak conscience, ye sin against Christ.

13. Wherefore, if meat make my brother to offend, I will eat no flesh while the world standeth, lest I make my brother to offend.

Eating meat sacrificed to idols was an issue in the Corinthian congregation not because it was sinful to eat that meat, but because some could not eat it because their consciences were weak; and others, who supposed themselves to be defenders of the believer's liberty, boldly, publicly, and callously ate meat offered to idols in the presence of the weak. The Corinthians asked Paul about this matter, which he took as an occasion to instruct them concerning the liberty of the believer in Jesus Christ. To begin, the apostle put aside the specific question regarding eating meat offered to idols. He is like a mother who deals with two squabbling children, the one crying because his toy was taken away and the other repeating, "It's my toy." The mother puts aside the matter of whose toy it is and addresses the heart of the matter, the love of the brothers for one another. She says, "We all know it is your toy, but do you love your brother?"

So the apostle says in verse 1, "We know that we all have knowledge." We all know of this truth of Christian liberty, "but if any man love God, the same is known of him" (v. 3). Love for God is the first and great commandment. We cannot talk about liberty until we talk about a man's love for God. This is because the man who loves God is regenerated, and a man who does not love God is unregenerated. The unregenerated heart takes every bit of knowledge it has, even good knowledge, and uses it against the neighbor, especially against the brother. That without which there is no liberty is a man's love for God based on God's knowing and loving that man.

Having spoken of that principle, the apostle now returns to the specific question: "As concerning therefore the eating of those things that are offered in sacrifice unto idols." Again the apostle concedes the point: "We know that an idol is nothing in the world, and [we all know] that there is none other God but one" (v. 4). The apostle grants the point of the Corinthians' liberty and then issues a warning: "Take heed lest by any means this liberty of yours become a stumblingblock to them that are weak" (v. 9). Here he speaks of the limitation on the exercise of Christian liberty.

The Meaning

Paul speaks of "this liberty of yours" (v. 9). By implication he speaks of the liberty of every believer in Jesus Christ. The believer in Jesus Christ is free. Believers in the specific instance in Corinth were at liberty to eat meat that had been sacrificed unto idols. Furthermore, their liberty consisted not only in eating the meat, but also in eating the meat in the temple of the idol: "If any man see thee which hast knowledge [of his liberty] sit at meat in the idol's temple" (v. 10). So far does the apostle teach them their liberty that they may not only eat the meat, but they may also eat it in the idol's temple, reclining at a meal in the temple of the idol and eating the meat that had been offered in that temple to the idol.

My intention is not to spell out exhaustively the modern applications of that "liberty of yours." But if we understand what the idols of the modern man are, we can quickly see the temples of those idols and what eating meat in the temples of these idols means today. Modern man makes an idol out of money, and he builds massive temples to his idol in all the financial districts of his cities. Man builds temples to his idol mammon in the stores he keeps open on Sunday. Man builds temples to his idol mammon in the unions. Man builds temples to his idols of science in research facilites and of medicine in hospitals. Man builds temples to his idol learning and wisdom in the universities. He builds temples to his idol security in insurance programs and public safety nets. There is a plethora of modern idols and temples, so that man's cities are as given over to idolatry as was Athens in the days of Paul and the Roman forum in the days of Augustus. Christian liberty is to eat meat in those temples. Christians may use man's learning, insurance, science, and medicine and shop in his stores and buy and sell man's products.

The Greek word translated as "liberty" in verse 9 is translated everywhere else in the Bible as "authority." This is the same word Jesus used when he said to his disciples, "All power is given unto me in heaven and on earth" (Matt. 28:18). The word "power" is a translation of the Greek word meaning authority. When Paul refers to liberty as authority, he means that there is no sin whatsoever in a Christian's liberty. There is no condemnation to those who eat meat in the temple of an idol. Furthermore, he means that it is the right of the believer to eat meat in the temple of an idol. An authority is a right. That right is based on the word of God, which gives a person such liberty.

In Corinth the matter was eating things offered to idols and thus the difference for the Christian between eating one kind of meat or another kind of meat. To eat things offered unto idols was perfectly within the rights of the Corinthian believer. There was nothing wrong with it whatsoever. There was no sin in that eating. Indeed, it was part of the exercise of the share of authority that he had by virtue of being one with Jesus Christ by faith. Believers share in his authority, an authority that consists in using all things and partaking of all things for the glory of God because all things are God's, and the very purpose of God with the creation is his glory. Believers may use them now in Christ for God's glory because in Christ they have both the right and the ability to do that.

The word *authority* also speaks of the believer's liberty as freedom from any law but the law of the word of God. The word of God is authoritative in his life in everything that he does and in every sphere of his life. He is free because he is the Lord's bondman.

The word *authority* also speaks of the reality of his freedom. He is free to do as he pleases so long as what he pleases is in accordance with the word of God.

The Basis of Liberty

Liberty is based on knowledge: "if any man see thee which hast knowledge" (1 Cor. 8:10). Here Paul speaks of the believer's liberty as it arises out of some knowledge. This knowledge is the knowledge of faith. Faith is the certain knowledge of and holding for truth all that God reveals in his word.

The apostle specifically defines what faith knows as the basis of liberty: "We know that…there is none other God but one" (v. 4).

He refers to the triune God—Father, Son, and Holy Spirit—the triune God of whom are all things and we in him, so that we live by him and out of him.

Implied in the knowledge of the one God is that "we know that an idol is nothing in the world" (v. 4). The idols that men worship in their temples are nothing but the figments of the corrupt imaginations of their reprobate minds, whose spirits are at war with the living God, who hate God, hold the truth of God under in unrighteousness, and change the truth of God into a lie. That is where the idols originate. These idols are nothing. The natural man makes money, science, medicine, fortune, his bodily strength, and his figure his idols and builds temples to them. But they are nothing, because "there is but one God" (v. 6). We know that. Faith knows that.

This says something about the liberty of the believer. First, it is as precious as the will of the one only true God, that he be glorified by his people. Liberty is as precious as the will and glory of God. This is the reason the apostle defends liberty when it is threatened by those who deny it and attempt to bring the church into bondage to carnal commandments, which have a show of piety and religion but are nothing more than the commandments of men. When believers eat and drink and use the creation, when they exist, learn, and work in the creation to the glory of God, the will of God is honored and the goal of the one only true God in his glory is attained. Their liberty is not for themselves but for the glory of God. The liberty of believers honors the truth that the whole creation is subject to the will of God and not to any commandments of men. The precious liberty of the children of God is to glorify God in all things. They all know that there is only one God.

Second, liberty is based on the believer's knowledge—faith—that there is "one Lord Jesus Christ" (v. 6). There is one Lord. There is one man, Jesus Christ, to whom God gave all things and all authority. This one Lord Jesus Christ purchased his people by his blood. The liberty of believers begins in the blood of the cross of Jesus Christ, because by his blood he freed them from the condemnation of their sins. By that blood he bought for them the right to live again in God's creation and to use all things for the glory of God. Liberty is a blood-bought right. This is the point of the apostle in the words "for whom Christ died" (v. 11). Paul grounds the liberty of believers in the cross and in the justification of the cross that freed them from the condemnation of sin and guilt. Apart from justification by faith there is no liberty to any man because all men forfeited in Adam any rights and liberties.

Then too, because Jesus bought his people, he is their Lord. He alone controls them. His will alone is sovereign in their lives, so that they actually begin to live according to all the commandments of God and to fulfill the law in love.

Whether you partake of meat and drink or do not partake of meat and drink, and that includes all earthly things, does not commend you to God, but Christ's blood does.

This says something about your liberty: it is as precious as the blood of Christ. The right for you to use this world is a right that you have from the cross, not in yourself but from your Lord. It is a blood-bought right to use the things of the world free from scruples, free from worrying whether this or that thing affects your standing before God. Now in Christ you know it does not affect our standing before God. Your standing and commendation before God rest in the cross, and your whole life in God's creation and with his creation is by the power of the cross and the lordship of Christ Jesus.

The natural man does not have this right. He makes things his idols, but he does not have the right to these things, not one breath of air or one little crumb of bread, because he is a sinner and outside Christ remains a sinner before God. His life and use of all the things in the world are cursed by God.

This is how precious your liberty is. It is not a concept to be minimized, ignored, or curtailed. It is especially evil when liberty is abused in the service of what is wicked and as a cloak for wickedness, so that what is in fact evil is called a liberty. It is just as evil to deny to believers this liberty by making sin that which is not sin. The apostle does not curtail the liberty of the Corinthians one iota. "This liberty of yours," he says, "is blood bought for the glory of the triune God." He grants and even defends their liberty.

He also does not lay the blame for their problem on too much doctrine—knowledge—on which liberty is based. It is good to understand that this doctrinal ground for liberty that he describes in verses 4–8—one God, the idol is nothing, one Lord, meat's inability to commend us to God—is the Corinthians' own argument. Liberty is based on good doctrine. Liberty has a firm foundation in the truth. The doctrine cannot be blamed. That is the right and Spirit-approved foundation of all liberty.

The Warning

"But take heed lest by any means this liberty of yours become a stumblingblock to them that are weak" (v. 9). The apostle places a limit on the exercise of the liberty. He does not say to take heed that this liberty of yours be not extended too far. Rather, take heed lest this liberty of yours become the stumbling block, so that in *the exercise and use of liberty* you cause the weak brother to stumble.

Then in verses 10–11 Paul points out a concrete case: You who have knowledge sit in the temple of the idol eating meat, and a weak brother sees you. Seeing you eat, he is emboldened to eat too. Through your knowledge a weak brother perishes. Take heed.

The limit on your liberty is the weak brother. Not every carping critic is a limit on your liberty, but the weak brother is. He is a brother—a man, woman, or child—in the church. He is a brother because he is of one confession with you. He believes the very same doctrine you believe, that there is one God, our Father, and there is one Lord Jesus Christ. In general, this brother also confesses that the believer has liberty, that external things do not commend him to God, and that the use of them does not endanger his salvation. This is a good test of the brother: if the brother demands that the whole church conforms to his view of these things, either he is right and the matter is sin, or he is not weak but a Pharisee and is not promoting the law of God but his own carnal commandments, which have a show of godliness but deny the power of it. Such a brother is not to be yielded to a single inch.

But some brothers in Corinth were weak. They were not weak regarding liberty in general. They did not deny liberty to the believer, but they were weak in a certain particular application of the doctrine of liberty. They were weak in the application that liberty allows believers to eat meat offered unto idols in the idol's temple.

Furthermore, they were weak in their consciences. When Paul speaks of the "conscience," he more closely defines the weakness of the brothers (vv. 7, 10, 13). The conscience is God's courtroom within the believer. When God causes the gospel to be preached unto his people and grants them faith to believe the gospel, and they believe it, God justifies them in their consciences. He declares to believers by the gospel of Jesus Christ, "Your sins are all forgiven; you are righteous before me, and there is no condemnation to those who love God and are the called according to his purpose." God does that all in his courtroom in their consciences. The conscience is God's, not man's, not even the man whose conscience it is.

The weak brother has a weak conscience. The weakness is that God has not granted him the peace that belongs to the believer and the child of God to eat that meat. When he eats it, there is no voice from God saying to him, "There is no condemnation." But when he eats it he hears, "There is condemnation to you." He is weak.

He is weak because he lacks knowledge. The one who sits

in the temple has knowledge. By implication the weak brother does not have it. This is why he is weak. The weakness is not a lack of knowledge about Christian liberty generally, but lack of knowledge in a particular application of liberty. This is how the apostle defines the weakness when he distinguishes between one who has knowledge and one who does not have knowledge (v. 10). Because of the lack of knowledge, the weak brother viewed that meat in his conscience as meat that had been sanctified for the idol and thus as defiled by the idol. If he ate it, he would be defiled. God had not given him knowledge.

Now herein is the danger. If the weak brother sees his strong brother, who has knowledge and may eat freely, eat the meat offered to the idol, the weak brother says to himself, "I may eat because my brother eats." He eats and he perishes, because his conscience does not testify that there is no condemnation to him in that eating. This is the reason the apostle says, "Take heed" (v. 9).

Take heed lest by your liberty you embolden your weak brother to eat what his conscience does not allow him to eat, to do what his conscience does not let him do. Take heed!

The Ground

The first ground of this warning is the command of God. God says to you about your liberty, "Take heed." You have liberty in many external things, but you do not have the liberty to use liberty to destroy a brother. A callous and injudicious use of liberty in the face of the weak brother is specifically forbidden by God. It is not liberty. It is sin. God says, "Take heed."

Second, you must take heed and you can take heed because you are dealing with a matter of liberty. Whether you eat or not does not commend you to God. If I must have something, that is a sorry form of "liberty." That is not liberty but bondage. But Paul speaks of liberty. Whether you eat or not matters nothing for your salvation. If you can eat without condemnation, you can also refrain from eating for the brother's sake for God's glory.

Third, you can take heed to the limit the apostle places on the exercise of your liberty because he grounds this taking heed in love. Love really is the ground for limiting the exercise of your liberty. This is obvious when in verse 11 the apostle calls the weak man a "brother." He is not a neighbor or a stranger but a brother, a fellow man in the church, a fellow believer who is one in the confession of one God our Father and one Lord Jesus Christ and the things that do matter for salvation.

If he is a brother, you must love him. A man who has liberty says he loves God. This is a principle of his liberty. But no man loves God who does not love his brother. A man who says he loves God and will not love his brother is a liar, and he is deceived (1 John 4:20–21). The man who loves God loves his brother too.

Love for the brother is the limit on the exercise of liberty. In esteem for the brother as precious and dear, you give up the use of liberty. You do not thereby give up your liberty, because your liberty does not stand in the use of a thing, but in Christ and in the love of God and the brother. In your determination to do good to the brother as someone who is precious and dear, you give up the exercise of your liberty. In your seeing that the brother is a brother who is loved by God, you give up the use of your liberty.

That is what one who gives up the exercise of his liberty in some specific situation says about brothers in Christ. Their eating does not commend them to God, but Christ's blood does. That is what Paul means in 1 Corinthians 8:11 by "for whom Christ died." The most important consideration in limiting the exercise of your liberty is not that you love the brother, but that God loves the brother. God loved him so much that he appointed him to salvation and sent his own precious Son to die for the brother. Whether that man eats like you can eat or cannot eat does not commend him to God. The blood of Christ commends him to God. He stands before God—as you the strong stand before God—not because he eats but because Christ died for him.

Since Christ died for that brother, he also has liberty. He has the liberty not to eat. That was bought for him too. The death of Christ that purchased your liberty to eat purchased for the brother liberty not to eat. The meat does not commend him to God. The weak brother's life, in which he cannot eat, is out of faith too. If he eats, he does not eat out of faith. If he does not eat out of faith, it is sin to him.

His life is also ruled by the love of God, which is faith. If he hears in his conscience from the God of his salvation, whom he loves, "Do not eat," and then he eats because he sees you eat, he does so against the God whom he confesses to love. This is sin to him. In the exercise of your liberty, you have become a stumbling block to your weak brother.

This is the scene the apostle paints in verses 10–13. Put yourself in Corinth in AD 50 in the temple of Aphrodite, the goddess of love. You may sit at meat in that temple and eat the meat offered to Aphrodite. You may do so because there is one God, our Father, and one Lord Jesus Christ. You have knowledge, but not everyone has knowledge. Some are weak.

The weak brother sees you exercising your liberty and eating the offered meat in Aphrodite's temple. The weak brother is "emboldened" (v. 10). "Emboldened" does not mean that he suddenly realizes by your callous example that he too has liberty, so that by your rash and unthinking exercise of your liberty you grant that man the freedom that God withholds from him. Rather, being emboldened means that by your example he builds a false foundation for his liberty. His foundation is not knowledge, but the example of the strong one's eating the meat offered to that idol. He takes that example and says, "If you can eat, I can too." And he eats. He eats apart from faith, and that is sin, because everything that is not out of faith is sin.

The weak brother perishes. "Through thy knowledge shall the weak brother perish, for whom Christ died" (v. 11)? The apostle does not say that the elect of God fall away, for that is impossible. But he speaks from the viewpoint of that man's spiritual life. The apostle refers to that brother's conscience and the testimony of his conscience. That false foundation does not give peace of conscience. The man who goes against his conscience is in a terrible way, for the conscience is the voice of God. Since there is no justification to him in his eating and thus no peace with God in his eating, he perishes. In his mind he is thrown into doubts, disquiet, and trouble. He has no peace and no rest with God because he ate not out of knowledge but because of another's bold, public, and callous use of liberty.

Take heed lest this liberty of yours become a stumbling block to him who is weak!

This is what the apostle means by "offend" in verse 13. To offend means to cause one to stumble spiritually. A brother may not stumble to his eternal perdition, but he stumbles so that his conscience is troubled and he has no peace with God.

The Meaning of "Take Heed"

Take heed does not mean that you limit the exercise of your liberty, which is as precious and dear to you as the glory of God and the blood of Jesus Christ, because of a domineering, censorious, and Pharisaical member of the church. There is a vast difference between a weak brother and a Pharisee. We know the Pharisees. John came not eating and not drinking, and they said, "He has a devil; he is a crazy man" (John 8:52). Jesus came eating and drinking, and they said, "He is a glutton and winebibber" (Matt. 11:19; Luke 7:34). Those accusers were Pharisees. Today also, if you do or if you do not do, they will have something critical to say. Your liberty is not limited by a Pharisee.

Take heed also does not mean that you limit the exercise of your liberty, so that you do not incur the displeasure of anyone and retain the favor of everyone. Some people abuse the apostle's teaching and maintain this. They say that when you make someone displeased with what you do that you "offend" him. Thus the believer is thrown into fits because he has to suppose that whenever there is any possibility of an "offense" he cannot exercise his liberty. This idea virtually takes liberty away from the believer. However, to displease someone is not the biblical idea of offend. To offend a brother means to cause him to stumble spiritually.

You can easily tell the difference between a weak brother and a displeased member. The weak brother will be tempted to do what you do. The displeased member will carp about what you did and never dream to do it himself. He can be safely ignored in his carping criticism and be told to keep quiet and exercise some Christian charity with the liberty with which God has made you free.

The weak brother limits your liberty in love. You are gentle with him. With great care you handle him. The censorious we rebuke: "There is one Lord, and you are not him." The weak brother is the limit on your liberty

The apostle means by "take heed" to listen and be careful. He intends to warn the members of the church against a public, callous use of liberty. It was well known in Corinth that there was a weak brother in the church. Against that well-known fact some callously used their liberty. They did that proudly, supposing that by such a bold example they could grant the brother some instruction and the liberty that God had withheld from him. They did that puffed up with the conceit that by such a bold use of their liberty they were defending Christian liberty. Against such thinking the apostle warns, "Take heed!"

Take heed also means to recognize that there is this difference: not everyone has knowledge. This is God's will. He put that distinction between believers. To take heed means to recognize that the scruple of the weak brother has to do with his conscience because of a lack of knowledge. This is liberating. While refraining from your use of liberty, you can simultaneously instruct the weak brother in such knowledge, praying that God will grant it to him. You can teach him about his liberty in Jesus Christ, and he can grow in his knowledge and overcome his weakness. The weak brother can become a strong brother. This is another difference between a Pharisee and one who is weak. The weak are teachable, but the Pharisee is wise in his own conceits.

Take heed also means that the exercise of your liberty must always be edifying and never destructive toward the brother. It means that you recognize that your liberty can become a sin. It is not a sin as such to eat meat in the idol's temple. It becomes a sin when you smite the weak conscience of your brother with your liberty. This is what Paul says. "Take heed...when ye sin so against the brethren, and wound their weak conscience, ye sin against Christ" (vv. 9, 12).

It is a sin not only against the brother, but also against Christ. It is like this: You have two slaves, both bought at the auction by one master. You take them to your estate and remove their shackles. As soon as you remove their shackles, the one slave smites the other slave. That is what the apostle warns against. Take heed lest your liberty, blood bought, becomes the occasion to smite the weak conscience of the brother.

CHAPTER 26

SUPPORT OF THE GOSPEL MINISTRY

1 Corinthians 9:14

---

14. *Even so hath the Lord ordained that they which preach the gospel should live of the gospel.*

In chapter 8 Paul spoke of walking in the excellent way of love as that applies to the whole subject of the Christian's liberty. He laid down the principle that the Christian, redeemed by Jesus Christ and engrafted into him by a true faith, has liberty. Christians are free to love, serve, and glorify God. They are also free from the doctrines of men that have a show of humility but are fundamentally carnal. Never once in that section did the apostle encroach on the believer's liberty in Jesus Christ. The believer is free in Christ; he is not a servant of other men. He is the Lord's.

Paul also explained the fundamental principle of that liberty: "If any man love God, the same is known of him" (v. 3). The principle of liberty is God's love of the believer in Jesus Christ, according to which he redeemed the believer from all his sins and made him free by God's pardoning grace.

The apostle taught a limit on the exercise of liberty. The limit is the weak, uninstructed brother. Because the one who loves God also loves his brother, in love for the weak brother the believer will freely forgo the exercise of his liberty. He never gives up his liberty, because that is a gift to him from Jesus Christ, but he gives up the exercise of that liberty. He has a right to something from Christ, but he does not exercise it when he pays attention to the weak, uninstructed brother.

Now the apostle applies that principle to himself as an apostle of Jesus Christ. He says, "Am I not an apostle?" (9:1). He also extends the application to other ministers of the gospel. He speaks of Cephas and of Barnabas, who was not an apostle but a minister (vv. 5–6), and of "others" (v. 12). The apostle and all ministers of the gospel have the right to a life in this earth. A minister has the right to eat and to drink like other men (v. 4). He has the right "to lead about…a wife" (v. 5) and therefore to have a home and family life and to devote time to the running and enjoyment of that home and family life. He has a right to have children and to support and rear those children. He has a right "to forbear working" (v. 6). Paul does not mean forbear to work at all but to forbear manual labor in the interest of the gospel, that is, manual labor by which a man would ordinarily support his earthly life.

Yet the apostle never used his right. He had to labor with his own hands, making tents in order to live. He writes more about that in 2 Corinthians 11:8–9, where he says, "I robbed other churches, taking wages of them, to do you service. And when I was present with you, and wanted [lacked enough to eat and could not support my earthly life], I was chargeable to no man: for that which was lacking to me the brethren which came from Macedonia supplied: and in all things I have kept myself from being burdensome unto you, and so will I keep myself." The Corinthians did not support Paul, and he had to take wages from other churches. He robbed them so he could do the Corinthians service.

The Bible says more about that situation in Acts 18:2–3. The apostle came to Corinth "and found a certain Jew named Aquila, born in Pontus, lately come from Italy, with his wife Priscilla; (because that Claudius [the emperor] had commanded all Jews to depart from Rome:) and came unto them. And because he was of the same craft, he abode with them, and wrought [worked]: for by their occupation they were tentmakers." The apostle as a minister of the gospel was not supported. He had to work, and when his own work was not enough, he had to rob other churches.

Corinth—wealthy, powerful, and gifted—could not find it within herself to support her minister.

This is not God's will. Paul's situation is not to be the standard. He makes a broad and timeless application in 1 Corinthians 9:14: "Even so hath the Lord ordained that they which preach the gospel should live of the gospel." Walking in the way of love, love of the Lord, love of the gospel, and love for the ministry of the gospel, will issue forth in its material support.

The Meaning

In verse 14 the apostle speaks of the ministry of the gospel. This is clear because he speaks of those "which preach the gospel." They are called and ordained men who in their office carry out the work of preaching the gospel. He specifically refers to himself as an apostle and preacher, to the brethren of the Lord, to Cephas, Jude, and James, to Barnabas, and to unnamed others (vv. 5–6, 12).

The ministry of the gospel is the office in the church for the proclamation or preaching of the gospel. The ministers declare authoritatively in the name of God the truth of the gospel. Gospel means good news. The gospel is good news from God concerning his Son Jesus Christ. The gospel is conceived by God, is from God, and is God's own message. The gospel comes as a light in darkness to God's people in the world.

The content of the message is Jesus Christ. The gospel declares from God to his people that Jesus Christ is the fulfillment of God's promise to save his people from their sins, that Jesus Christ is the seed of the woman, and that all of God's promises are yea and amen in him. The gospel declares that Jesus was born of the seed of David, that he became a man, that in his flesh he suffered his whole life long, especially under Pontius Pilate, and that he was crucified, dead, and buried. The gospel declares that the Son of God not only died, but also arose and that his resurrection is the proof that Jesus Christ has the power to save. The gospel declares that Jesus ascended to heaven, where he sits now at God's right hand. The gospel declares that he will come again to judge the living and the dead.

That gospel, therefore, declares that in Jesus Christ God made satisfaction for the sins of his people and that he has confirmed the new covenant. At the heart of the gospel stands the cross on which Jesus Christ accomplished the full will of God for the salvation of his people. The resurrection declares that the cross was effectual to accomplish perfect salvation.

The gospel, then, includes the whole of revealed truth. The whole of the Bible is the gospel, as the whole Bible has only one subject: Jesus Christ as the salvation of God's people, as the provision from God for his people to reconcile them to himself and to save them.

The gospel was an event that took place in Jesus Christ when he was born of a woman, when he died on the cross, and when he was raised from the dead. That gospel as an event comes to his people by the preaching. The gospel must be declared. It must be declared by the church through her preachers, for how can they preach unless they be sent?

That gospel preaching is the means unto your salvation. If you do not understand this point about the gospel, verse 14 does not make sense to you. That gospel, that saving event, as that saving event comes to you through the preaching, is the power of God to save you from death unto eternal life, to save from guilt to righteousness, to save from pollution to holiness, and to save from bondage to freedom. The gospel is a power because when the gospel comes by a preacher, Christ comes; when Christ comes, God comes to you and by his own word saves his people.

WALKING IN THE WAY OF LOVE

He calls out of darkness, turns from sin, sets on the way of righteousness, works faith, imputes righteousness by faith, and so strengthens faith that it sanctifies the whole life of the believer. The gospel preached does that.

The gospel comes from God. By the preaching of the gospel, those who sit in darkness see a great light; those oppressed by their sin and guilt are forgiven; those in bondage to various lies and errors are made free; and those who are afflicted by a host of various trials, tribulations, and situations are comforted. God does that by the preaching of the gospel.

There is no gospel apart from preaching. This is the utterly unique work of a gospel minister. He is the only person in the congregation who can preach.

These preachers are the interest of the apostle.

Paul declares that the gospel is supported when the preacher of the gospel is supported: those who preach the gospel "should live of the gospel" (v. 14). Many try to distinguish here and say, "I support the gospel, I love the gospel, but I don't like that preacher of the gospel." People said that about Paul. He reveals that as part of the problem in Corinth when he says, "Mine answer to them that do examine me is this" (v. 3). This is the beginning of the defense of his liberty and an apology for his ministry.

In the congregation of Corinth the issue was not that the members would not support a minister. Paul indicates this in verse 12: "if others be partakers of this power over you." Some preachers in Corinth were being supported. Paul mentions this in 2 Corinthians 11:13 and calls them "false apostles, deceitful workers" who transform "themselves into the apostles of Christ." So today, many spurious and unfaithful preachers are lavishly supported.

The apostle does not allow a distinction between the gospel and the preacher of the gospel, that is, that you can support the gospel but not a particular preacher because he does not please you. The support of the gospel is the support of the preacher of the gospel. You must support the minister who has been lawfully called by God through the congregation and whose office and sacred privilege it is to declare the gospel in the name of God in and to a congregation.

The Application

This has wide application. The apostle is not interested only in himself and Barnabas. He says that he does not write these things for himself and he would rather die than be chargeable to any man (1 Cor. 9:15). Paul is interested in the broad application of the principle that the support of the ministry of the gospel consists in the support of the preachers of that gospel. This includes the local church's support of her preacher. This includes domestic and foreign mission preachers. This applies to the emeritus ministers of the gospel and to ministers who labor in the seminary and train other men to preach the gospel.

The apostle's words can also be applied to the support of the Christian school, because the Heidelberg Catechism ties together intimately the support of the Christian school and the ministry of the gospel: "that the ministry of the Gospel and schools be maintained."[1] If we will not teach our children in a Christian school, how many of those children will become ministers of the gospel? The failure to support the Christian school is virtually to condemn the ministry of the gospel to a slow and agonizing death for lack of men. The apostle's words have a massively broad application.

His word about supporting the ministry of the gospel applies to the ministry of the *gospel*, not to every man with a message. The church may not support a man who does not preach the gospel. It would be like a wife's giving money to some slick salesman who tells lies about her husband and gets her to buy all sorts of things that she does not need. The church is called to support the

---

1 Heidelberg Catechism A 103, in Schaff, *Creeds of Christendom*, 3:345.

ministry of the gospel. If a preacher does not preach the gospel and he belongs to the church, he either repents or is eventually excommunicated.

When the apostle teaches that the Lord ordained that those who "preach the gospel should live of the gospel" (v. 14), he indicates very clearly that he means material support, although that is not the only way to support the gospel ministry. You support the gospel in your prayers. Paul says, "Brethren, pray for us, that the word of the Lord may have free course, and be glorified, even as it is with you" (2 Thess. 3:1). You support the gospel by diligent attendance at the worship services and hearing the gospel. But material support is basic. If a man will not give a dollar for the gospel, or worse he gives it kicking and screaming, he will not pray for the gospel. It is not surprising that he is not at the worship services very often either. Indeed, how foolish if a man would fervently pray, "O Lord, send the gospel," but he never opens up his wallet to give for the gospel.

The necessity for the material support of the gospel is clear from 1 Corinthians 9:4–5, where Paul writes that a preacher has power, or liberty, to eat and to drink, to lead about a wife, and by implication to have a family, which he must support. That the apostle refers especially to material support is clear when he writes, "We have sown unto you spiritual things, is it a great thing if we shall reap your carnal things?" (v. 11). Furthermore, in verse 14 he refers to the material support of the gospel when he speaks of the preacher's living by the gospel and compares this with a man who goes a warring, takes care of a vineyard or a flock, or plows and reaps, or to an ox that eats from the corn it treads (vv. 7, 9–10). A man who plows a field lives by plowing, which means that he eats by that work; so also a minister lives by the gospel.

This is a word to ministers first: "Preach the gospel." No minister who does not preach the gospel may expect support. More than that, the apostle says to ministers, "Devote yourselves to the preaching of the gospel so that you live of the gospel, and it may be said of you that it is your life in a similar way that a farmer's farm is his life, or as it may be said that a man's business is his life." The text calls ministers to live in continuous meditation on the word of God, week in and week out to prepare for the gospel preaching, so that the preaching of the gospel is not an aside to his office and the preparation for preaching on Sunday is not the last thing he gets to during the week. A man who will not so live by the gospel ought to be ashamed to pick up his paycheck, just as a bricklayer ought to be ashamed if he laid a shoddy wall that fell over with the first wind.

The text is also an exhortation to the congregation as a whole to pay its minister so he can live from his salary and devote himself to the gospel free from worldly cares.

The text exhorts the individual member of the congregation to support the ministry of the gospel. This means, practically and simply, to pay the church budget. It will not do as an excuse to become principled about *how* the money for the budget is collected. In some congregations the support of the gospel ministry is done through a church budget. This is not the only way, and other congregations do it differently. But a church budget is a perfectly proper and orderly way to collect money for the support of the gospel ministry. This is not a restriction on your giving. If the Lord has opened up the windows of heaven to you, you ought to give more than the budget. The budget is a bare minimum.

Consider how much of the church budget goes for the support of the gospel ministry. There is the portion that goes for synodical assessments to support foreign and domestic missions, seminary professors and students, the catechism committees, and the committees for contact with other churches. It is virtually all, in one way or another, directly or indirectly, the support of the gospel ministry. Then there is a portion for the support of the local minister and payments for the church building in which the congregation worships and the gospel is preached. There is the support of the evangelism efforts in the local congregation

WALKING IN THE WAY OF LOVE

through books, websites, magazines, articles, and many other ways. The whole budget is virtually for nothing else.

When Paul says, "They which preach the gospel should live of the gospel," he says to the members of the congregation, "Pay your budget. Pay it promptly. Pay it without the deacons having to knock on your door. Pay it year in and year out." The payment of the budget is the bare minimum of what the apostle means. If you are delinquent in paying the budget, year in and year out, you are not supporting the gospel ministry.

This also speaks of the attitude of the giver. The Lord does not merely want dollars. He can get dollars from wherever. Besides, they are all his anyway. The Lord exhorts the congregation to give willingly because it is for the gospel. Do you love the gospel? Do you desire for yourself and your children that the gospel will continue for your spiritual growth, life, and salvation? The Lord ordained that those who preach the gospel should live by the gospel.

The Reason

In the context the apostle points to the reason for the support of the gospel. He writes in verse 14, "Even so..." Even so, what? Even so the Lord ordains. The context is full of reasons for the support of the gospel ministry in its broadest application.

Paul gives examples in verse 7. "Who goeth a warfare any time at his own charges?" Must a soldier who goes to war pay for his gun and bullets, uniform and boots, food and drink, and transportation and lodging? No, the government who sends him to war pays for him to war. The kingdom of Jesus Christ must pay for its warriors. The minister is your soldier who goes a warring in the fights of the kingdom of Jesus Christ. "Who planteth a vineyard, and eateth not of the fruit thereof?" To change the example, who would plant a large garden full of tomatoes, cabbages, beets, carrots, and potatoes and not eat any of it? "Who feedeth a flock, and eateth not of the milk of the flock?" Who would care for a flock of sheep and would not drink the milk from the ewes to quench his thirst? Who would milk cows and not dip into the cold storage tank on Sunday for a large pitcher of creamy milk for his family?

Let's put the apostle's reasons in other terms: who would start a business, attend and build the business, labor in it from sunup to sundown six days a week, and never take a paycheck from the business?

Examples are good, but the word of God is decisive. The apostle says that. "Say I these things as a man? or saith not the law the same also" (v. 8)? Paul points to two texts in the law of God.

First, there is the law of Moses in Deuteronomy 25:4: "Thou shalt not muzzle the mouth of the ox when he treadeth out the corn." The cruel, stingy, and heartless farmer in Israel would use the ox to plow his fields, to pull his carts, to harvest his grain, and to thresh the grain, but would not even give the ox a mouthful of grain during his arduous labors. Man is so cruel and stingy that God had to legislate that the Israelite could not muzzle the mouth of his ox. The law was ordained for the sake of ministers: "Saith he it altogether for our sakes. For our sakes, no doubt, this is written" (1 Cor. 9:10). Paul has in view the stingy treatment of the ministry of the gospel. There is a call for a new mission field and the complaints are, "Oh, more dollars!" God says, "Do not muzzle the ox's mouth."

In light of the apostle's treatment in Corinth, where "others" were paid but he was not, and in light of the law about the muzzle on the mouth of an ox, forbidden is any attempt to control the mouth of the minister by his material support. There is the obvious thinking forbidden by the Old Testament law: "We'll starve him out." Or, "We appreciate that he never preaches about the particular sins that are near and dear to us and does not condemn any of the ungodly associations that we keep. We will make sure he gets a lot of supper." Thou shalt not muzzle the mouth of the ox.

The apostle continues that metaphor of the ox and that law: "We have sown unto you spiritual things, is it a great thing if we shall reap your carnal things?" (v. 11). Was it such a big deal that after the farmer had used the ox all year to plow his field, tread the grain, haul his carts, and the farmer reaped a huge profit from the ox's labor, that the ox ate a few mouthfuls of grain?

Paul here disabuses the church members of the notion that in their material support of the gospel ministry they pay for the ministry as an employer pays an employee. The wage is comparable to the work. The laborer works forty hours and gets forty hours of pay. In the support of the gospel, there is no correspondence between what spiritual things the ministry of the gospel sows and what the ministry of the gospel reaps.

The ministry of the gospel sows spiritual things. Believers reap from that sowing the spiritual harvest of salvation. When the gospel comes, salvation comes. When the gospel comes, they reap rewards unto eternal life for themselves and their children. The ministry of the gospel gets some carnal things in return.

But there is a second reason drawn from the law of God in verse 13: "Do ye not know that they which minister about holy things live of the things of the temple? and they which wait at the altar are partakers with the altar?" Second Chronicles 31 demonstrates that it was the priests' right to eat from the altar. King Hezekiah entered the temple and saw the temple courtyard full of huge mounds of gifts for the temple. Hezekiah "questioned with the priests and the Levites concerning the heaps." Azariah the chief priest answered him, "Since the people began to bring the offerings into the house of the LORD we have had enough to eat, and have left plenty: for the LORD hath blessed his people; and that which is left is this great store" (vv. 9–10). The priests had plenty to eat.

This passage also points out that the support of the gospel is tied to the spiritual attitude of the people. Before Hezekiah went through the land and destroyed all the idols, the priests did not have enough to eat and were starving because the idols had to be fed. In 1 Corinthians 9:13–14 the apostle Paul makes this same connection between material support and the attitude toward the gospel: "They which minister about holy things live of the things of the temple," and "they which preach the gospel should live of (out of) the gospel." This means that when the gospel is preached and lays hold on the hearts and lives of the people of God—as it did in Hezekiah's day after he smashed the idols and reinstituted the true worship of God—the gospel *itself* creates the desire and willingness to support the gospel. The minister literally lives *out* of the gospel. The gospel feeds itself.

For the very same reasons, "even so hath the Lord ordained" (v. 14). The Lord ordained. The Lord of heaven and earth—whose is all the gold and the silver; who bought his people not with cheap gold and silver but with his precious blood and redeemed their whole lives—likewise says about their lives, "They are mine." He says "mine" over their houses, bank accounts, and entire lives in the world. He says to them now in the use of their material things, "Support the gospel. I ordain that they who preach it shall live of it."

The Blessing

Because the Lord ordained it, there is a blessing in supporting the gospel. If the calling were from men, you would not have to listen. As it is from the Lord, there is the word that a man reaps what he sows. If you are only interested in sowing carnal things, so that what is most important to you is carnal things that perish with the using, you should not be surprised that you reap only carnal things.

The Lord is not mocked. He gave his people his gospel. What a gift! With the gospel comes salvation and eternal life for them and their children, their friends, and the generations to come. The question of the text is, is the gospel of any worth to you? Are the seeds sown by the gospel of any value? Do you reap spiritual things in the gospel? Is it a great thing if the ministry of the gospel reaps your carnal things?

There is an implicit warning in the words of verse 14: "They which preach the gospel should live of the gospel." If the church and her members do not support the gospel, it will die. That is, those who preach the gospel will die. When they die, there goes the gospel. It is very simple.

The Lord says too that he multiplies those carnal things so that you reap in the material support of the gospel a reward that is far and above what you give. You reap spiritual and eternal things, salvation and everlasting life. The Lord will see to it. That is the reason he ordained for his churches that those who preach the gospel shall live of it.

CHAPTER 27

MOTIVATION OF
THE GOSPEL MINISTRY

1 Corinthians 9:16–18

---

16. For though I preach the gospel, I have nothing to glory of: for necessity is laid on me; yea, woe is unto me, if I preach not the gospel!
17. For if I do this thing willingly, I have a reward: but if against my will, a dispensation of the gospel is committed unto me.
18. What is my reward then? Verily that, when I preach the gospel, I may make the gospel of Christ without charge, that I abuse not my power in the gospel.

In the context the apostle answers those who have examined him regarding his practice of not being paid in Corinth for preaching the gospel. He also points out that this was not what the Lord willed in the church. He willed that those who preach the gospel live of the gospel. Paul establishes this practice on the basis of the inspired word of God that the ox may not be muzzled and that the priest who ministered at the altar lived of the altar. Ministers must be paid so they can live from their work in the gospel. He establishes this same principle on the ground of sound wisdom: no one goes to war of his own charges; no one plants a vineyard and does not eat the grapes or drink the wine;

and no one takes care of a flock and does not drink the milk of the flock.

In order to remove suspicion from himself, Paul denies that he wrote and preached regarding the necessity of supporting the gospel ministry so that the Corinthians would start supporting him. "I have used none of these things: neither have I written these things, that it should be so done unto me" (v. 15). "None of these things" refers to his established practice of preaching without payment in Corinth. "That it should be so done unto me" means that he did not intend that they start paying him.

Then he speaks very strongly: "For it were better for me to die, than that any man should make my glorying void" (v. 15). He means that it is better for him to continue unpaid, and not being paid he starve to death, than for any man to charge him with making merchandise of the gospel and thereby making groundless and baseless his boast.

The apostle in his preaching of the gospel had a boast, which he calls his glorying. He wills that no man be able to deprive him of his boast. It is his personal boast. In explaining his boast, he also explains the motivation of the true gospel ministry everywhere.

The application to the minister today is that he must be able to say, "I do not preach the support of the gospel ministry because I desire the congregation to do so to me." It is an established fact in Reformed churches that no preacher should ever be unpaid. It is an established practice in Reformed churches that ministers should be adequately paid. The Lord so ordained, and the Reformed faith established that in obedience to the Lord's command. There are very few churches where so few support so heartily the ministry of the gospel.

The minister must also be able to say that he did not so preach the gospel in view of his paycheck. Regardless of pay or no pay, he must have the same motivation as the apostle so that no man be able to rob him of his glorying.

The application of the text is to the church herself. She is heir of the apostolic commission to preach the gospel, the task that she carries out through her ministers. This must be her boast, and no man should be able to deprive her of it. Regarding the church, the question that brings this out is, why do you support the ministry of the gospel? Why do you pay for ministers and missionaries, build schools, and support all the kingdom causes? What is your motivation? It must be the same motivation as the apostle's.

There is also a broad application. The apostle sets himself as an example and leads in the churches regarding the use of his rights. Do not forget the subject is still Christian liberty. He says that he did not so use, or fully use, or abuse his liberty in the gospel.

Ministry of the Gospel

The apostle's concern in verses 16–18 is still the ministry of the gospel. His ministry and that of every gospel preacher involve the preaching of the gospel. The apostles gave up the ministrations to the poor in order not to neglect the ministry of the word and prayer. The minister of the word has as his chief calling to labor in the word and doctrine. The apostle repeatedly emphasizes this. He says, "A dispensation of the gospel is committed unto me." "I preach the gospel of Christ…without charge." I have "power in the gospel." "I preach the gospel" (vv. 17–18). All of this simply emphasizes that preaching is his main task, and so it is always with the ministry of the gospel.

The ministry of the gospel is the service of the word carried out by men authorized and qualified by Jesus Christ to speak in his name the word of the gospel. They say, "Thus saith the Lord," and declare the truth, and through them Christ himself speaks and saves his people through that word.

The apostle reveals something more about the ministry of gospel when he says it is a setting forth. This comes out in a more literal translation of the phrase in verse 18 that the King James Version renders as "when I preach the gospel, I may make the gospel of Christ without charge." A more literal translation is "in order that I set forth the gospel of Christ, preaching freely." The preaching is the setting forth of the gospel of Christ. This setting forth is the authoritative teaching, presenting, showing, or establishing of the gospel of Jesus Christ. When the preacher preaches, he declares to everyone in the audience and to everyone where the gospel is set forth. Yet that gospel is not good news intended for everyone, but is only for God's people in the world, his elect. It comes to them from God by means of the ministry of the word preached to all men without distinction.

The apostle calls the gospel he preaches the gospel of Christ. "I...make [set forth] the gospel of Christ" (v. 18). Setting forth the gospel is not laying out a ten-step plan for the improvement of life, society, or the world. It is not either the setting forth of the apostle's or man's wisdom. Preaching the gospel is setting forth Christ. In the gospel Christ is set forth as the full and saving revelation of the triune God, whom to know is life eternal. In the gospel the person, natures, and work of Jesus Christ are set forth as the only Savior and the only work of salvation. He is set forth as the Son of God who became flesh, died on the cross, and accomplished salvation.

Setting forth includes the call of the gospel that declares from God that this Christ must be believed and that calls all men everywhere to repent and to believe in him. In the gospel the promise is set forth that all who do repent and believe shall certainly be received in mercy, and the warning is sounded that whoever does not repent and believe will be judged by that gospel.

The ministry of the gospel includes the instruction of the disciples of Jesus Christ in his will for their lives as that follows from and adorns the gospel.

The gospel in short is the preaching, the setting forth, of the whole counsel of God as it is revealed in the sacred scriptures.

The gospel brings liberty. This is part of the apostle's point when he brings up in verse 18 the subject of "my power [literally, my liberty] in the gospel." When the gospel comes and calls God's people out of darkness into God's marvelous light, it brings liberty. The gospel of Christ brings liberty from the Old Testament ceremonial and civil laws. The gospel brings liberty from the guilt of sin by declaring to God's people that for the sake of Christ's death all their sins are forgiven. The gospel brings true freedom from bondage to sin. Freedom is not the ability to choose this or that or to do this or that. This is the devilish imitation of freedom with which the devil tempted Eve in the beginning and for which Adam grasped and brought himself and all his posterity into bondage to sin and Satan. Freedom is to be free from the bondage of sin and to be free to do the will of God. Freedom is to be a son of God. The gospel calls out those sons of God in principle already in this world. This is the power of the gospel. It is power to create in the hearts and lives of God's children the reality that they are sons of God. This ministry is Paul's concern.

It is a ministry that resided in him and that now is committed to the church. The ministry of the gospel does not reside in a man anymore. The power and the right to preach reside in the church as the gathering of believers and their seed. They carry that out by calling and ordaining men to preach the gospel.

A Glorying Ministry

The apostle speaks of a reward if he preaches willingly and thus carries out his stewardship willingly. "If I do this thing willingly, I have a reward...What is my reward then?" (vv. 17–18). "Willingly" means that he does it with readiness of mind, zeal, and a whole heart. He contrasts that with unwillingness. Unwillingness is doing something simply under necessity. Paul has a reward if he does this thing willingly.

What is the reward? That reward, as all rewards mentioned in the Bible, has nothing to do with merit. It does not have to do with the minister's, Paul's, or the church's earning something from God. That is not the biblical idea of reward. Any reward is always of grace. When we have done all that is our duty to do, we are unprofitable servants, or as the apostle says, "For though I preach the gospel, I have nothing to glory of" (v. 16).

The reward is the payment Paul received in the preaching of the gospel. He was not paid a wage for his labor in the gospel, but that does not mean that he did not have payment. He had wages. They were the wages of which he could not be deprived by any man.

In those wages Paul had a boast: "It were better for me to die, than that any man should make my glorying void" (v. 15). In explaining the reward, he also explains that the ministry is a glorying ministry.

Paul's payment was very strange. He asks, "What is my reward then? Verily that, when I preach the gospel, I may make the gospel of Christ without charge, that I abuse not my power in the gospel" (v. 18). The apostle's argument is undoubtedly clipped, and perhaps another translation will help us understand what he means. "What are my wages? This: when I preach the gospel, I set forth the gospel of Christ freely, or I set forth a free gospel of Jesus Christ, even unto not abusing my power in the gospel."

The words "without charge" modify the gospel. Paul's reward was that when he preached the gospel, he preached a free gospel, a without-charge gospel. How much did he do that? He did that to the point that he did not abuse his liberty in the gospel, so that although he had the right to be paid he never was paid. That was proof that he set forth the gospel of Christ as a free gospel. In this he gloried.

The motivation of the gospel ministry is much more than

necessity or fear of woe. Sometimes ministers have to be reminded of that: "You are charged to preach the gospel. Preach it! You have a dispensation, a stewardship, and God gives you woe if you do not preach the gospel. God's people want to hear the gospel, and if you do not preach the gospel to them, God pronounces a woe on your ministry." But fear is not a lasting teacher of duty. The motivation of the gospel is the wages, not the wages that men pay, but that when a preacher of the gospel preaches he sets forth a free gospel.

First, the reward is that a minister may preach the gospel freely. This means that the gospel itself has laid hold on the preacher and church and saved them. It is not a piece of merchandise that they hawk, but the truth that saved them. This is a wage that pays eternally. The preaching of the gospel is its own reward. The fact that the church has the gospel and is able freely to proclaim it from the pulpit, in evangelism, in the homes, and on the mission fields as that which they actually believe is the wage. We have the gospel. Isn't it a grand gift to have the gospel for ourselves and our children in a world of darkness and in an age of apostasy? We reap eternal rewards from the gospel. We have the privilege, the sacred calling from God to preach it.

Second, the reward is that when the church preaches the gospel through her preachers and in all her gospel endeavors, she sets it forth as a free gospel. This means that when the gospel is preached, it is not preached to earn a wage. They say about a man that you can tell when he is in the right job if he says, "I love this job." Although he gets paid for the work, he loves the work. He did not go into it because he wanted to get rich or to make something of himself in the world, but he loves the work. This is why he does it. The wage is extra. When the gospel is set forth as a free gospel, it is not set forth to garner a wage.

If it is not set forth as a free gospel, the gospel is in jeopardy. This is why Paul says: "If I do this thing willingly, I have a reward" (v. 17). He must preach the gospel, but if he preaches willingly, he has a reward because he sets forth a free gospel. The idea is that the power of the gospel makes the one who sets it forth do it willingly and not to garner a wage. If one preaches to garner a wage, the gospel is in jeopardy because that gospel does not live in that man's soul and he will prostitute it for his own purposes. If the church pays its minister a lot of money, he will preach a lot. If he receives little, he will preach little. If he is not paid at all, he preaches not at all. The gospel is in bondage to a wage and to those who pay the wage. The gospel is not free.

Third, setting forth that gospel as a free gospel also means that the gospel comes utterly free. It comes and it cannot be purchased. That is because of what the gospel essentially is. It is the saving knowledge of God in Jesus Christ. The gospel was bought with the blood of the Son of God. The gospel cannot be bought with silver and gold, and in that sense it is free. When the gospel comes, it cannot cater to the interests of a portion of the congregation and be bought by a section of the congregation for its own purposes. The moment one tries to do that, he makes void the gospel. The minister who allows that to happen sells the gospel and makes it void, even though he may preach it formally correct.

The apostle's boast is that he sets forth a free gospel. The gospel itself compelled him willingly to preach it and to preach it as free gospel.

To drive home the point that no one could make his glorying void or charge him that he made merchandise of the gospel (that he preached the gospel to get something from somebody), the apostle says, "I will not take a wage, lest any man make my glorying void." No one could accuse him of making merchandise of the gospel. That was his wage; he set forth a free gospel.

That has to be the motivation of the preacher: he must set forth a free gospel. The gospel is not bound; it is the servant of no one. It commands and has authority first over the preacher, then over all to whom it comes. That is what the gospel is; it is free. It is free as God himself. That free gospel is the power of God unto salvation because it saves whom he wills.

This also speaks to the church to set forth a free gospel. The church pays for her missionaries, professors, and preachers. I suppose the church could send a missionary out and say, "You cannot take any scrip or purse, and you will be supported by those to whom you come." The church does not do that. She pays for the support of the gospel ministry of the church, because she would have a free gospel without charge.

There are other ways in which the gospel can be bound by earthly considerations. The gospel can be a slave not only to money, but also to numbers. The gospel can be a slave to what we perceive as fruits or results. The gospel can be a slave to getting a return on the investment. But it is a free gospel. The apostle is saying that our zeal and willingness in the gospel cannot depend on earthly calculations or results. He preached a free gospel, not an enslaved one. By this he was motivated in all his preaching. In this he gloried, and so does every true minister and church of Christ.

A Necessary Ministry

The gospel ministry and minister are also motivated by necessity: "For though I preach the gospel, I have nothing to glory of: for necessity is laid on me" (v. 16). Paul means that if he discharges his office and preaches the gospel, he is doing nothing but what the Lord strictly enjoined on him and what is his duty from the Lord. If he preaches the gospel perfectly and faithfully, he has done nothing extra but only what is necessary.

This applies to the church. If the church faithfully preaches the gospel through her ministers and carries out the ministry of the word, she has nothing in which to glory. Necessity is laid on her.

The ministry of the gospel is necessary. That necessity Paul speaks of proceeds from God's counsel, which is the necessity of all things. The necessity of the ministry of the gospel is that it is the means God has ordained to perfect all things. It is not merely the means to perfect a certain people, but it perfects all things.

Paul calls this ministry, the laying on him the charge to preach the gospel, "a dispensation" (v. 17). "Dispensation" does not mean a span of time, but stewardship, as this word is translated everywhere else in the Bible. A stewardship is committed to Paul. When God gave the gospel to the apostle to preach it, he was given a stewardship. The ministry of that gospel is itself temporary. It does not last into eternity. In heaven and in the new heaven and earth there will be no need for ministers, because we will know God face to face and know even as we are known. Rather, the ministry of the gospel is the instrument to gather the elect and to advance God's kingdom, and on that everything waits.

Jesus said in his sermon on the last things shortly before his death, "This gospel of the kingdom shall be preached in all the world for a witness unto all nations; and then shall the end come" (Matt. 24:14). The goal of all things waits on the preaching.

When Peter explained the apparent delay of the Lord's return, he said, "The Lord is…longsuffering to us-ward [to his elect], not willing that any should perish, but that all should come to repentance" (2 Pet. 3:9). The coming of the Lord comes in the way of the preaching and ingathering of God's elect.

In the vision of the opening of the seals in Revelation 5, the first horse that runs is the white horse, the preaching of the gospel.

The necessity of the preaching is not that everyone will get a chance to hear, and neither did this motivate the apostle's zealousness. That is Arminian and man-centered. The necessity is that the gospel, being controlled by the will of God, is the instrument whereby God calls his elect out of darkness into his marvelous light, and calling them out, God works the end of all things.

The apostle says that in view of that necessity he preaches. His motivation in the ministry of the gospel is the realization of that necessity. Preaching is willed by God. Paul says that necessity is laid on him. The idea is that the knowledge of that necessity—the urgency of it, the source of it, and the goal of it—is laid on him.

The church must view herself as being in possession of the gospel by a gracious bestowal of God. She does not have it by her choice, but because it was committed to her. In the giving of that gospel, God laid a stewardship on the church. If she is doubtful about whether or not she has the gospel, she cannot preach it. If she supposes that the gospel she received is only a form of the gospel, one form among many forms, she cannot preach it as necessary. Only if she believes that the Lord committed to her the gospel and along with that gave a stewardship is there an urgency in the preaching of the gospel, because it belongs to stewards that they must be found faithful. If there is a stewardship, there will be a judgment from the Lord and an investigation of what his stewards did with this most precious treasure of his household.

The same thing goes for the preacher. When he is called and ordained, a stewardship is committed to him. This says something to both the church and the minister. To the minister it says that he cannot withdraw from his calling as steward of the gospel. These verses are the ground for the Reformed understanding that the call to the ministry is for life. He cannot withdraw when he chooses, has obstacles, is vexed, or is tried.

This is the reason the call to the gospel ministry is so sacred for the church. The church cannot play fast and loose with the call without doing incalculable harm to herself. The call and its order of nominating, electing, approbating, and installing are sacred. Through that call the minister carries out the stewardship that has been committed to the church.

By calling the ministry a stewardship, verse 17 commands the church that has received the gospel to preach it. She cannot hide it, be embarrassed by it, or change it. The truth of that gospel does not belong to her but is God's, and it is not up for debate or negotiation. Stewards are simply to discharge their office faithfully.

Furthermore, belonging to the necessity of gospel preaching is what the apostle says next: "Woe is unto me, if I preach not the gospel!"(v. 16). Paul had to preach the gospel, the church with the gospel must preach it, and the minister who receives the gospel must preach it, or God will curse them. To the Protestant Reformed Churches this means that they have received the gospel as it has advanced and developed through history, as it has been shaped and hammered and sharpened to a razor's edge. This is the gospel they have received. This is not a generic gospel but a very sharp gospel. They have received the gospel of Jesus Christ as it is set forth in the sacred scriptures and systematized in the Reformed creeds. That is the gospel that has been fought for in controversy in the past and in these churches. God says to them, "Preach the gospel. And if you do not, I will curse you."

If the churches do not sharply set forth the gospel from the pulpits, in magazines and pamphlets, through evangelism committees, on the mission fields, in the seminary and schools; if they muzzle it, are ashamed of it, turn their backs on it; then the woe of God comes on them.

The same thing holds for preachers. They have a stewardship. It belongs to stewards that they must be found faithful. Every minister will answer for what he did with the gospel. Necessity is laid on him. Woe is he if he does not preach the gospel. In all of his studies, pastoral work, visits, preaching, and catechism instruction, he has only one word, and that is the gospel. If he and the churches are faithful, they have nothing about which to glory. Necessity is laid on them.

A Broad Application

There is also a broad application to all of us about our lives in the gospel. The Holy Ghost set forth the apostle as an example to the Corinthians and to us of the proper use of our liberty. We all grant that Paul had the right to be paid, especially in his abundant labors in the gospel and in light of his faithfulness. We all grant that he should have been paid. Which of us would not give huge sums to have him preach for us? But he used none of those things. So concerned was he for the gospel and that it be preached unconstrained that he did not "abuse," which means to use fully, his power and liberty in the gospel (v. 18). No one could doubt that. No one abounded more than he did in the gospel. No one had a deeper understanding of the mysteries of the kingdom of God than Paul. He had a right to be supported, but for the gospel's sake he did not use his right.

This is a word to us. It is a larger point that cannot be missed in these verses. Paul did not make his labor and zeal in the gospel dependent on someone's honoring his rights, recognizing his labors, or even thanking him for them. Not infrequently he received the very opposite of thankfulness. Yet he labored willingly. Nor did he did write this so that it be so done unto him. He would rather die than that any man would make his glorying vain. His was such a holding of the gospel that he gloried in it and nothing else unto not fully exercising his rights, in short, giving them up.

This applies to all our work, specifically regarding money. Any man who does anything for money will pierce himself through with many sorrows. This applies not only to the gospel ministry, but also to any line of work. We do what we do because the gospel of Jesus Christ has come and in its coming freed us from the bondage of sin and set us in the glorious liberty of the sons of God, who are free to love him and to love his gospel. In all our labors we are called to serve not mammon but God and to seek with all our material labors the kingdom of heaven first. The school, the church budget, and the gospel come before anything else.

Paul did not make his zeal and labor in the gospel dependent on payment from men, even though it was his right to ask for wages. He labored for the gospel's sake. That means that in his work he was wholly motivated by the love of God, love of Christ, and love of the church. That was its own reward. This speaks to us about our whole walk in the way of love, love for the gospel. We may often give up or at least not exercise fully our rights. If we use our rights—liberties—in any other way than wholly motivated by love for God and for the neighbor, that is a kind of abuse of them and completely out of harmony with the gospel. Every liberty we receive in the gospel is received for the sake of the gospel, and any time the exercise of that right may hinder the gospel, we must forgo our rights and willingly suffer for the gospel's sake.

Is that not what the gospel declares? Jesus Christ, who was in the form of God and thought it not robbery to be equal with God, made himself of no reputation. Willingly he who was rich became poor for our sakes. This is what the gospel and Christ in the gospel teach. He who had the right to all things restored what he did not take away. He exchanged the sapphire throne for the stable floor.

Further, whatever our calling, our labor in that calling must be willing. The gospel does this when it comes. It makes us willing in the day of God's power. In other words, you do not love your husband because he loves you but because the gospel says, "Love him." Especially the mother embodies this. She does not labor because her wage compensates her for it, but because she glories in the gospel of Jesus Christ. This is the more excellent way.

This is our calling in the gospel. When it comes, it not only sets us free, but also calls us to suffer even the loss of our rights for the gospel's sake. In this we honor the gospel.

CHAPTER 28

ACCOMMODATING
OURSELVES TO ALL MEN

1 Corinthians 9:22–23

---

22. *To the weak became I as weak, that I might gain the
weak: I am made all things to all men, that I might by all
means save some.*
23. *And this I do for the gospel's sake, that I might be partaker thereof with you.*

In verse 19 the apostle says that he is "free from all men." With
that phrase he describes again the liberty that he has in Jesus
Christ. He is free from all men, but he is the Lord's bondman. As
the Lord's bondman he is wholly owned by the Lord. Applying
this to his work as an apostle, he is wholly subject to Jesus Christ
and not to men. In this way he is free from all men.

This is true not only of the apostle, but also of all believers.
Being owned body and soul by Jesus Christ, they are free from all
men. They are free from the opinions, condemnations, and judgments of men. Especially in their consciences they are free from
men because their consciences are not ruled by men but by God
through Jesus Christ by his grace.

Although Paul was free from all men in his ministry, he carefully accommodated himself to others. The particular instance
of that accommodation is that he did not use his power in the

gospel to be paid, lest he hinder the gospel. The idea is not that if he would receive payment others could bring a charge against the gospel. Rather, the idea is that he did not hinder the gospel by making his labor in the gospel and his bringing the gospel depend on payment for his work. The Corinthians did not pay him. He neither demanded payment from them nor refused to preach. Because Paul accommodated himself in that way, no one could make his glorying vain—the glorying that he did not preach the gospel for money but in the service of Jesus Christ exclusively.

From that specific example the apostle makes a general application, as he frequently does throughout the book of Corinthians. He says, "Though I be free from all men [and I demonstrated that in not being paid for preaching the gospel], yet have I made myself servant unto all, that I might gain the more" (v. 19). In this instance he was only doing what was his settled practice. That practice was to accommodate himself. Freely of his own will he subjected himself to all men. He was not under the power of anyone because he was the Lord's bondman. Yet he so lived his life as though he were subject to the inclinations of everyone.

In verses 20–22 he gives instances of his practice of accommodation. "Unto the Jews I became as a Jew...to them that are under the law, as under the law...to them that are without law, as without law...to the weak became I as weak." He was a chameleon of sorts.

In that practice the apostle was an example for us to follow in accommodating ourselves to all men. This accommodation called for by the way of love is the main thought of verses 22–23.

All Things to All Men

When the apostle says in verse 22, "I am made all things to all men," he refers to his accommodation. Here he explains what he said in verse 19: "Though I be free from all men, yet have I made myself servant unto all, that I might gain the more." We cannot understand what he means in verse 22 unless we understand what he means in verse 19 by "I made myself servant [or slave] unto all."

He was not in fact the servant of all men. He was the servant of Jesus Christ. He establishes this fact when he says he was free from all men. There was one from whom he was not free and from whom he never wished to be free, Jesus Christ. He was owned by Jesus Christ in life and death, in his ministry, and in his personal life. He labored solely under the power of God's grace and in the interest of the gospel of Jesus Christ.

Although he was free from all men, yet he made himself servant unto all men. "Servant" means slave. It was his own settled decision in his life to subject himself as a slave to all men. A slave is one who is owned body and soul by another. The apostle made himself a slave to all.

When he calls himself a slave, he also indicates what motivates him. A proper, Christian servant labors out of love for his master, as part of his honoring all authority for God's sake. A Christian slave does everything in love first for God and second for the one he serves. Paul was governed by a deep love for others to subject himself to their needs. He was motivated by love for them and concern for their welfare. The Bible teaches this as the essence of a slave's duty. This is what the apostle means by his becoming a servant.

That practice necessarily involved the apostle's accommodating himself to others. When he says, "I am made all things to all men" (v. 22), he describes what is involved in being a slave. A slave must accommodate himself. Literally, "I was made" means I became. To accommodate yourself means to become adjusted to, to adapt to, or to be reconciled to another. A slave is owned by the one he serves, and the slave adjusts himself to the needs, desires, and inclinations of his owner. This is the slave's life. A slave modifies his behavior to bring it into conformity with the one he serves.

When Paul became all things to all men, he means that in whatever particular situation he found himself, he accommodated himself to that situation. He assumed an appearance that changed with the context. He accommodated himself to the needs, welfare, and benefit of others. That is why he says "as." He does not say, "To the Jews I became a Jew or to the weak I became weak." He says that he became "as" a Jew and "as" weak. He assumed that appearance and mode of life.

To guard against misunderstanding and to ward off the idea that this was a new kind of bondage in which he was subject to the opinions and inclinations of men, he says he did it freely. Free from all men, he became a slave to all and became all things to all men. Because it was out of love, he also did that freely. He was not compelled to it. Because it was out of love, it was always subject to God and to the will of God.

He indicates specifically what he means by his accommodation of others when he says he became as a Jew, as under the law, as without law, and as weak. This is a representative, not an exhaustive, list. First, he says to the Jews that he became as a Jew. Implied is that to the Gentiles he became as a Gentile. Jew and Gentile are the two great divisions of the human race. When Paul says Jew and implies Gentile, he means the Jewish and Gentile modes of life. There are things that belong to being a Jew and things that belong to being a Gentile that do not belong to the gospel. There are things that belong to being an American, an Eastern European, or an Asian that do not belong to the gospel. In the United States there are things that belong to being a Southerner and a Northerner that do not belong to the gospel. These things do not belong to the gospel, but they belong to the context into which the gospel comes.

Paul could move in either Jewish or Gentile society with equal ease, and no one knew the difference. When he became as a Jew, no one could tell that he was equally at ease in the agoras of Athens or on the hill of the Areopagus, speaking to the skeptics and philosophers. He could fit in equally well in suburban America, the Deep South, the Midwest, Asia, and Europe.

Giving another example, he says that he became to those under the law as under the law and to those without the law as without the law. These two ideas belong together, and this pair intensifies the apostle's point. Some would have no objection to the apostle's saying to the Jew, "I became as a Jew," and to the Gentile, "I became as a Gentile." They would not object to saying that in Europe one can live as a European, in America live as an American, and in Asia live as an Asian. But Paul makes his point about accommodating ourselves to others very sharp. To those under the law he became as under the law, and to those without law he became as without law.

By under law and without law he refers again to a great division in the human race. In the Old Testament the great division of the human race was into Jew and Gentile. To that division corresponds the similar division between those with law and those without law. In the new dispensation this division between law and no law would be akin to the difference between those raised in the church and those raised outside the church. Paul could talk to someone who had never heard a "thee" and a "thou" in their whole life, and he did not make it a matter of principle. He could speak equally well to one who had never heard a syllable of the gospel and to those who grew up with the gospel as the very air they breathed. He could preach in the synagogues of the Jews and quote Moses, and he could speak on Mar's Hill in that most idolatrous of cities, Athens, and quote Greek poets.

To ward off the charge that he taught a new kind of licentiousness or promoted an unprincipled life, Paul says that he is "not without law to God, but under the law to Christ" (v. 21). He does not advocate that to gain the heathen you become a heathen, to gain the lawless you become lawless, or to gain those outside the church you live as one who lives outside the church. He keeps his accommodations wholly subject to the law and to Christ.

Continuing his examples of what it means to accommodate ourselves to others and at the same time showing how far this is necessary, he says, "To the weak became I as weak" (v. 22). Here he makes another point about accommodation that is necessary also in the church. The weak are not unbelievers but believers and fellow members of the congregation. They are Christians. They have faith, but their consciences are weak. They do not yet have from God the testimony in their consciences that gives them the kind of liberty that another believer may be able to exercise. To the weak Paul became as weak. If a man in the church thinks it is sin to grill on Sunday, and because he sees you grill on Sunday he is tempted to grill too, you must accommodate the weak brother.

The weak brother is not the Pharisee who attempts to lord it over the church of Christ by his own laws. Take the example above about grilling. The Pharisee would reveal himself not by grilling on Sunday but by raising a storm of controversy about your grilling on Sunday. To that man there is no yielding, as Paul did not yield to the Pharisees who spied out his liberty with Titus and tried to compel him to be circumcised (Gal. 2:4).

The accommodations of which Paul speaks involve both life on the mission field and life in the established church. Paul makes this application because the Corinthians did not think it was necessary in the church to accommodate to anyone. They used their liberty so brazenly that they trampled on the weak brother and destroyed him, as long as they could use their liberty.

A host of things are implied in accommodation of the weak. To children you become as a child. They are weak. To the old you become as the old. To the foolish you become as foolish.

When Paul says, "All things to all men" (1 Cor. 9:22), he shows how far this accommodation goes. It has no limit regarding earthly contexts and circumstances of the gospel. If we can, without doing injury to the gospel, we must become all things to all men.

For the Gospel's Sake

What makes this necessary? The gospel itself does: "This I do for the gospel's sake, that I might be partaker thereof with you" (v. 23). Paul freely accommodated himself for the sake of the gospel. He considered nothing in his life or person sacred in comparison with the gospel. The gospel so controlled every aspect of his life that any part of it could be given up for the gospel's sake.

Notice, he does not say that he accommodated the gospel. Not once did he accommodate the gospel. In another place he expressly denies that he accommodates the gospel: "As we were allowed of God to be put in trust with the gospel, even so we speak; not as pleasing men, but God, which trieth our hearts" (1 Thess. 2:4). "Pleasing" means accommodating oneself to the desires, opinions, and interests of others. Paul did that with his own person and situations, but never with the gospel. He did that with his own person in the interest of preaching an unaccommodated gospel.

Accommodation is a massive theme today. Read a mission book; accommodation is often the main theme, or the book has some section devoted to this theme. The writers will use words such as *cross-cultural missions, context, contextualization,* and *adaptation.* None of the words are in themselves bad, but often the content put into them is wrong. What is usually meant is that because some particular culture or group does not understand or will not understand a particular aspect of the gospel, you put it away and do not bring it up, or that some culture's peculiarities mean that you accommodate the gospel. If it is too hard or offensive or causes too much trouble or will not convert enough people, get rid of that aspect of the gospel. So the gospel is adapted and accommodated to men, which is unfaithfulness toward God, who gives the gospel to be preached fully to all men everywhere without accommodation. These promoters of accommodation do not accommodate themselves but the gospel.

To accommodate the gospel is shameful dissimulation with

the gospel. The gospel is no longer free but is in bondage to man. The gospel is also in that way not the gospel. The gospel cannot be bound, and if a man tries to bind it, he tries to bind God.

There is not even a hint of that kind of dissimulating accommodation of the gospel in these verses. In the epistle to the Corinthians, the apostle never accommodates the gospel. He binds on new converts the gospel regarding marriage, the laws of chastity and holiness, worship, sacraments, discipline, and all the scriptural truths.

It is exactly because the gospel is not bound to some particular form or mode of life, or to some particular culture, no matter how ancient or advanced, that the preacher of that gospel can freely become all things to all men.

The gospel cannot be accommodated because of what the gospel is. It is the word of God. As the word of God it is as unchangeable and eternal as God himself. The gospel is as authoritatively powerful as God himself. To accommodate it would be for man to assume authority over the gospel. No man, no church, no missionary has the power or the right to accommodate the gospel.

Man can only be a "partaker" of the gospel (1 Cor. 9:23). In other words, the apostle means that the gospel accommodates man to it. The gospel does not change. Man must change. The gospel does change men. This is its power. When the gospel comes, it lays hold on men, women, and children in their particular context, and it changes them in the depths of their beings, in their thinking, priorities, lives, and beliefs.

In the process it turns the world upside down. The apostles were charged as those who "have turned the world upside down" (Acts 17:6). This is what the gospel does.

We recognize at the same time that there are nonessentials, things that can freely be given up in a particular context. Whether the church uses an organ or not and takes the offerings with bags or plates are of no account. By agreeing that these are nonessentials, you agree that these things have nothing to do with the gospel.

Thus the accommodation of the apostle that he exhorts on the church never touches one point of the gospel. He demonstrated that in his life. When the Judaizers wanted to bring the church back into bondage, the apostle waged war on them. When Peter dissembled regarding the gospel and accommodated himself to the Judaizers, Paul publicly rebuked Peter to his face. The accommodation touches no point of the gospel.

Accommodation is not a judicious silence. The implication of Paul's accommodating himself for the gospel's sake is that he accommodated himself to others and became all things to all men in order to speak, not to keep silent. Some suppose that they do what the apostle exhorts here when they fellowship and make friends with enemies of the gospel, who assault the gospel and live contrary to the gospel, and they say nothing and claim to become all things to all men. Judicious silence in these circumstances is contrary to the gospel. The apostle does not mean that he accommodates himself to others in order to retain their good will, but he does it for the gospel's sake.

First, for the gospel's sake means that the gospel sanctions this liberty. The gospel gives to the apostle and to believers the right and the obligation where necessary to accommodate themselves for the sake of the gospel. This is in harmony with the gospel.

To put it in Paul's terms: being free from all men and a servant of Jesus Christ, he did nothing else but the will of Jesus Christ, in which he followed the example of his Lord. Paul was a good servant of his master. Jesus Christ as the Lord of all, who was in the form of God and thought it not robbery to be equal with God, in the incarnation made himself of no reputation and took on him the form of a servant (Phil. 2:6–7). He was not a servant. He was the Lord. He took the form of a servant. Jesus Christ came meekly and lowly and bearing the burdens of his people.

This is what a slave does. Jesus was a burden bearer; he bore the burden of the sins of his people.

That is also what Christ exhorted on his apostles and thus on all his disciples by his example when he laid aside his garments, wrapped himself in a towel, carried the bowl of water, kneeled down, and washed his disciples' feet (John 13:4–5). He became their servant and taught his disciples to do likewise. The Son of man came not to be ministered unto—to be served—but to minister. He served in particular by giving his life a ransom for many. At the cross Jesus Christ served his people. He did that because he was wholly the servant of the triune God. He did that in love for God and in love for his people.

This is in distinction from those for whom all their desires and modes of life are principles. There is seemingly nothing on which they can accommodate themselves. Their desires, wills, and wants are seemingly everywhere and at all times synonymous with a gospel principle, and with them, then, there is no liberty. Not so the apostle, who accommodated himself to all men for the gospel's sake. He would not hinder the gospel. He would allow nothing to stand in the way of the gospel.

Second, for the gospel's sake means that the gospel liberates God's people to do this. No man ever does this of himself, because it is contrary to the natural man. He would rather mock the Jew, look down on the Gentile, be completely lawless, and beat up the weak. The natural man never accommodates himself to anyone. He would rather die and go to hell than to accommodate himself. That hatred of the neighbor, revealed in his treatment of the neighbor, is nothing except the revelation of his hatred of God whom he cannot see. The gospel not only sanctions accommodation, but also gives to God's people the spiritual resources to do it. The gospel makes them willing and able to do it in love for God and in love for the neighbor.

Third, for the gospel's sake means that the apostle accommodated himself in the interest of preaching the gospel. He did not accommodate himself to avoid ridicule or persecution, to shamefully dissimulate, to rack up numbers in missions, or to reach some artificial goals in evangelism, but to preach. He did that to preach in order to be a "partaker thereof with you" (1 Cor. 9:23). Being a partaker refers to the effect of the gospel preaching. He accommodated himself in order to preach the gospel, so that the gospel might make men partakers of it. There was a danger that he would get in the way of the gospel. He did not want to do that, so he accommodated himself.

He did not accommodate himself to make men more easily accept the gospel. No man accepts the gospel. No amount of accommodation can make a man accept the gospel. The apostle's experiences teach that. There was no one who was more careful to accommodate himself to others, and there was no one who was stoned more often, beaten more frequently, or in prison more often than the apostle Paul. His accommodations served the preaching. By Paul's preaching, God through the gospel made men partakers of the gospel. Paul accommodated himself in order to preach the gospel, so that the preaching of the gospel would make men partakers of its salvation and benefits.

Paul accommodated himself to "all men" (v. 22), that is, to all kinds of men—Jew and Gentile, those under the law and those without law, the weak and the strong—because the gospel is for all kinds of men. A Jew needs the gospel to free him from self-righteousness. A Gentile needs the gospel to free him from his ignorance and wicked ways. One under law needs the gospel to teach him the essence of his salvation, and one without law needs the gospel to free him from his lawlessness. The weak needs the gospel to make him stronger; the strong needs the gospel to teach him not to trample on the weak. All men need the gospel. Apart from it they perish.

To Save Some

Paul accommodated himself in order to preach the gospel to all "that I might by all means save some" (v. 22).

He was not mistaken or caught up in false mission zeal that God by the preaching of the gospel intends to save every man. He preached in order to "save some." With that one word, "some," he places the whole of his ministry under the will of God. Let the preaching go out wherever and to whomsoever God in his good pleasure sends it to save some. Paul preached to gain that "some," as he says, "For the elect's sakes" (2 Tim. 2:10).

With the word "gain," he accommodates himself to the Corinthians. Every Corinthian would instantly understand that he referred to business profits. They knew how to make a profit because they were hard-working businessmen. They worked hard in order to gain. The apostle says that the gospel is his currency and men's souls are his profit. "I am made all things to all men, so that the currency of the gospel goes out and returns a profit." What kind of businessman would invest his precious currency in some business venture and then bungle it all up by his boorish, foolish, and insensitive behavior?

Paul accommodated himself because he would not allow himself to stand in the way. He was utterly convicted that there is only one power that saves men, namely, God in Jesus Christ by the gospel. In order that the gospel could be preached wherever God in his good pleasure sends it for the salvation of his elect people, the apostle accommodated himself.

In that he calls all God's people, in the interest of the gospel, not to stand in the way of the preaching of the gospel, but to accommodate themselves to all men, becoming slaves to them all.

CHAPTER 29

A LESSON FROM THE OLYMPICS

1 Corinthians 9:24–27

---

24. *Know ye not that they which run in a race run all, but one receiveth the prize? So run, that ye may obtain.*
25. *And every man that striveth for the mastery is temperate in all things. Now they do it to obtain a corruptible crown; but we an incorruptible.*
26. *I therefore so run, not as uncertainly; so fight I, not as one that beateth the air:*
27. *But I keep under my body, and bring it into subjection: lest that by any means, when I have preached to others, I myself should be a castaway.*

The world is familiar with the Olympics. Every four years athletes from around the world gather to compete in their chosen specialty. In those games there is a lesson that the Holy Spirit will have the believer and church learn. If any pay attention to the Olympics, they must not miss the Spirit's lesson for Christians. That lesson is not what the Olympics itself would teach, that is, how to get along and have peace. That lesson of the Olympics is thoroughly anti-Christian because those Olympic Games are devoted to world peace in this age and apart from and in opposition to the gospel of Jesus Christ. Over against that

407

lesson Christians rejoice in the spectacle of the simmering hostilities between the nations at these games, because it means that the nations have not yet given up their warfare and turned all of their hatred on the church.

Neither is the lesson of the Olympics purely negative: that we are reminded about the vanity of striving after gold or admonished that bodily exercise profits little. This admonition is implied when the apostle says in verse 25, "They [strive] to obtain a corruptible crown." They do all that for the corruptible. What vanity.

Yet the apostle draws his and the Holy Ghost's lesson from the athletes who competed for that corruptible crown. Those athletes were the ones who strove for mastery. They competed year round in the various cities of the Roman Empire. Rome was addicted to her sports. Any city worthy of the name had a sports arena, in which athletes ran and boxed and competed. Every four years as the grand culmination of all those competitions the Olympiad was held, where the athletes of the empire strove for the coveted victor's wreath.

Therein is the Spirit's lesson for Christians. The athlete who aimed to compete in the Olympics was "temperate in all things" (v. 25). What is the Christian to do in his life of liberty wherewith Christ has made him free? The broadest application of the truth of the Christian's liberty in Jesus Christ is that the Christian likewise is called to be temperate in all things.

Temperate in All Things

The lesson the Holy Spirit draws from the Olympic athlete is temperance. That temperance is the main subject is clear from the words of verses 24–27. The apostle explicitly mentions temperance in verse 25: "Every man that striveth for the mastery is temperate in all things." The one who strives is the athlete. In verse 26 the apostle mentions that the runner does not run uncertainly and aimlessly, and the boxer does not fight beating the air but with the purpose to land his blows. Both are examples of temperance. The temperate man keeps his eye on the prize and runs and fights with a purpose. In verse 27 the apostle says, "I keep under my body, and bring it into subjection." There is temperance again. Keeping under the body and bringing the body under subjection are aspects of temperance.

The word translated as "temperance" means inner strength. This inner strength is illustrated in an earthly way by the athlete at the top of his game, here the Olympic athlete. He has an inner drive and complete control over his body, and by rigid discipline he bends his whole life to the purpose of competing in the greatest games and winning the prize. He eats, drinks, sleeps, and even relaxes for the Olympics. The world describes this temperance of the athlete by the words *dedication, hard work, discipline, drive,* or *determination.* The athlete in the Olympics devotes his entire life—often from youth—to competing in the games. His appearance in those games is not strictly the product of his superior bodily strength and athleticism—natural giftedness—but is especially due to his temperance. The gifted athlete without temperance squanders all his gifts. The athlete of moderate giftedness by means of temperance achieves more than someone might think from a strict assessment of his gifts.

Regardless, the Olympic athlete subjects his body to hard training, his life to strict regimentation, and his cravings to a strict diet. By a calculated use of all things he is prepared. Now he is running for the gold. Now he is in the ring, landing crushing blows against his opponent. There is a lesson for the Christian in the temperance of these athletes.

The temperance that the apostle notices in the athlete and the temperance that he exhorts on the Christian are different kinds of temperance. The temperance of the Christian is not merely the inner, psychological-physical drive and strict external discipline. One may be the most disciplined person in the world and be utterly intemperate insofar as the apostle is concerned. He exhorts on the Christian a spiritual temperance. This temperance is the fruit of the Spirit by which the elect, justified believer can subject his whole life to Jesus Christ and moderate and discipline himself according to the will of Jesus Christ.

Temperance is not simply earthly moderation, although certainly a man given to earthly excesses has a slim claim to spiritual temperance. Temperance is not either a merely earthly and external discipline or regimentation of a man's life and the life of his family. Temperance also has nothing to do with the temperance movement, which makes rum the devil's drink and demonizes what God calls good and made for man to make his heart glad.

Because temperance is the Spirit's fruit, the natural man is utterly devoid of temperance. Man, the intemperate beast, is a spiritually drunken glutton. He utterly lacks self-control. He is a slave to sin, to his passions, lusts, and desires. Consequently, the natural man is full of sin, a sinner out of control, although externally he may be the most disciplined person in the world.

This is true because he is a child of Adam and is judged in Adam, who was intemperate in the garden. God gave Adam everything. He had an exquisite, strong body. He had a lovely wife, perfect herself and in all things an exact complement to him and one with whom he could fellowship. He lived in a lush garden full of trees beautiful to look at and good for food. In the center of the garden he had a home, and in the midst of it he could walk with God in the cool of the day. Adam was king of creation. His goodness and glory consisted in nothing less than God's own image. He had God's word as well, which instructed him on the way of life in the garden. But Adam would be God too. He would not be ruled by the word of God for his life but rebelled against that word. Intemperate man!

For that sin he was judged and brought under the power of sin, so that all he could do was sin and especially his will was bound under sin. For that sin all his posterity likewise were condemned to the bondage of intemperance.

Temperance is a fruit of the Spirit in the justified believer. This is implied by the apostle in the words "preached to others" (v. 27). The reference is to the justifying gospel of the cross of Jesus Christ believed by faith. Because God forgives the sins of believers, also their intemperance, in the cross and imputes to them the righteousness of Christ by the preaching of Christ crucified, he also blesses them with the gift of temperance by freeing them from the bondage to their passions and lusts.

Believers must understand that they have received the gift of temperance because they are justified. Freed from the guilt of sin, the guilt of their original sin in Adam, and the guilt of their own actual sins, also their intemperance, they are free from being slaves to sin and from the dominion of sin. Being justified, they have the right to new lives of temperance. Apart from faith in the one, perfect sacrifice of Christ, it is utterly worthless to speak of temperance. Because they are justified, they are actually given that gift, so that they begin already in this life to live the life of the new heaven and earth, lives of temperance wholly regulated by the will of God.

Temperance is inner spiritual strength in the justified believer. The strength is grace. Grace is a power. The strength is the Spirit of Christ. By means of that strength the believer is able to subject his life to Christ and discipline his life by the will of Christ.

The apostle defines temperance more closely in verse 27: "I keep under my body, and bring it into subjection." The natural man was a slave to sin; after being regenerated he is in subjection to Jesus Christ. Since subjection is a heart matter in which the believer loves the authority of Christ over his life, wills that authority, and willingly places himself under that authority, temperance begins with that attitude of the regenerated heart. Temperance is a part of the believer's hardy love for Christ. Temperance proceeds from love, and love is manifested in temperance. In love for Jesus Christ, the believer subjects himself to

Christ. In love for him, the believer moderates, regulates, and disciplines his life according to Christ's will.

Subjection is a heart matter and as such is invisible. Yet that subjection always manifests itself. The manifestation of the believer's subjection to Christ in his heart the apostle mentions in the phrase, "I keep under my body." "Keep under" means discipline. The disciplined person regiments and organizes his life. Paul makes the object of his discipline the "body" not because discipline is limited to the body—in fact temperance begins in the heart of a man—but because the body is the instrument of one's life in the world. The body does whatever the one who is controlling it demands the body to do. To the natural man who is under the subjection of sin—intemperate—the body is the instrument to sin. The temperate Christian disciplines his body and thus makes his whole body and the life of that body subservient to the will of Jesus Christ, so that his body and consequently his whole life become the instruments of righteousness.

The apostle speaks of temperance "in all things" (v. 25). Temperance is not a compartment of a believer's life. No, he must be temperate in *all* things. A man intemperate in one thing is intemperate in his whole life. Observe the drunkard.

The temperate believer is wholly temperate. By "all things" Paul makes temperance the quality of the believer's entire life, so that the believer's life consists in temperance. Paul did the same when he reasoned with the skeptic Felix about "righteousness, temperance, and judgment to come" (Acts 24:25). Paul reasoned of righteousness because the believer has it only by faith in Jesus Christ, of temperance because it describes the entire life of the justified person, and of judgment to come because that will be the end of the believer's life when he will have received the crown of glory that fades not away.

The intemperate man in his drink drinks to excess, is a drunkard, and will not be subject to Christ and moderate his life by the will of Christ. While he may not be drunken when he takes a drink of alcohol, he will not be sober for Christ's sake and in love for Christ, himself, and his family. Temperance is not the mere abstinence from alcohol. To abstain from something apart from Jesus Christ is wicked. Temperance is the thankful use of alcohol as God's gift to make the believer's heart glad.

The sluggard is intemperate in his work. He will not be regulated in his life by the will of Christ that if a man will not work, he will not eat (2 Thess. 3:10). In love for Jesus Christ and for his fellow saints, for whom he never has a penny and always desires theirs, he will not work.

The unmarried man who has a sex life is a fornicator. The married man who has a sex life apart from his wife is an adulterer. They will not be chaste and will not subject that aspect of their lives to Jesus Christ and his will. Whether he views pornography on the Internet, purchases a whore off the street, buys her at a bar for the price of a meal and a few drinks, or divorces his wife and marries another, the sin is the same and all is intemperance.

The man who loves his wicked acquaintances or wicked children more than God, so that he fellowships with the impenitent, helps the ungodly, and loves those who hate the Lord (2 Chron. 19:2), is intemperate in his friendships.

The man intemperate with food—he lives to eat—commits a kindred sin to drunkenness. He neither eats to stay alive, nor eats to enjoy the good things God gave to man, but he lives to eat because his god is his belly. Such is the man who will not give up his Sunday job or a lucrative and secure union job because he will not starve for Christ's sake. For the sake of his full belly and pleasant earthly life, he will abandon the church, his family, and every good thing. He is intemperate.

Is the one who is outwardly regimented and physically and mentally disciplined in his earthly life necessarily temperate? The successful, disciplined, hard-working businessman who does everything for himself is as intemperate as the drunk in the gutter, because he is as devoid of love for Christ, is driven by love for money, and pierces himself through with as many sorrows as the other does because of his booze.

The individual who exercises religiously and either does not eat enough or eats way too much and throws it up is intemperate, even though today there are fancy names for the sin, such as anorexia and bulimia. Those who engage in those activities are less akin to athletes and more to drug addicts, individuals who will not be subject to Jesus Christ and to the calling to eat for his sake. She may lie to herself: "I am very disciplined. I exercise frequently. I can control myself. I can control the most basic of all my desires," but she is not in control. The sin is intemperance.

The monks who regimented their lives and beat up their bodies, slept on boards, wore hair shirts, observed strange hours, and lived in odd places were intemperate because they did it for themselves and not unto Christ, for obtaining righteousness and not because they were righteous by faith.

The remedy to such intemperance in anything, and thus a lack of temperance in all things, is repentance and believing in Christ Jesus for the forgiveness of your sins, for righteousness, and as the ground of your deliverance from the power of those sins. From him also receive Christ's Spirit and word and the grace to be temperate, and in temperance to subject yourself in the entirety of your life to the spiritual discipline of Jesus Christ. For the drunkard, be sober for Christ's sake. For the glutton, eat for Christ's sake. For the anorexic, eat for Christ's sake. For the one driven by his passions, regulate and rule those passions for Christ's sake. Thus you are temperate in all things: the lesson of the Olympic athlete for Christians.

To Obtain a Crown

The athlete is temperate in all things "to obtain a corruptible crown" (v. 25). The athlete wants to run in the race. He wants to run in the greatest of races, the Olympiad. Once there he wants to win. The boxer trains to step into the greatest ring on earth and there to land his blows with devastating power and win. He disciplines himself and pays assiduous attention to his regimen and diet in order to compete in those international games, to pummel his opponent, and to have his arm lifted as the champion.

So also the purpose of the believer's temperance is to run the race. His running is not in an earthly race, not the earthly fight of the boxer in a ring, but his running and fighting consists of the whole Christian life. Just as the intemperate athlete is flabby and out of shape at race time and cannot run, so the intemperate Christian cannot run the Christian race.

The apostle describes the Christian life as a race and thus as a grand contest, in which Christians are set when God regenerates them and to which they are appointed in election. It is a race that begins with regeneration and ends in heavenly glory.

It is called running because it takes exertion, a great deal of spiritual energy, and stamina. It is also called fighting because we are bloodied and swollen from trading punches continually with the enemy. It is the great boxing match with our opponents: sin, Satan, and the whole world.

In a sense every believer has the same basic calling as a Christian: to be sorry for his sins, to confess Jesus Christ in the world, to live according to his will, and to hate and fight sin. That contest has only one great object all through its course: to keep the faith.

In another sense each one has this calling in harmony with the station that God has given him in the world. The Spirit points to the apostle as an example, and he says not only "I therefore so run," but also "when I have preached to others" (vv. 26–27). The calling of the apostle was not only to be a believer and a Christian, but also specifically to be that as a preacher of the gospel and an apostle of Jesus Christ. Each individual believer receives from Jesus Christ a particular station and calling in life, which is his race and his contest—the mother, the father, the child, the laborer, the employer, the elder, the deacon, the minister, and whatever calling God gives in this life. Temperance serves the purpose that we live in those callings and run in them.

It is impossible to fulfill our callings apart from temperance. For example, the drunkard cannot be a father and a husband and a worker. He can pretend for a while, but he does not do what God calls him to do; he does not run. Why is he not running? He cannot run, because he is intemperate. The man who strives for mastery is temperate in all things. The intemperate man who claims to be a Christian is like the runner who runs in circles. He never goes around the track from start to finish, but he runs in circles on the infield. He wastes all of his time and energy. The intemperate man is like the boxer who pounds the air with his hands, and while he is flailing about his opponent lands blow after blow, leaving him broken and bloody. How can a carnal, earthly minded, and sensual man, entangled in the world's affairs, run the Christian life?

Temperance serves the athlete's contest. Temperance serves the Christian's calling to run the Christian life and to fight the Christian battle of faith.

That running is to obtain. The Spirit makes this point with a rhetorical question: "Know ye not that they which run in a race run all, but one receiveth the prize?" (v. 24). Even though a huge pack of runners goes out for a race, only one receives the prize. For years they train. When they run the race, they run to win. The man who enters the cross-country race just to be in the race is not running to obtain, and that shows. He only trains for a couple of months, part time, and he comes in last place.

When Paul says in verse 24, "So run, that ye may obtain," he refers to the manner of the Christian's running. He says, "Be temperate in order to run. When you run, run to obtain." Temperance serves the running. Apart from it no one will run. Running temperately ensures that the manner of the running is to obtain. God sets his people on the course of the Christian life and sets them in the Christian boxing ring and says, "Run to obtain. Press on to perfection. Land your blows. Win!"

"Now they do it to obtain a corruptible crown" (v. 25). Today athletes run to obtain a little gilded medal. In the days of the apostle, they ran to obtain a small wreath. Those prizes are corruptible, and all the glory of their victories is corruptible. Who can remember who won the bobsled race in 2006? Nobody can, because the athletes' crowns and glory are corruptible. Yet for years the athletes regimented their lives to obtain those corruptible crowns and glory.

Christians run to obtain "an incorruptible [crown]" (v. 25). The crown is incorruption. What we obtain at the end of our running and our great contest in the ring is incorruption! It is incorruptible because it consists in immortality and eternal life. Incorruption is the complete and utter freedom from the possibility of sin, so that we cannot die and cannot sin, and we will serve God perfectly all the days of our everlasting life. The crown is incorruptible because it is beyond the possibility of sin and death.

It is called a crown because it is glory. What the athlete wants in the Olympics is not the little gold medal, but particularly the glory—the thrill of victory when in that brief moment he stands in glory with all the crowds cheering. If he does all that for what is corruptible, how much more the Christian, who obtains an incorruptible crown? There is a glory that awaits the believer, a glory that has never entered into the heart of man to conceive, that never fades away, and in comparison to which all of the sufferings of this present life are not worthy to be compared (1 Cor. 2:9; 1 Pet. 1:4; Rom. 8:18). When you give up corruptible things, you receive in exchange an incorruptible crown. When you are weary in the contest with sin, Satan, the world, and the relentless onslaught of the flesh, the word of God is that there is a crown of glory waiting at the end of the contest. Run to obtain!

Belonging to the temperance of the Christian athlete is his understanding that he has this incorruptible crown in store for him. He has that promise by virtue of God's regeneration, by which God made him temperate and set him in this greatest of races. There is a crown at the end of the race.

When the apostle says that many run and only one is crowned, his point is not that Christians have to push others out of the way because only one will get the crown. His point is how believers run the Christian life. They run to obtain so that in the same way that the athlete runs with the glory of victory in his mind's eye, the Christian runs in view of that incorruptible crown.

Because that crown is called incorruptible, it is not earned by running. The crown is merited only by the death of Jesus Christ. Only he can merit incorruption. The incorruption that he earned is eternal life, living and reigning with Christ in glory. The crown is appointed to some men. Speaking of eternal salvation, God says, "It is not of him that...runneth, but of God that sheweth mercy" (Rom. 9:16). The apostle places the cause of salvation in eternal election. In Ephesians 2:10 the apostle says that believers are "created in Christ Jesus unto good works, which God hath before ordained that we should walk in them." So Paul traces the source of all their good works to God's eternal counsel for their salvation. Believers are appointed to those good works and according to that eternal counsel are given those good works by God. The believer does not receive the crown because he runs. He receives it at the end of the running, in the way of running, so that both the running and the crown are gracious gifts of God.

At the end of the running God's people receive the glory and incorruption, so that the temperance by which they run is a gift, the running in the way of which they receive the crown is a gift, and the crown received at the end of the running is a gift.

Now so run that you may obtain. This is the lesson from the Olympian.

The Calling to Believers

This same lesson the Spirit urges on the believer.

If the Christian says, "I am not going to run, to strive, to discipline myself under Jesus Christ or his word. I will live my life as I please. I am going to keep on going in the same old way," then Paul and the Holy Spirit warn that Christian that in that way he will not obtain. So run that you may obtain.

If one says that this exhortation to run conflicts with the doctrine of grace, so that the exhortation implies that the running itself obtains the crown, this is mistaken. Exhortations in scripture are not implicit conditional theology. As proof the Holy Spirit presents the apostle Paul, as the Spirit presents him throughout 1 Corinthians and elsewhere in scripture, as the example of temperately running the race. No one in the whole world taught more clearly that the believer's salvation is dependent solely on the grace of God—rooted in election, grounded on the death of Jesus Christ, and given by the gift of grace. Who also ran and labored more than he did? Run to obtain.

I can also appeal to your experience, as Paul appealed to his. Does the believer who knows the graciousness of his salvation, especially that the incorruptible crown of glory was merited by the death of Christ and not by the believer's works, run in order to merit the crown of glory? This kind of thinking is far from the believer's mind. It is exactly because he knows that Christ merited the crown for him and calls him to run that he runs. Run to obtain.

The apostle warns about the seriousness of refusing to run. Refusing to run involves intemperance, for the intemperate cannot run and will not run. The one who will not run also will not run to obtain. The apostle warns about not learning this lesson from the Olympics. "I therefore so run...but I keep under my body, and bring it into subjection: lest that by any means, when I have preached to others, I myself should be a castaway" (1 Cor. 9:26–27).

Paul does not mean that he doubted his salvation or his obtaining the crown. Later he wrote, "I have fought a good fight, I have finished my course, I have kept the faith: henceforth there is laid up for me a crown of righteousness" (2 Tim. 4:7–8). He did not doubt that. Besides, such a thought is utterly foreign to scripture, which speaks very clearly of the preservation of the saints, whom God elects, justifies, and glorifies.

But the apostle casts himself in a figure and speaks of himself impersonally. He teaches about the seriousness of the lesson and the urgency of the calling to run to obtain.

First, he teaches that there is a casting away that does not end in perdition. This casting away Peter and David experienced in their utterly lamentable and melancholy falls. They did not watch and pray in order not to enter into temptation. They would not be temperate and engage in spiritual exercises, and consequently they fell deeply. What a waste, what a beating of the air to no purpose, and what a running about aimlessly. This is the reason God calls the intemperate person a wastrel. He throws away things. He wastes his family, his marriage, and his job, as Adam did his. He might not be damned, but what a chastisement! Be temperate in all things. Run to obtain.

Second, the apostle teaches that this lesson exempts no one. Even he, so advanced in the way of sanctification and temperance, learned this lesson. He ran, kept under, and pounded his body into submission not to himself and his lusts, but to Christ; not by bodily exercise, which profits little, but by spiritual exercises.

Speaking by this figure, he also speaks of the result of intemperance. He teaches that intemperance is a sin. The intemperate athlete cannot run, and therefore he is not crowned. The intemperate human is damned. Intemperance is not a vice, a habit, or a bad way of life; it is a sin. The intemperate man who continues impenitently in intemperance will not obtain but is cast away. In his being cast away he reveals himself as one who is not subject to Jesus Christ and thus is utterly the slave of his passions.

Be temperate to run. Run to obtain an incorruptible crown.